BLEEDING AFGHANISTAN

BLEEDING AFGHANISTAN

WASHINGTON, WARLORDS, AND THE PROPAGANDA OF SILENCE

Sonali Kolhatkar and James Ingalls

Foreword by David Barsamian

SEVEN STORIES PRESS
NEW YORK TORONTO LONDON MELBOURNE

A Seven Stories Press First Edition

Seven Stories Press
140 Watts Street
New York, NY 10013
http://www.sevenstories.com

In Canada:
Publishers Group Canada, 250A Carlton Street, Toronto, ON M5A 2L1

In the UK:
Turnaround Publisher Services Ltd., Unit 3, Olympia Trading Estate, Coburg Road, Wood Green, London N22 6TZ

In Australia:
Palgrave Macmillan, 627 Chapel Street, South Yarra, VIC 3141

Library of Congress Cataloging-in-Publication Data

Kolhatkar, Sonali.
Bleeding Afghanistan : Washington, warlords, and the propaganda of silence / Sonali Kolhatkar and James Ingalls. -- 1st Seven Stories Press ed.
p. cm.
ISBN-13: 978-1-58322-731-2 (pbk. : alk. paper)
ISBN-10: 1-58322-731-8 (pbk. : alk. paper)
1. Afghanistan--History--1989-2001. 2. Afghanistan--History--2001- 3. United States--Foreign relations--Afghanistan. 4. Afghanistan--Foreign relations--United States. I. Ingalls, James. II. Title.

DS371.3.K65 2006
327.73058109'0511--dc22 2005036504

College professors may order examination copies of Seven Stories Press titles for a free six-month trial period. To order, visit www.sevenstories.com/textbook/, or fax on school letterhead to (212) 226-1411.

Book design by Jon Gilbert
Printed in the USA

9 8 7 6 5 4 3 2 1

CONTENTS

FOREWORD by David Barsamian vii

INTRODUCTION xi

PART ONE: HISTORICAL CONTEXT

1. Destroying a State: U.S. Policy Before September 11, 2001 3

PART TWO: REGIME CHANGE AND ITS CONSEQUENCES

2. Bombs, Threats, and Torture: Afghanistan Becomes a U.S. Target 41
3. Replacing One Brutal Regime with Another: The Return of the Warlords 85
4. A Client "Democracy": Reshaping Afghan Politics 117

PART THREE: RHETORIC VS. REALITY

5. "Liberation" Rhetoric and Burqa Obsessions: Objectifying Afghan Women 169
6. The Propaganda of Silence: The Mass Media and Government Impunity 197
7. Power, Prestige, and Pipelines: The Uses of Afghanistan 223

EPILOGUE

From the Belly of the Beast: Activism and Solidarity 251

NOTES 263

ACKNOWLEDGMENTS 295

INDEX 297

ABOUT THE AUTHORS 315

FOREWORD
BY DAVID BARSAMIAN

Most Americans have been inside their own burqas when it comes to Afghanistan. The level of knowledge about the country is minimal. When it comes to U.S. involvement, the levels of ignorance and amnesia are astounding.

Five years after the U.S. invaded Afghanistan and effected "regime change," Sonali Kolhatkar and James Ingalls break what they call the "propaganda of silence" with their acutely timed *Bleeding Afghanistan*. The Taliban are resurgent and "anti-American anger is boiling over." How are these developments explained by Washington, its satraps in Kabul, and the corporate media? These problems, they say, are caused by "outsiders" and "agitators." Yet, without irony, officialdom exempts U.S. and NATO troops from these labels.

The Afghan people, meanwhile, are extras on an American-produced movie about getting "bad guys, dead or alive." The cast, led by Hamid Karzai, dutifully recites lines extolling the virtues of their occupiers, with an allowance for an occasional murmur about the "collateral damage" when it becomes conspicuous.

Since the late 1970s, Afghans have been mere figures in Washington's imperial calculations. The country was infamously used as a pawn against the Soviets. The repercussions of U.S. policy in the recruiting, financing, training, and arming of what Eqbal Ahmad has called "the most fanatical elements in the Muslim world to fight in the great jihad" against the Soviets, are with us today. Once the USSR was driven out, the emboldened jihadis only gathered momentum.

The widespread crimes of the warlords, *jang saalaraan*, paved the way for the rise of the Taliban. As Ingalls and Kolhatkar point out, Dostum, Sayyaf, and others have not been held accountable, and the impunity has scarred the Afghan political landscape. As Human Rights Watch reports, "up to 60 percent of deputies in the lower house of parliament are directly or indirectly connected to current and past human rights abuses."

Karzai, in his ubiquitous shawl and karakul hat, has rewarded some of the warlords with government positions and a permanent get-out-of-jail-free pass. Karzai, it must be added, in a ringing affirmation of his confidence in his fellow Afghans, surrounds himself with American bodyguards. A marked man, he does not stray too far from Kabul.

The U.S. presence in Afghanistan, like all imperial and colonial projects, is accompanied by lofty rhetoric about noble goals. Echoing the British "white man's burden" and the French *mission civilatrice,* the rhetoric of the new wars is about democracy and freedom. Yet the U.S invasion and occupation of Afghanistan had an extra fillip: women's liberation. As Arundhati Roy observed: "We're being asked to believe that the U.S. Marines are actually on a feminist mission." It's hard to know whether to laugh or cry.

One of the heroes of the book is Malalai Joya, the young member of the Afghan parliament. Her courage in raising inconvenient facts about the rehabilitated warlords to directly to their faces in parliament is one of the most stirring and inspiring moments recounted here. The authors observe that Joya, "speaking for millions of Afghans, pointed out a reality that defies the U.S.'s rhetoric of 'liberation,'" which "simply returned a different set of misogynists to power." Joya's life has been threatened many times but she remains steadfast and defiant. Wouldn't it be something if Laura Bush, that great champion of Afghan women, invited her to the White House and honored her? And while the First Lady is at it, maybe she could celebrate the exemplary work of the Revolutionary Association of the Women of Afghanistan (RAWA).

The book's focus on RAWA is both illuminating and important. That the authors are themselves involved with the organization gives their perspective depth and urgency. Ingalls and Kolhatkar warn us against stereotyping Afghan women and seeing them just as victims. We should be wary, they advise, "not to fall into the same traps of exploitation and sensationalism that the mainstream media and conservative and liberal groups are guilty of. Objectifying Afghan women by their clothing is not an appropriate way for progressives to draw attention to the suffering of Afghan women. . . . Thousands of Afghan women have bravely marched with bare faces and fists in the air in their political demonstrations, demanding their rights."

Largely ignored today even by progressive voices, Afghanistan dropped off the media's radar screen once the main event in Iraq was launched. Corporate embedded reporters preferred the "action" in storied Baghdad over Gardez in Afghanistan. Fixated on Iraq, reporters assigned Afghanistan the role of sideshow, an afterthought in the Bush Wars.

In Kabul, in late May 2006, an accident involving a U.S. military vehicle led to multiple civilian deaths as American troops fired into crowds. The U.S. media described what happened as a "riot." Journalists were stunned to hear the "natives" chanting, "Death to America." Their tone was one of surprise. After all, the country, with a few blemishes here and there, was a "success" story. The BBC did provide some background. It reported that "life is not good" in Afghanistan. There is an "underlying sense that people are dissatisfied." There is "growing frustration" and "40 percent of the population is hungry." Afghan civilian deaths as a result of U.S. bombings and shootings surely number in the many thousands. Does anyone count or care? And the survivors? If they are lucky, hundred-dollar bills are thrown at them.

Today Afghanistan is ranked by the UN as the second worst country in the world to live in—after Sierra Leone. Much of the donor money entering the country goes to security and drug eradication programs. Many of the aid projects are riddled with corruption and amount to shoddy and incomplete work. Kabul is a capital city with luxury villas and grand hotels charging over $1,000 a night, while much of the population lives in squalor with less potable water and electricity than before the U.S.-led attack. Afghans are indeed "enduring" freedom.

Well documented and carefully researched, *Bleeding Afghanistan* is a book long overdue. It fills a huge void in information on and analyses of Afghanistan. As the authors remind us, "Living in the belly of the beast . . . it is up to us as Americans to change our government's policies."

Boulder, Colorado
June 2006

INTRODUCTION

If you ask an average citizen of the United States, "When did the U.S. first get involved in Afghanistan?" they will probably answer, "right after September 11, 2001." A May 2004 editorial in the *Free Lance-Star* of Fredricksburg, Virginia, is an example of this view:

> Before September of 2001, most Americans would have been hard pressed to find the country on an unlabeled map. Vaguely we might have remembered the Russians were embroiled there for a while, or recalled pictures of the giant, ancient stone Buddhas blown up by the Taliban. . . . Then [after the 9/11 attacks] the brutalities of the Taliban government, its support of terror, its oppression of women, and its iron grip on the people snapped into focus. That government fell in October of 2001, and since then, the United States and other countries have been working to resuscitate the gasping nation.[1]

All too often, discussion of Afghanistan as it was prior to 9/11 focuses exclusively on the crimes of the Taliban. A particularly far-reaching view might touch upon the 1979 Soviet invasion and the civil war that followed, but never with an honest assessment of the U.S. role. The *Free Lance-Star* mentions "25 years of civil war" and the "irrigation systems destroyed by the Russians or the Taliban." We get the sense that things were going badly in Afghanistan before 9/11, but the United States was only a helpless and casual observer of the horrors visited on Afghans by the Soviet Union and the Taliban. After the World Trade Center and the Pentagon were attacked, the U.S. had had enough, and finally decided to do something about the festering problem caused by others. "[S]ince then, the United States and other countries have been working to resuscitate the gasping nation." Now, as a result of U.S. actions, "[s]ome good things are happening."[2]

U.S. citizens truly concerned with how Afghanistan became the way it is, and what role our government played, might be interested to learn about the U.S. response to the Soviet invasion of 1979. They might want to know about the destruction wreaked on Afghanistan in the '80s and early '90s by U.S.-backed fundamentalist militias, which set the stage for the Taliban taking power in 1996. The *Free Lance-Star* does not go into that story.

This ignorance of history becomes more deliberate and subtle as we move from the average U.S. citizen to elite intellectuals and decision-makers. An example is the prevalent use of the phrase "failed state" to describe Afghanistan before the post-9/11 U.S. intervention. Rachel and Michael Stohl wrote in the Center for Defense Information newsletter in October 2001, "Afghanistan is an all too graphic example of a failed state whose internal situation has dramatically confronted the rest of the world." British Prime Minister Tony Blair told reporters, "it is important . . . that we help [Afghanistan] to go from being a failed state, failing its region and its people, to a state that offers some hope of stability and prosperity for the future."[3] Like "terrorist," the "failed state" label is almost always used in judgment and is reserved for weak states that affect powerful ones, especially when an excuse is needed to intervene in the affairs of the former. Powerful countries whose democratic institutions garner less than 50 percent participation, or those that regularly break their international treaty obligations, have not failed at statehood. Wealthy states that invade and occupy poor ones in violation of the international system are certainly states whose "internal situations dramatically confront the rest of the world," in the words of Rachel and Michael Stohl, but they are never called "failed states." The U.S. has never been a "state that offers some hope of stability and prosperity for the future," to Afghans, Palestinians, Haitians, Iraqis, and others, yet nothing is proposed by other world leaders to deal with the U.S. "failure" to stem the horrible effects of decisions made by its managers.

The real concern with weak "failed states" is the unpredictable ways they can hurt the powerful. According to the London *Economist*, Afghanistan is "still capable in the future of visiting its failures violently upon the West," as in the 9/11 attacks, planned or at least inspired by Osama bin Laden and other international renegades harbored in Afghanistan. The 2002 National Security Strategy of the Bush Administration declares, "America is now threatened less by conquering states than we are by failing ones." (It is not clear to us when in the recent past the United States was truly threatened by "conquering states.")[4]

In this view, "failed states" always require intervention; they "have to be rescued" (*Economist*). The U.S. was advised by Council on Foreign Relations Fellow Sebastian Mallaby to include as part of its imperial mission fixing "failed states": "U.S. foreign policy must . . . respond to . . . the growing danger of failed states." Martin Wolf of the London *Financial Times* admonished that, for "failing states . . . policies should cut out the poison before it festers."[5]

One reason the "failed state" label is convenient is that it focuses on *local* shortcomings, problems with the "failed" government, with the geographical region the state occupies, or with the people being governed (e.g., poor education, backward culture), rather than on any external actors or externally driven trends that may have catalyzed the failure. A 2003 RAND study, *America's Role in Nation Building*, partially funded by the Department of Defense, makes clear that the failure of Afghanistan was far from purely indigenous, but ignores entirely the crucial U.S. role. According to the study, Afghanistan is a "weak state pulled apart by *its neighbors*. The 1979 Soviet invasion sparked a period of civil war and unrest that lasted over twenty years. After the Soviets withdrew, various factions occupied and then lost control of the capital, Kabul, until the rise of the Taliban in 1996 [emphasis added]."[6]

Conspicuously absent are the *origins* of the "various factions," conveying the impression that they were home grown, part of the fabric of Afghan society. The only other actors named are the Soviet Union, "its neighbors," and the Taliban. In fueling the Afghan civil war that destroyed state institutions and killed or forced into exile millions of moderate Afghans who might have helped rebuild the country, Washington bears a large share of the responsibility for its destruction.

Suppressing the U.S. decisive role allows a study on U.S. "nation-building" to include Afghanistan.

Contrary to the mainstream picture, the late-20th-century Afghan "state failure" is the direct result of destructive U.S. policies, in addition to the destructive policies of the Soviet Union and other Afghan neighbors. In this book, we start off by reviewing the pre-9/11 history, concentrating on the role of U.S. policies in furthering the destruction of Afghanistan. In the 1970s, the country went from a "neutral" constitutional monarchy dependent on both Soviet and U.S. aid, to a Soviet client "democratic republic." The Soviets made the first move in violating the sovereignty and human rights of the Afghan people. But, *during the 1980s, U.S. intervention was used exclusively to increase the likelihood that the Soviet-backed state of Afghanistan as it was currently composed would fail.* The U.S. policy of the 1980s had serious repercussions that still echo today. The crucial U.S. role in bringing terrorists to Afghanistan and strengthening fundamentalists is almost never admitted. When it is recognized, it is rarely judged harshly.

While visiting Afghanistan in 2005 we met Mariam, a 44-year-old woman whose tragic story is typical. In the 1980s her brother, a political prisoner, was killed, and her husband, an educated and politically astute man, was taken away one day by armed men loyal to the warlord Gulbuddin Hekmatyar. The men entered her home and beat her and her children, and raped her teenage daughter. She never saw her husband again. Mariam explained to us why her husband was targeted:

> . . . my husband was educated, he was a political person—Hekmatyar did not want any political, educated people. My husband was not the only person they killed. They killed so many educated and political people like him. . . . He wanted to kill off all the educated and political people in Afghanistan.[7]

Like Mariam's husband, thousands of educated Afghans were disappeared by the forces of Hekmatyar (and other U.S.-backed fundamentalists such as Abdul Rasul Sayyaf).[8] Hekmatyar received the bulk of

U.S. funding during the Soviet occupation and was the most vicious of all the warlords, having gained notoriety for throwing acid in the faces of women who refused to veil themselves.[9]

Even as the Soviets finally withdrew their forces in the early 1990s, leaving behind a puppet regime, U.S. support to fanatical warlords continued. The period from 1992 to 1996, after the Soviet Union left and before the Taliban took power, is considered the most violent in recent Afghan history. Weapons supplies were never confiscated, refugees were never repatriated, and criminals were never tried. During this time, the dismantling of Afghan state institutions by the U.S.-backed Mujahideen was finalized. In April 1992, after the Soviet puppet Najibullah was deposed, Mujahideen factions entered Kabul and declared themselves leaders of the country. With vast stores of rocket launchers, grenades, and other weapons, they began fighting one another, turning the nation's cities and provinces into killing fields. In Kabul alone, tens of thousands were killed. The bombed-out shells of buildings and bullet-ridden walls of the city today are a visible testament to the horrors of those four years.

Between 1992 and 1996, Western governments and the Western media turned their backs on Afghanistan. Media coverage during that period of violence and chaos dropped by more than two-thirds compared with the period of the Soviet occupation. It was also during this period that a severe erosion of Afghan women's rights began. Most Americans attribute women's oppression to the Taliban, but the Taliban simply formalized into law a legacy begun by U.S.-backed fundamentalists. There was little ideological difference between the U.S.-backed Mujahideen leaders and the Taliban. The infamous Ministry for the Promotion of Virtue and Prevention of Vice, which controlled women's dress codes and the lengths of men's beards, originated during the Mujahideen government in the early 1990s. Rape was a common tool of war for the U.S.-backed fundamentalists. An Afghan in Farah Province who identified himself simply as Qasimi told us:

> Young women who did not want to be raped by the fundamentalists threw themselves off the top floors of tall buildings and

> preferred death to rape. . . . Many families who had daughters didn't want fundamentalists to rape them. So when the fundamentalists attacked their homes, they would kill their own daughters because it was better for them to die than to be raped by these criminals.[10]

In 1996, the Mujahideen factions were forced out of Kabul by a new group of fundamentalists calling themselves the Taliban. The Clinton Administration, eager to see the embarrassing factionalized violence of U.S. protégés come to an end, initially condoned, and even encouraged the Taliban, despite knowledge of their totalitarian vision for the country. This vision was borne by women in particular, but all Afghans faced severe repression. Armed with weapons, satellite telephones, and brand-new Japanese pickup trucks, the Taliban took over the majority of Afghanistan with terrifying speed, forcing their Mujahideen opposition to put aside all differences and form a "United Front" that held onto a small part of Northern Afghan territory. They would come to be known as the "Northern Alliance," and ally once more with the U.S. against this new "enemy."

U.S. responsibility for the rise to power of the Taliban includes direct support in the form of a pipeline deal between the Taliban and a U.S. corporation (Unocal). The al-Qa'eda attacks on U.S. embassies in 1998 resulted in cruise missile strikes against Afghanistan, followed by the hypocritical late denunciation of the human rights record of the Taliban, useless and hurtful sanctions, and a revival of backing to the Northern Alliance. Time and again, the actions of the United States either encouraged or prolonged the war in Afghanistan and the suffering of Afghans.

After the tragic events of 9/11, media attention to Afghanistan dramatically increased, and the U.S.'s "War on Terror" was launched with Operation Enduring Freedom. America's air war killed thousands of Afghans, sowed thousands of cluster bomblets, which added to the existing land-mine problem, and starved unknown numbers of people in the brutal winter months because the bombs cut off aid. Meanwhile, the ground war allied U.S. troops with members of the Northern

Alliance and other local warlords, who were eager to see the Taliban vacate the territories they had once claimed. Afghans warned the U.S. to not repeat the mistakes of allying with fundamentalists, but once again the fate of civil society was less important than "getting the job done," which was defined narrowly in terms of toppling the Taliban government. Within two months, the Taliban retreated and Northern Alliance members began reestablishing themselves into positions of power and repeating their criminal acts.

Meanwhile, on the political front, Afghanistan's government was redesigned by the U.S. with the pliable puppet, Hamid Karzai, as president. The elderly ex-king, Zahir Shah, was supported by many to lead Afghanistan's interim government, but U.S. Special Envoy Zalmay Khalilzad ensured that Shah was undermined and replaced by Karzai, in a move that U.S. media all but completely missed. Prominent members of the Northern Alliance were repaid for their help in toppling the Taliban with high-ranking positions in the interim government, while most ordinary Afghans were excluded. Khalilzad, eventually named U.S. Ambassador to Afghanistan, emerged as the real power broker in Kabul, while Karzai remained sequestered under the protection of U.S. soldiers.

With the return of the warlord and a U.S. puppet in Kabul, Afghanistan was also subjected to the return of Islamic law. Enshrined in Afghanistan's new constitution, Sharia Law continues to be abused by fundamentalist clerics appointed by Karzai, with women as the primary victims. Women's self-immolation in the conservative city of Herat reached shocking proportions, greater than during the Taliban's rule. Today Kabul's prisons are filled with women convicted for the "crimes" of refusing to marry the man their families picked for them, and running away from home.

Afghan women have been exploited by both liberal feminists and conservative warmongers. Feminist groups in the U.S., horrified by the Taliban's institutionalized misogyny, began rallying around the cause of Afghan women and supported an anti–"gender apartheid" campaign that simplistically condensed Afghan women's oppression to the forced wearing of the *burqa*. On the other end of mainstream U.S. politics, women in the Bush Administration used a propaganda campaign designed to take advantage of Afghan women for U.S. benefit. In the end both liberals and conservatives took up the cause of Afghan women as a justification for war and regime-change. Meanwhile, the life-risking political work of women's rights activists on the ground in Afghanistan, who opposed both U.S. imperialism and Islamic fundamentalism, was ignored.

The U.S. was less likely than the warlords to earn the hatred of ordinary Afghans—until stories of abuse by U.S. soldiers began to emerge. Sexual abuse and torture of prisoners in Afghanistan predated the infamous Abu Ghraib scandal in Iraq. The *New York Times* reported the murder of two Afghan men, Dilawar and Habibullah, in terrifying detail, at the hands of American soldiers while in U.S. custody.[11] Afghans responded to this incident, coupled with reports of U.S. abuse of the Holy Koran, with violent protests across the country in 2005. Instead of addressing its own behavior, the Bush Administration attacked *Newsweek* for reporting the story of Koran abuse.

The U.S. media have acted in near lockstep with U.S. policies in Afghanistan by providing mostly favorable coverage of U.S. actions, and dropping coverage when convenient. U.S. news outlets have also rarely explored the reasons why the U.S. went to Afghanistan and established military bases in the country and surrounding region. While left-wing commentators jumped to conclusions regarding oil interests, the real reasons are numerous and more complex than just oil.

Meanwhile, mainstream media discussion of the Afghan state failure seldom implicates foreign powers. But troubling questions persist regarding U.S. culpability. After all, the warlords who once ruled Afghanistan and who are back in power would never have been able to wreak so much havoc on Afghan people without being armed and trained by the United States. As the "war on terror" occupied the headlines, our newspapers failed to scrutinize either the past and current empowerment of fundamentalists or the manipulation of Afghan "democracy" by U.S. players for U.S. benefit. On the eve of the Pentagon's "Operation Enduring Freedom" in October 2001, women's rights were touted as a reason to fight the Taliban, and most Americans sympathetically supported a "war to liberate women." But what of our role in helping destroy women's rights in Afghanistan through the support of fundamentalists? What about the continued oppression of Afghan women in post-Taliban Afghanistan?

Surveys have revealed that the majority of Afghan people want justice for the warlords' destruction of their country.[12] But Americans are not calling for justice for the *warlords in Washington* who engineered a cruel fate for the Afghan people for two and half decades. There is a "propaganda of silence" surrounding the historic and current role of the U.S. government in Afghanistan. This book is intended to break that silence and lay bare the systematic actions of successive U.S. administrations that led to the suffering of the Afghan people.

Today Afghanistan is known as the "sick man" of Asia.[13] In 2005, the United Nations Development Program office in Kabul collected statistics for the first time on Afghanistan, and ranked Afghanistan 173rd out of 178 countries in the UNDP human development index.[14] The statistics on health, literacy, employment, and lifespan, especially for women, have changed little since the fall of the Taliban. A typical Afghan woman cannot read or write, and if she is lucky enough to survive childbirth, she may live to the age of forty-five. These grim facts rallied the sympathy of the world to help the people of Afghanistan after September 11, 2001. Billions of dollars of aid were promised and pronouncements were made never again to forget about the Afghan people. But several years later, little attention is paid to Afghanistan globally or in the United States. Polls reveal that today Americans are less interested in Afghanistan than Iraq,[15] where standards of living, although deeply impacted by war, are still decades ahead of Afghanistan.

Our goal with this book is to survey the current political discourse on Afghanistan and place it in a context that is critical of the decisions made in Washington. We draw from the work of mostly mainstream reporters and analysts, as well as declassified U.S. government documents. We supplement this with our own observations made during our visit, and information and comments gleaned from hours of recorded interviews with Afghan political activists, journalists, lawyers, refugees, teachers, students, government officials, and others. We believe that informed citizens can change the world and we hope that this book spurs your interest in Afghanistan whether you are an activist, student, teacher, politician, or simply a concerned American. More importantly, we hope it will spark some action to change the U.S. patterns of behavior in Afghanistan.

PART ONE

HISTORICAL CONTEXT

CHAPTER ONE

DESTROYING A STATE

U.S. POLICY BEFORE SEPTEMBER 11, 2001

How did Afghanistan arrive at its present condition? And what responsibility does the U.S. government bear? To answer these questions we need to go back at least two and a half decades to the late 1970s, when the Soviet Union invaded and began an occupation of Afghanistan that would last ten years. With the Cold War between the U.S. and the USSR in full swing, Afghanistan became the perfect battleground for the world's two superpowers to fight a proxy war that would decide once and for all who would dominate global politics. The U.S. chose to arm and train an indigenous force, supplemented by fighters from around the globe. The ruthlessness of the seven fundamentalist Mujahideen parties that the U.S. backed, and the effects they would have on Afghan society once in power, was never a consideration for U.S. policy makers. The people of Afghanistan paid a heavy price—thousands of dissidents and intellectuals were disappeared, hundreds of thousands became refugees, and any progress made by women's rights advocates in the context of an already conservative Muslim society was set back decades.

THE 1970S: SOVIET AND U.S. INVOLVEMENT ESCALATES

Since 1919, Soviet influence in Afghanistan had always been greater than that of the United States. The two neighbors had been allies since Afghanistan became formally independent from Britain, and the Soviet Union was the largest foreign donor to Afghanistan. Second to the amount of Soviet aid was U.S. aid. As it had been a "buffer state" between Britain and Russia, Afghanistan was now considered a buffer between U.S.-backed Iran and Pakistan, on one side, and the Soviet Union on the other.

By the 1970s, the Soviet Union was becoming increasingly involved in the politics of Afghanistan. Left-leaning political parties were a natural conduit for Soviet influence (real and alleged). The Progressive Democratic Party of Afghanistan (PDPA, referred to by some as the "Afghan Communist Party") was formed in 1965 and became the most popular leftist organization in the country. By the early 1970s, PDPA had split into two factions, Parcham (Banner), "the foremost and probably best organized leftist group" according to U.S. political officer Albert Fairchild, and Khalq (the Masses). Parcham was led by Babrak Karmal, who after the 1979 Soviet invasion became their puppet leader. The party was "pro-Soviet and follow[ed] the Moscow line." To some, it was also backed secretly by the Royal family to provide a "lightning rod for dissent," earning it the derogatory name "Royal Afghan Communist Party." Fairchild asserted that this theory "cannot be entirely discounted." For example, the Parcham party was allowed to publish its own newspaper for over a year, whereas Khalq had its newspaper banned immediately. Khalq was headed by Noor Mohammed Taraki, who also became president, coming to power in a Soviet-backed coup in the late 1970s. There was apparently very little difference between the two parties, other than "personality differences between Taraki and Karmal." According to Craig Baxter, however, "Taraki [Khalq] favored a Leninist-type party based on the working class, while Karmal [Parcham] wanted a broad democratic front. Supporters of Khalq were primarily Pashtuns from rural Afghanistan, while Parchamis tended to be from urban areas." Fairchild noted in addition that "Khalq has been very active among the Turcomen [*sic*], Uzbek, and Panjshiri [a Tajik subgroup] ethnic minorities."[16]

The Afghan king Zahir Shah was ousted in 1973 by his cousin Daoud, who had the backing of the military and the Parcham faction of the PDPA. Daoud, who abolished the monarchy and formed a republic, was also said to have had Soviet backing. Still, a declassified U.S. Department of State cable expressed little serious antagonism to the coup.

> Daud [*sic*] seems unlikely to make any major shifts in Afghan policies, but there could be some changes in emphasis. . . . Daud may be a little harder to deal with than was Prime Minister Shafiq or the King. He is likely to be more suspicious of U.S. motives, somewhat less cooperative, and a bit more pro-Soviet. Nevertheless, on the issues that affect U.S. interests—continued Afghan independence, stability in the area, and narcotics—there is no reason to think he will reverse Afghan policies.[17]

Here "independence" means independence from the Soviet Union. So long as Daoud's behavior coincided with the interests of the United States, there was no problem. In 1977 the State Department commented favorably on his improved ties with the U.S.-backed dictatorship in Iran, saying that he had "made significant contributions to the improvement of regional stability—thereby helping to fulfill [a] principal U.S. objective."[18]

In April 1978 Daoud was killed in a coup by the military, in collaboration with the PDPA. Noor Mohammed Taraki, head of the Khalq faction of the party, became president, prime minister, and chairman of the Revolutionary Council. The PDPA presidency was far from popularly supported, even among those who might be considered favorable to progressive politics.

After the Taraki coup brought the PDPA officially to power, the U.S. State Department began to worry about the blow to U.S. credibility represented by a "communist" government in Afghanistan. A Department memo to Secretary of State Cyrus Vance read, "Pakistan, Iran, Saudi Arabia, and others of our friends in the area will see the situation clearly as a Soviet coup. On the domestic front, many Americans will see this as an extension of Soviet power and draw the parallel with Angola, Ethiopia, etc."[19]

The precise nature of the U.S. response is unknown, because Freedom of Information Act requests for crucial records pertaining to U.S. support for Afghan rebels during this period have been denied.[20] But at least one Washington policy maker has claimed that U.S. support for Islamic extremists was not a consequence of the December 1979 Soviet invasion, but predated it. President Jimmy Carter's National Security Adviser Zbigniew Brzezinski told an interviewer in 1998 that the U.S. began covert support for Afghan rebel groups based in Pakistan by mid-1979:

> According to the official version of history, CIA aid to the Mujahideen began during 1980, that is to say, after the Soviet army invaded Afghanistan, 24 Dec 1979. But the reality, secretly guarded until now, is completely otherwise: Indeed, it was July 3, 1979 that President Carter signed the first directive for secret aid to the opponents of the pro-Soviet regime in Kabul. And that very day, I wrote a note to the president in which I explained to him that in my opinion this aid was going to induce a Soviet military intervention. . . . We didn't push the Russians to intervene, but we knowingly increased the probability that they would. . . . It had the effect of drawing the Russians into the Afghan trap . . .[21]

Perhaps unknown to Washington, the Soviets were just as worried by the path Taraki was taking. According to Steve Galster of the National Security Archive, "Soviet officials thought the Khalqi leadership was moving too fast with its reforms and urged Taraki and Amin to moderate the pace of change and broaden their political base by including noncommunists in the government."[22] Taraki's deputy Hafizullah Amin was especially bothersome to the Soviet government, who at one point labeled him a "CIA agent."[23] Amin murdered Taraki and took power in November of 1979, "riding roughshod over tradition and tribal and ethnic autonomy."[24] One month later, the Soviets invaded. After assassinating Amin in December, Soviet troops entered the country and installed Babrak Karmal, the former Parcham leader who had been in exile in Moscow, as their puppet president.

Afghans today uniformly condemn the Soviet occupation. Toufiq, our driver and guide in Herat and Farah, related a common saying among Afghans:

> The Soviet Union came to Afghanistan under the banner of three slogans:
>
> We will give food to the people
> We will give clothes to the people
> We will give homes to the people
> But instead of food they gave us bullets
> Instead of clothes they gave us coffins
> Instead of homes, they gave us graveyards[25]

THE 1980S: MAKING AFGHANISTAN FAIL

To the United States, the December 1979 Soviet invasion of Afghanistan was a serious blow to its credibility in South Asia and the Middle East, especially after the Iranian revolution next door toppled the Shah, a U.S. client, early the same year. It did not look good to have one client state and one nonaligned state, both on the border of your chief enemy, fall to hostile forces. Some in the Carter administration were concerned about the possible threat it posed to U.S. control of Middle East energy reserves, or at least that is what they said publicly. President Carter declared that the invasion of Afghanistan "has brought the Soviet military forces to within 300 miles of the Indian Ocean and close to the Straits of Hormuz, a waterway through which most of the world's oil must flow." He was concerned that the Russians were "attempting to consolidate a strategic position" near the Middle East reserves "that poses a grave threat to the free movement of Middle East oil." To Carter, "An attempt by any outside force to gain control of the Persian Gulf region will be regarded as an assault on the vital interests of the United States of America, and such an assault will be repelled by any means necessary, including military force." It is not clear if Carter really felt that Middle East oil was threatened by the Soviet move, or if he was just trying to rally the public in favor of the proxy war that the U.S. was running behind the scenes.[26]

Some in the United States saw the Soviet invasion as a gift. To Brzezinski, the Russian move was a blunder that the U.S. had to use to its fullest advantage. "The day that the Soviets officially crossed the border, I wrote to President Carter: We now have the opportunity of giving to the USSR its Vietnam War."

As the U.S. invasion did for Vietnam, the Soviet attack on Afghanistan and the U.S. counterattack decimated the country. Afghanistan expert Barnett Rubin wrote, "The painstakingly constructed state shattered when Soviet-supported Communist elite tried to use that fragile apparatus as an instrument of massive, coercive social change. The coherence of the society that tried to resist that onslaught and the invasion that followed was shattered not only by the Soviet counterinsurgency strategy but also by the way that Pakistan used U.S. and Saudi aid to the Afghan resistance."[27]

Here the term "Afghan resistance" refers to the seven Islamist "Mujahideen," or "jihadi," groups based in the Afghan refugee camps in Pakistan that received the bulk of U.S. and Saudi monetary, military, and logistical support via the Pakistani Inter-Services Intelligence Directorate (ISI). The amount of U.S. and Saudi assistance to these groups started at around $30 million in 1980 and increased to over $1 billion per year in 1986–89. Unfortunately, the jihadis are often considered to represent the entire resistance movement, despite the fact that there were many Afghans who resisted the Soviets that had nothing in common with the jihadis politically. For example, the Revolutionary Association of the Women of Afghanistan (RAWA), whose struggle for women's rights naturally put them at odds with the Islamist parties in Pakistan, was one of many secular organizations that encouraged the Afghan people "to unite and fight for the independence of our beloved country" against the occupation. Unlike the Islamists, their aims were not to bring about a return to a conservative, misogynist order, but "to build a society in which oppression, torture, execution, and injustices must be replaced by democracy and social justice." But the goal in sponsoring the Mujahideen was to make the Soviets pay a price, not to offer an alternative political structure for the Afghan people. The only Pakistan-based party that was not fundamentalist was the National Islamic Front of Afghanistan, led by Syed Ahmad Gailani, the head of the Qadiri Sufi order. Although this was still a religious party, the Front was considered "the most liberal and closest to the old royal regime of all the parties," and thus might have been the least harmful. But this party "had no strong foreign support."[28]

The commander receiving by far the most U.S. aid was Gulbuddin Hekmatyar, today working to bring down the U.S.-backed regime of Hamid Karzai. As a Kabul University engineering student in the early 1970s, Hekmatyar organized attacks that consisted of throwing acid on unveiled women's exposed faces or legs and sometimes even shooting at their legs. The CIA admitted to his "vicious" and "fascist" tendencies, but perhaps because of these tendencies he was expected to be the most effective against the Soviets. The goal of U.S. aid, according to Barnett Rubin, was "a military victory dominated by the forces of Hikmatyar [*sic*]." Hekmatyar was extremely useful to Pakistan not only because he was rabidly anticommunist, but also because he was antinationalist. Afghan fundamentalists like Hekmatyar readily allied themselves with the fundamentalist Zia ul Haq regime in Pakistan, rather than support ethnic Pashtun nationalism and separatism for the Pashtuns living in Pakistan's Northwest Frontier ("Pashtunistan"). "Both the ISI and the CIA considered him a useful tool for shaping the future of Central Asia," says Rubin.

Hekmatyar's violence was not directed only at the Soviets or their cohorts. During the resistance war, he assassinated other rebel leaders inside Afghanistan, and conducted a "reign of terror against 'insufficiently Islamic' intellectuals" in the refugee camps of Pakistan. In testimony before the U.S. House of Representatives, Rubin reported that hundreds of innocents were killed by order of Hekmatyar. "Hekmatyar has committed these crimes on the territory of Pakistan with complete impunity . . . for ten years while continuing to receive American aid." Among the murders attributed to Hekmatyar's purges were Faiz Ahmad, the husband of RAWA's founding leader Meena, in November 1986, and Meena herself in February 1987.[29]

It was not only Afghan Mujahideen who were harnessed by the U.S. and its allies (Western Europe, Saudi Arabia, Pakistan, Egypt, and China) to fight the Soviet Union. "Jihadis" were recruited from around the globe to fight in the "holy war" against the atheistic communist invaders. One "man the west could use" was Osama bin Laden, the son of "Saudi Arabia's richest building contractor." During the 1980s, bin Laden "raised money and supplies for Afghan . . . mujahedeen [*sic*]. He raised huge sums from oil-rich Arabs in Persian Gulf states, contributed millions from his own fortune and even brought in heavy equipment from his family's company to help build camps, tunnels, military depots and roads for the Afghan forces." In 1984, he founded Makhtab al Khadimat, "a group that recruited and trained Muslim volunteers from Egypt, Algeria and other countries to fight in the Afghan war." Some of the money funneled by the CIA to the Mujahideen "may have gone" to this group, according to the *New York Times*. Makhtab al Khadimat later "was to play a major role in raising the concept of global holy war to a reality over the next decade, eventually becoming the organization known as al-Qa'eda."[30]

Many who write about the anti-Soviet war, such as Paul Berman in his book *Terror and Liberalism*, refer to the U.S. support for indigenous and expatriate fundamentalist fanatics in Afghanistan as a well-meaning deed that backfired:

> A thousand commentators have pointed out, in retrospect, that Ronald Reagan's policy in Afghanistan back in the 1980s did lead to difficulties in later years, which is indisputable. In Afghanistan . . . America's beneficiaries turned out to be America's worst enemies. The world is full of back-stabbing sons-of-bitches: such is the lesson of modern history . . .

Berman dismisses the U.S. responsibility for providing material and moral support for the largest global nongovernmental terrorist network in history by blaming those who got the money and weapons, and absolving their funders. He and others disregard the intentionality of the U.S. government in building a coalition of terror to bleed the Soviets.[31]

The use of extremists is a standard imperial tool to invalidate, destroy, or cause a government to "fail." The single-minded nature of extremists and their unwillingness to compromise ensures that they can be trusted to follow a single purpose: hurt the enemy, regardless of the consequences. The excuse commonly given for this reprehensible tactic as used in Afghanistan is that the United States did not expect to beat the Soviets militarily, and thus the best they could do was to make the Russians pay a price. According to

Barnett Rubin, "... no one in the United States or Pakistan believed that they would drive the Soviets out of Afghanistan and set up a new government.... Most officials assumed that the mujahidin [*sic*] would lose." In memos, the U.S. State Department expressed the belief that the rebels were "fragmented, lack[ed] effective national leadership, and certainly [could not] force a Soviet withdrawal." In that case, one would think the most effective solution to the occupation would be to support a political alternative to the puppet government, instead of an unlikely military victory. On the contrary (Rubin): "The United States was particularly indifferent about which groups [among those it was funding] might have more popular support, be more amenable to a political settlement, or be more likely to form a stable government."[32]

The primary concern in Washington was the Soviet presence and its threat to U.S. interests. The price of this for the Afghan people was never considered. Progressive or secular groups interested in regaining control over their country—exiled supporters of the ex-king Zahir Shah, nationalist anti-imperialist activists, anti-Soviet progressive or moderate intellectuals—might not be willing to draw enough blood. To the U.S., Afghans were cannon fodder and mattered only so much as (1) they could impose a cost on the Soviet occupiers, and (2) their suffering could be used for anti-Soviet propaganda. Milton Bearden, CIA station chief in Pakistan from 1986–89, responsible for the covert action program to arm the Mujahideen during that period, characterized the relationship between the U.S., the USSR, and the Afghan people as follows: "The United States was fighting the Soviets to the last Afghan."[33]

It should be mentioned that the U.S. approach contradicted the wishes of its own people. In a Gallup poll taken on 11–12 January 1980, 52 percent of respondents favored a U.S. reaction to the Soviet invasion of Afghanistan that included "economic and diplomatic pressure," while only 30 percent favored a military-type response (21 percent wanted to "send arms" and 9 percent to "send troops"). The remaining 18 percent either had "no opinion" (13 percent) or thought the U.S. should "do nothing" (5 percent). This is probably one reason why U.S. material aid to the Mujahideen remained covert until the mid-1980s. The chief public response to the Soviet invasion was the U.S. boycott of the summer Olympic games in 1980 and halfhearted sanctions on agricultural and other exports. In opposition to the bulk of the population, however, there was bipartisan near-universal support of the Mujahideen from U.S. officials. Republican Senator Hatch praised the "freedom fighters" for their "determination and raw courage." Democratic Senator Bill Bradley envisioned the Mujahideen groups "developing a modern concept of an independent, neutral Islamic state," against all odds. He urged that they be recognized as "the sole legitimate representative of the Afghan people."[34]

The bipartisan support for the Mujahideen had a few exceptions in elite circles. James Nathan, a political scientist at the University of Delaware, criticized the politicians for wanting to put Afghan lives on the line to fight Washington's war. In a prophetic *New York Times* opinion piece in 1980, before U.S. material support for the Mujahideen was overtly acknowledged but was still being debated, he wrote, "to aid the Afghans now is not to offer them a better chance of relief from oppression but rather to improve their prospects for near-extinction. To intensify Afghan suffering in the hope of making the Soviet Union pay a price verges on a kind of racism." But it is easier to destroy a state than to build a new one, and U.S. planners exempted themselves from doing the latter, while concentrating on the former.[35]

1990–96: DISINTEGRATION

> Far more innocent civilians died in Kabul [during the 1990s] than in the United States on September 11. Although it took longer than one day to kill them, the agony of those burned, mutilated, and shattered, and the endless grief of their survivors, is just as real.[36]
>
> —BARNETT RUBIN

When the Soviets finally withdrew in February 1989, 1.5 million Afghans were dead, 5 million were disabled, and another 5 million were refugees. Russian Foreign Minister Eduard Shevardnadze told the Supreme Soviet in 1989 that their invasion of Afghanistan "violat[ed] the norms of proper behavior and disregard[ed] the values common to all mankind. We committed the most serious violations of our laws, our party, and public norms." As Shevardnadze apologized for his country's role in the destruction of Afghanistan, U.S. President Ronald Reagan authorized an increase in funding to the Mujahideen and rejected moves towards peace. The Afghan president at the time, Dr. Najibullah, while certainly a Russian puppet, supported reconciliation with his enemies and a role for the former king Zahir Shah in a proposed coalition government. He said he was prepared to step down if he lost elections. A ceasefire offer from Russian president Gorbachev was declined by the U.S., who wanted to prolong the bloodshed until the last trace of Soviet influence was expunged. Assistant Secretary of State John Kelly made it clear in written testimony to the House Foreign Affairs Committee that "we believe that no stable political settlement is achievable as long as the Najibullah regime remains in power." Kelly cited "two key premises" on which the U.S. government based its political strategy in Afghanistan: "the Afghans themselves should determine their own future"; and "our own diplomatic efforts will support the Afghan resistance."[37]

To Washington, the continuation of war was equated with "diplomacy." The seven Pakistan-based parties were likewise equated with "the Afghan resistance," and the varying degrees of fundamentalism they espoused were taken to represent the opinions of all Afghans. While denouncing Najibullah, the United States offered no political alternative to him, other than the seven groups, few of which were aligned politically with most Afghans. For example, none of the U.S.-backed groups even suggested reconciliation with the deposed king. The political head of Burhanuddin Rabbani's supposedly "moderate" fundamentalist faction Jamiat-i Islami said, "Most Mujahideen are against the participation of the king, and we are also against him." But the king was considered by many Afghans to be "the only hope." A "prominent Afghan journalist" told the *New York Times*, "It shames me to admit it, for I demonstrated against him when I was a young man, but the King should come back. This alliance [between the seven parties] is no alliance." Even a staunch supporter of the Pakistan-based groups, Sayed Bahauddin Majrooh, head of the Afghan Information Center, proposed that a post-Soviet government might include "four or five political personalities in exile" in addition to the Mujahideen leaders, implying a role for the former king, then in exile in Rome. Referring to the Pakistan-based factions, Majrooh's son Naim commented, "The seven of them sitting in a room cannot decide the future, cannot impose a government on the people of Afghanistan." Majrooh was killed on order of Gulbuddin Hekmatyar soon after he published a poll taken among Afghan refugees in Pakistan finding that 70 percent favored the king's return.[38]

Washington's blanket endorsement of the extremists had the effect of "weaken[ing] and undermin[ing] secular nationalist leadership, and fragment[ing] power in every locality" of Afghanistan. Hekmatyar, the primary U.S. beneficiary, gleefully encouraged this process. Most of his time during the 1980s had been spent not fighting Soviets or government troops but in consolidating his power and grooming himself for his expected coronation. The huge caches of arms he had accumulated were not used in battle so much as hoarded "to gain a military edge over rival parties." Apparently the CIA and its allies in Pakistan were too enamored of Hekmatyar to stop their support, although U.S. policy was always to publicly disavow aiding him. The *New York Times* put it this way: "Administration officials said little if any of the $300 million in aid the United States covertly grants the guerrillas annually goes intentionally to Mr. Hekmatyar. But he appears to be amply supplied by the Pakistani military intelligence agency," which was of course "amply supplied" by the CIA. Not only was the ISI giving the bulk of the U.S. aid to Hekmatyar, but "reports from the field" asserted that the CIA was "directly involved" in planning at least some of his military campaigns. According to Barnett Rubin, "ISI—and CIA-sponsored military activity increasingly took the form of encouraging individual commanders to fire rockets into Kabul city, where they mainly killed civilians. Commanders with greater power and a strategic vision resisted this policy, but those who followed it, including Hekmatyar's commanders, were paid for each rocket fired."[39]

The major cities of Afghanistan, which had remained relatively unscathed during the Soviet occupation, now became the targets of a multiyear siege of highly populated areas. Assistant Secretary of State Kelly justified the siege as part of a strategy "of choking the Regime-controlled locales" by attacking targets within the cities as well as supply lines to the North, "forcing the Soviets to maintain a high level of resupply and preventing the regime from enlarging significantly the areas which they control."[40] Under the direction of Washington, the civilian death toll rapidly escalated, as "more than 90 percent" of the rockets fired hit "nowhere near military targets." *New York Times* correspondent John F. Burns had "seen these rockets kill as many as 40 people in a single blast." According to Burns, at least a thousand civilians were killed in Kabul during the first year after the Soviet withdrawal. Citizens of Kabul understood who was ultimately responsible for the onslaught: "Many Afghans began to see the United States . . . as a distant power that sanctioned the routine killing of civilians."[41] To keep up with the attacks, Soviet airlifts in aid of Najibullah's government were now filled mostly with weapons, instead of food. The Associated Press reported, "an estimated 2 million people in Kabul face a winter of scarce food and fuel unless the Communist government changes its priority of supplies,"[42] which would have meant losing the war. The starvation of Afghans was a predictable consequence of the U.S.-backed siege, part of the "choking" strategy that necessitated "a high level of re-supply."

Before the 1991 Gulf War, the Pakistan-based Mujahideen continued to be treated en masse as representatives of the Afghan resistance. Administration officials made every effort to deflect criticism of the extremist leaders. An example is the following exchange during a House of Representatives subcommittee hearing between Representative Lee Hamilton from Indiana, chairman of the subcommittee, and Assistant Secretary of State John Kelly.

> MR. HAMILTON: Can you say that a large part of our support . . . are [*sic*] really going to fundamentalist Moslem leaders?
>
> MR. KELLY: Let me say in general terms that most of the people in the Mujahideen are what might be termed fundamentalist Islamic believers.
>
> MR. HAMILTON: . . . [W]e have a lot of trouble with fundamentalist leaders in other areas of the world.

> MR. KELLY: Well, let me talk for a minute about fundamentalism. Where I grew up in the South being a fundamentalist was not a very bad thing. I knew a lot of fundamentalist Baptists and a lot of other fundamentalists. So I guess maybe a better word would be an extremist, somebody who wants to impose his religious beliefs on another by force, or something like that.
>
> MR. HAMILTON: Do these people want to do that?
>
> MR. KELLY: There are certainly some people in Afghanistan who do want to do that.
>
> MR. HAMILTON: How about the ones we are supporting? Do they want to do it?
>
> MR. KELLY: We think that the bulk of them are reasonable people, Mr. Chairman.[43]

After the 1991 U.S. assault on Iraq (Gulf War), Washington was forced to reconsider its unconditional support for two of the groups. Gulbuddin Hekmatyar, the primary beneficiary of U.S. support, and Abdul Rasul Sayyaf both denounced the U.S. aggression and offered support to Saddam Hussein. This was an embarrassment for the George H. W. Bush administration. Having refused to say anything negative about Hekmatyar in the 1990 Committee hearing, Kelly was forced the following year to admit to the House, "he is a person who has vehemently attacked the United States on a number of issues . . . I think he is a person with whom we do not need to have or should not have much truck." This public denunciation did not yet lead to a weakening of Hekmatyar's power. According to Rubin, "Just when the State Department began to try to turn U.S. policy away from the support for Hikmatyar that the CIA still urged, Saudi Arabia [a close U.S. ally] increased its aid to Hikmatyar as the strongest Sunni force while Arab volunteers continued to flock to both him and Sayyaf."[44]

An agreement with the Soviets on "negative symmetry," i.e., the mutual end of support to the Mujahideen and the Najibullah Government by December 1991, was hailed as a diplomatic triumph for the new post–Cold War Washington/Moscow alliance. In reality the "symmetry" was a fallacy, since U.S. associates Saudi Arabia and Pakistan had no intention of withdrawing support from their favorite factions, including Hekmatyar, so the shelling of Kabul continued. At the same time, the end of the Russian aid that was sustaining the Afghan government meant the government lost its influence with certain commanders that it had earlier bought with arms, food, and fuel. Predictably, most of the Soviet-backed militias, including that led by the powerful warlord General Abdul Rashid Dostum, defected to the Mujahideen, and the government crumbled in a few months. Najibullah fled his post on April 16, 1992.

Almost immediately, Washington lost all concern for the deepening crisis for which it was in large part responsible. Apparently it was somehow expected that the commanders who had been groomed by U.S. and Pakistani intelligence to oust the regime would magically unite and rebuild the country. State Department spokesperson Margaret D. Tutwiler made a public plea, "I don't know who all is armed there, but people who are armed . . . please don't resort to violence"—words that sounded as though they came from a helpless outsider, not a State Department that was responsible for instigating and funding the arms and aid pipeline to the Mujahideen for more than a decade. The truth is that the Bush administration didn't care anymore what happened in Afghanistan. Privately, officials and experts admitted that the "basic expectation is that Afghanistan is headed for a protracted internal power struggle." The *Economist* noted a few months after Najibullah was ousted that Afghanistan was already "more divided" than ever, due to "the emergence of three strong men" (Hekmatyar, Ahmed Shah Massoud, and Dostum). What should have been a period of rebuilding became a new, more vicious war. An unidentified source told *New York Times* correspondent Thomas Friedman that

> [with the Russians and Najibullah gone] most people in the U.S. government have long since come to the conclusion that our objectives in Afghanistan are pretty limited. . . . What we basically want is an Afghanistan that does not destabilize its neighbors, like Pakistan and the Central Asian republics, where we really do have important interests and we don't want a boiling Afghanistan exporting radicalism.[45]

The "current policy" of the U.S., as described by journalist Radek Sikorsky, was to "go back to treating Afghanistan as the backwater it was before the Soviets invaded." The *Los Angeles Times* agreed with this approach, explaining, "What happens there—at least for now—stops well short of being a vital national interest." For the U.S., perhaps that was true, but for the Afghan people, it was the beginning of yet another era of devastation.[46]

On April 26, 1992, Hekmatyar's army tried to occupy Kabul, but was rebuffed by the forces of Ahmed Shah Massoud and General Dostum. "Throughout the day, two rival rebel groups filled the virtually empty streets with the thunder of tanks, rockets, and rifle fire," reported the *New York Times*. Two days later, a few of the fundamentalist Pakistan-based groups, along with Dostum, declared themselves a "government." The president of the coalition was Sibghatullah Mojadedi (who would later be appointed chair of the 2003/4 Constitutional *Loya Jirga,* head of Afghanistan's "Reconciliation Commission," and head of the Upper House of Parliament). Burhanuddin Rabbani succeeded Mojadedi as president on June 28. Margaret Tutwiler said, "We welcome this development and hope the presence of [the Mujahideen government] will help stabilize the situation." U.S. delegates traveled to Kabul in June "to discuss establishing diplomatic relations" with the new "government," and make plans to reopen the U.S. embassy in Kabul, which closed when the Soviet troops withdrew in 1989.[47]

What was the new government, which was "welcomed" by the United States, like? "Their first taste of Islamic government has left some Kabulis yearning for the old communism," reported the *Economist*. This was especially true for women. The Afghan "Ministry for the Promotion of Virtue and Prevention of Vice" became well known under the Taliban, but was in fact originally formed by the U.S.-recognized government of Rabbani. Afghan women were subject to Taliban-like restrictions immediately. "One of the first edicts" put forward by Rabbani "is for women to wear the traditional Muslim dress and to cover their heads in public. Young university women . . . are back to wearing their mothers' old chadors just to be allowed inside the campus." Similar conditions would garner global outrage under Taliban rule only four years later. A decree issued by the Rabbani government in August 1993 formalized and extended the earlier edicts so that they were virtually indistinguishable from strictures made famous under the Taliban.

> Women do not need to leave their homes at all, unless absolutely necessary, in which case they are to cover themselves completely; are not to wear attractive clothing and decorative accessories; do not wear perfume; their jewelry must not make any noise; they are not to walk gracefully or with pride and in the middle of the sidewalk; are not to talk to strangers; are not to speak loudly or laugh in public; and they must always ask their husbands' permission to leave home.[48]

It would be another eight years before the Taliban were defeated and these decrees finally lifted (2001).

In addition to the oppressive restrictions on women's dress and behavior was the escalation of violence between the formerly U.S.-backed factions, who, we must remember, were chosen by the CIA and ISI not for their skills at diplomacy or nation building but for their ruthlessness and desire for power. Within an hour of the April 29, 1992, takeover by the new regime, Kabul was attacked again with rockets "presumably fired by Mr. Hekmatyar's forces." Hekmatyar refused to join the new government because of the presence of Dostum, a "traitor" who had worked with the Soviets. The bombing continued off and on for months, reaching a climax by late summer. *Time* magazine described a city "completely isolated, its transport and communications links cut," with "no power or water." In huge numbers, residents were trying to escape. "Foreign embassies and U.N. personnel are seeking evacuation, while perhaps 100,000 more citizens have fled" in the week leading up to August 24. By early September, the Associated Press wrote that "Kabul is a city haunted by fear, blasted and burning from rockets randomly fired by rebels on its outskirts," led by Hekmatyar.[49]

Now that the U.S. was no longer backing the siege of Kabul, it was condemned in the strongest terms by the State Department. Once encouraged as part of a strategy of "choking Regime-controlled locales," Hekmatyar's attacks were now called "savage" and "ruthless" and denounced because of the "tremendous suffering" they caused. An October 2, 1992, statement by Department Spokesman Richard Boucher noted that Hekmatyar was acting "in pursuit of personal ambitions," as if his atrocities had been acceptable when he was acting in pursuit of CIA ambitions. Boucher made assurances that the United States "will continue to oppose anyone who uses violence to subvert the political process, which we believe is central to resolving the Afghan conflict." No one in the media commented on the irony of this statement.[50]

Hekmatyar was not the only Mujahideen commander with violent extremist tendencies. Rabbani and company also had no problem targeting civilians. In February 1993, when the ethnic Hazara militia, Hisbi-i Wahdat, sided with Hekmatyar, Massoud and Sayyaf sent their troops on a rampage through a Hazara civilian neighborhood in southwestern Kabul. As Michael Griffin notes, "Government forces and their allies entered the Hazara suburb . . . killing—by local accounts—'up to 1000 civilians,' beheading old men, women, children, and even their dogs, and stuffing their bodies down the wells, '60 at a time.'"[51]

In March 1993, Hekmatyar reconciled with Rabbani, agreeing to become prime minister of the Mujahideen "government." Massoud and Dostum boycotted the peace talks (held in Pakistan) and then Massoud refused to let Hekmatyar back into Kabul to take his post, so Hekmatyar resumed his attacks on the city. On New Year's Day 1994, because of his own rivalry with Massoud and his effective exclusion from political power (Rabbani had given him the figurehead title "President of the Northern Alliance"), Dostum joined Hekmatyar in bombing Kabul.

From April 1992 to February 1995, *before the Taliban took power,* at least 25,000 civilians were killed in Kabul by indiscriminate shelling by Hekmatyar, Rabbani, Massoud, Dostum, and others, according to Western agencies. Local accounts put the figure as high as 50,000. Hundreds of thousands were injured, and over 1 million people were displaced. In addition, thousands of people were "disappeared" by armed men affiliated with the warring parties. According to Amnesty International, "In much of the country, leaders of armed political groups act as Islamic judges and order punishments such as amputation, stoning and 'executions' with no legal safeguards against their arbitrary decisions." Amnesty International described numerous horrific cases of violence against women and girls, including rape and torture. Apparently, "rape is . . . condoned by most [factional] leaders as a means of terrorizing conquered populations and of rewarding soldiers."[52]

Approximately 80 percent of Kabul had been reduced to rubble by early 1995, when the Taliban first started bombing the city. John F. Burns wrote, "whole neighborhoods look like Hamburg or Dresden after World War II bombing raids." Amnesty International blamed the foreign powers that had originally supplied the Mujahideen against the Soviets for catalyzing the destruction: "Afghan civilians have paid a terrible price for international involvement in their country's affairs. As the country descended into violence and lawlessness, the armed Afghan factions gained confidence and military might from the unconditional and uncritical support of foreign powers backed up by endless supplies of arms."[53]

If Afghanistan ever deserved the label "failed state," it was most appropriate in the years 1992–96, when U.S. eyes were averted while U.S. weapons were eliminating the buildings, institutions, and people required for the survival of the State of Afghanistan. In his book *Reaping the Whirlwind* Michael Griffin surmised that in Kabul, "The point, it seemed, was to kill off the city and all of its attitudes and skills; to wipe the slate clean; to quell government itself, in fact." He summarized the destruction of Kabul under the Mujahideen: "No city since the end of the Second World War—except Sarajevo—had suffered the same ferocity of jugular violence as Kabul from 1992 to 1996. Sarajevo was almost a side-show by comparison and, at least, it wasn't forgotten."[54]

Taking Griffin's reference to the former Yugoslavia a little further, we can compare the U.S. responses to the war in Bosnia with the response to the war in Afghanistan, which occurred around the same time. In the first conflict, Washington bore little direct responsibility and had little connection to the factions initially; in the second conflict it bore direct responsibility and probably still had influence with some warring parties (despite claims to the contrary). Intervening in Bosnia was considered important to U.S. national interests, whereas Afghanistan was ignored. In 1992 the Bush administration promoted a court to try war crimes by parties to the war in Bosnia. In doing so, the administration said it was sending "a clear message that those responsible for the atrocities and gross violations . . . must be brought to justice."[55] No such court was supported for Afghanistan, where, according to the *New York Times*, "the onus for fueling a murderous war falls on the U.S. and Pakistan."[56] Perhaps that is why there was no Bush action to investigate war crimes or bring criminals to justice. Moreover, Washington all but refused to take any responsibility for the condition of the ruined nation. Between 1992 and 1995, the U.S. spent approximately $2.2 billion toward UN peacekeeping and humanitarian assistance in the former Yugoslavia.[57] During the same period, the U.S. gave only $237.7 million in assistance to Afghanistan.[58] In February 1995, the head of "a major international relief agency" asked a State Department official for help "deal[ing] with the massive social problems engendered by the war" in Afghanistan, and was rebuffed. "When I mention Afghanistan in Washington these days, people ask me: 'Where's that?'"[59]

1996–98: THE TALIBAN: A "PREFERABLE ALTERNATIVE"

> When we knew that Najibullah was finished and the Mujahideen were coming, we were so happy. We said, "Now things will be better," but they weren't. They were much, much worse. The Mujahideen turned out to be nothing but terrorists. Now, again, we have somebody else coming, the Taliban, and we ask, "Will it be better, or will it be worse?"[60]
>
> —JAMILA KARIM, AFGHAN WOMEN'S ASSOCIATION EMPLOYEE, KABUL, 1995

In late 1994, a new generation of fundamentalists appeared. They called themselves the Taliban and, with the full backing of Pakistan (it is believed that the Taliban replaced the incompetent Hekmatyar as clients of the ISI), they rolled into Afghanistan in brand-new Japanese pickup trucks, with rocket launchers and satellite telephones, bringing a new era of terror for the Afghan people, especially Afghan women. At first welcomed by many Afghans who had suffered under the Mujahideen, the Taliban soon became known as equally brutal leaders, imposing the same harshly repressive conservative edicts as the Rabbani government and exhibiting the same disregard for civilian lives. The Taliban were able to take control of a much larger part of Afghanistan—as much as 90 percent—than any single jihadi group. But their war crimes and oppression were as worthy of denunciation and calls for justice as those of the Mujahideen. The U.S. government, mostly silent on Mujahideen crimes, eventually became one of the most vocal critics of similar crimes when committed by the Taliban—but not initially.[61]

In 1995 the Taliban, like their predecessors, engaged in a relentless assault on Kabul. For nearly one and a half years, the movement took over the bombing of the city from Hekmatyar, who had already reduced most of it to rubble. When he saw he was outgunned, Hekmatyar attempted a belated union with Rabbani, Massoud, Dostum, and Sayyaf, and was sworn in officially as prime minister of the Mujahideen "government" in June 1996. But the writing was on the wall. With full support from Pakistan, the Taliban had conquered most of the other major cities in the south and east of the country, and on September 27, 1996, Rabbani's group was forced to flee and the Taliban took control of the capital.

Confidential documents from the period show that U.S. government emissaries had already met with Taliban officials many times prior to the capture of Kabul. While the movement was described as "secretive," and meetings with their representatives left "more questions than answers," the administration was familiar with the impact the Taliban had already made in areas under their control, as well as their stated goals. A January 1995 secret cable from the U.S. Embassy in Islamabad described the Taliban as "well-armed, militarily proficient, and eager to expand their influence." In cities that they conquered prior to Kabul, and in the capital, the Taliban were making a name for themselves. In Kandahar, the first city to fall under their influence, the movement practiced "a heavy-handed style of conservative Islam" with a cruelty that was well documented in the cable. They had "restrict[ed] women to the home, closed girls' schools, and carried out criminal punishments including execution and amputation," according to the *Washington Post*. (It is almost never mentioned that the U.S.-backed Rabbani government had implemented these same measures, but perhaps with less success.) A cable in February described a meeting between U.S. embassy officials and the mayor of Kandahar, who outlined the goals of the Taliban. "[We] seek to establish one government . . . and restore peace to the country. The first objective will be disarmament of all the commanders, after which shariah [*sic*] law will be established." The Pashtun-based movement had little tolerance for ethnic diversity. "Asked about relations with the Shi'a, Tajiks, Uzbeks, and other ethnic and religious minorities," the mayor responded, "Anyone who gets in our way will be crushed."[62]

The day after the Taliban took Kabul, the State Department instructed the Islamabad Embassy on "Dealing with the Taliban." The administration wanted to

> engage the new Taliban "interim government" at an early stage to: demonstrate . . . willingness to deal with them as the new authorities in Kabul; seek information about their plans, programs, and policies; and express [U.S. Government] views on areas of key concern to us—stability, human rights, narcotics, and terrorism.

Although the State Department mentioned human rights as one of four "areas of key concern," it was not discussed further in the six-page instructions to the Islamabad Embassy, showing how insignificant the topic was really considered. The other three concerns were touched on at least once more in the cable. The Clinton administration appeared eager to build ties with the new Afghan "government." If asked about opening the U.S. Embassy in Kabul, officials were instructed to tell the Taliban that they "would like to re-open our embassy here, when security permits . . . In the meantime, we would like to make frequent trips to Kabul to stay in contact with your government."[63]

Overall, Washington seemed pleased. An article in the *Washington Post* told how "U.S. officials and experts" believed that the Taliban "capture of Kabul . . . represents the best chance in years of ending the anarchy," despite the fact that, "it also could be the prelude to the construction of a particularly strict Islamic state." The newspaper conveyed "the U.S. point of view" that "a Taliban-dominated government represents a preferable alternative in some ways to the faction-ridden coalition" led by Rabbani. A *Los Angeles Times* editorial argued that "The American aim [in Afghanistan] was ultimately met by the Taliban." As *Post* analyst Michael Dobbs explained, "the country had lost much of its strategic importance since the collapse of communism. But it has remained a potent source of instability in Central Asia," a place where Washington now had significant interests (i.e., oil and natural gas reserves and strategic positioning with respect to China and Russia; see below and Chapter 7). So long as the Taliban resisted Russian, Iranian, or Chinese influence, brought the country under unified control, and confined their mayhem to *within* the borders of Afghanistan, they were acceptable to the U.S.[64]

The Clinton State Department was, like the Carter, Reagan, and Bush Departments before it, unconcerned with the human rights consequences of having armed fundamentalists in charge of Afghanistan. Within hours of its takeover of Kabul, the Taliban hunted down former Soviet-backed president Najibullah and tortured and hanged him in public. There was talk of segregating women from men in the capital, dismissing women from work, and confining them to their homes. According to the *Post*, "nearly half of the civil servants in the city" were women, and they "might have to be dismissed." State Department spokesperson Glyn Davies disregarded any allegations of Taliban violations: "We've seen some of the reports that they've moved to impose Islamic law in the areas that they control, but at this stage we're not reading anything into that. I mean, there's on the face of it nothing objectionable." The polite regard and unwillingness to challenge the Taliban on their human-rights record implied that it would take far more than "a heavy-handed style of conservative Islam" to raise objections in Washington.[65]

More important interests were at stake. The Central Asian republics, recently independent from Russia, presented new strategic opportunities because of their location on the borders of Russia and China, and economic opportunities because of the untapped oil and gas wealth underground. The possible stabilization of war-torn Afghanistan by the Taliban was expected to yield a windfall for a U.S.-based oil company, Unocal, who wanted to build natural gas and oil pipelines from Turkmenistan to Pakistan via Afghanistan. Even before the Taliban captured Kabul, the United States had put its weight behind the pipeline project. In 1995, President Clinton personally convinced Turkmen president Saparmurat A. Niyazov to sign a contract with Unocal. On April 21, 1996, U.S. Assistant Secretary of State for South Asia Robin Raphel announced in Islamabad, "We have an American company which is interested in building a pipeline from Turkmenistan through to Pakistan." Nine days later in Moscow, Raphel told Russian Deputy Foreign Minister Albert Chernyshev that the U.S. "now hopes that peace in the region will facilitate U.S. business interests like the proposed Unocal gas pipeline." This was while Rabbani was nominally still the head of the country. To secure the World Bank loans that would fund the project, Afghanistan needed a stable government that was internationally recognized. Five months after Raphel's tour, when Kabul fell to the Taliban, State Department spokesman Glyn Davies expressed "our hope . . . that the new authorities in Kabul will move quickly to restore order and security and to form a representative interim government." Chris Taggart, executive vice president of Unocal International Energy Ventures, agreed, "If the Taliban leads to stability and recognition then it's positive."[66]

In lieu of humanitarian and infrastructure aid to Afghanistan or efforts to disarm the warring factions, Washington chose to support a corporate venture that would entrench in power one or another abusive fundamentalist government. Like the backing of fundamentalist fanatics against the Soviet invasion, this was rationalized as U.S. "assistance" to the destitute country. A Congressional Research Service paper of August 2003 described the pipelines as a form of aid:

> In an effort to find a long-term solution to Afghanistan's acute humanitarian problems, the United States has, when feasible, tried to promote major development projects as a means of improving Afghan living standards and political stability over the long term. During 1996–98, the administration supported proposed natural gas and oil pipelines.[67]

One of the supposed goals of the pipeline was to create "an incentive for the warring factions to cooperate." It is impossible to take this seriously. Anyone with knowledge of the Afghan factions Unocal was trying to deal with could see that under their rule political stability and improved Afghan living standards would be impossible. Knowing the kind of atrocities that all of the contending groups had committed—whether it be Hekmatyar, Dostum, Massoud/Rabbani, or the Taliban—Unocal was still prepared to deal with any faction that wound up controlling the country. Marty Miller, vice president in charge of the project, has said, "We are fanatically neutral when it comes to politics." It didn't matter who was in power, only that they had total control, and their government was internationally recognized. John Maresca, vice president of international relations for Unocal, told the U.S. Congress that the company had "the same relationship" with the Taliban as it had with "all the factions" in Afghanistan. That is, "we have talked with them, we have briefed them, [and] we have invited them to our headquarters to see what our projects are." When challenged on the human rights record of the Taliban, Maresca said, " I don't think either faction here has a very clean human rights record, to tell you the truth." Unocal never approached exiled moderate Afghans such as Zahir Shah because they had no chance of coming to power in the middle of the war, even though the former king was considered by many Afghans the leader "who can most successfully address the problems facing Afghanistan today." Men with guns were the only leaders worth considering by Unocal.[68]

This situation was standard for the company, notorious for having abusive governments as business partners. At the same time the Afghanistan deal was being made, Unocal was being brought to court for allegations of "forced labor, rapes and a murder" along the route of the natural gas pipeline in Burma owned by a subsidiary. In December 2004, Unocal as much as admitted its guilt when it agreed to settle out of court and pay damages to fifteen Burmese villagers.[69]

In general, human rights outcomes bear little on corporate decisions. Making the point explicit, Maresca said, "I am not here to defend the Taliban. That is not my role. We are a company that is trying to build a pipeline across this country." Congressman Dana Rohrabacher (Rep.), a staunch supporter of the Mujahideen extremists, who had been grilling him on the human rights record of the Taliban, accepted Maresca's corporate logic: "I sympathize with that."[70]

Less than a month after the Taliban took Kabul, forces loyal to Rabbani began a counteroffensive, "making it unlikely that the Taliban [could] consolidate their military gains or establish the nationwide peace that some had imagined." Clinton's advisers "began to have serious questions about the benefits that would come from Taliban control," and the decision was made to "keep the Taliban at arm's length." In addition to being "policy correct," according to a Clinton official, the shift was considered "politically correct." The administration wanted "to distance itself—particularly during the presidential campaign—from a movement that has barred women from working and girls from going to school." A more conspicuous inclusion of women's rights in public statements regarding the Taliban was due in large part to the activism of U.S.-based organizations such as the Feminist Majority and the National Organization for Women, who criticized the pipeline deal with the misogynist Taliban. Since the president's reelection depended on his maintaining a facade of respect for women's rights (he had a 27 percent lead over Republican challenger Bob Dole in polls among women), he did not want to appear too tolerant of the Taliban.[71]

Nevertheless, even though Clinton cooled his rhetoric supporting the Taliban, the bargaining chips of aid, pipelines, and recognition by the U.S. would not be abandoned for another couple of years. The administration "left the door open to working with the Taliban if certain conditions are met." Assistant Secretary of State for South Asian Affairs Karl F. Inderfurth had confidence in the fanatical movement: "The Taliban will not change their spots, but we do believe they can modify their behavior." In January 1998, U.S. ambassador to the United Nations Bill Richardson became the highest-level U.S. official to visit Afghanistan since Secretary of State Henry Kissinger in 1974. Richardson was to "deliver a stern message to the Taliban militia that they will never gain wide international recognition or aid so long as their repression of women continues." Nevertheless, he showed that Washington was still ready to work with them, promising "U.S. funding to help rebuild the country's war-damaged infrastructure if the Taliban seriously engaged in peace talks and improved its treatment of women."[72]

1998–2001: ROGUE STATE*

Afghanistan is ruled by a rogue regime, the Taliban.[73]
—ZALMAY KHALILZAD AND DANIEL BYMAN, 1999

Throughout the 1990s, the extremist training camps in the border regions with Pakistan continued to thrive. The terrorist networks that operated them had of course been built with the connivance of the CIA and the Pakistani ISI, when terrorism was part of a strategy to combat the Soviet occupation. Essentially the U.S. "invested" in terrorism in the 1980s, and the Afghan people reaped the "dividends," most horribly in the 1992–96 period. In 1993, the United States too felt the effects of its 1980s policies when the World Trade Center in New York was bombed by soldiers of the Afghan war. This was followed by the 1996 bombing of the Khobar Towers complex in Saudi Arabia, which had been occupied primarily by U.S. troops; the bombings of U.S. Embassies in Kenya and Tanzania in 1998; the October 1999 attack on the USS *Cole*, docked in Yemen; and finally the September 11, 2001, destruction of the World Trade Center towers and attack on the Pentagon in Washington, DC. These attacks were supposedly carried out by men connected with the al-Qa'eda organization of Osama bin Laden.

Founded in Afghanistan in 1988, al-Qa'eda was an outgrowth of the group Makhtab al Khadimat, which bin Laden formed in 1984 to help the CIA's anti-Soviet efforts. Bin Laden returned to Saudi Arabia in 1989 but left for Sudan in 1991 because of his opposition to U.S. troops, which the Saudi royal family had allowed in their nation during the Gulf War. At the request of the United States, his Saudi citizenship was revoked in 1994 and Sudan expelled him in 1996, so bin Laden went back to Afghanistan, living in hiding on the sufferance of the Taliban. Bin Laden, and others like him, set an example in the 1990s of outspo-

---

* Parts of this section originally appeared in James Ingalls, "'Smart' Sanctions on Afghanistan," *Z Magazine*, March 2001.

ken resistance to U.S. military and economic control of the Middle East, and a denunciation of the corrupt regimes that assured U.S. control. In doing so, he echoed the concerns of many people in the Arab and Muslim world. His message, probably more than the terrorism he sponsored or inspired, was initially what led the United States to request that the Saudi and Sudanese governments ostracize him.

After the August 7, 1998 embassy bombings, the United States under President Clinton went from a policy of polite diplomacy towards Afghanistan to a policy of threats, aggression, and sanctions. The first U.S. response to the bombings was the equally criminal August 20 cruise missile attacks on the al Shifa pharmaceuticals plant in Khartoum, Sudan, and on Zhawar Kili al Badr training camp near Khost, Afghanistan. The Sudan attack leveled the plant, a supposed site of bin Laden's fledgling chemical weapons program. Later analysis showed no evidence that the plant had ever produced a precursor to the VX nerve agent as alleged. Instead, "The factory supplied 50 to 60 percent of Sudan's pharmaceutical needs, as well as exporting products abroad." Before the bombing, the plant was a main supplier of important medicines for UN programs in Africa and the Middle East, in addition to producing over half of Sudan's painkillers, antibiotics, and medicines to treat malaria.[74]

The Afghanistan attack consisted of about fifty cruise missiles, fired at the compound of a training camp in Khost, where "several hundred" terrorist leaders, including bin Laden, were supposedly gathering. The site was "effectively a military cantonment, away from civilian population centers and overwhelmingly populated by jihadists," according to CIA evidence reviewed by the 9/11 Commission. National Security Adviser Sandy Berger claimed that the attack did "moderate to severe" damage. But an Afghan news agency said that 21 people were killed and 53 wounded. Apparently, bin Laden had left hours earlier, but the attack was praised in the U.S. The missile attacks were meant to show, in the words of Defense Secretary William Cohen, that "there will be no sanctuary for terrorists and no limit to our resolve to defend American citizens and our interests, our ideals of democracy and law against these cowardly attacks." It is interesting that the embassy bombings were "cowardly attacks," while the cruise missile responses that, in the case of Sudan, eliminated over one half of the medicine production for that poor country, are considered acts of "defense."[75]

There was an interesting effort by the Clinton government and some legal experts to cast the missile strikes as acts of "self defense" consistent with international law. Ruth Wedgewood, a law professor at Yale and visiting scholar at the Naval War College, described the attacks as "pretty close to classic Article 51," referring to the clause in the United Nations charter that describes the right of a state to defend itself while under attack. Bill Richardson, outgoing U.S. ambassador to the UN, filed a brief with the UN Security Council stating that "We have convincing evidence that further such attacks [as the embassy bombings] were in preparation from these same terrorist facilities. The United States, therefore, had no choice but to use armed force to prevent these attacks from continuing." But "evidence that further such attacks" may occur is not the same as being *under* attack. Furthermore, in the case of the Sudan factory, the evidence was fabricated. By Washington's logic, surely Sudan had the same right to bomb the U.S.? The Taliban thought they had that right too. Syad Abdullah, a senior Taliban leader, told the *Los Angeles Times*, "America has declared war on us. We will take revenge. If we had these sort of missiles, we would launch them against America."[76]

Ian Lesser, a senior analyst with the Rand Corporation, explained that the legality argument hinged on the fact that the U.S. was not trying to assassinate anybody. "The administration is being very careful to distinguish between an attack on infrastructure and not on Osama bin Laden himself. We don't assassinate. As an instrument of foreign policy we don't do that." But not all members of the U.S. government agreed with that premise. "[L]awmakers who had expressed strong support for the strikes . . . said . . . that they will not consider the mission a complete success unless it becomes clear that the missiles inflicted sizable casualties." Senator John McCain complained that "Just hitting physical structures is not particularly impressive." According to the *9/11 Commission Report*, the original purpose of the attacks was indeed "to kill bin Laden and his chief lieutenants," but the strikes were desirable "whether or not there was firm evidence that the commanders were at the facilities." The *Los Angeles Times* agreed that it was important simply to show "that the military reach of the United States is long and that its knowledge of terrorist hiding places and activities can be exact and devastating."[77]

On October 15, 1999, the U.S. sponsored a resolution (1267) in the United Nations Security Council that imposed sanctions on the Taliban, banning flights outside Afghanistan by the state-owned airline Ariana and freezing Taliban assets. President Clinton was deliberately forcing Afghans to pay a price to teach the Taliban a lesson. In a November 19 statement he warned, "The people of Afghanistan have already paid a high price in isolation because of the Taliban's continued harboring of this terrorist, and that toll will now increase."

The sanctions were achieved with the cosponsorship of Russia on the Security Council. Russia was once again involved with Afghan politics, but now supporting the anti-Taliban factions who had helped end the Soviet occupation and driven out their puppet Najibullah. Russia found common cause with its former enemies because the Pakistan-sponsored Taliban were gaining adherents and allies with radical Islamists in the former Soviet republics of Central Asia, which threatened to destabilize the mostly Moscow-friendly regimes there.

A report published on December 8, 2000, by the UN Office for the Coordination of Humanitarian Affairs, entitled "Vulnerability and Humanitarian Implications of UN Security Council Sanctions in Afghanistan," studied the effects of the 1999 sanctions on the people of Afghanistan. This was made public while the Security Council was considering a more stringent sanctions resolution offered by Washington. The report found that "the direct impact of sanctions on the humanitarian situation in Afghanistan is limited but tangible." A case study of the effect of sanctions on Indira Gandhi Paediatric Hospital in Kabul demonstrated that the ban on Ariana flights had "cut the main supply link" between the hospital and the outside world. Because of the war, malnutrition, and drought, the hospital continued to operate at full capacity, but under poor conditions. The report noted that

> Sanctions have contributed to a deterioration of the standard of care provided in the hospital. The loss of the airlink seems to have constrained the hospital from restocking with essential drugs from its previous main supplier. Children's families are being asked to purchase medicines themselves at a time of economic crisis, when the majority of the Kabul population barely has the means to obtain food, let alone medicine.

Before the sanctions were imposed, an estimated 10 percent of the medicines used in the hospital were bought by patients. A little over a year later, 50 percent of the medicines had to be bought from the bazaar, and the rest had to be donated by aid agencies.[78]

A UK Defense Ministry Web page published in March 2002 described efforts by British soldiers to refurbish Indira Gandhi Hospital after the Taliban's defeat. With no mention of the role of more than two years of UK-supported sanctions, the article described the horrible conditions the soldiers found:

> The most basic medicines and equipment were lacking, and over 240 children were being treated in only 150 beds. At least one child patient was even having [sic] to sleep on a window sill. Most of the staff had not been paid for a long time, but continued working regardless, to do what they could for the children.[79]

On December 19, 2000, the sanctions were intensified in SC Resolution 1333. The goal of the sanctions, according to U.S. Ambassador to the UN Nancy Soderberg, was "convincing the Taliban leadership to turn over the terrorist that we seek;" they were primarily a response to the October bombing of the military vessel USS *Cole* in Aden harbor, Yemen. In addition to reinforcing the October 1999 ban on flights and closure of foreign offices of Ariana, Resolution 1333 introduced an arms embargo against the Taliban. Unlike many other sanctions regimes, these "smart" sanctions were supposedly calculated to not affect the dire humanitarian crisis in Afghanistan, despite evidence to the contrary. When asked if the people of Afghanistan would suffer, Ambassador

Soderberg dismissed the suggestion. "These sanctions, we have very specifically targeted to not have an impact on the humanitarian situation on the ground."[80]

It is true that the *wording* of the sanctions resolutions was targeted only at the Taliban, and did not literally impose hardships on ordinary Afghans. In fact, the second resolutions seemed to do what should have been done for years to the Taliban—eliminate their ability to wage war and to produce and sell the opium that financed them. Their adversaries, the old Mujahideen factions under Massoud, Dostum, Ismail Khan, and others—now calling themselves either the "United Front" or "Northern Alliance"—were not similarly targeted. This was deliberate, and was the Security Council's contribution to the anti-Taliban war. According to the *9/11 Commission Report*, "The aim of the resolution was to hit the Taliban where it was most sensitive—on the battlefield against the Northern Alliance." To cut off weapons flows and drug money to the Taliban and not to the Northern Alliance legitimized the behavior of the latter group, and ignored the plight of *their* victims. Human Rights Watch argued in a letter to the Security Council prior to the vote, "it is particularly unfortunate that the present discussion is limited to the Taliban's role in harboring Osama bin Laden . . . and does not directly address the grave abuses that continue to be perpetrated against the country's own civilian population . . . [by] *all* warring factions [emphasis added]."[81]

In Secretary-General Kofi Annan's November 20, 2000, report to the UN General Assembly and Security Council, he lamented that

> The tendency persists to see Afghanistan as a series of compartmentalized problems, be they narcotics, terrorism or refugees, and to seek to solve them in isolation rather than through a comprehensive approach. It is to be hoped that the Security Council . . . resolutions and decisions . . . will be . . . taken in the context of, rather than being a substitute for, a comprehensive strategy to bring about a lasting solution to the Afghan conflict.[82]

The new sanctions showed the contempt in which the Security Council must have held Annan's words. Indeed, U.S. ambassador Soderberg saw no problem with a compartmentalized approach, admitting that the sanctions constitute "a single-purpose resolution aimed at terrorism. The other issues [we leave] to others."

"Other issues" left to others included diplomacy and humanitarian aid. According to Annan the sanctions were "not going to facilitate peace efforts, nor our humanitarian work." It is significant that the sanctions were imposed only one month after Annan's personal representative, Francesc Vendrell, had obtained the first-ever written commitment by both the Taliban and the Northern Alliance "to seek a political settlement through an uninterrupted process of negotiations under United Nations auspices [Annan]." The *Economist* predicted that Vendrell's "tenuous effort at peace-broking . . . is likely to be an early casualty" of the sanctions. Indeed the Taliban immediately shut down the UN mission in Afghanistan and exited from the negotiations. Russian Ambassador Sergei Lavrov, the current president of the Security Council, somehow excused this by blaming the Taliban for promising "on many occasions to begin the negotiating process, and each time . . . [breaking] their word."[83]

The Chinese ambassador abstained from voting on the sanctions because Afghanistan is "facing a serious humanitarian situation," and the sanctions "would undoubtedly make that situation even worse." Kofi Annan summarized: "The accumulated and direct effects of conflict, compounded by extreme poverty and profound underdevelopment, contribute to a situation that has resulted in Afghans being amongst those who are least able to enjoy their rights, including the right to life." According to a 1997 UNICEF study, children in Afghanistan were twice as likely to die before their first birthday as those in other South Asian countries, and Afghanistan's maternal mortality rate was the second highest in the world. The Food and Agriculture Organization declared Afghanistan to be one of the three hungriest countries in the world. Around 70 percent of Afghans were estimated to be undernourished—more than twice the prewar figure from 1979. During 1999 and 2000, at least 140,000 Afghans were displaced internally due to armed conflict.

Afghans in Pakistan, Iran, and other nations constituted the largest single refugee group in the world since 1979. Nearly 50,000 new refugees fled to Pakistan from September to December 2000 alone.

The *Economist* also predicted that another "casualty of the American and Russian plan to get tougher with the Taliban . . . is likely to be the UN's own humanitarian efforts in Afghanistan." It was common knowledge that millions of Afghans depended critically on international humanitarian organizations for much of their food, health care, and shelter needs. Those organizations were unanimous in their opposition to the new sanctions. Oxfam warned that the resolution "threatens to deepen this already desperate humanitarian crisis." Eight French aid groups, including Action Against Famine, Medecins du Monde, and International Medical Aid, sent a letter to French Prime Minister Lionel Jospin, expressing fears that the sanctions "will worsen the humanitarian situation" in Afghanistan. The UN Coordinator for Afghanistan, Erick de Mul, complained that "The ability of ordinary Afghans to withstand any kind of deterioration in their situation after twenty years of war is extremely limited, and seemingly innocuous actions can have a serious impact on the lives of millions of people."[84]

RAWA published a statement on their Web site, admonishing, "UN sanctions on the Taliban will not solve the problems of Afghanistan." They suggest instead that the UN impose sanctions on the governments that are "directly influencing the internal affairs of Afghanistan," providing military and financial support to either the Northern Alliance or the Taliban. To RAWA, both the Taliban and the Northern Alliance were "war criminals," and "it is the proper time for the U.S. and other countries that have fostered these fundamentalist parties to apologize to the Afghan people and take steps toward healing old wounds."[85]

By March 2001 the value of the Afghani, the national currency, decreased from 70,000 to the dollar to 80,000 to the dollar, due to the sanctions. Since most commodities were imported, prices of daily necessities were steadily rising. In March a pound of sugar cost 20 cents, compared to 16 cents in December. For a country where those who actually had a job made only about $10 a month, inflation of the prices of basic commodities was debilitating. Meanwhile the Taliban were unaffected. "Before the sanctions they drove around in the latest vehicles, and now they are still driving around in the latest vehicles," said the director of an Afghan aid organization.[86]

It was difficult to see how the United States expected the sanctions to make any difference to the Taliban. As of March 30, *Radio Free Europe* reported that there was "still no UN presence in Pakistan" to ensure that the sanctions preventing arms flows to the Taliban were observed. Pakistan's token efforts to comply with the sanctions amounted to reducing the staff at the Taliban consulate in Peshawar, but little else. When Russia tried to get the Security Council to impose sanctions on Pakistan to stop them from supporting the Taliban, the newly sworn-in George W. Bush administration refused, because Pakistan was a country "which Washington considers an ally."[87]

The pre-9/11 Bush policy took a step backward and once again renewed some of the polite diplomacy of the early Clinton years, including a donation of $43 million in food aid (mostly government-subsidized surplus wheat) as a token of appreciation for the Taliban reduction in Afghan drug production. New diplomatic visits to Afghanistan and to the refugee camps in Pakistan sent a message that the U.S. was beginning to engage the Taliban again.[88] For example, four U.S. diplomats were sent to Afghanistan on what was called a "humanitarian mission." According to Pakistan's *Dawn* newspaper, "Diplomatic sources . . . point out that the mission shows an important shift in U.S. policy towards the Taliban . . . [S]ince the arrival of the Republican administration, there have been signals from the U.S . . . that it may be willing to review its tough stance."[89] At the same time the U.S. continued the sanctions and covert moves to capture or kill bin Laden. Like Clinton, Bush seemed not to be troubled by most things the Taliban did, only their support for bin Laden.[90]

The people of Afghanistan seem to have always been pawns of outside powers. Even the language typically used to describe the political condition of the country reflects the way it affects outside countries. It was a "buffer state" when there was more than one empire vying for influence. It became, alternately, a "failed state" and a "rogue state" in the

1990s, when no country cared what happened inside its borders. Both latter phrases inappropriately mask the crucial U.S. role in bringing terrorists to Afghanistan and strengthening fundamentalist forces. A better term might be "destroyed state," which points to the wrecked condition of the country, but also to the responsibilities of outsiders. After 9/11, the U.S. unleashed once again many of the same fundamentalist and warlord armies to eliminate the weak Taliban government. They were given a place in the new government, entrenching their violent hold indefinitely over the suffering people of Afghanistan. Given that human rights and women's rights were never before of concern to U.S. policy makers, post-9/11 U.S. policy should have been viewed with a great deal of skepticism.

PART TWO

REGIME CHANGE AND ITS CONSEQUENCES

CHAPTER TWO

BOMBS, THREATS, AND TORTURE

AFGHANISTAN BECOMES A U.S. TARGET

After September 11, 2001, Afghanistan was transformed from a "rogue state" ruled by a brutal regime hostile to U.S. interests into a nation occupied by Western forces and ruled by a puppet leader. The "regime change" was brought about by U.S. firepower from the air and Afghan warlord armies on the ground. Both tactics achieved Washington's goals with a low cost in American lives, but the Afghan people were not so lucky. They suffered first from the destructive U.S. onslaught, and then from the reestablishment of oppressive Northern Alliance leaders into positions of status and power in the new U.S.-backed regime, as we will see in Chapter 3. The decision to bomb Afghanistan had less to do with a war on terrorism than with the need to demonstrate U.S. willingness to respond violently when attacked, as described in Chapter 7. While the U.S.'s violent response surely ended the freedom that anti-U.S. terrorists Osama bin Laden and al-Qa'eda had enjoyed under the Taliban, the bombing itself was an act of terror.

AFGHANISTAN BECOMES A U.S. TARGET

The seeds of the post-9/11 United States military strategy in Afghanistan can be found in cabinet-level documents from both the Bill Clinton and George W. Bush Administrations. The 1998 U.S. Embassy bombings and the U.S. "retaliation" to them changed the status of Afghanistan in Washington, DC. Prior to that, the Clinton administration was content to let the Taliban institute a reign of terror and gobble up territory. In fact, at one point U.S. officials found it desirable to have the Taliban control all of the country, because an internationally recognized government would enable World Bank funding for Unocal oil and gas pipelines. But eventually, Osama bin Laden's presence in Afghanistan and the continuing refusal of the Taliban to submit to U.S. authority put the country on a list of potential U.S. military targets.

It is not clear, however, that Washington was waiting for an *excuse* to hit Afghanistan, and that the 9/11 attacks were a convenient pretext, as some have claimed. Unlike Iraq, where successive U.S. administrations agreed that controlling that country's oil required military intervention and regime change, the Bush administration before September 11, 2001, did not seem to have Clinton's enthusiasm for demonizing the Taliban or bin Laden as he had done after the 1998 embassy bombings. Both administrations did threaten to attack Afghanistan, although the Bush threat was made only privately before 9/11. But those threats focused on getting the Taliban to follow U.S. orders concerning bin Laden or demonstrating that the U.S. "arm was long," not ending the Taliban government. Even after 9/11, the overthrow of the Taliban was almost an afterthought precipitated by the need to show dire consequences for attacking the world's only superpower. It is undeniable in hindsight that bin Laden was a danger to the U.S. population, and post-9/11 investigations have revealed that this was well known by both Clinton and Bush. So a pretext for invading Afghanistan could have been manufactured easily prior to 9/11 if the U.S. had really been interested. No spurious claims to nonexistent "weapons of mass destruction" (as in Iraq) or "ethnic cleansing" (as in Serbia/Kosovo) were required. Prior to September 2001, however, despite the wishes of a few advisers, the Bush administration was more interested in attacking Iraq than Afghanistan.[91]

The Washington policy maker most outspoken on military action in Afghanistan was Richard A. Clarke. Clarke, the counterterrorism coordinator (or "czar") on the National Security Council for both the Clinton and early G.W. Bush Administrations, advocated a strategy to destroy the bin Laden network after the August 1998 embassy bombings. This had some influence on Clinton's policy, and later became a blueprint for the Bush response to the 9/11 terrorist attacks. It was Clarke who suggested that the al Shifa pharmaceuticals factory in Sudan be destroyed in 1998, with no demonstrable evidence that the factory was ever involved in a bin Laden chemical weapons operation. He presented the target to his team and was "met with skepticism," according to one of the participants. Clarke "brushed aside those concerns and said the decision to strike had already been made. The officials had been summoned . . . not to pass judgment on the target, Clarke told them, but to help prepare paperwork."[92]

In late 1998 Clarke presented to his working group a "Political-Military Plan *Delenda*" to "immediately eliminate any significant threat to Americans" from bin Laden. The word *delenda* refers to the Latin phrase from ancient Rome, *delenda est Carthago* (Carthage must be destroyed), connoting the wish to obliterate a bothersome rival. The plan was not adopted formally, although some of its suggestions would be carried out or attempted a few years later in response to the 9/11 attacks. The "most fully articulated element" of Clarke's proposal was an "ongoing campaign of strikes against bin Laden's bases in Afghanistan or elsewhere . . . [H]e argued that rolling attacks might persuade the Taliban to hand over bin Laden and, in any case, would show that the [cruise missile] action in August [1998] was not a 'one-off' event." Full details of Clarke's "*Delenda*" are unavailable, since Freedom of Information Act requests for the classified document have been denied.[93]

Clinton never acted on most of Clarke's military recommendations, but did follow his advice to authorize efforts to assassinate Osama bin Laden. On the ground, the CIA had been empowered by Clinton in late 1998 to use its "tribal assets" (Mujahideen groups with CIA contacts from the 1980s) to try to capture or kill bin Laden. In February 1999, the CIA was also authorized to work with the Northern Alliance to do the same. The Alliance, led by Ahmed Shah Massoud along with other former commanders from the ousted Rabbani government such as Abdul Rashid Dostum, was now in a losing battle with the Taliban and controlled only about 10 percent of Afghanistan. Once used by the U.S. in the early 1990s to eject the Soviet-backed Najibullah, but then considered too chaotic to govern in Kabul, these men were once again being purchased by Washington to help root out bin Laden (another former U.S. ally). In September 2000, U.S. unmanned aerial vehicles (UAVs) flew missions from Uzbekistan into Afghanistan to try to locate him. Throughout the year 2000, according to *Time* magazine, "two U.S. Navy submarines" were stationed in the northern Arabian sea "ready to attack [him with cruise missiles] if bin Laden's coordinates could be determined" by either the Northern Alliance or the UAVs. This exercise of U.S. air power in tandem with Northern Alliance forces on the ground foreshadowed the twin strategies used by the Bush administration to remove the Taliban in late 2001.[94]

After the October 2000 destruction of the USS *Cole* in Yemen by supposed members of an al-Qa'eda cell, it was expected that a harsh military response would follow. A U.S. Navy official told United Press International that a "'very severe' military response" was in the works. "We are going to find out who's responsible, get the U.S. public behind the response, and that response will be very, very heavy." A U.S. diplomat told the *Far Eastern Economic Review*, "We are determined to make life very, very difficult for the Taliban in every field—political, economic, military and in terms of their foreign relations—unless they hand over bin Laden." As described in Chapter 1, the 1999 sanctions on the Taliban were worsened in December 2000. A possible strike against bin Laden's training camps in Afghanistan by a coalition that included the U.S., Russia, Uzbekistan, Kazakhstan, and Kyrgyzstan was entertained by Washington, according to the *Review*, but Clinton didn't want to get involved in a war at the end of his presidential term.[95] A second Clarke paper, *The Strategy for Eliminating the Threat from the Jihadist Networks of al Qida* [*sic*], declassified in April 2004, was written in December 2000 to summarize the posture of the outgoing Clinton administration to the new George W. Bush administration. Clarke's recommendations included "overt U.S. military action to destroy al Qida [*sic*] command/control and infrastructure and Taliban military and command assets." In addition, the document advocated "covert U.S. assistance to the Northern Alliance to oppose the Taliban militarily." This program "would allow Masood [*sic*] to stay in the fight with the Taliban and al Qida as a credible, conventional threat." Here the intent was to prolong the Afghan war—and, in effect, Afghan casualties—so that al-Qa'eda was distracted from committing terrorism against U.S. targets. An unnamed "counterterrorism official" (maybe Clarke) told *Time* magazine later that the plan was "[to] keep [al-Qa'eda] on the front lines in Afghanistan. Hopefully you're killing them in the process, and they're not leaving Afghanistan to plot terrorist operations." Clarke's objective was, in effect, to trade Afghan casualties for those of U.S. citizens. A similar strategy to covertly aid "the Taliban's foes" was developed independently by the CIA and distributed as "draft legal authorities" in spring 2001. Again, the goal was to lengthen the war. In fact, it was "expressly stated that the goal of [U.S.] assistance was *not* to overthrow the Taliban," but to make them pay a price for harboring a U.S. enemy. Like in the 1980's proxy war against the Soviets, a war would have once more been promoted in Afghanistan to bleed a U.S. rival. Success was assured as long as the criminals remained within Afghanistan and targeted only the Afghan people. From Carter to George W. Bush, the pain of innocent Afghans has always been a price worth paying to further U.S. interests.[96]

On January 25, 2001, Clarke gave his paper to Bush National Security Adviser Condoleezza Rice, along with his 1998 "*Delenda.*" Rice ignored it and instructed him to start a "policy review process" and reanalyze the situation from scratch. Then on May 29, Rice once again directed Clarke to draft a "presidential directive" that would present "a range of options for attacking bin Laden's organization." The draft he delivered was "essentially similar to the proposal he had developed in December 2000 and put forward to the new administration in January 2001." A "frustrated" Clarke asked to be removed from his position as counterterrorism czar, since the administration was not "serious about al-Qa'eda."[97]

Clarke's later draft, circulated in June 2001, contained language directing Secretary of Defense Donald Rumsfeld to "'develop contingency plans' to attack both al-Qa'eda and Taliban targets in Afghanistan." Aside from Clarke's proposal, there were still no concrete plans to invade Afghanistan. Many 9/11 conspiracy theorists claim that Washington was looking for an excuse to invade Afghanistan prior to 9/11, but there is no evidence that Bush or his cabinet was pursuing

Clarke's recommendations seriously yet. According to the 9/11 Commission, "Secretary Rumsfeld did not order his subordinates to begin preparing any new military plans against either al-Qa'eda or the Taliban before 9/11." Even so, the Clarke proposal was a "draft presidential directive," so U.S. diplomats probably knew about it and used it to effect with the Taliban and their backers in Pakistan. On June 18, Condoleezza Rice met with Pakistani foreign minister Abdul Sattar and "really let him have it" on the Taliban harboring of al-Qa'eda, or at least this is what she told the 9/11 Commission in her defense. In July, administration officials warned another Pakistani diplomat, former foreign secretary Niaz Naik, that the U.S. was considering military action against the Taliban. Often Naik's account, reported in the BBC Online article "U.S. 'planned attack on Taliban'," is used as *evidence* for secret U.S. battle plans. The article supposedly quotes Naik in the headline, but it is not clear whether those are really Naik's words or a BBC interpretation. Furthermore, Naik is not directly quoted anywhere else in the article. A London *Guardian* piece on the same meeting between U.S., Russian, Pakistani, and UN officials actually quotes Naik:

> The Americans indicated to us that in case the Taliban does not behave and in case Pakistan also doesn't help [them] to influence the Taliban, then the United States would be left with no option but to take an overt action against Afghanistan . . .

As far as we can tell from available evidence, Naik was simply warned in the hopes that he would convince his government to threaten the Taliban to expel al-Qa'eda. There is no evidence that the U.S. was actually willing to carry out its threat. According to Naik, "Russians [who were also at the meeting] were trying to tell the Americans that the threat of the use of force is sometimes more effective than force itself."[98]

After the 9/11 attacks, there was little question that Washington would respond with force. Initially, however, it was not clear what the target of the response would be. In fact, U.S. policy makers had to restrain themselves from attacking Iraq. National Security Council discussions, as recounted in Bob Woodward's book *Bush at War*, paint a picture at odds with the view that Afghanistan was a longtime target and Washington had been waiting for an excuse to invade. If that can be said of any country, it was Iraq. Deputy Secretary of Defense Paul Wolfowitz had a semireligious "belief that Iraq was behind 9/11," completely out of touch with the facts. Then–Secretary of State Colin Powell said that Wolfowitz was interested in "using [9/11] as a way to deal with the Iraq problem." Richard Clarke relates a conversation he had with Wolfowitz after 9/11: "I began saying, 'We have to deal with bin Laden; we have to deal with al-Qa'eda.' Wolfowitz . . . said, 'No, no, no. We don't have to deal with al-Qa'eda. Why are we talking about that little guy? We have to talk about Iraqi terrorism against the United States.'"[99] Notably, Vice President Dick Cheney, Secretary of Defense Donald Rumsfeld, and Wolfowitz had all been involved in U.S. Iraq policy at least as far back as the first Gulf War (1991). According to Woodward, all three tried to push cabinet discussions in the direction of attacking Iraq. In the end, to quell domestic and international expectations, and to maintain credibility in the face of an outside attack, it was decided that Afghanistan had to be the first step in what was termed the "Global War on Terrorism." Iraq would be the second step. Reportedly it was Bush who came up with this scheme: "Start with bin Laden, which Americans expect. And if we succeed, we've struck a blow and can move forward" to Iraq. It took four days of deliberations for the Bush administration to decide *not* to invade Iraq.[100]

Once Afghanistan was determined to be a target, the earlier recommendations of Clarke and others were dusted off the shelf and finally received Bush's consideration. As mentioned above, this included attacking the Taliban using the Northern Alliance and U.S. air strikes. The CIA had begun shipping cash, arms, and supplies to the Northern Alliance on September 13, giving the group's war against the Taliban a new lease on life. Air strikes took a little longer to organize. Afghanistan's landlocked status required U.S. troops to be stationed nearby and fighter planes to fly in the airspace of neighboring countries. Basing rights in Uzbekistan and the right to overfly Pakistan had to be negotiated. At the time, the dictator of Uzbekistan was more than happy to have a long-term U.S. military presence. This has since changed—Islam Karimov expelled U.S. troops in 2005 (see Chapter 7).

Pakistan, the main supporter of the Taliban, had to be treated more delicately. Pakistani support for the U.S. war would mean the end of a project the ISI had worked on for decades—the insertion of a pliant regime in Afghanistan. As noted in Chapter 1, this would have solved the "Pashtunistan" issue in addition to ensuring that Pakistan would never have to fight a war on two fronts. (Part of the reason why India supported the Northern Alliance was to keep Pakistan vulnerable to such a contingency.) President Pervez Musharraf agreed surprisingly quickly to support the U.S., provided sanctions on Islamabad (because of its nuclear weapons program) were lifted and new U.S. aid was forthcoming. Musharraf also needed assurance from Washington that the Northern Alliance would not rule Afghanistan. Another reason for Pakistani persistence in supporting the Taliban was the fear of an uprising from Pakistan's fundamentalist clerics and their followers. While there was indeed a backlash against Musharraf, it was not as powerful as feared. A U.S. Defense Information Agency source asserted that

> [T]he vast majority of Pakistanis are firmly in support of President Musharraf [ending support to the Taliban]. . . . [T]here is no division within the military. . . . Almost all of Pakistan's traditional tribal leaders have also pledged support. Only a few fringe Islamic political figures are protesting, but . . . these politicians are corrupt and discredited.

Musharraf judged that ending support for the Taliban was in "Pakistan's self interests," because the country would be

> assisted by the U.S. . . . for its commitment in the struggle [against the Taliban and al-Qa'eda]. Musharraf and other Pakistani leaders see this as an opportunity for a better future and expect concrete forms of assistance to help Pakistan climb out of the terrible economic condition the country presently is in.

If this is true, then perhaps Pakistan could have cut off ties to the Taliban years before, if pressured in a similar manner by the U.S., and offered similar economic support. That is, if the U.S. had really been interested in promoting democracy and ending terrorism in Afghanistan. It took an attack on U.S. soil to get Bush to think about ending the Taliban regime, and even then all U.S. actions were calculated to advance U.S. foreign policy objectives, not the safety and well-being of Afghans.[101]

BOMBING AFGHANS TO SAVE THEM

September 11, 2001, cast an intense spotlight on Afghanistan, the nation that Amnesty International had designated "the world's largest forgotten tragedy." Not since the December 1979 Soviet invasion did Afghanistan receive so much international attention. About the same size and population as Iraq, the country turned out to be a convenient testing ground for the Bush administration's concepts of "imperial democracy" and "nation building lite," which were to be implemented later in Iraq, albeit with more resources and attention. The Afghan people were the perfect experimental subjects—impoverished, oppressed, and willing to accept any alternative to the Taliban. The alternative presented to them by the U.S. was called Operation Enduring Freedom.

On October 7, 2001, less than a month after 9/11, the U.S. began bombing Afghanistan. The country had survived three invasions by Britain and one by the Soviet Union. Destroyed by 22 years of recent war (including the Soviet invasion), Afghans were under attack yet again, this time by the current superpower.

Bush often spoke as if the goal of the bombing had been to convince the Taliban to perform a specific task. At a September 17 National Security Council (NSC) meeting, Bush ordered Colin Powell to "issue an ultimatum against the Taliban today warning them to turn over bin Laden and his al-Qa'eda or they will suffer the consequences. If they don't comply, we'll attack them." Bush's intent was "to have them quaking in their boots." The added possibility that the U.S. would obliterate the Taliban was also considered. As Bush said to the NSC, "Our goal is not to destroy the Taliban, but that may be the effect."[102] Publicly, however, the war was described as a necessary evil to bring terrorists to justice. On September 20, Bush declared that "They will hand over the terrorists, or they will share in their fate." Some speeches specified only tactical goals, or goals that would weaken the Taliban's ability to wage war, but not necessarily eliminate them. In his October 7 public announcement of the beginning of U.S. air strikes, President Bush said the U.S. would "attack the military capability of the Taliban regime." On October 29, he said the U.S. aim in Afghanistan was to "dismantle Taliban defenses, [and] . . . destroy al-Qa'eda training bases." On November 6, the objective was to get "the Taliban to hand over al-Qa'eda, the leaders, to release those who are being detained, and to destroy any terrorist training camps."[103]

Despite public pronouncements that the outcome of the war depended on the contrition of the Taliban, the truth is that nothing the Taliban did or said would have ended the U.S. air raids. Bush was steadfast in rejecting any approaches by the Taliban that might have led to a less destructive result. After about a week of bombing, the Taliban offered to hand over bin Laden, provided the U.S. stopped their attack and presented them with evidence that he was responsible for 9/11. This was rejected by Bush:

> There's no need to negotiate. There's no discussions [*sic*]. I told them exactly what they need to do. And there's no need to discuss innocence or guilt. We know he's guilty. Turn him over. If they want us to stop our military operations, they've just got to meet my conditions. Now, when I said no negotiation, I meant no negotiation. . . . There's no negotiation—they must have not heard—there's no negotiation. This is non-negotiable. . . . There's nothing to negotiate about. . . . [T]here is no negotiation, period.[104]

Two days later, a senior Taliban official in Pakistan "appealed for an American bombing pause in Afghanistan while moderates in the Taliban government sought to persuade . . . [Taliban supreme leader] Omar to agree to a formula for the handover" of bin Laden. But the Bush administration was not really seeking the capture of bin Laden or justice for 9/11 so much as it was trying to show its power. In the view of the *New York Times*, "A bombing pause . . . could be seen as compromise or weakness by the United States."[105]

Behind closed doors, the rhetoric was even more bellicose. Cofer Black, head of the CIA's Counterterrorism Center, told Russian officials on September 18, "We're going to kill them. We're going to put their heads on sticks. We're going to rock their world." Bush declared at a September 13 NSC meeting, "We are going to rain holy hell on them." Admiral Sir Michael Boyce, chief of the British Defense Staff, emphasized on October 28 that it was not just the Taliban and al-Qa'eda who were targets of the bombs, but every single Afghan. "The squeeze will carry on until the people of the country themselves recognize that this is going to go on until they get the leadership changed" (*New York Times*, October 28). Bush too held the Afghan people responsible for the presence of bin Laden and company. At one point, he advised his staff to "Tell the Afghans to round up al-Qa'eda. Let's see [al-Qa'eda members], or we'll hit them hard." Bush left no doubt that he was using the air war on Afghanistan as an example to the rest of the world. "We're going to hurt them so bad so that everyone in the world sees, don't deal with bin Laden." This should not be taken literally, since Osama bin Laden was a key player in the U.S.-backed Afghan jihad. What Bush really must have meant was, "don't cross the United States." To Washington, bin Laden's real crime was disrespect.[106]

In the end, the U.S. bombing raids on Afghanistan resulted in at least as many Afghan civilian fatalities as the 3000 U.S. civilians killed on 9/11. A systematic study of press reports and eyewitness accounts by Professor Marc Herold of the University of New Hampshire revealed that between 3,000 and 3,400 civilians were killed directly by Operation Enduring Freedom.[107] Several incidents documented by Human Rights Watch of U.S. bombs killing civilians highlighted the brutality of the campaign and disregard for the lives of the people supposedly being "liberated." On the night of October 21, 2001, twenty-three civilians, mostly children, were killed by three consecutive bombing raids on the village of Thori between 10 p.m. and 1 a.m. One day later, between 25 and 35 Afghan men, women, and children from the village of Chowkar-Karez were killed by the U.S. in an hour-long attack that began at 11 p.m. A Human Rights Watch investigation revealed that "many of the people in the village . . . ran out of their homes, afraid that the bombs would fall on the homes. All witnesses stated that aircraft then returned to the area and began firing from guns. Many of the civilians were killed from the firing." Defense Secretary Donald Rumsfeld refused to respond to the bombing and gunning of Chowkar-Karez: "I cannot deal with that particular village." But later, Pentagon officials informed CNN that Chowkar-Karez was "a fully legitimate target" because it was a nest of Taliban and al-Qa'eda sympathizers, a claim refuted by the Human Rights Watch investigation. The Pentagon finally explained Chowkar-Karez in simpler terms: "The people there are dead because we wanted them dead."[108]

A few days later, the entire village of Kama Ado and 115 to 155 of its residents were wiped out by U.S. bombs. Initially the Pentagon denied that anything happened at the village. This was refuted by Richard Lloyd Parry, an investigative reporter for the London-based *Independent,* who personally saw the corpses, interviewed local witnesses to the bombing, and found a remnant of a U.S. Surface Attack Guided Missile in the wreckage.[109]

In November 2001, the civilian deaths continued: the village of Mudoh near Tora Bora was bombed. "A new cemetery carved from a rocky bluff where the village once stood holds the remains of 150 men, women, and children . . . they were killed, and the village obliterated, by American warplanes." According to the *Los Angeles Times,* "the carnage at Mudoh is the residue of a bombing campaign that, while exceptionally accurate, nonetheless killed, at minimum, hundreds of civilians and wounded thousands more."[110]

In December 2001, as thousands of Afghans fled the southern region of Kandahar, heavily bombed because it was a Taliban stronghold, an ambulance driver noted that "we are receiving five or six bodies each day, half of them military and half civilians." According to a refugee from Kandahar who fled the bombing, "There are a lot of casualties, they are martyrs, and they are mostly civilians."[111]

U.S. bombing raids seemed to have been based on shaky intelligence and rumors, revealing a reckless unconcern for Afghan lives. The *Los Angeles Times* visited 25 bombing sites in Afghanistan to find that "U.S.

warplanes killed and maimed civilians because of unreliable intelligence, stray ordinance and faulty targeting, or because enemy fighters mingled with civilians." In early 2002 the *Washington Post* reported a U.S. strike on a group of peasants collecting scrap metal: "The Pentagon has said the missile was fired on the strength of intelligence suggesting the men were al-Qa'eda leaders, feeding speculation that a tall man among them might have been bin Laden." At a Pentagon briefing, Rear Admiral John Stufflebeem, the deputy director of operations for the Joint Chiefs of Staff, admitted that "we do not know who were the individuals at the strike site." The "tall man" who they thought might be Osama bin Laden turned out to be an Afghan man by the name of Mir Ahmad. Despite that, Stufflebeem went on to justify the attack, saying, "The indications were there, that there was something untoward that we needed to make go away."[112]

Within days of the start of Operation Enduring Freedom, the U.S. began dropping cluster bombs over Afghanistan. Condemned by human rights groups worldwide, the cluster bomb used by the U.S., the CBU-87, consists of 202 bomblets that are deployed over "areas as large as the size of several football fields," which "saturate an area with explosives and tiny flying shards of steel." On October 25, 2001, Joint Chief of Staff General Richard Myers acknowledged, "Yes, we have used cluster bomb units. . . . There have [*sic*] not been a great number of them used, but they have been used." Between October 2001 and March 2002, the U.S. dropped 1,228 cluster bombs containing 248,056 bomblets over Afghanistan. Supporting the U.S.'s use of cluster bombs, the British Secretary of State for Defense Geoff Hoon said they were used only on a "limited number of occasions against the particular military threat of armored vehicles." But because the bombs scatter over such large areas, civilians are extremely vulnerable, no matter how precise the deployment. For example, in the western Afghan village of Shaker Qala a cluster bomb attack on October 22, 2001, killed nine civilians and injured fourteen. It was estimated that up to 200 bomblets failed to explode, leaving residents fearful of leaving their homes.[113]

Cluster bombs routinely leave behind unexploded bomblets, killing civilians long after the attacks are over. While manufacturers and governments routinely report a 5 percent failure rate on cluster munitions, foreign agencies engaged in clearing landmines and other unexploded ordinance report a much higher failure rate of up to 30 percent.[114] Conservative estimates put the numbers of unexploded cluster bomblets at about 12,000, but it is likely that the U.S. bombs left behind at least 25,000 bomblets (using a conservative estimated failure rate of 10 percent for 1,228 bombs dropped) throughout Afghanistan. Within four months after the attack on Shaker Qala, twelve more civilians died as a result of unexploded cluster bomblets.[115]

According to the United Nations Mine Action Programme, Afghanistan is one of the most heavily land-mined countries in the world. Between March 1978 and December 2000, at least 2,812 people were killed by mines and thousands more injured. The U.S. use of cluster bombs only worsened these statistics, given that cluster bomblets are more lethal than land mines. In Herat, between October 2001 and June 2002, unexploded cluster bomblets killed 44 percent of their victims while mines killed 21 percent.[116]

In November 2001, Physicians for Human Rights (PHR) called on the U.S. to immediately stop using cluster bombs in Afghanistan. Leonard S. Rubenstein, Executive Director of PHR, said, "The world has condemned the use of antipersonnel land mines. It is now time for all nations, including the United States, to recognize that both antipersonnel mines and cluster bombs are indiscriminate and cause a devastating civilian toll." PHR also called on the U.S. to clear all the unexploded bomblets deployed in Afghanistan. Predictably, the U.S. did not respond to either the moratorium or the request for clearance. In 2002 the United Nations Mine Action Programme began the daunting task of clearing the U.S.'s unexploded ordinance, estimating the total number to be 25,000.

In addition to those who were killed directly as a result of bombs, unknown numbers of Afghan civilians died of starvation during the winter of 2001 when the U.S. army refused to pause its bombing campaign in response to a request by foreign aid agencies wanting to distribute desperately needed food and medicines. Jonathan Steele of the London *Guardian* estimated that "as many as 20,000 Afghans may have lost their lives as an indirect consequence of the U.S. intervention." Steele takes into account massive dislocation, cold, disease, and a cutoff in aid supplies. Even the most conservative estimate of about 10,000 indirect deaths "clearly exceeds the scale of those killed by bombs."[117]

Prior to the U.S. invasion, Afghanistan was receiving 20,000 to 25,000 tons of food aid per month through the UN World Food Program. When the bombs began dropping, that aid was abruptly halted, jeopardizing the lives of millions of Afghans. The UN Human Rights Commissioner, Mary Robinson, made an ardent plea, calling on the U.S. to suspend air strikes for a short time: "All I can say is that there is a desperate situation for hundreds of thousands—perhaps up to 2 million—of the Afghan civilian population who desperately need food." Because of the halt in food aid, the need increased from 25,000 tons to 50,000, according to the UN. The UN also estimated that $584 million in food and water aid was needed before the onset of winter—the U.S. had pledged only $320 million. The U.S.'s response to Afghan starvation was to air-drop food parcels. Somehow this was expected to address the food needs of 7.5 million Afghans (roughly one-third of the country's population) estimated to be at risk. These food drops were roundly criticized by international aid agencies because they did little to address the overwhelming need. Julian Filochowski, director of Catholic Agency for Overseas Development, explained how unlikely it was that the food would actually reach starving Afghans, "Showering Afghanistan with food parcels is rather like showering London with gold coins hoping that they will reach the homeless, the widows, and those in need." Christian Aid called the food drops "misguided," and said they "divert attention from the real crisis and devalue the very concept of humanitarian aid." Doctors Without Borders called food drops "a purely propaganda tool, of little real value to the Afghan people."[118]

Not only did the food drops do little to address starvation, they actually increased the risk to Afghans. To look for food packets, people had to risk stepping on unexploded bomblets or landmines. In a grotesque coincidence, the food packets were roughly the same size and color as cluster bomblets. In an embarrassing admission of the dangers of cluster bombs, the U.S. was forced to broadcast radio messages warning people to not confuse the bomblets with food packets:

> Attention, noble Afghan people. As you know, the coalition countries have been air dropping daily humanitarian rations for you. The food ration is enclosed in yellow plastic bags. They come in the shape of rectangular or long squares. . . . In areas away from where food has been dropped, cluster bombs will also be dropped. The color of these bombs is also yellow. All bombs will explode when they hit the ground, but in some special circumstances some of the bombs will not explode.[119]

Referring to the confusion of food packets with bomblets, U.S. Congresswoman Cynthia McKinney asked a pointed question to the House International Relations Subcommittee on International Operations and Human Rights: ". . . how in the world can a 300 billion dollar a year military machine not see to it that the food packets and the bomblets from the cluster bombs they are dropping are not the same color? Is it that they really just don't care?"[120]

Explaining the difference between the terrorist attacks on 9/11 and the U.S. attacks on Afghan civilians, Kenton Keith, spokesman for the U.S.-led coalition, said, "We do have an overriding imperative . . . and that is to root out international terrorism . . . we do not deliberately target civilians . . . and al-Qa'eda did deliberately target civilians on Sept. 11th."[121] Yet, the villagers of Chowkar-Karez are dead because the Pentagon says it "wanted them dead." And it was the intention of military planners that the bombing "will carry on until the people of the country realize" that they need to "get the leadership changed."

Perhaps even worse than the admission that slaughtering innocents is a military objective are assertions by some liberal commentators that it was some sort of development aid. *Nation* writer Christopher Hitchens hailed the U.S. actions in Afghanistan as success in "bombing a country back out of the Stone Age."[122] It is comforting to know that villages like Chowkar-Karez, Kama Ado, or Mudoh were sacrificed for a good cause. Strangely, Janat Khan, the mayor of Mudoh, was not happy with his village's role in bringing Afghanistan "out of the Stone Age." "No one should ever have to bury a baby's hand," he told reporters as he recovered fragments of corpses in the aftermath of U.S. bombing.[123]

The *New York Times*' Nicholas Kristof had another justification for the murder of civilians:

> One of the uncomfortable realities of the war on terrorism is that we Americans have killed many more people in Afghanistan than died in the attack on the World Trade Center. . . . So what is the lesson of this? Is it that while pretending to take the high road, we have actually slaughtered more people than Osama bin Laden has? Or that military responses are unjustifiable because huge numbers of innocents inevitably are killed? No, it's just the opposite. Our experience there demonstrates that troops can advance humanitarian goals just as much as doctors or aid workers can. By my calculations, our invasion of Afghanistan may end up saving one million lives over the next decade.[124]

By this logic, innocent civilians were killed by the U.S. to save the lives of others. In other words, we were bombing Afghans in order to save them. It is highly probable that Osama bin Laden felt the same way about the 9/11 casualties.

MILITARIZED AID: BUYING HEARTS, MINDS, AND INTELLIGENCE

In addition to bombing, a second major component of U.S. military strategy is the militarization of aid, exemplified in the air by the food drops, and on the ground by so-called "Civil Affairs Units" or "Provincial Reconstruction Teams" (PRTs). PRTs are considered by military experts to be at the "forefront of a worldwide trend toward integrating military and humanitarian work,"[125] and serve a combination of military, humanitarian, economic, and public relations goals for the Pentagon. Each PRT consists of a group of fifty to five hundred troops whose mandate ostensibly includes security and reconstruction. As of September 2004, there were twelve PRTs operating within Afghanistan, of which nine were run by the U.S., two were run by other members of the U.S.-led coalition, and one by the International Security Assistance Force (ISAF).[126]

On the surface, the PRTs embody benevolent-sounding objectives: "there is need for an alternative force to keep the peace and help with the reconstruction of the country. . . . [S]uch a force does now exist, in the form of the Provincial Reconstruction Teams (PRTs)."[127] PRTs, we are told, benefit the Afghan people because they "have helped promote security, stability operations, reconstruction. . . . This effort should lead to the ultimate objective of this operation—the ability of the Islamic Transition Government of Afghanistan to effectively govern and care for its own people."[128] But PRT overtures toward providing security and reconstruction are token efforts. In reality, the PRTs are focused on other, more useful goals for the U.S. First, they are an effective, if unethical, tool for manipulating poor and starving civilians by dispensing aid in exchange for information and good behavior. According to a soldier who headed a PRT in Afghanistan, civil-military integration is "a military tool to achieve military ends . . . and the humanitarian side of it is a positive byproduct."[129] Second, PRTs are intended to enhance the image of the U.S. army as a benevolent force in the lives of the Afghan people.

The problem with "integrating military and humanitarian work" is that reconstruction tasks and relief work are performed by *combat forces* alongside military operations. In addition, the reconstruction costs of PRT-led projects are prohibitive: according to Refugees International, a typical PRT may build a handful of schools, worth $10,000 each, while spending $10 million a year in personnel and support costs. Aid agencies that are experienced and dedicated to small reconstruction projects are far more cost effective.[130]

In fact, the aid component of PRT work is redundant. Even though one of the goals of PRTs is ostensibly to "expand reconstruction programmes [*sic*] beyond large cities,"[131] there were already operational humanitarian aid efforts in many Afghan provinces, a number of them active for decades. The commander of Combined Task Force Thunder, Army Col.

Gary Cheeks, explained that while PRTs "will continuously conduct combat operations, our main effort will be the reconstruction of Afghanistan and building its capacity for economic growth and prosperity."[132]

In the best-case scenario, one might expect PRTs to conduct reconstruction projects where it is too dangerous for aid agencies.[133] But they generally operate in relatively safe cities like Kunduz and Bamian. As a result, aid workers have been the most vocal critics of the PRTs. InterAction, a coalition of 159 organizations including Doctors Without Borders, CARE, and Oxfam America, "does not believe the military members of the PRTs should be engaged in humanitarian and reconstruction activities."[134] Instead, the aid community simply wants military forces to stick to providing security. Rafael Robillard, the director of a coordinating body of international aid agencies in Kabul, summed up the frustration of many aid workers:

> I was talking to one civil affairs guy, and we were looking at a kindergarten the American military was building, and the soldier turned to me and said, "Why aren't you guys doing anything about disarmament?" I could not believe it. The military is building kindergartens, and they are asking me, a civilian aid worker, to do disarmament! The world is upside down.[135]

InterAction called on the PRTs to take security more seriously than humanitarian aid. Paul Barker, the country director for CARE, called the conflict between PRTs and aid workers "unnecessary. . . . There are plenty of aid agencies in Afghanistan who have lots of experience and who can build schools and clinics and village water supplies. What we are not able to do and what we wish the military would do is focus on improving the security environment."[136]

Another consequence of militarizing aid is that people's suffering is extorted for strategic gain. The PRTs, which "double as intelligence-gathering operations,"[137] use aid and reconstruction projects as military tools to elicit information, force compliance, and deal with local threats to U.S. soldiers. In spring 2004, the U.S.-led military coalition air-dropped leaflets that read: "In order to continue the humanitarian aid, pass over any information related to Taliban, al-Qa'eda or Gulbuddin organizations to the coalition forces."[138] After aid agencies expressed outrage at the leaflets, they were quickly withdrawn. Aid is often used to bribe Afghans who provide information on the Taliban or al-Qa'eda. "The more they help us find the bad guys the more good stuff they get," explained one Army lieutenant.[139] One military news Web site summarized a common military response to rockets fired at the U.S. Bagram Air Base:

> American commanders have learned that there are ways to get the locals to talk, and identify the people firing the rocket[s]. The most useful method is to halt reconstruction projects, or shut down the weekly bazaar (where local Afghans can sell goods to the thousands of troops and civilians on the base). Either of these moves costs the local Afghan economy thousands of dollars a week. In a country where $20 a month is a good salary, that kind of loss is felt.[140]

An American identifying himself as the "regional counter-terrorism director" in the Goshta district, concurred: "It's all part of the same picture. If people cooperate with us and make their areas secure, we help them."[141]

Conversely, the consequences of not cooperating include threats of violence, leading to outright abuse. Colonel Terry Sellers, U.S. Army commander in the Uruzgan province, threatened, "The tribal elders know where the Taliban are. If they do not want their asses whipped, they will have to start cooperating with us."[142] After discovering Afghans were using radios to pass on information about U.S. troop movement, Sergeant Donald Thomas told one group of villagers that if they "want this village to stand like it is," they would voluntarily produce the radio, the laser pointer, and every weapon in the village within twenty minutes. "I will destroy these houses if they lie to me," he warned. Ultimately, the PRTs fall back on "standard tactics of military power to achieve their aims: intimidation, overwhelming force, hands tied behind backs, and faces in the dirt."[143]

The militarization of aid has had direct consequences on real aid workers by undermining their credibility and impartiality in delivering aid to local populations. Even worse, it puts them in danger. When humanitarian aid is distributed by military forces, and especially when Afghans are abused and manipulated in the process, humanitarian aid workers are more likely to be considered military targets. While the American Forces Press Service claims that "civil affairs soldiers work to make areas safe for civilian aid organizations to work,"[144] according to one aid worker, "the deliberate linking of humanitarian aid with military objectives destroys the meaning of humanitarianism. It will result, in the end, in the neediest Afghans not getting badly needed aid—and those providing aid being targeted."[145] When we asked the NATO spokesperson in Kabul, Major Karen Tissot Van Patot, about these concerns, she denied them: "we have very clear tasks and functions and they do not conflict with the humanitarian functions as I am aware." However, the targeting of aid workers by anti-U.S. elements in Afghanistan is now commonplace. In 2004 alone, at least 24 aid workers were killed, including five members of Medecins Sans Frontieres/Doctors Without Borders (MSF).[146] This led the Nobel Prize–winning organization to pull out of Afghanistan after 24 years of service. Diderik van Halsema, a Communications Officer of MSF, reflected on the decision to leave:

> [T]he Taliban, whilst claiming responsibility for the assassinations, falsely accused us several times of working for American interests. Ironic given that MSF has worked extremely hard to maintain its independence and distance from the coalition forces and has been repeatedly critical of their attempts to link military objectives with the provision of "humanitarian" assistance. Through these accusations, we are vulnerable to further attack.[147]

The departure of real aid workers ensures that the U.S. remains in control of distributing aid and leading reconstruction efforts in provincial areas, thereby increasing civilian dependence on them. One official said that PRTs have "put a human face on the American presence." But, "despite our name, we're not really here to do reconstruction. We are here to reinforce Afghan authority"[148] Given that a significant portion of the Afghan central government is beholden to U.S. concerns, this really means U.S. authority.

TERROR IN THE COUNTRYSIDE

> They gave me medicine and also a radio and corn seed. He asked if we needed anything. I said, "We don't need anything. Don't humiliate us. Don't rob our country. Don't commit crimes. We don't need anything."[149]
>
> —AFGHAN VILLAGER IN URUZGAN PROVINCE RELATING HIS CONVERSATION WITH A PRT HEAD

In May/June 2004 Australian filmmaker Carmela Baranowska was embedded with U.S. Marines in the remote and dangerous Afghan province of Uruzgan. She was the only independent reporter that year to witness the Marines in their "hunt for Taliban and al-Qa'eda." During a subsequent trip to Uruzgan, she followed up on the ugly consequences of their actions. Her 45-minute documentary "Taliban Country,"[150] recorded on a handheld digital camera, earned Baranowska the Walkley Award—the Australian counterpart to the Pulitzer prize—for her "exceptionally courageous report."

While embedded with the Marines, Baranowska documented groups of U.S. soldiers brutally kicking down doors of mud homes. In one incident, they arrested a young man named Janan, frightened and alone inside a mud compound. Janan was turned over for interrogation to Jaan Mohammed, the local warlord collaborating with the U.S., who accused him of being a member of the Taliban. Janan's "crimes" included being found with nine AK-47 rifles and two grenades. "In a country awash with weapons and in a major operation involving a convoy of Humvees, helicopters, and up to 50 Marines, this number is hardly significant," reported Baranowska.

To investigate the aftermath of U.S. search operations, Baranowska headed back to the same province independently a few weeks later. She found Janan and interviewed him. He insisted that his village was not a stronghold of the Taliban:

> This isn't the Taliban's territory. The Taliban come here but they don't stay. If one night they do come and confront us or someone else . . . we're like lambs to the slaughter. . . . The Taliban come two or three days before the Americans, then the Americans just arrest you and me and hassle us normal people going about their business. They don't have the means to arrest the Taliban. They're usually three days late so they just hassle us. . . . I was really scared of the Americans.

Instead of searching for and arresting Taliban and al-Qa'eda members, the U.S. military is being used, either naively or knowingly, by warlords and their militias to punish vulnerable Afghans based on their ethnicity and tribal allegiance. According to Janan, the reason his village was being targeted by the U.S.'s collaborator, Jaan Mohammed, was that it belonged to a "different tribe," and that villages sharing Jaan Mohammed's tribal affiliation had never been searched by the U.S. Baranowska interviewed several Afghans from other villages who described ongoing abuse by Jaan Mohammed and his men, including the interrogation and beating of children as young as seven. Ordinary Afghans are caught between the Taliban, the local warlords, and the U.S. military, fearing brutal reprisals from all three. One village elder expressed his frustration:

> Never in the world have the Taliban come to us, nor have we helped them or set eyes on them. We have tribal enemies. We have no place in government and no role in voting. The skies have fallen upon us over and over. The hardships we have suffered this time around would never be suffered by infidels. I asked the [U.S.] interpreter, "what crime have we committed?" This [abuse] is based on tribal issues but it's as if we're harboring al-Qa'eda.

He expressed relief that only 35 men from his village were arrested—in a neighboring village, all the men were arrested. One man who was arrested, Wali Mohammed, spent three nights in detention. He described his treatment to Baranowska:

> They fingered us, beat us and humiliated us. . . . There was no food. My legs gave way. We were asking desperately for food. There was nothing. They gave us water, but spilt it over our mouths, noses and eyes. They shoveled snuff up our nostrils and into our eyes . . . this type of cruelty has never been done to us or seen by us. . . . They were all Americans. . . . They were all laughing and mocking. It wasn't one, it was more than 20 Americans . . . they disrespected us and undermined our dignity. They brought shame on us before the whole world. They'll show the world our naked bodies . . . they took our picture.

Wali's elderly father, Noor Mohammed Lala, had a similar experience:

> I was imprisoned too. No Muslim should suffer that. They tied my hands and then they put me in a container. They removed my clothes. I pleaded through an interpreter that it was against Islam. "Don't make me stand here naked." But they said no. I said "for the sake of Allah and the Koran, don't do this." . . . I was told to look up and put my hands on the container. I couldn't see behind me, but someone was fingering me. Some of them were pulling my testicles . . . my bottom was wet. I wouldn't be a Muslim if I lied to you. When I put on my clothes I rubbed it off . . . and this happens when I am old, white-bearded, with no teeth . . . this outrage happened to me.

The thirty-five men arrested, including Wali Mohammed and his father, were accused of providing food and shelter to al-Qa'eda and Taliban forces. Their humiliation was expressed by the village elder: "we are all dead, all dead. We have no more honor. We'd prefer death to this humiliation." Baranowska also discovered that whole villages were being abandoned as people fled to other villages or to Pakistan, unable to live with the shame of the abuse they suffered at the hands of the U.S. "You [Westerners] humiliate my elders, my tribe and my land. So again you bring violence to my Afghanistan," said another man.

Human Rights Watch exposed the behavior of U.S. troops in their report "Enduring Freedom: Abuses by U.S. Forces in Afghanistan."[151] According to the report, the U.S. military routinely uses force (beatings and other harsh treatment) during arrests, often captures innocent civilians, destroys Afghan homes and property in the course of its raids, and is often manipulated by its warlord colleagues against local rivals. A UN official complained about the "use of cowboy-like excessive force" against residents "who generally turn out to be law abiding citizens," as well as "blowing doors open with grenades, rather than knocking," and mistreating women and children.

The report cites many shocking cases of people's lives destroyed by U.S. forces. One example was Ahmed Khan, whose house was shot at from helicopters, and raided by U.S. troops. His home was destroyed and looted, and he and his two sons arrested and taken to Bagram Air Base. During the raid, a father of four children, Niaz Mohammed, was sleeping outdoors guarding the grain harvest when he was shot in the back by U.S. forces. Khan and his sons were eventually freed, having been deemed innocent. He now looks after Niaz Mohammed's children, saying, "We will forgive America when they pay for his life."[152]

U.S. Special Forces were guilty of cruel and inhumane treatment of villagers in southeastern Afghanistan. An Army psychological operations officer witnessed a Special Forces member "throughout the day . . . punching people, slapping them, pulling his M-9 [pistol] out and threatening to shoot the village people." He also witnessed the same Special Forces soldier take a blindfolded man whose hands were bound behind a wall. "For the next one to two minutes, you could hear the sounds of someone being beaten. After that, [name deleted] brought him out [bleeding from the] mouth and/or nose."[153]

Reports of physical abuse, torture, and sexual humiliation continue to trickle out of Afghanistan via the media and are far too numerous to mention. Clearly, U.S. military forces operate with impunity and a dangerous unconcern for Afghan civilian lives. Given that most foreign reporters have left Afghanistan, it is likely that only a small percentage of the incidents of abuse are even reported.

PROVOKING ATTACKS

A prominent news story in 2005 highlights a new tactic initiated by the U.S. military to fight the Taliban. In October 2005, U.S. soldiers burned the bodies of two dead Taliban fighters in an incident captured on video by Australian journalists John Martinkus and Stephen Dupont. It was attributed to the U.S. soldiers' cultural ignorance, and the soldiers were disciplined.[154] Cultural ignorance and racism is common among U.S. soldiers, but the body-burning was accompanied by a loudspeaker message intended to incite Islamic sensibilities, and inflame fear of and/or anger toward the United States:

> You allowed your fighters to be laid down facing west [toward Mecca] and burned. You are too scared to come down and retrieve the bodies. This just proves you are the lady boys we always believed you to be. Your time in Afghanistan is short. You attack and run away like women. You call yourself Talibs but you are a disgrace to the Muslim religion and you bring shame upon your family. Come and fight like men instead of the cowardly dogs you are.[155]

According to Dupont, who captured the burning on film, the message was put forward by Psychological Operations officers, not the less-experienced men who actually burned the bodies:

> [T]he psychological operations unit, who were [*sic*] responsible for the broadcast along with some other broadcasts to the Taliban, they're quite well aware of [the provocative nature of the message]. They're older guys. That's their job. . . . They use it as a weapon.

Dupont told an interviewer that the message was part of a calculated strategy to provoke Taliban attacks.

> They deliberately wanted to incite that much anger from the Taliban so the Taliban could attack them. . . . [The U.S. was

> trying to] smoke them out. They want the Taliban to fight them because they can't find them otherwise.[156]

Sometime near the end of the year 2004, the Taliban had begun engaging in more clandestine suicide and other attacks on mostly "soft" (nonmilitary) targets. According to *Asia Times*, "A new generation of mujahideen not known in Afghanistan, including Arabs, Pakistanis, Afghans and others, was selected and kept at remote positions" throughout the south and east of the country. After hitting their targets, (nonsuicide) attackers would quickly blend into the population, making it difficult for U.S. soldiers to strike back. These "Iraq-style" tactics were much more organized and decentralized than in the first few years after the U.S. invasion, making it impossible to fight the Taliban militarily.[157]

Instead of following up on attacks using law-enforcement techniques, the Pentagon devised a new military approach that includes threats and provocations directed against the potential support system for the new Mujahideen: the Afghan population itself. The message broadcast while the Taliban bodies burned was an instance of the U.S. using this technique to promote fear, anger, and violent reprisals. Dupont said,

> It's a really crazy situation. And, you know, the fact that they're announcing these kind of, you know, sort of incredible statements, I think, says a lot about the war that's going on there. I mean, they really want to be attacked. That's the only way they can find them.[158]

The messages and other provocations fall under the rubric of Psychological Operations, described by the U.S. Special Operations Command Web site as "force multipliers that use nonviolent means in often violent environments." Despite this benign description, psychological operations can still terrorize civilian populations, and make formerly tolerant citizens support a violent response to the U.S. presence. The techniques "rely on logic, fear, desire or other mental factors to promote specific emotions, attitudes or behaviors."[159] In this case the "specific behaviors" promoted are attacks on U.S. soldiers.

One region where U.S. psychological operations took a particularly vengeful cast was in Korengal valley in Kunar province, where a U.S. helicopter carrying nineteen soldiers was shot down in June 2005, the "worst single loss of life in Afghanistan" for the Americans since they invaded in 2001. Lt. Col. Jerry O'Hara, chief spokesman at the U.S. base at Bagram, declared that, "We're not letting go of that area." The U.S. broadcast a message to the residents of the valley:

> if they [the people of Korengal] are not going to comply with the demands of expelling the enemy from their villages then we will be forced to continue to pursue the enemy relentlessly until the elders either force them to leave or the hand of our national security troops force [*sic*] them out. The people of Korengal are either with the people of Kunar or against them.

Sam Zarifi of Human Rights Watch said that the message "contains a barely veiled threat of collective punishment," which is "a violation of the Geneva conventions and other laws of war." Afghan officials who were recruited to broadcast the message "said they were not happy about the language, which they described as 'how the foreigners speak'." One official warned that "it will make things worse," meaning the message would make villagers less supportive of the U.S. As mentioned above, this is in fact their purpose.[160]

The technique is apparently working. About 30 percent of the Afghan population now believes that attacks on U.S. forces "can be justified," according to an ABC News poll.[161] Unless the Taliban make up one-third of the population, which is unlikely, those who support attacks on American soldiers include many average Afghans who are not part of the Taliban insurgency. But the U.S. military does not ask whether those who attack them at any given moment are Taliban fighters or average Afghans who have taken up arms against Americans insulting Islam and threatening their villages. Furthermore, many Afghans support the insurgents. According to one Lance Corporal operating in Korengal Valley, "[The villagers] always tell us that there are no insurgents, yet we're always getting attacked every time we come here."[162] Brig. General

James Champion made it clear that attacks on U.S. troops can often be blamed on the U.S. presence itself. "I think we're initiating the overwhelming majority of the actions. . . . [They] would not be firing the first shots if we weren't in the area looking for them."[163]

ENEMY COMBATANTS, EXTRAORDINARY RENDITION, AND INDEFINITE DETENTION

Since 2001, hundreds of men, and even some boys designated as "enemy combatants" for the Taliban or al-Qa'eda, have been arrested by the U.S., imprisoned, tortured, and in a few cases, killed. For the first few years there were no opportunities for third parties, such as human rights organizations or lawyers, to determine whether those arrested and detained were in fact linked in any way to the Taliban or al-Qa'eda, or if they were even guilty of any crimes. While in U.S. custody, many were subjected to horrifying torture and humiliation. Most were rounded up and sent to Bagram Air Base, Kandahar base, and other bases in Afghanistan. Several hundred were transported to Guantánamo Bay in Cuba, where they were imprisoned without any sort of trial. Some were exported to prisons in countries like Egypt or Jordan, where torture of suspects is government policy and is not subject to public scrutiny. Some were imprisoned directly by the U.S. in secret international prisons.

The exporting of prisoners to countries that are known to have atrocious human rights records is called "extraordinary rendition." About 150 prisoners have reportedly been "rendered" for interrogation (and likely torture) in prisons run by the host countries but financed, and sometimes directed, by the CIA.[164] According to Jane Mayer of *The New Yorker*, "upon arriving in foreign countries, rendered suspects often vanish. Detainees are not provided with lawyers, and many families are not informed of their whereabouts."[165] In 2002, a Syrian-born Canadian engineer, Maher Arar, who was returning home after vacationing with his family in Tunisia, was apprehended while in transit in the U.S. He was rendered to a Syrian prison, where he was imprisoned for ten months in an underground cell three feet wide, six feet long, and seven feet high. He was physically and psychologically tortured during his interrogations.[166] After his eventual release, Arar filed a lawsuit against the U.S. government for his arrest and torture.[167]

It came to light in late 2005 that the CIA has been directly hiding and interrogating prisoners in a secret international prison system that spans eight countries, including a prison in Afghanistan code-named "The Salt Pit" and several unnamed "Eastern European democracies." Of the approximately one hundred men being held directly by the CIA, thirty are considered "major terrorism suspects," while the rest have "limited intelligence value."[168]

Closer to Afghanistan, many repressive Central Asian republics have been firmly enrolled in the U.S.'s war, in particular Uzbekistan. Before September 11, 2001, the U.S. State Department's Human Rights Report began with the declaration that "Uzbekistan is an authoritarian state with limited civil rights."[169] While the report detailed some human rights violations by the Islamic Movement of Uzbekistan (IMU), the bulk of repression was government sponsored. Subsequent State Department human rights reports consistently open with the exact same sentence.[170]

Human Rights Watch has singled out the so-called "moderate" Uzbek government for abuse of prisoners and civilians:

> Torture and ill-treatment in prisons was rampant, and there were several shocking reports of deaths in custody from torture in prisons. [There were] hundreds of reports of beatings and numerous accounts of the use of electric shock, temporary suffocation, hanging by the ankles or wrists, removal of fingernails, and punctures with sharp objects. Human Rights Watch received credible reports in 2000 that police sodomized male detainees with bottles, raped them, and beat and burned them in the groin area.

According to a forensic report commissioned by the British Embassy in August 2002, two prisoners were even boiled to death.[171]

State Department reports themselves cite Human Rights Watch's documentation on Uzbekistan's torture. According to the Institute for Foreign Policy Analysis, "this places the United States in the uncomfortably familiar position of its principal military ally in a Muslim region being a corrupt, secular authoritarian opposed by Islamic fundamentalist forces."[172] Yet, not only was the U.S. government closely allied with Uzbekistan, there was substantial evidence that detainees captured by the U.S. were being turned over to its Central Asian friends for "detention and interrogation" as part of the "rendition" program.[173] President Bush dismissed concerns about torture and abuse in Uzbekistan, saying, "we seek assurances that nobody will be tortured when we render a person back to their home country." Clearly the benefits of Uzbek friendship far outweighed human rights issues. General Myers said the United States had "benefited greatly from our partnership and strategic relationship with Uzbekistan," and brushed aside human rights violations, saying, "in my view, we shouldn't let any single issue drive a relationship with any single country. It doesn't seem to be good policy to me."[174]

The main U.S. prison for terrorism suspects that is known to the public is in Guantánamo Bay, Cuba. Initially, Camp X-ray became the detention center for more than seven hundred men and boys representing 44 countries.[175] As of this writing, about five hundred prisoners remain in captivity in a more permanent structure called Camp Delta.[176] One Afghan man, Alif Khan, described the manner in which he was transported to Guantánamo after being picked up by U.S. forces:

> They put cuffs and tape on my hands, taped my eyes and taped my ears. They gagged me. They put chains on my legs and chains around my belly. They injected me. I was unconscious. I don't know how they transported me. When I arrived in Cuba and they took me off the plane they gave another injection and I came back to consciousness. I did not know how long the plane was flying for. It might have been one day or two days. They put me onto a bed on wheels. I could sense what was going on. They tied me up. They took me off the plane into a vehicle. We [went] to a big prison and there were cages there. They built it like a zoo.[177]

The Pentagon denied that any prisoners were injected while being transported to the U.S. base on Cuba. Consistent with Khan's description, media outlets like the BBC reported that prisoners were "housed in cells measuring 1.8 by 2.4 meters (six feet by eight feet) with open, chain-link walls, a concrete floor and wooden roof."[178] The cages, which Human Rights Watch's Jamie Fellner called "a scandal,"[179] were mistaken for dog kennels, according to one journalist.[180]

What was even more scandalous was the Bush administration's circumvention of international law and the Geneva Conventions. In designating the hundreds of captured men and boys as "enemy combatants" rather than "prisoners of war," the U.S. circumvented legal restrictions on treatment of prisoners. Under the Geneva Conventions, "*any person captured during a war*" (presumably this includes "enemy combatants") are

> entitled to humane treatment, understood at a minimum to include basic shelter, clothing, food and medical attention. In addition, no detainee—even if suspected of war crimes such as the murder of civilians—may be subjected to torture, corporal punishment, or humiliating or degrading treatment. If captured fighters are tried for crimes, the trials must satisfy certain basic fair trial guarantees.[181]

Human Rights Watch stated that, according to the Geneva Conventions' definition, al-Qa'eda members may perhaps not qualify as "prisoners of war" because they "neither wear identifying insignia nor abide by the laws of war," but Taliban soldiers could qualify: "captured fighters are considered prisoners of war (POWs), if they are members of an adversary state's armed forces, or are part of an identifiable militia group that abides by the laws of war."[182] This is extremely generous to the U.S., and a dangerous precedent. In this interpretation, the U.S. does not have to distinguish between suspected al-Qa'eda members and ordinary civilians, since neither groups wear "identifying insignia."

In refusing to distinguish between al-Qa'eda members, Taliban soldiers, and ordinary civilians, the U.S. expressed open contempt for the

Geneva Conventions and other internationally accepted standards of war. The Bush administration claimed it had the legal authority to ignore the Geneva Conventions. This was based on the U.S. Congress's near-unanimous decision on September 18, 2001, to authorize

> all necessary and appropriate force against those nations, organizations, or persons he [Bush] determines planned, authorized, committed, or aided the terrorist attacks that occurred on September 11, 2001, or harbored such organizations or persons, in order to prevent any future acts of international terrorism against the United States by such nations, organizations, or persons.

Arguing thus that the prisoners had no legal right to attorneys, and that the U.S. Constitution did not apply outside U.S. borders, the imprisonment of the "enemy combatants," even those who were U.S. citizens, evolved into indefinite detention. To justify this legal black hole, Defense Secretary Rumsfeld informed us that the detainees are "very tough, hard-core, well-trained terrorists."[183] A year later, Bush assured us that "the only thing I know for certain is that these are bad people."[184] Without any legal method of verification, we are left to take the Bush administration officials at their word and assume that all five hundred remaining prisoners in Guantánamo, as well as hundreds more around the world held in custody without trial are "terrorists."

U.S. JUSTICE: BLIND, BOUND, AND GAGGED

In 2003 the Bush administration finally agreed to begin trials of some "enemy combatants" it had captured. But civil rights advocates were not celebrating—Bush's idea of justice was a secret military tribunal where suspects could be convicted with a two-thirds majority (convictions in civilian courts must be unanimous) and defendants are not guaranteed the right to appeal the court's decision. The order for military tribunals was first signed into law only two months after 9/11 and included the possibility of conducting trials outside the U.S.

One former military prosecutor explained that from the perspective of the president, "the easy way to go is a military commission" because "you have unfettered discretion" and "the most significant aspects of judicial review are curtailed."[185]

Proponents of this ominous method, such as John Dean, a Nixon-era White House counsel, claimed that suspects would actually have *more* rights within secret military tribunals because the secrecy would protect intelligence sources from revenge attacks. Dean says, "President Bush's order makes clear that he wants due process and the right to counsel for terrorists." By using the word "terrorist," Dean revealed that he had already made up his mind about the guilt of the detainees. A similar attitude was openly expressed by top government officials, including Vice President Dick Cheney, who said, "They don't deserve the same guarantees and safeguards that would be used for an American citizen going through the normal judicial process."[186] Then–Attorney General John Ashcroft agreed: "Foreign terrorists who commit war crimes against the United States, in my judgment, are not entitled to and do not deserve the protections of the American Constitution."[187] Clearly, the suspects were "guilty unless proven innocent." In 2004 the Bush administration announced that six of the detainees would face military tribunals. Salim Ahmed Hamdan, a former detainee, is challenging the legality of the tribunals.[188]

Three years after U.S.-run Afghan prisons started to be filled with "enemy combatants," the U.S. finally began releasing significant numbers of men. In January 2005, about 81 men were released from prison bases in Afghanistan to "help a reconciliation drive with former Taliban regime members sought by both President Hamid Karzai and the American military."[189] Four months later, 85 more "suspected Taliban militants" were released from Bagram and a base in Kandahar. Since their incarceration at Guantánamo in 2002, about 180 prisoners have been released, and 76 transferred to prisons in other countries as part of the rendition program.[190]

Afghan authorities had been negotiating with the U.S. over Afghan prisoners, and Supreme Court Chief Justice Fazl Hadi Shinwari claimed that U.S. authorities had "pledged to free all their remaining Afghan prisoners."[191] According to Reuters, "U.S. forces in Afghanistan have been stepping up releases of prisoners who are not seen as security threats, in line with efforts to encourage reconciliation in the country." The release of men from Guantánamo and U.S.-run Afghan prisons begs the question of why hundreds of men were imprisoned, some for years, in the first place. If they were in fact suspects who were a danger to the U.S., or had information on future terrorist attacks, then why were they suddenly released in a goodwill gesture?

After their release, several men confirmed the horrific abuse they and others had faced during their time in U.S. custody. Abdul Rahman, an Afghan man among those released, admitted that he had been abused during his three years in the Guantánamo prison but wouldn't share details. "There was a lot of bad treatment against us, but this is not the time to tell you. . . . Everybody in the world knows what kind of jail it is. I can't talk about it now." Perhaps Rahman was complying with Chief Justice Shinwari, who warned, "Don't tell these people the stories of your time in prison because the government is trying to secure the release of others, and it may harm the [chances of winning the] release of your friends."[192] A Kuwaiti former detainee, Nasser Nijer Naser al-Mutairi, described abusive practices that were consistent with findings of the International Committee of the Red Cross (see below). He also revealed that, on occasion, prisoners courageously stood up to the prison guards by organizing camp-wide hunger strikes. During al-Mutairi's three-year imprisonment there were three major hunger strikes at Guantánamo.[193]

NORMALIZING TORTURE

The only outside organization that was given rights to visit the Guantánamo prisoners was the International Committee of the Red Cross (ICRC). Breaking with their usual silence on political matters, the ICRC publicly denounced the U.S.'s detention of the more than 600 prisoners, saying, "One cannot keep these detainees in this pattern, this situation, indefinitely. . . . The open-endedness of the situation and its impact on the mental health of the population has become a major problem."[194] According to the *New York Times*, "in 18 months, 21 detainees have made 32 suicide attempts" and there is a "high incidence of such events, as well as the number of detainees being treated for clinical depression."[195] While the ICRC did not criticize the physical conditions at the camp, one lawyer representing some of the detainees alleged that they were being subjected to torture.[196] British citizen Moazzam Begg wrote a letter during his imprisonment that apparently "got past U.S. authorities by mistake," in which he claimed that he was being tortured to gather intelligence:

> I was physically abused, and degradingly stripped by force, then paraded in front of several cameras toted by U.S. personnel. . . . [I was] denied natural light and fresh food for the duration. . . . I was subjected to pernicious threats of torture, actual vindictive torture and death threats—amongst other coercively employed interrogation techniques. . . . The said interviews were conducted in an environment of generated fear, resonant with terrifying screams of fellow detainees facing similar methods. In this atmosphere of severe antipathy towards detainees was the compounded use of racially and religiously prejudiced taunts. This culminated, in my opinion, with the deaths of two fellow detainees, at the hands of U.S. military personnel, to which I myself was partially witness.[197]

With the U.S. government refusing outside scrutiny, the two deaths that Begg refers to cannot be verified or investigated.

E-mail messages between FBI officials obtained by the American Civil Liberties Union (ACLU) confirmed Begg's assertion that serious methods of torture were being practiced in Guantánamo. The e-mails included a previously unpublicized report by an FBI agent "who witnessed 'numerous physical abuse incidents of Iraqi civilian detainees' at Guantánamo including choking, beatings and placing lighted cigarettes inside ears." One incident described a detainee who "had been left in a room at near 100 degrees Fahrenheit and had pulled out his hair during the night," while others were "shackled hand and foot in fetal positions for 18 to 24 hours, forcing them to soil themselves."[198] The report also described how "female interrogators forcibly squeeze[d] male prisoners' genitals."[199] U.S. Attorney General Alberto Gonzalez was publicly skeptical about the FBI report. But Gonzalez has also declared of the "war against terrorism" that it "renders obsolete Geneva's strict limitations on questioning of enemy prisoners."[200]

Former U.S. Army Muslim chaplain James Yee spent several months in Guantánamo administering to the prisoners. In his book, *For God and Country: Faith and Patriotism Under Fire,* Yee confirmed much of what Begg and other prisoners have related. Furthermore, he came to the conclusion that at Guantánamo, "U.S. soldiers would systematically use Islam as a weapon against prisoners,"[201] including the mishandling of the Koran and verbal taunts against Islam. Among the physical abuses he witnessed was a common practice called "IRFing" (IRF stands for Initial Response Force), carried out by six to eight guards against a single prisoner:

> A detainee had refused to go to recreation after a guard had performed what was known as the "credit card swipe." To search for contraband or weapons hidden in the prisoners' bodies, the guards felt under the detainees' genitals and pressed their fingers inside the buttock crack. This type of physical contact is not acceptable under Islamic law, and the detainee had pushed the guard away from him. . . . [I]mmediately eight guards were summoned . . . and put on riot protection gear. . . . After they suited up, they formed a huddle and chanted in unison, getting themselves pumped up. They rushed the block, one behind the other, where the offending detainee was. . . . The team leader in front drenched the prisoner with pepper spray and then opened the cell door. Others charged in and rushed the detainee with the shield as protection. The point was to get him to ground as quickly as possible, with whatever means necessary—shields, boots, or fists. . . . The guards then dragged the detainee from his cell and down the corridor. . . .

> The detainee who had been IRFed appeared literally crushed under the weight of the guards' anger and brute force. . . . [IRF-ing] was being used against prisoners in locked cells . . . with extraordinary frequency.[202]

Yee also documented alarming cases of depression and other psychological distress among prisoners. About twenty of the "most traumatized" detainees were housed separately in Camp Delta, as many of them had reverted to childlike behavior: "they would respond to me in a child-like voice talking complete nonsense. Many of them would loudly sing childish songs, repeating the song over and over. . . . They'd lie on the floor or on their beds, drawing pictures."[203] Such behavior is known as "regression" and can be a psychological response to trauma.

At Bagram Air Base and other Afghan bases where prisoners are detained before being transported to Guantánamo, additional allegations of humiliation and torture have surfaced. U.S. military police described "a policy that detainees were hooded, shackled and isolated for at least the first 24 hours, sometimes 72 hours of captivity."[204] Strikingly similar to the images of Iraq's Abu Ghraib prison, U.S. soldiers had photographed themselves "standing with their weapons pointed at the heads of handcuffed and hooded or blindfolded detainees . . . and, in one case, pressing a detainee's head against the wall of a 'cage' where he was brought for interrogation." Unlike the Abu Ghraib photos, these were not released to the public, in order to "protect the privacy" of the Afghan victims. Some soldiers apparently destroyed many photos after the Iraq scandal: "I realized there would be another public outrage if these photographs got out, so they were destroyed," said one soldier.[205]

The techniques of torture and humiliation used by U.S. soldiers sometimes had dire consequences. In December 2002 at Bagram, Afghanistan, two Afghan men named Dilawar and Habibullah died in U.S. custody and have been the subject of detailed reports in the *New York Times*. Even though autopsies and soldier testimonies pointed to homicides, initially the Army attributed their deaths to "natural causes" and recommended closing the cases without bringing any criminal charges. Recent army investigations reveal that the men died from being "chained to the ceiling, kicked and beaten by American soldiers in sustained assaults that caused their deaths." Interrogations were marked by the frequent use of a particularly debilitating strike above the prisoner's knees called the "common peroneal strike," designed to "tear up" the legs.[206]

U.S. soldiers shared testimonies that revealed unbelievable and inhuman cruelty, tinged with racist and bigoted language in the interrogation of Dilawar. One MP described what happened after Dilawar was struck on the knees while shackled:

> He screamed out, 'Allah! Allah! Allah!' and my first reaction was that he was crying out to his god. . . . Everybody heard him cry out and thought it was funny. . . . It became a kind of running joke, and people kept showing up to give this detainee a common peroneal strike just to hear him scream out 'Allah.' . . . It went on over a 24-hour period, and I would think that it was over 100 strikes.[207]

One U.S. soldier, Willie Brand, admitted to striking Dilawar thirty-seven times, which resulted in "destroying his leg muscle tissue with repeated unlawful knee strikes" over a period of five days, according to the *New York Times*. Dilawar's injuries from the attacks were so severe that one coroner testified that his legs "had basically been pulpified" and the Army report cited a medical examiner who confirmed that "even if he had survived, both legs would have had to be amputated."

The tragedy of Dilawar's death is compounded by the senseless manner of his capture. Dilawar, a shy man, drove his newly acquired used taxi cab past a base used by American troops. He was transporting three passengers to earn gas money for a trip to bring his sisters home for the Eid-al-Fitr holiday. Local commanders stopped his car and arrested all four men. While his passengers were sent to Guantánamo and imprisoned for a year, Dilawar died at Bagram, simply for being in the wrong place at the wrong time. A sergeant who remembers Dilawar testified that by the time he was taken into his final interrogations, "most of us were convinced that the detainee was innocent."[208]

Another man, Habibullah, died from a pulmonary embolism caused by blood clots in his legs resulting from the beatings. His autopsy showed "bruises or abrasions on his chest, arms and head. There were deep contusions on his calves, knees and thighs. His left calf was marked by what appeared to have been the sole of a boot." When Habibullah's body was found, a medic recalled "it looked like he had been dead for a while, and it looked like nobody cared."[209]

A total of eight deaths in U.S. custody, between mid-2002 and December 2004, are under investigation.[210] Notably, these deaths occurred nearly a year before the now-famous torture scandal of Abu Ghraib prison in Iraq. Brand was the only soldier, as of this writing, to be prosecuted for either the murder of Dilawar or Habibullah. However, the Army report states that four military interrogators assaulted Dilawar and one other Afghan with "kicks to the groin and leg, shoving or slamming him into walls/table, forcing the detainee to maintain painful, contorted body positions during interview and forcing water into his mouth until he could not breathe." According to the *New York Times*, in fall 2004, "Army investigators implicated 28 soldiers and reservists and recommended that they face criminal charges, including negligent homicide."[211] According to data released by the government in 2005, 65,000 men were taken prisoner in Afghanistan and Iraq. Of these, 108 died in U.S. custody, "most of them violently."[212]

In March 2005, the UN Human Rights investigator in Afghanistan, M. Cherif Bassiouni, filed a report that described the human rights situation for all of Afghanistan. In addition to violations of human rights by Afghan commanders, the report drew attention to "arbitrary arrest, illegal detentions and abuses committed by the United States-led Coalition forces." He noted allegations of

> forced entry into homes, arrest and detention of nationals and foreigners without legal authority or judicial review, sometimes for extended periods of time, forced nudity, hooding and sensory deprivation, sleep and food deprivation, forced squatting and standing for long periods of time in stress positions, sex-

> ual abuse, beatings, torture, and use of force resulting in death.[213]

In one graphic example,

> a district governor from Paktia province who was assisting the Coalition forces was arrested, gagged, hooded and taken to a base in Urgun, where he was beaten, forced to stand in a stress position for a prolonged period of time, exposed to the cold, and denied food and water. He also reported the torture and sexual abuse of up to 20 other persons. When his identity was confirmed five days later, he was released, although the fate of the other detainees remains unclear.[214]

Near the end of his report, the UN investigator boldly asserted, "the Coalition forces' practice of placing themselves above and beyond the reach of the law must come to an end." The day that the report was released, Bassiouni's position as a UN investigator was dissolved at the behest of the U.S.—he was notified via e-mail. Bassiouni believed he was fired because the U.S. wished to hide abuses in Afghan U.S.-run prisons, where a transfer of as many as two hundred detainees from Guantánamo was planned. The Egyptian-born international law expert had been nominated for the 1999 Nobel Peace Prize for playing a crucial role in establishing the International Criminal Court. He had also served as chairman of the UN war crimes tribunal for former Yugoslavia[215]—a project that had served U.S. interests at the time. A State Department spokesperson explained the reason for Bassiouni's dismissal: "We came to the conclusion that more than three years after the fall of the Taliban, the situation had evolved. . . . It was felt . . . that the special mechanism of the independent expert was no longer needed."[216] At a time when shocking allegations of torture and abuse at the hands of U.S. soldiers abound, an independent UN investigator would have been in the best interests of the Afghan people. But since there were no more crimes of the Taliban for Bassiouni to highlight, he was no longer useful to Washington.

Today torture is seen as an acceptable means of treating people from countries like Afghanistan and Iraq. The Bush administration's insistence on reclassifying captured prisoners to avoid the requirements of the Geneva Conventions helps normalize the widespread use of torture. One reservist at Bagram Air Base said he believed "they could deviate slightly from the rules," and that "there was the Geneva Conventions for enemy prisoners of war, but nothing for terrorists." The detainees were to be considered "terrorists" until proved otherwise. If any of the guards developed a rapport with the detainees at Bagram, one of the sergeants would "sit us down and remind us that these were evil people and talk about 9/11 and they weren't our friends and could not be trusted."[217] One U.S. military policeman told the *New York Times* that the labeling of prisoners in Afghanistan as "enemy combatants" not subject to the Geneva Conventions made it easier to abuse them. "We were pretty much told that they were nobodies, that they were just enemy combatants," he said. "I think that giving them the distinction of soldier would have changed our attitudes toward them. A lot of it was based on racism, really."[218]

THE NEW WARLORDS

When they first appeared in the mid-'90s, the Taliban were originally viewed by many Afghans (and by Washington) as a source of potential stability; perhaps most Afghans today see the United States that way. An ABC News–sponsored poll found that, indeed, the people are more concerned about the Taliban and other Afghan warlords than they are concerned about the U.S., probably because of the well-known record of many years of violations by the Afghan groups.[219] Lt. General David Barno, commander of U.S. forces in Afghanistan from November 2003 to June 2005, explained why he thought the Afghans tolerated, and in some cases welcomed, U.S. forces.

> [O]ne great advantage we had militarily and for our overall policy objectives in Afghanistan was that the people there were sick and tired of war. They had been involved in 25 years of continu-

> ous conflict. . . . After all that tremendous experience, the people of Afghanistan simply did not want to fight anymore and were looking for a positive outcome, some ray of hope out there in their future . . . which helped us have a very favorable operating environment throughout most of the country—not a secure environment, but an operating environment where the Afghan people broadly were very supportive of that international aid that was coming in there . . . even if they didn't accept all the politics there.
>
> And I think that's an important distinction—25 years of conflict. Unlike in some other parts of the world where continuous fighting is still novel, here it's not novel anymore and people don't want to continue doing it.[220]

Barno's mentioning of "some other parts of the world where continuous fighting is still novel" might be a reference to Iraq, where the U.S. government does not have as "favorable [an] operating environment," as it has in Afghanistan. In other words, the U.S. exploited the war-weariness of the Afghan people to its own ends.

In the next chapter, we will see how Washington renewed the strength of Afghan warlords and did nothing to stop their taking over much of the countryside. But, even though Afghans fear the warlords more for the time being, there is no question that the United States military has established *itself* as a power to be feared in Afghanistan. American troops do not necessarily represent a respite from warlordism, but warlordism of a different stripe. As we showed in this chapter, the U.S. methods are not too different from those of earlier hated regimes. The Afghanistan Justice Project agrees:

> [T]he U.S. has replicated some of the same practices that characterized the PDPA and Soviet regime it opposed in the 1980s, as well as some of the brutal tactics employed by the feuding commanders during the early 1990s.[221]

In many Afghan villages the U.S. either bribes or terrorizes the people into siding with them or turning over anti-U.S. fighters. The U.S.

threatens and cajoles villages to provoke attacks, deliberately earning the enmity of Afghans. The U.S. engages in arbitrary and indefinite detention, torture, and extrajudicial killings. Like the Taliban, the Americans may one day be seen as an evil to be expunged.

CHAPTER THREE

REPLACING ONE BRUTAL REGIME WITH ANOTHER

THE RETURN OF THE WARLORDS

He told us his name was Qasimi. It was a false name, designed to protect him from the wrath of local warlords whom he criticized every chance he got. Qasimi was taller than the average Afghan, with a shabby but dignified combination of traditional Afghan and Western clothing. Like the other men we met he wore a turban on his head. Trained as a specialist in agriculture, he had been chosen twice by the people of the remote Farah province to travel the long journey to Kabul and represent them in the two historic *Loya Jirga* assemblies. He told us that he planned to run for Parliament when the time came. Although he could speak some broken English, he chose to communicate in his native Dari on the dusty banks of a canal from the Farah River, surrounded by endless miles of parched, tan-colored earth. We stood transfixed, as a dozen men and two women who were accompanying us sat on their haunches, their eyes squinting in the merciless sun. Some of the men carried rifles. As Qasimi began relaying Afghanistan's tortured history, they interjected with cries of "wah, wah!" and applause.

> In these 25 years of war, especially from the time of the Russians, and their puppet government, we have had war in Afghanistan and everything was destroyed. . . . The U.S. empowered the fundamentalists and armed them to destroy Afghanistan even more.
>
> After the Russians left, the Western world, and especially America, forgot about Afghanistan. Our people were struck by so much tragedy during the time of the fundamentalists.

> As our people became fed-up of fundamentalists, America helped another group with the help of the CIA and the ISI of Pakistan. This group was called the Taliban—they came to Afghanistan and took power.
>
> Some government officials in America said that the Taliban brought peace and security to Afghanistan. But that was not true. The Taliban perpetrated so much vigorous cruelty on women that we cannot forget this in the whole history of our country. They made a hell on earth for the men and women of Afghanistan.
>
> Repeating the previous experiment that America, the West, and other countries had with the fundamentalist government, after the Taliban was destroyed, they again brought them [the fundamentalists] back—these were very criminal, very bad people. Still these criminal people are in power.[222]

It was a history we heard from many of the people we met during our visit to Afghanistan in February 2005. Despite differences in education, age, vocation, gender, and class, most Afghans can relate an analysis of U.S. policy in Afghanistan that is similar to what Qasimi told us. It is the explanation of their lived experiences. The stories of loss and trauma that we heard varied little from the bustling streets of Kabul to the quiet isolation of Farah province. Women and men, young and old, poor and middle class, Afghans spoke of loved ones disappeared, assassinated, maimed, or recruited into war. Most were tired of the fighting and weapons that saturated their country, and preferred almost anything, even a temporary foreign occupation, to continued war. Despite their fear of warlords, they spoke with anger of war crimes, indicting and condemning the criminals, spitting out the word "Jang-saalaran" with vehemence. It was a word we heard often—literally meaning "warlords" in Dari. "The warlords have their hands soaked in the blood of the Afghan people," was a common refrain.

A "BARGAIN": WARLORDS AS ALLIES

At the core of U.S. policy in Afghanistan has been the empowerment of regional commanders and armed militias with atrocious human rights records. In engaging their help, the U.S. ignored everything but their willingness to act in U.S. interests. Since at least the 1970s armed men and their private militias have wielded unaccountable power in Afghanistan. Backed by the U.S. and its allies in the 1970s and '80s, the "Mujahideen" or "jihadis" were used to eliminate the Soviet occupiers. As described in Chapter 1, the United States ended its support for jihadi factions, and its concern for their actions, once the Soviet puppet Najibullah was ousted in 1992. After four years of fighting at a cost of fifty thousand lives, different jihadi factions were still trying to wrest Kabul from each other to see who would control the fledgling fundamentalist Islamic state, when the Taliban kicked them out in 1996 and garnered control over almost 90 percent of the country. During their war with the Taliban in the mid-1990s, groups led by commanders Ahmed Shah Massoud, Ismail Khan, Abdul Rashid Dostum, and Karim Khalili united to form the Northern Alliance, also known as the United Front. Alliance leaders hailed from the major non-Pashtun ethnic groups (Tajiks, Uzbeks, and Hazaras), in contrast to the mostly Pashtun Taliban. The group's military leader Massoud and titular head Burhanuddin Rabbani, had received money and weapons from the U.S. during the anti-Soviet war. From about 1996 until 1999, the Alliance received support exclusively from nearby powers such as Russia, Iran, and India. But in February 1999, Massoud was approached in secret by the Clinton CIA for help in finding and capturing or killing Osama bin Laden. He received money and logistical support from Washington, as well as indirect battlefield aid in the form of sanctions on the Taliban. The CIA maintained ties with Massoud until September of 2001. As related in Chapter 2, Counterterrorism Coordinator Richard Clarke proposed aiding the Northern Alliance militarily to "keep al-Qa'eda on the frontlines" instead of planning new attacks on the U.S., but neither the Clinton nor George W. Bush Administrations were to act on Clarke's suggestions until after 9/11. Al-Qa'eda managers must have similarly perceived the coincidence between Northern Alliance and U.S. objectives.

On September 9, 2001, Massoud was assassinated by al-Qa'eda operatives, two days before the 9/11 attacks.

Immediately after the 9/11 attacks, the Bush administration instructed the CIA to step up its support of the Northern Alliance. At that point the Alliance was in a losing battle (they only controlled about 10 percent of the country) and Massoud's successor Mohammed Fahim knew that U.S. backing could reverse their fortunes. Over the course of the war to oust the Taliban the CIA would give about $70 million in cash and truckloads of weapons to commanders in Afghanistan. According to Bob Woodward, "the president considered it one of the biggest 'bargains' of all time."[223]

FINDING PLIABLE PASHTUNS

In the beginning, the Northern Alliance was "the only real [U.S.] ally" with organized forces "on the ground" in Afghanistan. For weeks after 9/11, the CIA attempted a "southern strategy" of finding Pashtun warlords from southern Afghanistan who would work with the U.S. against the Taliban. But, as of October 23, Michael Gordon of the *New York Times* reported, "There is no 'Southern Alliance' or coalition of Pashtun tribes in the south that is prepared to take on the Taliban." There were two reasons that Washington needed representation in the Pashtun ethnic group for their war to succeed. First, most of the Taliban were Pashtun, so any attempt to overthrow them needed support from their major constituency. Second, the Pashtuns were the largest ethnic group in Afghanistan and in general most Pashtuns would not accept rule solely by the Northern Alliance. The U.S. needed Pashtuns to replace the Taliban.[224]

This didn't include Pashtun commanders who might be suspicious of U.S. motives. One of the most famous anti-Taliban Pashtun commanders who refused U.S. support after 9/11 was Abdul Haq. Like other warlords, Haq had earlier distinguished himself on the battlefield during the anti-Soviet war. In the 1980s he had received limited funding from Washington while working under Yunus Khalis, who formed a moderate splinter faction of Gulbuddin Hekmatyar's hard-line *Hisb-e-Islami* party. But after 9/11, Haq "mystified" U.S. intelligence agents by refusing U.S. money to follow Washington's bidding in the anti-Taliban fight. "Haq was not a CIA asset who took direction" (Woodward). His first mistake was criticizing the U.S. bombing, saying it "had only served to unite Afghans around the Taliban." Then he decided on October 21 to go in secret and with only nineteen soldiers into Afghanistan (he was based in Pakistan), to stir up anti-Taliban sentiment among Pashtuns. Haq's plan was leaked to the Taliban and they captured and killed him. It is not clear who leaked the information, but both the Pakistani ISI and the CIA were aware of the mission. Both had reasons not to want Haq to succeed—the ISI because of their connection to the Taliban; the CIA because Haq would not follow their program. The CIA refused to support Haq's plan, calling it "inadvisable," probably because it interfered with U.S. attempts to do the same thing. A CIA agent told the *New York Times* that in such cases either the U.S. calls the shots or the action goes unaided. "If it was our operation, we could say when it's time to go on stage, but it wasn't. He went on his own initiative."[225]

Abdul Haq was not treated well by the U.S. because it was feared that he might spoil their plans to impose a more pro-U.S. Pashtun leader on the Afghan people, namely Hamid Karzai. Coincidentally, Karzai was entering Afghanistan around the same time as Haq to organize opposition to the Taliban. A "minor Pashtun tribal leader," by the CIA's own reckoning, Karzai was living in Quetta, Pakistan. In mid-October, the U.S. Army flew him by helicopter to his home village of Tarin Kowt for the first time in over two years. He was "accompanied by American Green Berets" from the Army's 5th Special Forces Group "at all times." Two weeks later, "when it became clear that Taliban forces were closing in on his position," Karzai was flown to safety in Pakistan by another U.S. helicopter. Donald Rumsfeld remarked casually that Karzai was taken out of Afghanistan for "consultations." In reality, a "senior American military officer" explained, "If we had done nothing, he would have died," just like Abdul Haq. But the U.S. would not let that happen to Karzai who, of course, went on to become the U.S.-backed president in post-Taliban Afghanistan.[226]

Another anti-Taliban Pashtun development given little attention in the U.S. was the Peshawar Assembly held in the Pakistani border town on October 25–26, 2001. According to Pakistani reports, the meeting garnered over 1500 participants, but the *New York Times* counted only 700 delegates. The meeting was hosted by Pir Syed Ahmad Gailani, the head of a moderate Sufi sect and a former Mujahideen leader. Despite the fact that he was the most inclined toward secular rule of all the Peshawar-based Mujahideen leaders, Gailani received almost no funding from the United States during the anti-Soviet war. Gailani's proposal for a post-Taliban government included "[a] leadership council, with the [former] king as chairman . . . using 'capable technocrats' as functionaries. . . . [A] United Nations security force from Muslim countries would maintain law and order until a national army and police force could take over." Like Haq, the assembly made the mistake of calling for "an early end to American bombing" and criticized Washington's favoring of the Northern Alliance.[227]

Times reporter John F. Burns gave the meeting a negative spin, complaining that, "Little in the resolution appeared to advance by much the process of agreeing on the mechanics of a post-Taliban government," whereas "the Bush administration and its allies have been working to fashion a replacement government." How this took precedence over an Afghan-led effort was not explained. Burns made it seem as if the mostly-Pashtun Peshawar Assembly was illegitimate. The U.S. initiative, in contrast, would include "the country's many ethnic and political groups." Secretary of State Colin Powell pointed to the Peshawar Assembly as an example of Pakistan trying to manipulate Afghanistan again. "[W]e are not sure that Pakistan was the best place to have the overall meeting. . . . [T]he next government of Afghanistan cannot be dictated into existence by Pakistan." Instead, he advocated an "internationally blessed process," international relations code for a U.S.-blessed process. Powell did not mention that it was not Pakistan but the U.S. that was bombing the country and funding warlords, in effect "dictating into existence" a new government.[228]

The Pashtun most likely to unite Afghans against the Taliban was the former king, Zahir Shah. After 9/11, the United States encouraged Shah to work with the Northern Alliance to come up with an interim government to replace the Taliban. In exile in Rome, the eighty-seven-year-old Shah had been calling for a *Loya Jirga* (grand assembly) of Mujahideen and other exiles to solve Afghanistan's problems ever since the Soviet occupation. These calls had been rejected by warlords like Hekmatyar and Rabbani, primarily because as king he had always been antagonistic toward fundamentalists and "because they fought the Soviets and Communists to create an Islamic state," which would not be the case if Shah had been in the government. Besides, they did not want to share power with someone who was more popular than they were. Despite this enmity, on October 1, the former king and the Northern Alliance formed the "Supreme Council for the National Unity of Afghanistan," a less than amiable partnership. Rabbani and company gave "very lukewarm support" to the former king. "There is no question of a return to the monarchy," said Rabbani's foreign minister Abdullah Abdullah. "We would not agree to [him becoming head of state]. . . . We do not regard Zahir Shah as a savior." The Supreme Council did not last long. By October 15 the Northern Alliance had still not submitted their delegation list to Zahir Shah. Washington too was less than thrilled about the prospects of Zahir Shah as future leader of Afghanistan. In general, according to the Canadian magazine *Maclean's*, the Bush administration also gave a "lukewarm response" to "attempts to focus national reconciliation around" the ex-king. Like Abdul Haq, Shah had expressed reticence about the prospects of a U.S. invasion of the country; prior to the bombing he told a Congressional delegation that "he would prefer United Nations-led military support."

But, unlike Haq, the United States needed Zahir Shah to legitimize their plan to overthrow the Taliban, especially among the Pashtun population. So his initiatives were tolerated, even outwardly praised, so long as they served U.S. purposes. Colin Powell explained to a House of Representatives International Relations Committee, "The king will play an important role, not that I would expect him to become the chief executive of the next regime, but he brings a certain authority to the process and he will be able to rally all of the elements together." After the former king had helped rally Afghans behind the U.S., he and his supporters were cut out of anything but a figurehead role in the new Afghan government[229] (see Chapter 4).

AT THE GATES OF KABUL . . . AGAIN

By the first week of November 2001, the Northern Alliance, with U.S. help, was capturing more and more territory from the Taliban, until it became clear that they would reach the capital Kabul by the middle of the month. At a November 9, 2001, press conference with Pakistani president Pervez Musharraf, U.S. President George W. Bush said that the Northern Alliance would not be allowed to enter the city of Kabul: "We will encourage our friends to head south, across the Shamali Plains, but not into the city of Kabul, itself." Musharraf was against the Alliance entering the city, for purely political reasons—they were supported by India and Russia and might not be friendly to Pakistan. But the reasons he gave publicly were humanitarian and certainly touched on the well-justified fears of many Kabul residents.

> Kabul should not be occupied by the Northern Alliance . . . because of the past experience that we've had . . . after the Soviets left. There was [*sic*] total atrocities, killings, and mayhem within the city. And I think if the Northern Alliance . . . enters Kabul, we'll see the same kind of atrocities being perpetuated . . .

When asked if he agreed with this reasoning, Bush refused to answer: "I said one question."[230]

Since mid-October the U.S. had had to curb bombing around Kabul to ensure that the Northern Alliance did not have an easy road to the city, intentionally leaving it in the hands of the Taliban a little longer. There were two reasons for this. First, its ally Pakistan had "threatened to close its airspace to American aircraft and cancel support if the bombing allows the Northern Alliance to overrun Kabul." Second, "[T]he alliance could do Washington more harm than good if it rushed into the Afghan capital, since many Pashtuns might then rally around the only other force in the country that resists them, the Taliban." Most Pashtuns remembered the 1992 "government" by Rabbani et al., under which so many were killed.[231]

Unexpectedly, a string of Northern Alliance battle victories over the course of four days (November 9–13), fueled by Pashtun defections from the Taliban, gave the Alliance control of the northern half of the country, right up to the gates of Kabul. "A shift among Pashtun commanders previously aligned with the Taliban, which U.S. military officials expected would take much longer, happened suddenly, and fed an inexorable momentum for the Northern Alliance." Kabul was taken on November 13, against the wishes of the Alliance's backers, who wanted the new government in Kabul to be perceived as "broad-based" by the Pashtuns they brought on board. By November 15, U.S.-backed forces controlled nearly all of the country except the Taliban stronghold of Kandahar. On December 7, Kandahar also fell, "effectively leaving the Northern Alliance, its Pashtun allies and the U.S. in charge of the country. . . . Regime change had been accomplished 102 days after [9/11]."[232]

The Alliance's second entry into the Afghan capital after a five-year absence signaled their ambition to regain power. A close aide of Zahir Shah, Abdul Sattar Sirat, complained, "It is against the agreement they made with us. We did not expect that they would enter Kabul. We wanted Kabul to be demilitarized and that the . . . government . . . should come [about via] a political process." The takeover of Kabul before a government could be put together was also contrary to an agreement the Alliance had made with the U.S. and its Western allies. British Prime Minister Tony Blair was reportedly "embarrassed by the quick surrender . . . 24 hours after he predicted that [the Northern Alliance] wouldn't" take the capital. Still, Blair "expressed confidence" that the "the Alliance would honor the pledges they had made in return for . . . military support . . . [stating that] 'The basis on which that support was given was very clear.'"[233]

George W. Bush was forced to do damage control for the Alliance. Privately, he told his National Security Council, "We need to manage the publicity here. We need to emphasize the cowardly atrocities that the Taliban performed as they left the city." When Bush was asked at a press conference about reports of "violent reprisals" and execution of prisoners by Northern Alliance soldiers, he said,

> I have seen reports, which you refer to, and I also saw a report that said, on their way out of town, the Taliban was wreaking

> havoc on the citizenry of Kabul. And if that be the case . . . I wouldn't be the least bit surprised. After all, the Taliban *has been wreaking havoc on the entire country for over a decade* [emphasis added]. . . . I also saw reports . . . that in some of the northern cities, there was . . . a wonderful, joyous occasion as the citizens were free, free from repression, free from a dictatorial government. . . . [W]e will continue to work . . . with the Northern Alliance commanders to make sure they respect the human rights of the people that they are liberating.[234]

There are many factual errors in Bush's statement, but one in particular exposes the lie behind it. The Taliban only appeared in Afghanistan in 1994 and could not have been "wreaking havoc . . . for over a decade." Bush cleverly (or perhaps unwittingly) omitted the fact that the fundamentalist warlords who *were* wreaking havoc on the country included many of the men currently leading the Northern Alliance. He was certainly aware of the Alliance's record, having just heard president Musharraf of Pakistan recount it a few days earlier. In his attempt to use Taliban crimes to divert attention from the Northern Alliance, Bush was actually referring to Northern Alliance crimes.

In secret, the Bush administration was worried that the Alliance might form its own government in Kabul and throw into disarray their plans to build a U.S.-friendly government that wouldn't fall apart in a few days. A senior Bush administration official told the *New York Times*, "[I]t should be very clear to the Northern Alliance that you cannot have a declared government. We need the United Nations in, and we cannot have a vacuum of power." The administration wanted to "prevent a return to power of the same kind of government structure that was ousted by the Taliban in 1996," which would surely pave the way for a Taliban comeback. Unmentioned was the fact that that unwanted government structure came to power with the support of the U.S. taxpayer in the 1980s and early 1990s. It should be made clear that Bush and company had no problem with the Alliance as leaders *per se*, but it was important for both public relations and strategic reasons to have a government that appeared to be representative of the people of

Afghanistan. If the government was seen to be Northern Alliance–dominated, then the Pashtuns who had rallied behind the ex-king and Hamid Karzai might defect to the Taliban.[235]

"The fact is that Kabul fell much more quickly than any of us expected," a senior administration official told the *New York Times*. One theory for the quick turnaround, put forward by British military historian Sir John Keegan, was that the Alliance victories were "not due to superior weapons" as much as "a collapse of Taliban morale." Given the rapid series of Taliban commanders that defected to the Northern Alliance side, it is certainly plausible that the defectors saw massive U.S. support for the Alliance, plus the withdrawal of Pakistani support for the Taliban, and decided that they were on the losing side. If true, one has to ask whether the *current* hold that the Northern Alliance and other fundamentalist warlords have on the countryside is as inevitable as some people say.

The swift rout of the Taliban "perplexed, and in some ways even worried" U.S. planners who had expected a straightforward air war against a distinct army. The defeat of the Taliban meant the U.S. public would expect a ramp-down in the "war on terror," and a ramp-up of "nation building," and it would be more difficult to sell continued military activity in the country. On the contrary, military officials "sa[id] their mission . . . is still far from finished." President Bush's national security adviser Condoleezza Rice noted that "nobody is declaring any victory. . . . Loosening the grip of the Taliban was a means to an end, not an end in itself." Bush himself "had shown no signs of celebrating the Taliban's defeat, and had focused instead on the changing strategy." Even today, the U.S. military maintains a war footing in Afghanistan, engaging in an open-ended and nebulous "hunt for terrorists" in the countryside.

With memories of the crimes of warlords still fresh, Afghan civilians braced themselves after the fall of the Taliban for a resumption of the violence that marked the years 1992–96. In the north, revenge attacks by U.S.-backed warlords on the Pashtun population were commonplace, even though not all Pashtuns supported the Taliban. Thousands fled northern Afghanistan "telling tales of murder and rape and robbery."

One Kabul resident "did not feel safe at night as armed men allied to one or other of the many military commanders who fought against the Taliban are wont to take over the streets after dark."[236] In the months following the U.S. bombing, Northern Alliance forces carried out shocking violence and mass murder.[237] According to *Time*, "with warlords back in charge, some Afghans already miss the Taliban."[238]

Women's rights activists in RAWA made an "appeal to the United Nations and World Community" asking the UN to intervene to protect them from Northern Alliance commanders:

> The retreat of the terrorist Taliban from Kabul is a positive development, but [the] entering of the rapist and looter NA [Northern Alliance] in the city is nothing but a dreadful [*sic*] and shocking news for about 2 million residents of Kabul whose wounds of the years 1992–96 have not healed yet. . . . We would like to emphatically ask the UN to send its effective peace-keeping force into the country before the Northern Alliance can repeat the unforgettable crimes they committed in the said years.[239]

Three years later, in a comprehensive survey carried out by the government-funded Afghanistan Independent Human Rights Commission, 18 percent of respondents considered themselves the victims of Mujahideen crimes, compared to 11 percent, who saw themselves as victims of Taliban crimes.[240]

No sooner had the dust cleared in Kabul than the Alliance "began settling in as Afghanistan's de facto government" and "moved back into ministries they were forced to vacate in 1996." As the prospects of a political vacuum loomed large, Vice President Dick Cheney promised that ". . . the United States and our other coalition partners . . . will work with the United Nations and other international organizations to try to establish a secure, stable representative government. . . . Our interest is not in telling the Afghan people how they should govern themselves; those are decisions they'll have to make themselves." But in December 2002, only two weeks after Cheney's comments, at the behest of Washington, a group of handpicked Afghans met at a conference under United Nations auspices in Bonn, Germany, to decide who among them would wield power in the new Afghan government.[241]

Notably, almost all of the delegates at the Bonn Conference were stakeholders in Afghanistan who at one point or another had held positions of power. All of the delegates were either exiles or leaders of armed factions in Afghanistan. The Northern Alliance sent eleven delegates: the "Cypress Group" was a group of Afghan exiles with ties to Iran; the "Rome Group" was a group of Afghan exiles with ties to the former king, who was living in Rome at the time; and the "Peshawar Group" was a group of mostly Pashtun exiles based in Pakistan. Many of the politicians who attended the Peshawar assembly, such as Pir Gailani, the warlord Gul Agha Sherzai, and the ultrafundamentalist cleric Fazl Hadi Shinwari, were brought on board to form the new government, although only the fundamentalists, not moderates like Gailani, were given positions of power.[242]

Flown into Bonn in a British Royal Air Force jet,[243] the Northern Alliance dominated the gathering, and sought interim government positions as rewards for their role in toppling the Taliban. When the Northern Alliance didn't initially get what they wanted, they complained, demanding that their role in defeating the Taliban justified a political price. One warlord, Ismail Khan, sourly remarked that people outside the Northern Alliance "have just negotiated positions for themselves and have been unfair to others. . . . In allocating the key positions . . . the important role of those who have fought, have not [*sic*] been taken into account."[244] Ultimately, Khan and his colleagues were satisfied when government positions were dealt out to the various dominant parties, with over half of the positions going to Northern Alliance warlords.

ENFORCING INSECURITY

In backing the Northern Alliance militarily and supporting their role at Bonn, Washington once more unleashed brutal commanders and warlords not just on the Taliban, but on the Afghan people. Sarah Chayes of National Public Radio explained:

> Because they had reaped weapons and cash in the bargain [from the U.S.], the warlords were able to impose themselves as provincial governors, despite being reviled by the Afghan people, as every conversation I've had and every study I've done demonstrates.[245]

The U.S. ensured that its warlord partners were spared the glare of international oversight by working to restrict international peacekeepers to Kabul for more than two years after the fall of the Taliban. This had the effect of entrenching warlords in rural Afghanistan, where the overwhelming majority of Afghans reside. The *New York Times* wrote,

> As warlords have carved out chunks of Afghanistan after the fall of the Taliban, the lawlessness that gave rise to the strict Islamic movement in the mid-1990's has begun to spread, once again, across this country. The United States-led military campaign . . . has returned to power nearly all of the same warlords who had misruled the country in the days before the Taliban.[246]

As demonstrated over the years, the safety of the Afghan people has rarely been a serious concern in Washington.

As a result of the Bonn Conference, the United Nations established the International Security Assistance Force (ISAF) in December 2001 to "assist the newly established Afghan Transitional Authority create a secure environment in and around Kabul and support the reconstruction of Afghanistan."[247] At first, "the Northern Alliance and the Bush administration balked" at the idea of peacekeepers: the Alliance because they wanted to be the only armed force in the country; the U.S. because Washington hated working with international troops it could not control.[248] Yunus Qanooni, the Northern Alliance representative at Bonn, said, "We prefer that security is looked after by Afghan forces themselves . . . there is [already] complete security in Kabul."[249] In the end it was decided that the ISAF would consist of about 5000 troops from nineteen countries led by Britain, and would report to U.S. General Tommy Franks. But their mandate would be limited: the troops would be confined to Kabul, already the most secure part of the country. While ISAF forces would be restricted to the capital, U.S. forces would engage in a hunt for al-Qa'eda and bin Laden in the provinces. The ISAF was "noteworthy for what it will not do," that is, keep the peace outside of the capital, "where many Afghans live in a lawless no-man's-land largely cut off from international aid."[250] Compared with other postconflict environments, the international troop contingent in Afghanistan is pathetically small. For example, Bosnia, which is 13 percent of Afghanistan by population (and 8 percent of Afghanistan by area), has 18,000 NATO peacekeepers. To achieve the same ratio of forces to population as in Bosnia, Afghanistan would require about 134,000 troops.[251]

It was the opinion of many Afghans, aid workers, U.S. advocacy groups like the Feminist Majority, UN Special Representative Lakhdar Brahimi, and even Hamid Karzai himself, that the ISAF should have been expanded throughout Afghanistan. William J. Durch, codirector of the Project on the Future of Peace Operations, argued that Afghanistan needed a minimum of 18,500 international peacekeepers deployed throughout the country. At his last news conference before retiring, Francesc Vendrell, the second-in-command for the United Nations office in Afghanistan, asserted that the ISAF contingent should consist of "perhaps as many as 35,000 soldiers" and be spread throughout the country. Vendrell "concluded that a much larger foreign troop presence could be the crucial factor in creating stability and curbing the lawlessness." Such a move early on might have undermined the power of local and regional warlords before they fully entered the military vacuum left by the Taliban, but this didn't happen.[252]

The U.S. response to the idea of ISAF expansion was that American troops were not available for peacekeeping and since no other country had offered the troops or the money to do it, it was not worth considering. Defense Secretary Donald Rumsfeld remarked, "If it's appropriate to put in more forces for war-fighting tasks, the United States will do that [but] there are plenty of countries on the face of the earth who can supply peacekeepers."[253] When asked if he thought international troops should be used to bring peace and security to Afghanistan outside of

Kabul, Rumsfeld said, "There's one school of thought that thinks that's a desirable thing to do. Another school of thought, which is where my brain is, is that why put all the time and money and effort in that?"[254] To White House press secretary Ari Fleischer, U.S. troops were already bringing security. "The security of Afghanistan will best be obtained as a result of the United States having eliminated the al-Qa'eda and the Taliban and their ability to create insecurity." Besides the fact that U.S. military operations were probably never going to eliminate al-Qa'eda or the Taliban, Fleischer's point ignores the major ongoing cause of instability in the country, the U.S.-backed warlords.[255]

One thing is certain: having warlord armies as the only non-U.S. forces in the bulk of Afghanistan ensures little international accountability for U.S. troop operations in the countryside. ISAF expansion would have interfered with the U.S. hunt for al-Qa'eda and bin Laden. According to *Al Ahram Weekly* columnist Fahmi Howeidi, the "primary function of [ISAF] is to divert attention away from the military operations being conducted by U.S. forces in the Afghan countryside. In fact, as much as the hands of the international force are tied in Kabul, the Americans have a free hand elsewhere." The absence of peacekeeping troops, deliberately maintained by the Bush administration, ensured that the United States, rather than an international body, had control over most of Afghanistan.[256]

The official U.S. policy on Afghanistan's security, according to Rumsfeld, was "helping [Afghans] develop a national army so that they can look out for themselves over time." Since developing a national army and police force in a country flush with weapons and decimated by war is a time- and money-consuming effort, Rumsfeld privately "wondered why they couldn't just let the Afghan warlords create an army." In some areas of the country, this is indeed what has happened. While the national army is still in its infancy, local and regional warlords, many of whose private militias are well funded by drug revenues, easily filled the military vacuum left by the Taliban.[257]

Rumsfeld denied that security was even a problem, saying, "We keep reading today that the situation in Afghanistan is difficult and that the security situation is supposedly deteriorating. Most of the comments,

I suspect, are coming from people who are well-intentioned but may not be current with what's taking place on the ground, or may be looking at one particular portion of the country." The people he is referring to, those "not current" with the situation on the ground, include hundreds of Afghans and international aid workers interviewed by the Center for Economic and Social Rights a few months earlier. According to CESR's report, "People generally felt that the only hope for a sustainable peace was international intervention aimed at disarming warlords and maintaining security. Without exception, the interviewees favored extending international peacekeeping force beyond Kabul." In a public opinion survey of Afghans conducted by the Asia Foundation in 2004, Afghans cited security as the "greatest national concern" over all other factors. In our own discussions with Noorani, the editor of the independent weekly newspaper *Rozgaran* in Kabul, he said that ISAF expansion would be "very good for our people. . . . ISAF forces are welcomed by people more than U.S. troops because people think the U.S. has biased policies in Afghanistan—also the security would be better."[258]

On May 6, 2003, 300 Afghans held the first anti-U.S. demonstration in Kabul; lack of security was one of the main topics. The protesters "included government employees and university students" who "complained of growing insecurity, slow post-war reconstruction and delay in payment of state salaries by Hamid Karzai's U.S.-backed government," according to Reuters. One student chanted, "We don't want the Brits and the Americans! . . . We want security. They have failed to bring it to us and we want them out!" The protest was organized by the "prominent Afghan philosopher" Sediq Afghan, well known for his vocal denunciations of illegitimate governments in Kabul. The U.S. was not in good company: Sediq had in the past organized demonstrations against "the communist regime of the 1980s, the Mujahideen governments that replaced it, and also the Taliban."[259]

Interestingly, Rumsfeld's assertions about the security of Afghanistan could easily be refuted by the Bush administration's own State Department. On the one hand, a State Department fact sheet on Afghanistan released in 2003 painted a rosy picture of Afghanistan: "The country's security . . . is steadier than it has been in decades, thanks in particular to U.S. and coalition troops and increasingly, the presence of U.S.-led Provincial Reconstruction Teams in the countryside. . . . Afghans can look forward to a more prosperous and secure future." On the other hand, in a less conspicuous location of the department's Web site, Afghanistan has been the subject of an ongoing travel warning for U.S. citizens. The latest bulletin (updated January 2006) warns:

> The ability of Afghan authorities to maintain order and ensure the security of citizens and visitors is limited. Remnants of the former Taliban regime and the terrorist al-Qa'eda network, and other groups hostile to the government, remain active. U.S.-led military operations continue. Travel in all areas of Afghanistan, including the capital Kabul, is unsafe due to military operations, landmines, banditry, armed rivalry among political and tribal groups, and the possibility of terrorist attacks, including attacks using vehicular or other Improvised Explosive Devices (IEDs), and kidnapping. The security environment remains volatile and unpredictable.[260]

The Human Rights Watch World Report of 2003 contains an astute summary of the politics of security in Afghanistan and the U.S. responsibility. After 9/11, the report reads, "the United States, United Kingdom, and other coalition partners supplied warlords with cash, weapons, uniforms, and satellite telephones. . . . [In doing so,] the U.S., Iran, and Pakistan all actively supported local warlords in various regions of the country. . . . Local warlords with records of human rights abuses . . . all strengthened their grip on local power outside of Kabul." After the Taliban fell, "The official policy of these countries . . . was to work with President Hamid Karzai to help him strengthen his government and rebuild the country." But this official policy and the support of warlords were "contradictory, and worked to destabilize the country." "Few meaningful steps were taken by the United States, Iran, or Pakistan to counteract or blunt the effects of" supporting warlords. To "most nations" the security problems in Afghanistan would be solved by "police training and the rebuilding of the Afghan Army . . . despite the fact that these programs were poorly administered, did not have much effect beyond Kabul, and were considered to have little effect in the short- or medium-term." Finally, "International actors in Afghanistan resisted widespread calls to expand the ISAF peacekeeping force beyond Kabul. Instead, security outside Kabul was put in the hands of the local military forces that the U.S.-led coalition supported during the war against the Taliban." In the remainder of this chapter we relate some of the consequences of leaving "security" to the warlords.[261]

WAR CRIMES: MASS MURDER, REPRESSION, FIEFDOMS, AND FACTIONAL FIGHTING

> "Death by Container" has been a cheap means of mass murder used by both the Taliban and the Northern Alliance for at least five years.[262]
>
> —NEWSWEEK SPECIAL REPORT

Given the record of the Northern Alliance, Washington's support for them in 2001 meant the U.S. would be complicit once again in the mass murder of prisoners and civilians. It is notable that during the war against the Taliban, a condition for U.S. military support was that the Northern Alliance would accept a U.S.-imposed regime in Kabul. For the most part, the Alliance did allow this to happen. After the Bonn meeting, however, it appears that few further restrictions were imposed on the Northern Alliance or other warlords, and they were allowed free rein throughout the countryside.

War crimes by U.S.-backed commanders are neither new nor a secret to the U.S. government. One of the most horrible atrocities was the mass execution and disposal of prisoners. At a 1990 Congressional Subcommittee hearing on U.S. policy, Afghanistan expert Barnett R. Rubin spoke about the U.S.-backed anti-Soviet Mujahideen fighters:

> [O]ne commander ordered the summary execution of 650 government officials as "Communists" . . . there were also many rapes in Kunduz, for which the fighters were merely

> "reprimanded." . . . Another case . . . was the killing and mutilation of the garrison at Torkham [by the U.S. funded group Hisb-e-Islami, headed by Gulbuddin Hekmatyar]. Seventy-four of them were killed and their bodies dumped in tea crates inside Afghanistan.[263]

It was not just Hekmatyar who treated his prisoners atrociously. Seven years later, after the Taliban takeover, a brutal massacre by a Northern Alliance Commander was documented by Human Rights Watch:

> Some 3,000 captured Taliban soldiers were summarily executed in and around Mazar-e Sharif by Junbish forces under the command of Gen. Abdul Malik Pahlawan. The killings followed Malik's withdrawal from a brief alliance with the Taliban and the capture of the Taliban forces that were trapped in the city. Some of the Taliban troops were taken to the desert and shot, while others were thrown down wells and then blown up with grenades.[264]

The same thing happened in post-Taliban Afghanistan under U.S./Northern Alliance control. In January 2002 the Boston-based Physicians for Human Rights sent investigators to the Sheberghan prison camp in Kunduz and found 3000 starving and sick Taliban prisoners crammed into a space meant for 800—a clear violation of the Geneva Conventions on the treatment of prisoners.[265] But these 3,000 prisoners were considered the lucky ones. A recent documentary by Scottish journalist Jamie Doran and Afghan journalist Najibullah Quraishi entitled *Afghan Massacre: Convoy of Death* detailed the horrific murder of thousands of Taliban captives on their way to a prison at Sheberghan. The murders were carried out in late 2001 and early 2002 by troops loyal to the Northern Alliance commander and U.S. ally Abdul Rashid Dostum. As Doran and Quraishi discovered in the making of their documentary, thousands of Taliban prisoners had died of asphyxiation and gunfire on their way to the prison.

Screened by the European Parliament and on television stations around the world—with the exception of the U.S.—*Afghan Massacre* shows how Dostum and his forces were directly responsible for a mass murder of Taliban prisoners. The documentary eventually premiered nationwide in the United States on Pacifica Radio's *Democracy Now!* in May 2003, but neither commercial television networks nor PBS chose to air it.

Newsweek conducted extensive interviews with survivors, truck drivers, and local villagers and found that many of the prisoners who were crammed into containers transported by trucks, "licked and chewed each other's skin to stay alive."[266] *Newsweek* claims that their investigation did not reveal any U.S. complicity in the mass killings. They do admit, however, that "American forces were working intimately with 'allies' who committed what could well qualify as war crimes."[267] Furthermore, witness depositions given to Doran and Quraishi suggest that U.S. Special Forces redirected the containers carrying the living and dead into the desert and stood by as survivors were shot and buried.[268]

In the 2002 Emergency *Loya Jirga*, Dostum was rewarded with the post of deputy defense minister in Afghanistan's interim government, under the watch of U.S. Special Envoy Zalmay Khalilzad. As of this writing, he is the National Army chief of staff in the central government, appointed by President Karzai.

After the fall of the Taliban, Northern Alliance warlords obtained more power than the central government. Ismail Khan, known as the "Emir of Herat," controlled one of the largest private armies in the country, which was estimated in 2002 to be 30,000 strong.[269] This was twice the size of the Afghan National Army at that time.

Commander Abdul Rashid Dostum controlled the central northern provinces while General Mohammed Daud controlled the northeast. Commander Gul Agha Sherzai resumed his rule over the southern provinces, including Kandahar, for two years before being replaced by Yusuf Pashtun in 2003 in exchange for a post in the central government. However, Sherzai still remains in Kandahar as of this writing.[270] Meanwhile, the Karzai administration directly controls only a small region around Kabul, mainly with the help of 6,500 NATO (ISAF) troops.

One of the main functions of the warlords seems to be to keep the population in line and quell independent political organizing. According to Human Rights Watch, under Ismail Khan in Herat, "people are afraid to challenge the government, or even to engage in activity that might lead to harassment. Women avoid meeting with men in public, non-political civic groups have stopped gathering, and university students refrain from discussing political issues. There are no independent newspapers or local radio programs."[271]

Ismail Khan, described by Defense Secretary Donald Rumsfeld as an "appealing" and "thoughtful" person,[272] was criticized by Human Rights Watch for personally ordering many politically motivated arrests and beatings, particularly targeting Pashtuns. Khan enforced a "policy to create terror in the population in order to ensure their obedience and acquiescence." Torture inflicted upon detainees "range[d] from beatings—physical assaults with thorny branches, wood sticks, cables, rifle butts, and kicking, slapping, and punching—to more elaborate and severe torture techniques, such as hanging upside-down, whipping, and shocking with electrical wires attached to the toes and thumbs."[273]

A report released in July 2003 by Human Rights Watch (HRW) entitled "Killing You is a Very Easy Thing for Us" summarized the warlords' violence, describing a pattern of widespread abuse since 2002, including:

> . . . bus and taxi drivers . . . being hijacked or beaten for not paying bribes to soldiers and police; people . . . being arbitrarily arrested . . . accused of bogus crimes or "being a member of the Taliban," . . . arbitrary arrests of and death threats against journalists . . . detentions and intimidation of political opponents by government forces . . . impeding the delivery of humanitarian aid and keeping some refugees and internally displaced persons from returning to their homes.[274]

These crimes were not randomly committed by individuals taking advantage of wartime chaos. HRW went further in identifying those government officials and warlords responsible, as well as those who supported them:

> Serious human rights violations . . . are taking place throughout Afghanistan . . . in the southern province of Kandahar by troops under governor Gul Agha Sherzai; abuses in northern provinces around Mazar-e Sharif by troops under Atta Mohammad and Rashid Dostum; and continuing crackdowns on basic human rights by the governor of Herat, Ismail Khan . . . [T]he abuses described were ordered, committed, or condoned by government personnel in Afghanistan—soldiers, police, military and intelligence officials, and government ministers. *Worse, these violations have been carried out by people who would not have come to power without the intervention and support of the international community* [emphasis added].[275]

Political repression and human rights violations within the provinces are matched by factional fighting on the borders of warlord territories reminiscent of the years 1992–96. In the spring of 2002, about thirty people were killed in southeastern Afghanistan when 500 rockets were fired during a fight between warlords Padsha (Bacha) Khan and Taj Mohammad Wardak.[276] In March 2004, troops loyal to Ismail Khan in Herat fought a rival commander's troops, resulting in the assassination of Khan's son, the Afghan aviation minister. About a hundred people died in the clashes.[277] A month later, Northern Alliance strongman Abdul Rashid Dostum went as far as challenging the Kabul central government when he invaded Faryab province on horseback accompanied by trucks and tanks. The move was apparently in retaliation for Karzai's refusal to fire Dostum's main rival, the warlord Marshal Mohammed Fahim, the Afghan defense minister[278] (Faryab province was under Dostum's control in the early 1990s and is now ruled by Fahim's allies[279]).

Despite the renewed fragmentation of the country under the various repressive governors and their private armies, U.S. secretary of defense Donald Rumsfeld belittled concerns about factional fighting, asserting that the warlords were actually stabilizing the country:

> I do not believe that the threat to Afghanistan today is from factional fighting. Indeed, the reality is that in the bulk of the

> country the armies, the militias, the forces that exist there, *almost all of which have U.S. Special Forces involved with them and advising them and participating* [emphasis added], are by their presence contributing to stability.[280]

In some cases U.S. forces have even witnessed rival commanders' troops battling each other. One man whose brother was murdered in the 2002 battle between Padsha (Bacha) Khan and Taj Mohammad Wardak expressed frustration that the killings by U.S. allies were occurring in the presence of U.S. troops: "The Americans talk about the Taliban and al-Qa'eda. What is al-Qa'eda to me? This is my home, my children, my land and it is all in danger because of these fighters [the Northern Alliance] who are with the Americans." A U.S. military spokesperson at the site of the Khan-Wardak battle explained: "Our mission here is to capture or kill al-Qa'eda and senior Taliban. . . . Our secondary mission is to help to secure the country." When asked about factional fighting, the answer was dismissive: "I don't think it's for us to get into."[281] This is not surprising, since Secretary Rumsfeld considers factional fighting a positive stabilizing force, not to be interfered with.

CIVIL CRIMES: LAND, TAXES, AID, AND DRUGS

In a poverty-stricken country with few resources and no state monopoly over the use of force, economic power in Afghanistan can be acquired in only a few ways: stealing and controlling land, stealing taxes and revenues at borders and checkpoints, stealing humanitarian aid, and trafficking narcotics. In post-Taliban Afghanistan, warlords in the central government and local commanders have been using all four methods, always at the expense of civilians.

In one case of land appropriation, publicized by the rare instance of a UN official speaking out, Special Rapporteur on Housing Miloon Kothari accused the Education Minister Yunus Qanooni and Defense Minister Qasim Fahim of demolishing homes and creating a "culture of impunity."[282] According to Kothari, "ministers and people at the highest level are involved in occupying land and in demolishing the homes of poor people . . . some of whom have been there for 25 to 30 years."[283] In some cases homes were demolished with little or no notice, and while residents were still occupying them.[284] The Afghanistan Independent Human Rights Commission (AIHRC) released a report verifying the "destruction of houses and land property occupation, and forced selling of properties" by "cabinet members and . . . very high level officials and their relatives," which include the warlords named by Kothari.[285] In another case, the AIHRC listed twenty-nine senior officials and other powerful individuals in Sherpur who had received plots for nominal fees, including two former militia commanders, six cabinet ministers, the Central Bank governor, and the mayor. Additionally, thousands of returning Afghan refugees found their homes occupied by "commanders and their cronies."[286]

In defiance of the central government, warlords have also been appropriating hundreds of millions of dollars of revenue and taxes in the border regions under their control. Given the terrible state of the economy of war-torn Afghanistan, customs duties and border taxes are a main source of national revenue. Ismail Khan openly admitted to collecting $100 million a year in duties when he was governor of Herat. Compare this to Karzai's national operating budget of $460 million at the time, of which $340 million came from international donors.[287] Additionally, warlords have returned to their old practice of setting up illegal checkpoints to collect tolls from travelers and truck drivers. Under the Taliban the checkpoints were shut down, but now even the United Nations World Food Program was barred from delivering food to Kandahar because of bribes demanded at checkpoints.[288]

In addition to exacting illegal tolls on humanitarian aid deliveries, warlords often simply steal the aid and, in some cases, use it to buy political leverage. In a country dependent on foreign humanitarian aid for many years, the theft of food and other necessities means certain death for the intended beneficiaries. In the winter months after the fall of the Taliban, Northern Alliance warlords stole desperately needed relief goods that poured into the country.[289] According to journalist Ahmed Rashid in early 2002, "Afghanistan's lack of a nationwide peacekeeping force is allowing local warlords to jeopardize efforts to . . . deliver humanitarian supplies . . . Outside Kabul, warlords and bandits have become so pervasive that aid agencies are unable to deliver relief supplies to large swathes of the country." The only way to get aid to those who needed it was to use the warlords as go-betweens. After securing a 10–15 percent commission, the aid would be distributed by the warlords to those who promised to support them.[290]

As if stealing homes from the poor, revenue from the cash-strapped government, and food from the hungry were not enough, under the warlords the drug trade has been revived with a vengeance. After the terrorist attacks of 9/11, one of the many reasons given in the U.S. and UK to justify the bombing of Afghanistan was that it would curb drug production. According to President Bush, "it's important for Americans to know that trafficking of drugs finances the world of terror, sustaining terrorists."[291] Bush's ally Tony Blair also attempted to convince his electorate: "We act because the al-Qa'eda network and the Taliban regime are funded in large parts on the drugs trade. 90 percent of all heroin sold in Britain originates from Afghanistan. Stopping that trade is directly in our interests."[292] At the time these statements were made, drug production was actually greater in territories controlled by the Northern Alliance than under the Taliban.

UN sanctions supported by the U.S. in 2000 aimed at curbing terrorism and the drugs that financed it resulted in a Taliban ban on poppy growing. By 2001, drug production in Taliban-controlled areas had waned by 60 percent. But in areas controlled by the Northern Alliance, whom the U.S. was indirectly aiding, opium production continued to flourish.[293] According to the UK *Observer*:

> During the ban the only source of poppy production was territory held by the Northern Alliance. It tripled its production. In the high valleys of Badakhshan—an area controlled by troops loyal to the former President Burhanuddin Rabbani—the number of hectares planted last year jumped from 2,458 to 6,342. [Northern] Alliance fields accounted for 83 percent of total Afghan production of 185 tons of opium during the ban.[294]

Increased drug production under the Northern Alliance is not surprising. When the U.S. first armed the commanders commonly known as Mujahideen in 1979, Afghanistan acquired the status of number-one heroin producer within a few years. Trucks carrying weapons to the Mujahideen across the Afghanistan–Pakistan border would return to Pakistani laboratories laden with raw heroin. In the early 1980s Afghanistan's opium harvest doubled to 575 tons as a result of Mujahideen commanders forcing local peasants to grow poppies.[295] Apparently, "the CIA and its allies . . . tolerated the rise of the biggest drug empires ever seen east of the giant Colombian cocaine cartels" because they "regarded drug revenues as an important way to finance the war . . ."[296] According to a U.S. State Department estimate, Afghanistan's opium production was up to 900 tons by 1993, more than twice that of Iran and Pakistan combined. Writing in 1994, before the Taliban took power, Alfred McCoy, author of *The Politics of Heroin*, predicted that "the Afghan crop will soon exceed Southeast Asia's, and nearly double the supply of heroin for the world market," which indeed happened in 1998. The reason was not mysterious: "a mix [of] superpower confrontation and local ethnic conflict . . . facilitated formation of drug networks that can continue to grow."[297]

Within months of the fall of the Taliban and the revival of warlord control, drug production steadily increased nationwide from 185 tons in 2001 to 3,400 tons in 2002,[298] making Afghanistan the largest heroin producer in the world once again. In 2004 the UN reported that opium cultivation had increased by two-thirds, yielding 4,700 tons, despite bad weather and crop disease.[299] Remnants of the Taliban are reported to have long abandoned their poppy ban and are selling heroin to finance their insurgencies against the U.S. and its clients. In addition, media reports suggest that the drug trafficking is "funding the defiance of central government by local warlords."[300] Due to extreme poverty and the lucrative returns of the drug trade, most farmers are growing poppies even without direct coercion by the Northern Alliance.[301] This is no surprise, given that per hectare the value of opium is almost twelve times that of wheat.[302]

A March 2005 report by UN Human Rights investigator Cherif Bassiouni confirmed that local commanders gain economic independence through drug sales and warned of the threat it presented to the central government:

> The opium industry overshadows legal forms of agricultural production, fuels widespread corruption and provides increasing economic power to factional commanders and other local and regional leaders. The independent expert draws attention to the fact that drug trafficking has reached a crucial moment, when well-armed factional commanders, backed by huge drug profits, have increasingly taken on the characteristics of organized crime and present a significant threat to the new State.[303]

Bassiouni's report for the United Nations added that "problems faced by returning refugees and IDPs [internally displaced people] related to land claims, institutional corruption, abuse and violence" often happen at the hands of factional commanders who engage in "illegal land seizures, extortion and intimidation." He boldly recommended that "the removal of factional commanders and individuals associated with past human rights violations from positions of public authority must be a key government priority."[304]

CRIMES AGAINST WOMEN: RAPE, ABDUCTION, AND SELF-IMMOLATIONS

The Northern Alliance was initially presented as a feminist alternative to the Taliban and the U.S. media did not challenge this claim. On the contrary, the misogynistic track record of the Northern Alliance was chronically minimized or ignored. For example, right before the U.S. attack of 2001, the *New York Times* ran an article whose headline suggested a progressive feminist side to the Alliance: "Education Offers Women in Northern Afghanistan a Ray of Hope." But the content of the article demonstrated that the difference between the Northern

Alliance and the Taliban was insignificant and confined to tokenism (see Chapter 6).[305]

With the Taliban regime ousted, Afghan women did not face better times. One indication of this is the inability of women to conduct political demonstrations within Afghanistan. In November 2001, immediately after the fall of the Taliban, when international attention on Afghan women's oppression was at its peak and women were considered "liberated" from the Taliban, Afghan women attempted to organize a public demonstration for their rights in Kabul. They were immediately curbed by the Northern Alliance, who claimed that they couldn't guarantee the women's safety.[306] Nearly two years later, a thousand Afghan women attempted to march through the streets of Kabul to protest continued insecurity, but were forced to limit their demonstration to the Women's Park, a walled garden reserved for women and children.[307] This is in spite of the fact that Kabul is considered the safest region in Afghanistan, due to the presence of international peacekeeping forces.

Restrictions on political organizing are only the tip of the iceberg. Despite many promises of "liberation" by the Bush administration, the warlords have actually targeted Afghan women in a manner similar to the Taliban, and sometimes even worse. Only months after the Taliban's fall, there were cases of rape and mistreatment of women. Civilians have been fearful of speaking out about this—according to one community leader, "A lot of houses have been looted and a lot of women have been raped, but people are afraid to talk because they have been threatened. . . . They are afraid for their lives."[308] According to the UK *Independent*:

> [T]he Alliance feels the same way about women as the Taliban did—they are chattel, to be tolerated but kept out of real life. Instead of the religious police, the Alliance use shame as their weapon [*sic*]—to walk around in normal [nontraditional] clothes is to walk around naked, inviting ridicule on the husband who owns you.[309]

As in the 1980s and '90s, it is politically inconvenient to highlight women's oppression enforced by U.S. allies. In Herat, under the Northern Alliance commander and former governor, Ismail Khan, hundreds of girls and women committed suicide through self-immolation.[310] The suicides were thought to have been brought on by severe repression, which began soon after the fall of the Taliban and Khan's retaking of Herat. One doctor at a Herat Hospital commented, "During the Taliban regime, there were almost no cases like this. . . . Now, there are two or three burned women admitted each week."[311]

Nasreen is an eighteen-year-old woman living in Herat—she explained to us that Ismail Khan "didn't want women to . . . be more [*sic*] free. He said that . . . it's better that they would be in their houses than going [*sic*] outside."[312] As soon as Khan resumed power, men were forbidden from teaching women or girls in private classes, and boys and girls were not allowed to be in school buildings at the same time. One medic working for a foreign aid agency explained:

> The institutional repression of the [movement of women] is . . . a big factor because women are not allowed to go on their own in taxi cars, they are sort of socially policed if they are talking to other men, they have to be in the burqa, they have restriction on freedom to work. Just recently in Herat a women's shop which was employing a lot of women was closed. The driving school for women was also closed.[313]

Similar to the Taliban's restrictions, women in Herat were required to wear a burqa or chadori (full-length veil with only the face uncovered) when outdoors. Their dress was enforced by police, employers, and school administrators.[314] Herat also had a religious police and a "youth police" to subject women and girls to forced "chastity checks" via hospital gynecological examinations[315] in order to determine if they were "untouched."[316]

According to Human Rights Watch in December 2002, Taliban-style behavior was not limited to Herat:

> In Kabul, a reconfigured Vice and Virtue Squad (renamed "Islamic Teaching") . . . harasses women in Kabul's streets for "un-Islamic behavior," such as wearing makeup, and, in some instances, follows them home to castigate their parents or spouses. Women have reported being harassed and threatened by unidentified men for discarding particular aspects of the Taliban-mandated dress code. Outside of Kabul, women and girls have faced serious threats to their physical safety, including sexual violence. In the north, three rival forces have committed abuses against Pashtun civilians, including raping entire households and girls as young as fourteen. . . . [A]round the northern city of Mazar-e Sharif, factional rivalry between local commanders contributed to targeted attacks on women aid workers and rapes of women and children in displacement camps that had become militarized.[317]

In many cases the violence against women became even worse than under the Taliban. In 2003 Amnesty International published a 47-page report entitled "No One Listens To Us and No One Treats Us as Human Beings: Justice Denied to Women":

> Abuses perpetrated by armed groups against women and girls since the fall of the Taliban government in November 2001 include rape, abduction, and forced and underage marriage . . . the AIHRC [Afghanistan Independent Human Rights Commission] . . . indicates that the abuse of women by armed groups is so common that the body's research department has decided to maintain a separate category in its files for such incidents. . . . In parts of Afghanistan, women have stated that the insecurity and the risk of sexual violence they face make their lives worse than during the Taliban era. [After the Taliban,] women expressed a greater sense of fear and intimidation arising from the behavior of illegally and heavily armed groups in parts of Mazar-e Sharif and Jalalabad.[318]

In addition to abuse under Northern Alliance commanders, the report also implicates the Afghan National Army, specifically in instances of abusing women physically and transferring young girls from one army commander to another as "gifts." The overall situation for women deteriorated to such an extent that, according to one woman, "During the Taliban era if a woman went to market and showed an inch of flesh she would have been flogged—now she's raped."[319]

CHAPTER FOUR

A CLIENT "DEMOCRACY"

RESHAPING AFGHAN POLITICS

Three years after Operation Enduring Freedom began, the U.S. favorite, Hamid Karzai, won Afghanistan's first presidential elections. A year after that, the country held its first parliamentary elections. Both events took place in the midst of foreign occupation and an increasingly bloody insurgency. As of this writing, most of Afghanistan is still managed by troops fielded by the United States, NATO, Afghan warlords, or the resurgent Taliban. The elected government, itself a tool of the foreign powers, has little control over the Afghan countryside. We have to question whether this can truly be called a "democracy." In fact, for much of its existence as a country, the government of Afghanistan has been a client of global powers.

A BUFFER STATE

Since Afghanistan first became known by that name, it had been a weak state barely held together by a central government in Kabul. Like most south, central, and west Asian countries, the modern boundaries of Afghanistan were defined by European powers to benefit foreign interests, not those of the people living there. Sir Thomas Holdich wrote in 1901, "We have contributed much to give a national unity to that nebulous community which we call Afghanistan . . . by drawing a boundary all round it and elevating it to the position of a buffer state between England and Russia."[320] The term "buffer state" refers to the fact that the crown wanted a swath of populated land that would remain nominally independent to separate British-occupied India (now Pakistan) from Russian-occupied Central Asia. The Afghan people, "elevated" to buffer status by the imperial powers, would then fight to defend their nation from foreign encroachment, while English and Russian territory would remain intact. The boundary was negotiated in 1893 by Mortimer Durand, the foreign secretary of British India, and the Afghan king Abdur Rahman Khan. Percival Sykes, a member of British Army Intelligence at the time, commented,

> Durand thus secured for the [British] Indian Empire its most important achievement of external policy during the nineteenth century. He not only materially helped to end the long advance of Russia towards India, but removed a constant source of misunderstanding with that Empire.[321]

The borders were drawn to split the Afghan Pashtuns from their cousins in British-occupied India (now Pakistan); and the Afghan Tajiks, Uzbeks, and Turkmens from their cousins in Russian-occupied Central Asia. The Pashtun ethnic group, the largest, was chosen by the British to rule Afghanistan. The Afghan ethnic makeup ensured that the state would be difficult to govern by any one group, thus requiring a federated structure that was easily divided and susceptible to foreign influence. Captain C. W. Wade wrote in 1837, "whilst distributed into several states, the Afghans are, in my opinion, more likely to subserve the views and interests of the British Government." The legacy of this division continues today.[322]

Afghans celebrate Independence Day every August 19, the date in 1919 when the British Empire declared that it would "leave Afghanistan officially free and independent in its internal and external affairs."[323] As for most peoples who struggle against foreign rule, independence came at great cost for Afghans. Three major wars and a brutal British occupation consumed the preceding eighty-one years. In 1838 the Empire had installed by force a puppet monarch, Shah Shuja, in Kabul. The (British) governor general of India published the Simla Manifesto in 1838, outlining "the duty . . . of providing for the security of the possessions of the British Crown," which led to the decision to install Shuja and occupy Afghanistan. The puppet monarch was praised by the governor as a man "whose popularity throughout Afghanistan had been proved . . . by the strong and unanimous testimony of the best authorities." But as in the case of Hamid Karzai today, the "best authorities" tended to be outside the country. Shuja's popularity in his own country was largely a fiction—his real power came from his imperial benefactor. Indeed, the Manifesto stated that he was to be "supported against foreign interference and factious opposition by a British army," like the U.S.-paid mercenaries who still guard Karzai and the 20,000 "coalition" and NATO troops (mostly U.S., British, and Canadian) who currently roam the Afghan countryside. The strenuous attempt was made to show British policy decisions in the light of their benefit to Afghans. The governor general "rejoices that . . . he will be enabled to assist in restoring the union and prosperity of the Afghan people. . . . British influence will be sedulously used to further every measure of general benefit."[324]

Sir Henry Durand, who took part in those early British wars against Afghanistan, admitted the following in 1883 to his biographer (and son), Mortimer:

> [W]e had resolved to force Shah Shuja, a weakened worthless exile, upon the Afghan people, till then well disposed towards us; and this great and unprovoked injustice, the cause of all our subsequent troubles in Afghanistan, was to be effected by military measures of which the rashness and folly seem at the present day almost inconceivable.[325]

The "great and unprovoked injustice" Durand helped to carry out led to nearly a century of intermittent war.

After Afghanistan became fully independent in 1919 the country drifted into new relationships with all nearby powers (the Soviet Union, Persia, and Turkey) except British India. In 1923 King Amanullah (who came to power in 1919) signed a Treaty of Friendship with Russia, which, after the 1917 Bolshevik takeover, was once again an enemy of Britain. At the same time, Amanullah refused to accept the Afghan borders as drawn by England and Russia. On the east, he wanted to nullify the Durand Line (the border with British India) and reunite the Pashtun people. To the north, he began to look for ways to regain land lost in Central Asia. Amanullah "grew increasingly disillusioned with the Soviets, especially as he witnessed the widening oppression of his fellow Muslims across the border." Still, Afghanistan was to remain beholden to the Soviet government for decades, receiving huge gifts of "cash, technology, and military equipment" from the 1920s until the fall of the Soviet puppet Najibullah in 1992.[326]

The king pushed through rapid social reforms, going as far as to require European-style dress in the capital, Kabul. His reforms irked religious and military leaders, who saw them as weakening their power. A coup was staged and Amanullah was forced to abdicate in January 1929. The Tajik rebel leader Bacha-i-Saqqao became king for the next nine months. He was overthrown by Pashtuns, mostly from the British side of the Durand Line, led by Nadir Khan, who became King Nadir Shah.[327] It has been said that the coups by both Bacha-i-Saqqao and Nadir Shah were assisted by Britain, who disliked Amanullah's close relationship with Russia.[328]

In 1933, Zahir Shah became king at age nineteen when his father Nadir was assassinated. Because of his youth, two of his uncles ruled as prime ministers from 1933 until 1953. His cousin Mohammed Daoud served as prime minister from 1953 to 1963.

As regents, Shah's uncles and cousin began to imagine the reunification of the Pashtun people into "Pashtunistan." Decolonization of India by Britain in 1947, followed by the partition of India and Pakistan, gave the Pashtun people on the Pakistani side of the Durand Line new citizenship. Afghanistan was the only country in 1947 to vote against Pakistan joining the United Nations. In 1949 a *Loya Jirga*, or grand assembly, declared that Afghanistan recognized "neither the imaginary Durand nor any similar line." The British-drawn border would be a source of continuous tension between Pakistan and Afghanistan for the next five decades.

COLD WAR RIVALRY

From 1919 to 1973 the government of Afghanistan was mostly in charge of its own internal affairs while receiving significant amounts of military and financial aid from foreign powers. After World War II, superpowers played out their rivalries in Afghanistan in more subtle ways than fighting wars of conquest and drawing borders. Historian Nick Cullather notes, "The confrontation between colonizer and colonized, rich and poor, was with a rhetorical gesture replaced by a world order in which all nations were either developed or developing." Afghanistan was a prime example of this process. The competition to see which superpower could curry more favor with the royal family was used to some advantage by Afghan officials. At the same time, Afghanistan was becoming more, not less, dependent on foreign largesse, a situation that would prove unstable in the long run.

Perhaps the largest development project in the history of the country was the Helmand and Arghandab Valley Authority (HAVA) dam complex, begun in 1950 with U.S. aid and loans. Modeled after the Tennessee Valley Authority, HAVA was used to create dependency on the U.S. and garner leverage over Afghan policy, as well as to "buy hearts and minds" so that people would take the side of the U.S. against the Soviets. Tennessee-type dam projects in poor countries were considered by Washington to be a "weapon which, if properly employed, might outbid all the social ruthlessness of the Communists for the support of the peoples of Asia," according to historian Arthur Schlesinger.[329]

To Shah's uncles and Prime Minister Daoud, HAVA was a means of extending the power and prestige of the central government, and of promoting their goal of a strong Pashtun-dominated nation. According to Nick Cullather:

> Daoud's regime made no effort to disguise its chauvinism. Controlling positions in government, the army, the police, and the educational system were held by Pashtuns to such a degree that the appellation Afghan commonly referred only to Pashtuns and not to the minorities who collectively constituted the majority.[330]

Dam-building and valley-flooding were accompanied by huge relocation projects, and the forced settlement of Pashtun nomads, many of whom would normally spend part of their year in the Northwest Frontier Province of Pakistan. The nomads often took over land already occupied by Tajiks and Hazaras. The plan was to use the settlers "as a death squad to crush the uprisings of the non-Pashtun people."[331]

The Northwest Frontier Province of Pakistan, which had always been somewhat autonomous in practice, was considered a sort of buffer between Pakistan and Afghanistan. Its formal independence would have been a blow to Pakistan's security. In 1953 and 1954, Daoud paid tribesmen on both sides of the Durand line to influence the Pakistani government and disseminate propaganda in favor of Pashtunistan. In 1955, Pakistan closed the border to nomad traffic, simultaneously cutting off valuable trade that Afghanistan needed. In 1960, to further his goals for Pashtunistan, Daoud sent troops across the Pakistani border to stir up the Pashtuns again. Pakistan and Afghanistan severed relations the following year and Afghan exports of grapes and pomegranates suffered. Because of the deteriorating economy and the impasse with Pakistan, in 1963 Daoud was forced by the royal family to resign.

It was then that King Zahir Shah finally took actual power. The king immediately resumed relations with Pakistan, and the idea of Pashtunistan diminished temporarily as a threat to Islamabad's ownership of its Northwest Frontier. Pakistan would go on to search for ways to end the Afghan threat to its "buffer." Shah was overthrown by Daoud ten years later, and did not return to Afghan politics until late 2001, when his presence was required to legitimize the U.S. order in his country. The 1973 overthrow of the king and subsequent instability were used by the Soviets to manipulate subsequent Afghan leaders, and by Pakistan and the U.S. to stir fundamentalist rebellion. Once the Soviets invaded in 1979 and installed their puppet leaders, and the U.S. and its allies ramped up support for the resistance, direct foreign interference in Afghan politics became the norm once more.

TODAY'S PUPPET

> He spoke fluent English and seemed Western in his style, and many of his family members lived in the United States.
>
> —NEW YORK TIMES, DECEMBER 15, 2001

As Shah Shuja was to Britain and Najibullah was to the Soviet Union, Hamid Karzai was to the United States: an Afghan (Pashtun) with close ties to his external benefactors, installed virtually by decree after foreign troops occupied Afghanistan and removed his predecessors.

Just after the U.S. bombing campaign began in October 2001, reports began surfacing of Karzai as a "dissident" Afghan exile, who eventually "emerged as the Bush administration's main hope for forging a southern alliance against the Taliban."[332] The word "emerged" is appropriate. A National Newspaper Index search for Karzai's name in the *Christian Science Monitor,* the *New York Times,* the *Washington Post,* the *Los Angeles Times,* and the *Wall Street Journal* yields 273 instances from 1977 to 2004, 272 of which appeared after the U.S. began bombing Afghanistan.[333]

On October 18, 2001, the *New York Times* referred to Karzai as an "influential Pashtun chief" who was starting "a quiet rebellion" against the Taliban with U.S. support.[334] This gave the impression that Karzai must have had plenty of popular support among the Pashtun ethnic group—which comprises over 40 percent of the population—even though he was not well known internationally. But in February 2002, two months after he was established as interim chairman of the Afghan government, the Times asserted that a better description of Karzai's standing would be the exact opposite: "Mr. Karzai is a less formidable player at home than foreigners perceive him to be." Mohammed Fahim Dashty, editor of the *Kabul Weekly* newspaper, said, "I can understand why people in the U.S. were intrigued by Karzai, but people in Afghanistan are not impressed."[335] Meena Siddiqui, a human rights attorney in Kabul, told us, "When someone has not arisen from the people they cannot work on behalf of the people. Karzai had a good past, a good life, and ate well but he cannot do good for his people because he did not come from the people."[336]

Karzai was seen as a "compromise choice for interim leader, a Westernized tribal leader who was selected to satisfy the United States and the country's Pashtun majority,"[337] the two groups that mattered the most in Washington's calculations. He had visited the U.S. numerous times, speaking at conferences and testifying at Congressional hearings on the Taliban. But Karzai was also picked by the U.S. because of his longstanding connections to the U.S. intelligence establishment: "The Americans . . . knew Mr. Karzai, who had served as a funnel for covert American aid to the anti-Soviet Mujahideen in the 1980s."[338] In 1992 Karzai was appointed deputy foreign minister in the Mujahideen government but resigned two years later, in the midst of violent battles between the various factions. From 1994 to 1995, Karzai supported the Taliban, who had emerged from his home province of Kandahar. His brother Ahmed Karzai explained that "after he saw the Taliban as they really were, he cut all his ties in 1997."[339]

Karzai had no power base of his own, making him indebted to his foreign benefactors and to his military colleagues within Afghanistan, the Northern Alliance. According to the *New York Times*, "the anti-Taliban movement in the south led by Mr. Karzai and other Pashtun leaders would never have succeeded—or even come together—without the United States."[340] Zakia, a medical student at Kabul University, told us that, "every Afghan, even a child knows that he is a puppet of America. If America did not want to destroy the Taliban or set up the elections or create a government in Afghanistan and bring Karzai to the chair, it would not be possible. So everybody knows that he is the puppet of America and America can take him off the chair in one day."[341]

THE BONN CONFERENCE

The Bonn Conference, which ensconced the Northern Alliance in Afghan government, was where the U.S. arranged for Karzai to become interim president. Karzai, who was not even present at the conference, was allowed to address the opening session of the meetings via satellite telephone.[342] When the delegates voted for an interim president to hold the post for the next six months, Karzai initially received no votes. The votes went overwhelmingly to Professor Abdul Sattar Sirat, a member of the Rome contingent representing the former king. Sirat, an ethnic Uzbek who had been a justice minister when the king was deposed in 1973, "is almost certain to be the next leader of Afghanistan," reported the London *Guardian* on December 3. Sirat's connection to the king and lack of responsibility for the years of bloodshed after Shah's reign was probably what gave him his popularity among the delegates.

The other two contenders, Hamid Karzai and Burhanuddin Rabbani (president of the 1992–1996 Mujahideen government), were in competition for the support of the Northern Alliance. Karzai and prominent Alliance politicians Abdullah Abdullah and Yunus Qanooni were seen to be "exerting themselves at the expense of Mr. Rabbani, who had expected to return to his position as head of state." Rabbani had largely fallen out of favor with the Alliance, especially after his late-November 2001 "secret meeting in the United Arab Emirates with Lt. Gen Ehsan-ul Haq, newly promoted head of Pakistan's Inter-Services Intelligence (ISI) directorate," a move considered the ultimate betrayal of the Alliance to its enemies, the former sponsors of the Taliban. "Since then senior alliance figures have distanced themselves from Mr. Rabbani." Karzai gradually became "regarded by the alliance as likely long-term prospect as leader of Afghanistan."[343]

It wasn't just the Northern Alliance that favored Hamid Karzai. He apparently also "received the stamp of approval from Iran, Pakistan and Russia,"[344] in addition to that of his benefactors, the United States. Sirat, on the other hand, while he represented the popular (to Afghans) former king, would not have been acceptable to all outside powers, and certainly would not have been acceptable to the Northern Alliance, whom the U.S. and UN were intent on appeasing. Since he was an ethnic Uzbek, Sirat's ascension to head of state would have been against the standard practice: from Shah Shuja to Najibullah to Mullah Omar, all foreign-backed governments in Afghanistan deliberately had a Pashtun in charge, to guarantee the support of the largest ethnic group.

In the end, Sirat was "convinced" by the United Nations to step aside and allow Karzai to win the chairmanship. According to the *New York Times*, "all the delegates understood that the Americans wanted Mr.

Karzai . . . so on Dec. 5, they finally chose him." Haji Attaullah, a Pashtun delegate, complained later that the Bonn Conference "was only for show . . . the decisions had been made before."[345] Meanwhile, James F. Dobbins, the senior U.S. envoy there, called the conference "an outstanding success."[346]

Sirat later complained that in the Bonn meetings and in the 2002 Emergency *Loya Jirga*, "ethnicity became the main factor instead of professionalism and qualification." Referring to the UN special envoy Lakhdar Brahimi, who is Algerian, Sirat said,

> I will never allow myself to tell Algerians how to establish their political systems and run their country, but Mr. Brahimi intervened in the political life in Afghanistan and he supported ethnicity as the basis to get any position in the political and administrative affairs in Afghanistan. By doing that he endangered the national unity of Afghanistan.[347]

The Bonn Conference agreed upon what came to be known as the "Bonn Process," a series of four events designed to transform Afghanistan into a country consistent with U.S. interests. The initial conference established an interim cabinet and president until June 2002, followed by an "Emergency *Loya Jirga*," a "Constitutional *Loya Jirga*," and finally, presidential and parliamentary elections.

The path from the Bonn Conference to the 2004 presidential elections reveals deep political manipulation by the U.S. to ensure the same result: Karzai becoming the head of Afghanistan's fledgling government. Karzai's post-Taliban rise was purchased by allowing Northern Alliance warlords and regional militia commanders to regain military power in the countryside, and by granting them immense political power in government, squelching the hopes of most Afghans. Warlords dominated the four stages of the Bonn Process, effectively silencing the voices of civil society. Afghanistan's new constitution, with input from fundamentalist forces, heralded the return of Islamic Law, ushering in yet another ominous era for women. Afghanistan's first parliament in thirty years is made up of a majority of warlords and ultraconservatives.

This new Afghan "democracy" was ultimately not shaped by ordinary Afghans, but by the U.S. and its agent Zalmay Khalilzad.

ZALMAY KHALILZAD: AMERICA'S "VICEROY"

> The Clinton administration should appoint a high-level envoy for Afghanistan who can coordinate overall U.S. policy. This envoy must have sufficient stature and access to ensure that he or she is taken seriously in foreign capitals and by local militias. Equally important, the special envoy must be able to shape Afghanistan policy within U.S. bureaucracies.[348]

Zalmay Khalilzad is one of the few U.S. policy makers who publicly wrote his own job description and then got the job. No stranger to U.S. foreign policy circles, Khalilzad started off as an adviser to the Reagan administration on U.S. support to the Mujahideen in the 1980s, and ended up as a National Security Council staffer in the George W. Bush administration. After 9/11 he all but became the hypothetical envoy in the passage from his 2000 *Washington Quarterly* article with Daniel Byman, quoted above. In November 2003 he was promoted to U.S. Ambassador to Afghanistan.[349]

Sahar Saba of RAWA told us in March 2004, "People know very well that Khalilzad is the man behind the scenes. They know that he is really the man [who] decides what president Karzai has to do." Naimatullah Khan, a political commentator on Afghan affairs based in Quetta, Pakistan, told Agence France-Presse, "[Khalilzad] was undoubtedly the most influential person in Afghanistan. He was more than an ambassador." According to the BBC, "No major decisions by the Afghan government have been made without his involvement . . . he has sometimes been dubbed the viceroy, or the real president of Afghanistan." Habiba Sarabi, the first Minister of Women's Affairs and Afghanistan's first female provincial governor, spoke to us in her apartment in Kabul in early 2005, criticizing Khalilzad's "negative" influence on Karzai. "Sometimes he wants to show the people that he is more powerful than president Karzai because he is speaking [*sic*] strongly. I wish it not to be like this."[350]

"Zal," as his friends call him, was born in Afghanistan and first visited the U.S. as a teenager through an exchange program sponsored by the Quaker organization American Friends Service Committee. He eventually went on to pursue his doctorate at the University of Chicago and became a U.S. citizen in 1984. He urged the U.S. government to support the fundamentalist anti-Soviet Mujahideen as executive director of "Friends of Afghanistan" (a Mujahideen support group). He was also part of a group of policy makers who convinced Reagan to provide shoulder-fired Stinger missiles and other weapons to the Mujahideen.[351]

Formerly a Senior Analyst at the Rand Corporation, Khalilzad also headed the Bush-Cheney transition team for the Department of Defense, and has been a counselor to Secretary of Defense Rumsfeld. He served in the State and Defense Departments of the Reagan and Bush (senior) Administrations.[352]

Khalilzad is a longstanding advocate of U.S. global dominance. A founding member of the neoconservative right-wing think tank Project for a New American Century,[353] Khalilzad wrote (with contributions from officials such as Paul Wolfowitz and Dick Cheney) the Pentagon's 1992 Defense Planning Guidance, the draft of which called for the United States to "preclud[e] the emergence of any future potential global competitor." The draft, leaked to the press, stated that the United States "will retain the pre-eminent responsibility for addressing selectively those wrongs which threaten not only our interests, but those of our allies or friends, or which could seriously unsettle international relations." The document was "conspicuously devoid of references to collective action through the United Nations" and stated that "the United States should be postured to act independently when collective action cannot be orchestrated."[354] Khalilzad would certainly not permit true democracy to interfere with U.S. prerogatives.

Khalilzad was also associated with the energy giant, Unocal Corporation. The UK's *Independent* newspaper reporter Robert Fisk called Khalilzad a "former Unocal Corporation oil industry consultant"[355] More accurately, according to the *Washington Post*, Khalilzad was actually employed by the Cambridge Energy Research Associates in the 1990s, and "conducted risk analyses for Unocal" at the time that Unocal was engaging the Taliban on the construction of an oil and gas pipeline through Afghanistan.[356] We return to the Khalilzad-Unocal connection in Chapter 7.

From early 2002 to early 2005 Khalilzad held the real reins of power in Kabul. The following passage from the *New York Times* highlights the true nature of the relationship between Khalilzad and Afghan president Hamid Karzai.

> The genial Mr. Karzai may be Afghanistan's president, but the affable, ambitious Mr. Khalilzad often seems more like its chief executive. With his command of both details and American largesse, the Afghan-born envoy has created an alternate seat of power since his arrival [as U.S. ambassador] on Thanksgiving [2003].
>
> As he shuttles between the American Embassy and the presidential palace, where Americans guard Mr. Karzai, one place seems an extension of the other.
>
> Working closely with the Karzai government and the American military, Mr. Khalilzad ponders whether to push for the removal of uncooperative governors, where roads should be built to undercut insurgency, and how to ensure that the elements friendly to America gain ascendancy in a democratic Afghanistan. His overarching goal is to accelerate the country's rebuilding and securing, preferably on a timetable attuned to the American political cycle.[357]

In April 2005, Khalilzad was transferred from Afghanistan to the second country that has undergone a post-9/11 U.S. invasion and regime change: Iraq. There were mixed reactions in Afghanistan to his departure. According to the BBC, "there are some here who say Ambassador Khalilzad's departure is a good thing right now. . . . [S]ome analysts argue that it will make it much easier for [Karzai] to exert his authority, free from the shadow of the 'viceroy.'" Among the most sorry to see Khalilzad leave his country was ultraconservative Supreme Court

Chief Justice Fazil Hady Shinwari, whom Khalilzad helped to power. Shinwari has helped to return Afghanistan's justice system to a fundamentalist and often misogynist interpretation of Islamic law. In an open letter to President Bush, Shinwari pleaded against Khalilzad's reassignment, saying Afghanistan needed the ambassador "now more than ever," because "no one else can work as he has been doing."[358]

In a December 2005 profile on Khalilzad, *New Yorker* staff writer Jon Lee Anderson wrote that the ambassador "has a reputation both as a strategic thinker and as an operator, a man with extraordinary political instincts." An Iraqi political consultant told Anderson, "Zal makes it look like his suggestions are in the Iraqi interests. All the major players like him. [And he] knows how to play his Muslim card."[359] As we show later in this chapter, Khalilzad was skillful at working with Afghan "major players," mostly fundamentalists and warlords, compromising with them and convincing them that their interests (antiprogressive, for state control of private life) were shared by the United States. Khalilzad has many times ensured that Northern Alliance and other warlords have been legitimized as cabinet ministers, court officials, and regional governors, and their wishes for religion-based government enshrined in the Constitution. By giving them positions of power, Khalilzad has ignored the wishes of the majority of Afghans, who would rather see them on trial.[360] In addition, it was Khalilzad's idea for the Karzai government to offer amnesty to the Taliban. Khalilzad called this practice "co-optation in exchange for cooperation." RAWA called it a "treasonable alliance against our nation."

In Iraq, like in Afghanistan, Zalmay Khalilzad "often seems to be the one holding the government together." According to *Newsweek*, Khalilzad is "trying to repeat, in furiously accelerated fashion, the strategy he applied in Afghanistan . . . , where he cajoled the warlords—by a mixture of promises, military pressure and cash—to enter the political process." It is unlikely that this bodes well for the Iraqi people, but helping the people of Afghanistan or Iraq has always been incidental to Khalilzad's real goal: the promotion of U.S. power.[361]

MANIPULATING THE *LOYA JIRGA**

The concept of a *Loya Jirga*, a traditional Afghan assembly consisting of a gathering of regional delegates from all over the country, had been on the table since the early 1980s. Proposed by the ex-king Zahir Shah as a way to end the Soviet occupation through diplomacy, the initiative was not given a chance to flower until the United States needed it to legitimize their post-Taliban order. In his 2000 policy paper on Afghanistan, Zalmay Khalilzad had laid out the idea for the U.S. to "confront the Taliban," and supported the convening of a *Loya Jirga* for the "selection of a broadly acceptable transitional government."[362] Following the Bonn Conference, Khalilzad's prescription was closely observed.

The June 2002 Emergency *Loya Jirga* was to pick a "transitional" president and cabinet for the next two years, in anticipation of future presidential and parliamentary elections. According to two of the delegates, Omar Zakhilwal and Adeena Niazi, the meetings began optimistically:

> Delegates from all backgrounds—Pashtuns, Tajiks, Hazaras, and Uzbeks; urban and rural, Sunni and Shiite—sat together under one roof as if we belonged to a single village. Men and women mingled openly and comfortably. In tolerant and lively exchanges, we discussed the compatibility of women's rights with our Islamic traditions. Women played a leading role at these meetings. We were living proof against the stereotypes that Afghans are divided by ethnic hatred, that we are a backward people not ready for democracy and equality.[363]

The delegates had put together a "wish list focused on national unity, peace, and security." The list "emphasized access to food, education, and health services in neglected rural areas" but above all the delegates were united in "the urgency of reducing the power of warlords and establishing a truly representative government." Zakhilwal and Niazi wrote, "The sentiment quickly grew into a grassroots movement supporting the former king . . . as head of state. The vast majority of us

---

* Parts of this and the following section are based on James Ingalls, "The United States and the Afghan *Loya Jirga*: A Victory for the Puppet Masters," *Z Magazine*, September 2002.

viewed him as the only leader with enough popular support and independence to stand up to the warlords."[364]

In June 2001, when asked in a poll "who can most successfully address the problems facing Afghanistan today?" a plurality of Afghan people named their former king Mohammed Zahir Shah. Sahar Saba of RAWA explained to us why the former king was the first choice.

> [It is] because of the lack of a real political democratic alternative in Afghanistan. Everyone knows that the king is not really the best choice. It's not "he was the best and we would not have any other." But in this situation, the fundamentalists oppose him. We have a saying in Persian: "the djinn are afraid of the name of God." So the fundamentalists were afraid of the king—if he comes then he would destroy them. That is the reason why the majority of the people supported him. If you ask the people in Afghanistan they will say it's simply a comparison between bad and worse. The king was bad, but these fundamentalists are worse. But this doesn't mean if the Afghan people are in favor of the king then they want a kingdom and a monarchy and all. It's just the first step towards having a united Afghanistan. That's why RAWA [and Afghans] supported him and preferred him to the Northern Alliance and the Taliban.[365]

Unlike Hamid Karzai, Zahir Shah is well known, with a 40-year history as king of Afghanistan, including a record of animosity towards fundamentalists and warlords. Thus, Zahir Shah would have presented a minor challenge to U.S. control and a major challenge to some of the warlords, who were afraid of him. This immediately put him out of the running for interim president.

According to United Press International, "democracy nearly broke out in Afghanistan on Monday [June 10, 2002], but was blocked by backroom dealing to prevent former King Mohammed Zahir Shah from emerging as a challenger to Hamid Karzai."[366] Instead of beginning at 8 a.m. on June 10, as scheduled, the *Loya Jirga* was postponed until 10 a.m., but at 3 p.m. it was announced that the meeting would not convene at all until the following day. Zalmay Khalilzad, the U.S. special envoy to Afghanistan, told the press that the organizing commission decided to postpone the opening of the *Loya Jirga* "to ascertain the true intentions of the former King." Before Zahir Shah could make his own announcement, Khalilzad gave the answer: "The former king is not a candidate for a position in the Transitional Authority. . . . [H]e endorses the candidacy of Chairman Karzai."[367] At a 6 p.m. press conference, the former king, "looking grim," was flanked by Khalilzad and Karzai. He said nothing, but his chief of political affairs read a statement: "As I have always mentioned, I have no intention of restoring the monarchy and am not a candidate for any position in the Emergency *Loya Jirga*."[368]

Khalilzad explained, "Statements that were issued yesterday [June 9] that the former King might be, or is, a candidate for the post of President of the Transitional Authority . . . were inconsistent with earlier statements by the former King," which had caused "consternation and confusion"[369] among the *Loya Jirga* delegates. The "statements issued" were actually the former king's response to a BBC interviewer's questions. When asked if he would accept the job of head of state, he answered, "I will accept the decision of the *Loya Jirga*. . . . What the majority decides about the future of Afghanistan, and my role, I'll accept that."[370] Contrary to Khalilzad's assertion, this was consistent with at least one earlier statement, in which he said, "I will accept the responsibility of head of state if that is what the *Loya Jirga* demands of me."[371] Clearly, many delegates took these remarks to mean that the former king would stand for office if nominated. But Khalilzad was only interested in using Shah's popularity to legitimize Karzai. In a 1996 opinion piece in the *Washington Post*, Khalilzad said he saw the former king as "a symbol of national unity because of the support he enjoys along ethnic lines."[372]

According to UPI, the U.S. special envoy had "apparently brokered" a deal with the former king to withdraw his candidacy. So it was only natural that "some delegates . . . were angered by what they perceived to be a U.S. effort to front load the *Loya Jirga* to ensure that Karzai was reappointed."[373] Omar Zakhilwal wrote in the *Washington Post*, "Rather than address the issue democratically, almost two days of the six-day loya jirga were wasted while a parade of high-level officials from the interim government, the United Nations, and the United States visited Zahir Shah and eventually 'persuaded' him to publicly renounce his political ambitions."[374] It is well known that, if given the chance, Shah probably would have won a significant number of votes. UPI said that, "many delegates felt the highly popular ex-king would probably have had the votes to be chosen for a role in the transitional government, but had been prevented from declaring his candidacy."[375] According to the *New York Times*, Amanullah Zadran, the tribal affairs minister, "promised that he would take 700 delegates from the loya jirga to the former king's house on Tuesday to show the strength of support for his candidacy."[376] Shah was eventually relegated to the symbolic role of "father of the country."

When over 1,200 of the 1,500 delegates voted for Karzai on June 13, it came as no surprise. As the *New York Times* had reported in late May, "[Karzai] is expected to win an easy victory and lead the new government, Afghan officials and Western diplomats said."[377] The predictions of "Western diplomats" have a strange way of being fulfilled, especially after the careful intervention of the U.S. special envoy and other "high-level officials" to ensure that there was no real choice in the matter. After the vote, the *Times* noted that "the grand council did what had been expected of it today" by electing Karzai. Sima Samar, the interim Minister for Women's Affairs, commented wryly to the BBC: "This is not a democracy, it is a rubber stamp. Everything has already been decided by the powerful ones."[378] The "powerful ones," namely the U.S. government and its allies, have made sure that the leader of Afghanistan was not someone who could challenge their power.

AT THE MERCY OF WARLORDS

In the months leading up to the 2002 Emergency *Loya Jirga*, there was a marked increase in violence by various warlords and their armies. When UN election observers entered the city of Gardez, the local commander fired rockets at them.[379] Eight delegates to the *Loya Jirga* were murdered there in May. In February in Mazar-e Sharif, the city ruled by the Northern Alliance's Abdul Rashid Dostum, "armed men broke into the home of an Afghan aid worker and raped the women and looted all the household assets." In the same city in April, a UN employee was dragged from his bed and killed by gunmen.[380]

The delegate selection process leading up to the *Loya Jirga* was wracked with problems caused by the warlords. Afghan provinces had expected to elect their own delegates to represent them. But in many cases "independent candidates [were] . . . detained or beaten by local commanders intent on sending their own delegates to the loya jirga. More often, warlords simply drew up their own lists of delegates and insisted that the local populace approve them."[381] As a result many powerful commanders strong-armed their way into the political process. According to a UN election observer, "We have found some illegal methods in the elections and interference by the Northern Alliance, such as sending money and mobile phones to their supporters" to garner votes. One observer for the International Crisis Group claimed, "Just before the Loya Jirga . . . up to one hundred extra 'political delegates' were summarily added to the rolls." They were "mostly provincial governors and other political-military figures unwilling or unable to stand for election," whose presence on the ballot "constituted a blanket of intimidation upon the delegates."[382]

After the postponed opening of the council, followed by the announcement that Zahir Shah would have no place in the new government, the warlords were ecstatic. "[T]he atmosphere of the *Loya Jirga* changed radically. The gathering was now teeming with intelligence agents, who openly threatened reform-minded delegates, especially women. Access to the microphone was controlled by supporters of the interim government." One woman delegate told Human Rights Watch, "We are hostages of the people who destroyed Afghanistan. They are trying to hold us hostage to their power. There are petitions being circulated and we are pressed to just sign them without reading them." When she complained publicly, the delegate was later threatened with the words, "You either mend your ways or we will mend them for you." A Human Rights Watch press release attributed the problem to the inclusion of major U.S.-backed Northern Alliance figures in the meetings, people "widely held responsible for Afghanistan's devastating decade of civil war and ensuing atrocities" during the 1990s. According to the rules of the *Loya Jirga*, war criminals were to be excluded, but Human Rights Watch "is not aware of a single case in which this exclusion clause was used, despite the presence of some of Afghanistan's most abusive warlords among the delegates."[383]

Sam Zia-Zarifi of Human Rights Watch explained, "Warlords are making a power grab by brazenly manipulating the *Loya Jirga* selection process. If they succeed, Afghans will again be denied the ability to choose their own leaders and build civil society."[384] The CIA agreed. In a leaked report the agency warned, "Afghanistan could once again fall into violent chaos if steps are not taken to restrain the competition for power among rival warlords and to control ethnic tensions."[385]

After Karzai was picked as "transitional" leader and the *Loya Jirga* had nearly ended, on June 19 the new president unveiled his interim cabinet for the next two years, before the country's first elections. Predictably, most of the posts were awarded to warlord members of the Northern Alliance. The *Christian Science Monitor* called the new government "a rogue's gallery."[386] Human Rights Watch's Salman Zia-Zarifi said, "Afghanistan's warlords are stronger today than they were ten days ago before the *Loya Jirga* started." *Loya Jirga* delegates Zakhilwal and Niazi described their reactions:

> Our hearts sank when we heard President Hamid Karzai pronounce one name after another. A woman activist turned to us in disbelief: "This is worse than our worst expectations. The warlords have been promoted and the professionals kicked out. Who calls this democracy?" . . . The key ministries of defense and foreign affairs remain in the hands of Muhammad Qasim Fahim and Abdullah, both from the dominant Northern Alliance faction based in the Panjshir Valley. . . . Three powerful Northern Alliance commanders—Mr. Fahim, Haji Abdul Qadir and Kharim Khalili—have been made vice presidents. . . . These are the very forces responsible for countless brutalities under the Mujahideen government. . . . As the loya jirga folded its tent, we met with frustration and anger in the streets. "Why did you legitimize an illegitimate government?" one Kabul resident asked us. The truth is we didn't. . . . [W]e

delegates were denied anything more than a symbolic role in the selection process.[387]

It is significant that the *New York Times* and the *Washington Post* published separate accounts by Omar Zakhilwal criticizing the outcome of the *Loya Jirga* (the piece excerpted above was cowritten by Adeena Niazi), but both articles were published as "opinion" pieces, not as "news." So-called "news" articles instead focused on the chaos of the meetings, trivializing the controversies, yet praising the "balanced" outcome. The *New York Times* said that Karzai's cabinet "showed a careful balance of factions and ethnic groups. . . . Despite Mr. Karzai's declared intention of promoting professionals in his cabinet, his appointments clearly reflected the need to please the various regional and ethnic groups."[388] In this context, "various regional and ethnic groups" means "warlords." For example, the son of Ismail Khan, called "the strongman of Herat," was given the ministry of aviation and tourism. The newspaper rather nonchalantly noted that women's rights might get eliminated from Karzai's agenda: "The ministry of women's affairs was not mentioned for the new cabinet and may have been cut along with one of only two women ministers in the last government, Dr. Sima Samar." In the end, the ministry was not cut, but Samar was removed from her post because of "blasphemy" charges after making remarks on women's rights. Habiba Sarabi would replace Samar later that month.

J. Alexander Thier, a representative of the Brussels-based International Crisis Group, called the *Loya Jirga* an "enormous missed opportunity"[389] to weaken the power of the warlords. Referring to the *Loya Jirga*, Salman Zia-Zarifi from Human Rights Watch said, "Short term political expediency has clearly triumphed over human rights."[390] *The Guardian* of London complained that "The West Is Walking Away from Afghanistan—Again."[391] But these criticisms miss the point. By actively shaping events so that the politically weak Hamid Karzai was unchallenged by Zahir Shah, whom the "vast majority . . . viewed . . . as the only leader with enough popular support and independence to stand up to the warlords,"[392] the U.S. envoy was *taking* an opportunity. Far from "walking away," the West was deliberately manipulating the politics of Afghanistan so that a weak leader who depended on foreign backing and who needed to appease the warlords was installed. Following elimination of Zahir Shah from the running, it was impossible simply to allow the delegates, many of whom had a strong human rights agenda and were intent on weakening the warlords, either to vote or speak their minds freely and fairly.

First Khalilzad, and then Karzai, justified the inclusion of warlords in the new government as a choice between "peace" (warlords in government) and "justice" (warlords on trial). On June 10, 2002, Khalilzad commented: "The question really is how to balance the requirements of peace, which sometimes necessitates difficult compromises, and the requirements of justice, which require accountability."[393] Two days later, Karzai echoed Khalilzad in an interview with the BBC: "I said first peace, stabilize peace, make it certain, make it stand on its own feet, and then go for justice. But if we can have justice while we are seeking peace, we will go for that too. So justice becomes a luxury for now. We must not lose peace for that."[394] Just as the Taliban were once considered capable of "ending the anarchy" (bringing peace), the warlords were somehow expected to do the same.

THE NEW CONSTITUTION: A STEP BACKWARD FOR DEMOCRACY*

The Constitutional *Loya Jirga* of January 2004 was the third event in the Bonn Process, at which elected delegates from around the country were theoretically supposed to agree on a new constitution. It was not the first time Afghanistan had a constitution. In fact, the 2004 document is based on Afghanistan's first constitution from 1964, brought into force when Zahir Shah was still king.

Declassified records from the period of Shah's rule give a glimpse into the U.S. government perspective on the first Afghan constitution. In 1973, U.S. Embassy political officer Charles F. Dunbar cabled the State Department:

> Afghans have become acutely conscious, and indeed jealous, of

* Parts of this and the following section are based on James Ingalls, "The New Afghan Constitution: A Step Backwards for Democracy," *Foreign Policy in Focus*, March 2004.

> the personal freedoms guaranteed them under the 1964 Constitution. This consciousness has manifested itself in hitherto undreamed-of criticism of the government by members of parliament, students, and the free press. . . . Many educated Afghans carry the Constitution in their pockets and quote from it extensively.[395]

A 1970 analysis by Dunbar discussed "clerical unrest" and demonstrations by religious leaders against "atheistic communism," but concluded, "mullahs [religious leaders] probably did little to change the views of the segments of the society at which the communist appeal is aimed." Interestingly, the report also found that

> Religious conservatism, for the first time in many years, vividly demonstrated that it remains a force with which the government must contend. Nevertheless, the existence of a reasonably strong army, *the absence of outside assistance*, and a basically conciliatory government policy, has so far prevented the situation from getting out of hand. . . . [T]he demonstrations may ultimately come to be regarded as proof of the mettle of the society and the democratic experiment [emphasis added].[396]

Dunbar's mention of "the absence of outside assistance" to the mullahs is ominous in hindsight, given that the U.S. tipped the ideological scales in Afghanistan with billions of dollars worth of weapons and cash to religious fundamentalists in the 1980s, and again after 9/11. These artificial infusions of power to religious conservatives are the main reasons why they are forces to reckon within Afghanistan today.

Like the first two milestones in the Bonn Process, the 2004 constitutional meetings were notorious in that the Northern Alliance factions were allowed to participate as legitimate representatives of the people.[397] According to John Sifton of Human Rights Watch, the process of selecting representatives for the assembly was once again characterized by "vote-buying, death threats and naked power politics."[398] He recounted,

> [We] documented numerous cases of local military or intelligence commanders intimidating candidates and purchasing votes. In Kabul, guarded by international security forces, intelligence and military officials were openly mingling with candidates at an election site. Many candidates complained of an atmosphere of fear and corruption. In areas outside of Kabul, many independent candidates were too afraid to even run. In a few cases, factional leaders themselves were elected—despite rules barring government officials from serving as delegates. The majority of the 502 delegates to the *Loya Jirga* were members of voting blocs controlled by military faction leaders, or warlords. While some legitimate representatives were elected, they were outnumbered—and scared.[399]

On the floor of the assembly, a young delegate named Malalai Joya risked her life by denouncing the warlords present, calling for their trial for war crimes. Her microphone was immediately cut off and she became the target of death threats, leading the UN to provide her with bodyguards (see Chapter 5).

Meanwhile, warlords in Washington were engaging in their own form of intimidation, directed at the Afghan population residing in the extensive border with Pakistan. A week before the constitutional *Loya Jirga,* the United States began "Operation Avalanche," its largest military campaign in Afghanistan since the fall of the Taliban. The operation was part of a "security plan" to keep the *Loya Jirga* free from terrorist attacks, which had been rising dramatically throughout the country.[400] "We want to take the offensive . . . to keep them busy protecting and defending themselves," U.S. ambassador Khalilzad said. Here, "them" was intended to mean terrorists, but anyone in the way of Operation Avalanche was unlikely to be spared. The title was surprisingly frank in evoking the U.S. military as an unstoppable force of nature, indiscriminately destroying whatever is in its path. In the first week of the assault, U.S. forces proved that assessment correct, killing fifteen children in two separate aerial attacks aimed at single individuals. Lt. Col. Bryan Hilferty absolved the U.S. military by blaming the children for being in the path of Operation Avalanche: "if noncombatants surround themselves with thousands of weapons . . . in a compound known to be used by a terrorist, we are not completely responsible for the consequences." Hilferty did express regret for the massacres, but not because they were war crimes; rather, "such mistakes could make the Afghan people think ill of the coalition." After the first air raid killed nine children, the UN envoy to Afghanistan, Lakhdar Brahimi, said, "[it] adds to a sense of insecurity and fear in the country." The *Washington Post* reported that the U.S. air strikes, together with antigovernment terrorist attacks, "have cast a jittery pall over preparations" for the constitutional assembly.[401]

On January 4, 2004, in an act described by many as a positive step toward democracy, the gathered delegates accepted almost unchanged a draft constitution for Afghanistan presented to them by Karzai. U.S. ambassador to Afghanistan Zalmay Khalilzad wrote, "Afghans have seized the opportunity provided by the United States and its international partners to lay the foundation for democratic institutions and provide a framework for national elections."[402] Khalilzad did not comment on the undemocratic atmosphere of intimidation fomented by U.S. allies. In addition to its propaganda value as "proof" that U.S. actions lead to democracy, the constitution cements a political power structure that legitimizes the long-term intentions of the U.S. for Afghanistan.

Despite the fact that the constitution mandates a National Assembly, or Parliament, with the ability to enact laws, overwhelming political power is allocated to the president. A strong presidency is not necessary for democracy, but it is a lot easier for an external empire to exert control if one person holds most of the power. According to an op-ed in *Gulf News*, "A centralized presidency in Kabul must be the surest way of maintaining the Afghan government's support for U.S.-led policies . . . diluting authority is bound to bring in voices of dissent on matters [bearing on] Washington's interests."[403]

A paper by the International Crisis Group, a mainstream Brussels-based think tank (board members include Zbigniew Brzezinski, Wesley Clark, and George Soros), analyzed the draft constitution presented by Karzai to the delegates (this draft was accepted with minor changes).[404] According to the report, that version of the constitution "would fail to provide meaningful democratic governance, including power-sharing, a system of checks and balances, or mechanisms for increasing the representation of ethnic, regional and other minority groups." The ICG criticized "the manner in which the draft has been prepared and publicized, as well as its content," all of which "raise serious questions about whether it can become the first constitution in Afghanistan's history to command genuinely deep popular support." An earlier draft described a prime ministerial position to balance the power of the president. But, according to the ICG, president Karzai changed the draft because of a "strong desire . . . for a purely presidential system." Apparently it was not Karzai's idea alone. It is "the perception of many Afghans" that the notion of a strong presidency grew out of "the U.S. desire to ensure Karzai is in firm control, or at least unchallenged while he struggles to assert his authority over other powerful players."

Many Afghans also found fault with Karzai's draft. Controversy over presidential power actually threatened to shut down the constitutional *Loya Jirga* when 48 percent of the delegates boycotted the vote. Karzai was furious, declaring, "There won't be any deals on Afghanistan's system of government, neither with jihadi leaders nor with anyone else."[405] An interesting choice of words, since in the end it was a "backroom agreement" brokered by U.S. and UN officials that led to the withdrawal of objections to a strong presidency.[406]

Karzai and his backers in the U.S. and the UN portrayed the proponents of a more representative system as "rivals of Karzai, mainly from the Northern Alliance."[407] In other words, they are warlords with independent fiefdoms anxious to legitimize their power at Karzai's expense. While it is true that the warlords stand to benefit from a decentralized government, there are many problems with the view that a strong presidency is the only way to weaken the power of the warlords. First, it ignores the tacit legalization and bolstering of warlord power resulting from decades of U.S. strategic decisions, and puts the burden for disempowering them on Afghan shoulders. Second, while the lack of a prime-ministerial position ensures that a warlord figure will currently not be able to share power with Karzai, a presidency with few checks and balances makes more likely the takeover of Afghanistan by such a figure in the future (as in a Musharraf-style coup, or a Central-Asian-style authoritarian regime). And third, the boycott was instigated and joined by many Afghans who are not members of the Northern Alliance or other warlord factions. For example, Mustafa Etemadi, a member of the Shiite Hazara minority, who said, "We did not go to vote because our people's desires were not respected. We want far-reaching democracy in this country, we want our parliament to have more authority." Habiba, a teacher from Kabul, had a similar message: "We want a strong parliament alongside the president, equal rights for men and women, democracy among all the ethnic groups, and recognition of all the languages of the nation. The constitution is not for one tribe or one people, it belongs to all the people of the country."[408]

Although the assembly was dominated by Karzai and his U.S.-backed elite on one hand and the Northern Alliance warlords on the other, there were "less-powerful groups: women delegates, ethnic Hazaras, former Communists, and ethnic Uzbeks" who strove for a parliamentary system. They also fought for the few lines of the constitution giving women some recognition—women's rights are declared equal to those of men, and over 25 percent of seats in the lower house of parliament are reserved for women. In contrast, U.S. concerns at the constitutional *Loya Jirga* were strictly power-related, centering on the need to control the people with a dominant president. Other causes, such as human rights and bringing warlords to justice, were not considered important enough to advocate.

THE RETURN OF ISLAMIC LAW

Ultimately, the adopted constitution asserted equality for men and women, something that even the U.S. constitution does not claim: "The citizens of Afghanistan—whether man or woman—have equal rights and duties before the law" (Article 22). President Bush hailed the constitution as a victory for women's rights, claiming, "The amazing accomplishment . . . is that Afghanistan has a new constitution that guarantees full participation by women. . . . All Afghan citizens, regardless of gender, now have equal rights before the law."[409] Possibly negating any rights of women, however, is the ominous inclusion of the supremacy of Islamic law: "In Afghanistan, no law can be contrary to the beliefs and provisions of the sacred religion of Islam" (Article 3). Wasay Engineer, a member of the secular, prodemocracy Solidarity Party of Afghanistan, told us that his party tried to stop this, joining an effort to gather signatures from more than 150 delegates at the *Loya Jirga* who supported a secular government.[410] The petition was ignored and Afghanistan declared an "Islamic Republic." As if to underscore the danger for women under a nonsecular government, the chairman of the constitutional *Loya Jirga*, former Mujahideen president Sibghatullah Mojadedi, said to the women delegates at the convention, "Even God has not given you equal rights because under his decision two women are counted as equal to one man."[411] Like any religious framework, Islamic law is open to interpretation. The Taliban's official oppression of women invoked Islamic Sharia law and could be considered legal under this constitution.

The possibility that the supremacy of Islamic law could be used to further oppress Afghan women is quite serious, given the membership of Afghanistan's courts. Fazil Hadi Shinwari, an elderly ultrafundamentalist cleric with no training in secular law, was "appointed" Chief Justice of the Supreme Court by the Northern Alliance's Burhanuddin Rabbani in 2001 during the political vacuum left by the Taliban. Shinwari was reconfirmed by Karzai in 2002[412] despite the fact that he had shown his fundamentalist colors by upholding a 2001 charge of blasphemy against then–Minister of Women's Affairs Sima Samar, who said she did not believe in Islamic or Sharia law. (Blasphemy can carry the death penalty in Sharia law). Shinwari has revived the Taliban ban on cable television and has attempted to ban women from singing and dancing in public. He has declared that adulterers would be stoned to death, the hands of thieves amputated, and consumers of alcohol given eighty lashes. Speaking to a National Public Radio correspondent about the supremacy of Islam, he explained that "First, a man should be politely invited to accept Islam; second, if he does not convert, he should obey Islam. The third option, if he refuses, is to behead him." In an ominous throwback to the Mujahideen and Taliban Ministry for the Promotion of Virtue and the Prevention of Vice, the interim Afghan government under Karzai established a religious law-enforcement apparatus called the Accountability Department, which functions under the direct authority of Shinwari's supreme court.[413]

Since his appointment by Karzai, Shinwari has been consolidating his power and expanding the power of extremist advocates of Sharia law. According to a report by the International Crisis Group,

> Shinwari has rapidly placed political allies in key positions, even expanding the number of Supreme Court judges from nine to 137. Of the 36 Supreme Court judges whose educational qualifications are known, not one has a degree in secular law. Shinwari's actions, together with the re-emergence of a ministry to promote Islamic virtue, have added to fears that the judicial system has been taken over by hard-liners before the Afghan people have had a chance to express their will in a democratic process.

A draft of the Afghan constitution was closely examined by a group of "Islamic leaders from across the country" at a gathering organized by Shinwari. They concluded that "the only source of legislation in Afghanistan is Islamic Sharia Law" and, regarding women, "they should dress in an Islamic manner and observe hijab."[414]

The explicit inclusion of Islamic law also reduces the possibility of future secular advances in Afghan society. According to Article 35 of the constitution, "The citizens of Afghanistan have the right to form political parties in accordance with the provisions of law, provided that: 1. The program and charter of the party are not contrary to the provision of the sacred religion of Islam . . ." This could exclude political parties like the Solidarity Party that espouse secular government as part of their platform. Regarding education, Article 45 states, "The state shall devise and implement a unified educational curriculum based on the provisions of the sacred religion of Islam . . ." and Article 54 states that "The state shall adopt necessary measures to ensure . . . the elimination of traditions contrary to the provisions of sacred religion of Islam." Justices of the Supreme Court are given the choice between a "higher education in law or in Islamic jurisprudence." Most strikingly, the constitution bars any future changes that would impact the supremacy of Islamic law: "The provisions of adherence to the provisions of the sacred religion of Islam and the republican regime cannot be amended" (Article 149).

Claiming to speak for everybody, Chief Justice Shinwari said, "Only an Islamic government is acceptable to the Afghan people."[415] In fact, Islamic government is not necessarily a popular notion. A delegate from Farah province, Malalai Joya, explained to us that many of her constituents want a secular government:

> I wish that one day our government will be a secular government because . . . under the name of Islam, these criminals [warlords] did a lot of crimes against our people, especially against the women of Afghanistan. You should ask the poor people of Afghanistan . . . the women who do not have education . . . [who] know very well about these criminals—how they use the name of Islam and did crimes. This is the reason our people want a secular government.[416]

Islamic Sharia law has in many scenarios been interpreted most viciously against women and indeed, under Shinwari, it is being exploited to its fullest extent. Kabul's prisons are filling up with women in the years after the passage of the constitution. Meena Siddiqui, a human rights lawyer in Kabul, explained to us that

> if a woman's father says I will marry you to the butcher but she says no, I am an educated girl, I don't want to marry the butcher, she has to run away from home and take a job in a restaurant. They say this is a big crime in Afghanistan, if a girl runs away from her family for even one day or night, it's a big crime for a girl. I have seen a lot of cases like this where girls come to me and tell me that she [*sic*] has had violence committed against her in her house and she doesn't want to marry a certain man. That's why most women go to prison. . . . Clause 130

> of the Constitution says that if small crimes like this are not solved by the government, they should be given to the "Qazi"—the man who works in the Supreme Court—the chief justice like Shinwari. Due to Islamic rules, he orders her to prison.[417]

Article 34 of the constitution enshrines the "freedom of expression," but this means little under a fundamentalist court. Deputy Chief Justice Ahmed Fazel Manawi, in examining a draft of the constitution, declared that "Islamic values should be taken into consideration in the media. If the press publish something which is considered a crime under Islamic law, they will be considered criminals and questioned."[418] This was not an empty threat—journalists who question the current order are arrested and intimidated. "Killing You is a Very Easy Thing For Us," is the title of a Human Rights Watch report, referring to a threat received by an editor who published a political cartoon lampooning Defense Minister Fahim.[419] One story that received limited mention in the U.S. press was that of the editors of the weekly newspaper *Aftab*, Mir Hussein Mahdawi and his assistant Ali Reza. The two were arrested in 2003 for "blasphemy" after publishing an editorial entitled "Holy Fascism" criticizing the Afghan warlords and some mullahs for "crimes committed in Islam's name." The piece denounced many of the U.S.-backed leaders of the Northern Alliance, including then–vice president Abdul Karim Khalili. The journalists were released on orders from president Karzai, but the blasphemy charge was sustained. Karzai said he believed in press freedom but that "It is our job to protect the Afghan people's . . . religious beliefs. . . . We will naturally take measures whenever we see that the foundations of the Afghan people's beliefs are violated. This does not mean a disregard for the freedom of the press, it is rather respect for the freedom of the press."[420]

Some journalists in Afghanistan find fault with Karzai's notion of "freedom of the press." Noorani, the editor of an independent weekly newspaper, *Rozgaran* ("News of the Day"), has published strong critiques of the warlords. He told us that in retaliation:

> I have been threatened several times and they have created lots of problems for me. They have threatened me by telephone. . . . They have called me several times to make clear some points of Rozgaran because some of the figures have accused me or my paper for writing about warlords and about government. . . . They have warned me two times and if I get warned a third time, then they may close my publication. I rarely come to my office—only if there is very urgent work.[421]

Gulalai Habibi, the editor of *Shafaq*, is also the target of threats for openly writing about women's rights and the impact of warlords. She told us that despite the threats she plans to continue her life-risking work:

> I know that if I write against the warlords my life will be in danger and my family will be in danger, but what should we do? If our generation will not disclose their wrongdoings in Afghanistan, they will continue for more generations and then our country will be destroyed forever. . . . I am not afraid of them. Nobody is pushing me to do this—I feel compelled to do it.[422]

PRESIDENTIAL ELECTIONS: A WATERSHED FOR WASHINGTON*

The next step to a permanent post-Taliban government prescribed at the Bonn Conference was the 2004 presidential election (parliamentary elections, scheduled for the same time, were postponed several times and eventually rescheduled for September 2005). In the lead-up to the elections, there was much media hype surrounding the event. To the Bush administration and media pundits, presidential elections in Afghanistan were supposed to bring the country closer to being a "democracy," where people decided their own fate. *Business Week* described the elections as a "first test" of Bush's claim that Afghanistan and Iraq "are on the path to democracy." In a *Washing-*

* Parts of this section are based on James Ingalls and Sonali Kolhatkar, "Afghan Elections: U.S. Solution to a U.S. Problem," *Foreign Policy in Focus*, October 6, 2004.

ton Post opinion piece, Andrew Reynolds of the University of North Carolina similarly described the elections as a "Test for Afghan Democracy." In this view, any failure of the process would be caused by a lack of readiness of Afghanistan and its people for "democracy," not a failure of external players to fulfill their responsibilities to the country. What was being tested was solely the capacity of Afghans to embrace democracy. Indeed, *Business Week* described only indigenous threats to the elections exercise: "Power brokers are trying to cut deals to eliminate competitive elections. Violence against election workers and politicians is on the rise. . . . Hardly anyone expects the voting to meet international standards."

As if surprised by the fact that Afghans could want a voice in their country's future, George W. Bush touted the fact that over 10 million Afghans registered to vote as "a resounding endorsement for democracy."[423] But the *New York Times*' Paul Krugman didn't believe the numbers, suggesting that "what they call evidence of democracy on the march is actually evidence of large-scale electoral fraud."[424] As the registration polls closed seven weeks before the elections, election officials reported that the number of voting cards issued far exceeded the estimated number of eligible voters. Reporters for the *Toronto Star* spoke with a man who registered six times and heard reports of a woman who obtained forty registration cards while wearing a burqa.[425] A commonly cited statistic was the estimated 10 percent over-registration countrywide. According to *Business Week*, "some areas have registration rates as high as 140 percent of projected eligible voters." At a press conference in August 2004, Karzai was questioned about multiple registrations, to which he responded, "This is an exercise in democracy. Let them exercise it twice!"[426] This was definitely disturbing, and a blow to Bush's own propaganda citing ten million registered voters.

The focus on voter fraud, however, kept the emphasis on the *Afghan* failure to measure up to international standards. Few media outlets dared to blame the United States for the more egregious fraud of imposing early elections on a still war-ravaged country where Northern Alliance warlords legitimized by Washington continued to hold real power, regardless of who won the vote. The Afghanistan Research and

Evaluation Unit (AREU), in a report entitled "Afghan Elections: The Great Gamble," pointed out:

> Just as elections have the potential to be a catalyst for positive change, there is also significant risk that elections held before key conditions are in place will actually do more harm than good. There is a real danger that the enormous amounts of human and financial resources that will be spent on getting a president elected will be at the expense of the more important task of reforming and strengthening state institutions . . .[427]

More disturbing than ordinary Afghans registering multiple times were incidents of voter intimidation by election candidates and local commanders. Brad Adams, Asia director of Human Rights Watch, said, "Many voters in rural areas say the [warlord] militias have already told them how to vote, and that they're afraid of disobeying them."[428] In particular, Human Rights Watch found that warlord candidates in the north who have received U.S. support at one time or another—Abdul Rashid Dostum, Atta Mohammad, and Mohammad Mohaqqeq—engaged in bribery, threats, and the confiscation of voter-registration cards to ensure that rural civilians would vote for them. In the west, forces loyal to Ismail Khan "were continuing to threaten independent political activity and stifle free speech" up until his removal from the governorship of Herat in September 2004. In the southern province of Wardak, a local commander called a meeting of elders in September and threatened them to vote for Karzai. "He [the commander] told them, 'If you don't vote for Karzai, and then something happens to you, it will be your responsibility.'"[429] A September 2004 survey by the Human Rights Research and Advocacy Consortium made up of NGOs working in Afghanistan found that voter intimidation was more common in the southern and eastern provinces of the country. When asked who was responsible for the intimidation, 86 percent of respondents said "commanders."[430] Voter intimidation by warlords, directly linked to U.S. policy, was not as sensationalized by the media as were flaws in the average Afghan's ability to vote by the book.

In reality the Afghan presidential elections were not as much a test of "Afghan democracy" as of Washington's ability to impose its political order on a country. An editorial in *Newsday* held that "historic elections in Afghanistan and Iraq are key goals of U.S. foreign policy, especially for President George W. Bush, who is campaigning on his determination that they be held on schedule." According to Reynolds in the *Washington Post*, the elections were to be "a watershed moment [for Afghanistan], equal in importance to the post-Sept. 11 ousting of the Taliban." Since the warlords that run most of the country are as bad as or worse than the Taliban, the ousting of the Taliban was more a watershed for Washington than for the Afghan people. Likewise for the presidential elections.

For the Afghan elections to provide an effective showcase of U.S. foreign policy, it was imperative that the election process remain smooth and free of violence. In the lead-up to the polls, the antielection violence threatened by the Taliban and other groups largely did not materialize, due to a heavy military and police presence throughout the country. There were only "scattered rocket and grenade explosions across the country and a smattering of attacks on election sites." The United States and Afghan governments deployed over 100,000 security personnel (mostly Afghan, with 18,000 U.S. troops and 7,000 NATO forces backing them up) to polling places and at checkpoints on important roads. The deployment was part of "a sophisticated, nationwide security strategy."[431] In a year in which security had been "deteriorating," according to NATO public relations, with the number of violent attacks steadily increasing, it was notable that the U.S. waited until the election to show that all along it could have brought desperately needed security to the country. As expected, that level of security was not sustained after the election was over.

Over the months leading up to the elections, just as it had done in the earlier stages of the Bonn Process, the U.S. attempted to engineer a situation where the only real choice for the Afghan electorate was Hamid Karzai. This was accomplished by bolstering his standing with ordinary people and reshaping public perception. To do this, U.S. officials admitted in September 2003 that they "wanted to accelerate U.S. reconstruction efforts in a bid to ensure that Afghan people enjoy the benefits of the U.S.-backed rule of President Hamid Karzai before elections."[432]

Ensuring Karzai's success also meant eliminating any serious challengers to his candidacy. Zalmay Khalilzad was reported as saying, "Afghan warlords, whom Washington previously tolerated as allies against the Taliban, would be 'marginalized' if they continued using guns to impose their will."[433] The same day, President Karzai passed the "political parties law," which "bans political parties from having their own militias or affiliations with armed forces." Strangely, the law also banned "judges, prosecutors, officers, and other military personnel, police, and national security staff" from joining a party while still in office. This obviously narrowed the spectrum of possible challengers to Karzai's candidacy. Technically Karzai himself was ineligible to run for office, since the law also forbade parties that "receive funds from foreign sources." But apparently the U.S. is not regarded as a "foreign source."

To Afghans, the decree was long overdue. For example, the RAWA had for years called for "Debarment of higher-echelon individuals of Jihadi and Taliban parties from holding high public office," as well as "prosecution of all individuals who, during the past 23 years have committed high treason, war crimes, blatant violations of human rights and plunder of national assets." But it is not only the progressive organization RAWA that supports such goals. When asked in a survey if human-rights abusers should be removed from their posts in the government, 90 percent of Afghans replied "yes."[434]

But the political parties law was not calculated to bring justice to the Afghan people. According to some, Karzai's move was designed to prevent "Afghan warlords from using their private militias to intimidate voters,"[435] which is probably correct. But, more importantly for him, it also helped to eliminate much of his potential opposition. The law was formally approved a few days after members of the Northern Alliance militia, including officials in the defense ministry, declared that they would not support Karzai's campaign, but would run their own candidate instead. Karzai "reacted angrily" to the announcement, saying he was "fed up with coalition government." Washington was also worried. According to the *Washington Post,* "The threatened internal defection from Karzai comes at a critical time for Afghanistan's troubled transition to democracy, already a source of concern to the Bush administration, which strongly backs Karzai."[436] Rather than consider it a success of democracy, an increase in the number of candidates was seen as a threat to the "troubled transition to democracy."

The Bush administration also actively lobbied Karzai's opponents to not run. According to the *Los Angeles Times*, thirteen of the eighteen candidates complained about interference from Zalmay Khalilzad, the U.S. Ambassador. Khalilzad reportedly "requested" candidates to withdraw from the race, attempting to bribe them with positions in the Cabinet. Senior staff members of several candidates were described as "angry over what many Afghans see as foreign interference that could undermine the shaky foundations of a democracy the U.S. promised to build."[437]

While there were a total of eighteen candidates running, the U.S. media focused almost exclusively on Karzai, frequently dubbed "the favorite" in news reports. For the Bush administration it was imperative that their handpicked and well-trained candidate won. Not only would Karzai's victory cement the current order of U.S. influence, it would signal a victory for the "war on terror" as Bush defines it. Reynolds said, "Karzai's victory . . . would shine a ray of hope on an otherwise gloomy series of U.S. foreign policy misadventures."[438] This was a common assessment. The AREU concluded:

> There is a widely held perception that this enthusiasm for 2004 elections is a result of the Bush administration's need for a foreign policy and "war-on-terror" success ahead of the November 2004 presidential elections in the U.S., particularly as Iraq appears to be becoming less of a success by the day.[439]

AFTER THE ELECTION: DASHED HOPES

Unsurprisingly, Hamid Karzai won the elections with 55.4 percent of the popular vote, winning twenty-one of thirty-four provinces. The second-place candidate, Yunus Qanooni, got 16.3 percent of the vote.

Strictly in terms of voter participation, the presidential elections were a resounding success. According to the UN-administered Joint Election Management Body, over 8 million Afghans voted, more than three-quarters of the 10.5 million registered voters. Voter diversity was not quite as high, however. Even though women comprise approximately two-thirds of the population, they were 42 percent of registered voters on average. In some provinces in the southeast that figure dropped to 10 percent.[440] We spoke with ordinary citizens and civic leaders on the elections and found that Afghans were overwhelmingly appreciative of the ability to have a say in the leadership of their country and took pride in the high level of participation. "In my opinion the election was very good [because a] large amount of people participated," said Noorani, the editor of the Kabul-based *Rozgaran*.[441] In the remote Western province of Farah, Qasimi, an elected delegate to both of the *Loya Jirgas* and a candidate for parliamentary elections, characterized the elections as a "very important point in the history of Afghanistan". He boasted that "85 percent of the people in this area voted in the election. . . . In my village 2000 women and 1600 men registered." He beamed with pride as he emphasized that more women than men in his village showed the desire to vote.[442] Zakia, a Kabul Medical University student, told us, "as an Afghan woman I was proud to give vote to the person who I wanted to be the president of the country."[443]

A September 2004 report by the Human Rights Research and Advocacy Consortium describes interviews with over seven hundred Afghans "not heard or heeded in the corridors of power." Despite voter intimidation and threats of violence during the election, many of those interviewed reflected the belief that the elections would improve things significantly. One woman in Kandahar said, "If the new government is fair, it will bring great changes to our lives. We will feel more secure; women will be able to work without any fear; our country will be free from bad people." A man in Kabul expressed the hope that "If there is a permanent government, the guns will be collected [and] people will have jobs. Afghanistan will be a safe, comfortable society."[444]

Many Afghans, tired of decades of war, death, and destruction, saw the election as a way to send a message to Karzai that warlords must be removed from power. Just after polls closed, we wrote that the Afghan elections were "a cruel choice between two possibilities: a U.S.-controlled Hamid Karzai government with fascist fundamentalist warlords in subordinate positions; or a government completely controlled by the warlords. . . . It would be a mistake to say Afghans were charmed by Karzai."[445] Afghans simply picked what they viewed as the lesser of two evils, an assessment confirmed by our conversations with people in Afghanistan. Mehmooda, a member of the RAWA in Kabul, likened her group's situation to that of the "anybody-but-Bush" movement in the 2004 U.S. presidential election: "RAWA members voted for Karzai because he is not a warlord," she stated simply.

Wasay Engineer of the Solidarity Party of Afghanistan, one of many secular democratic parties, told us that most of the members of his party voted for Karzai because they saw the election as a "big struggle against the fundamentalists. . . . In these twenty to thirty years of war, our people have seen what they did in Afghanistan, how they destroyed the country and now people are fed up with them so that is why they didn't vote for them." Malalai Joya, a parliamentarian from Farah Province and a delegate to the Constitutional *Loya Jirga,* concurred with this logic. "In the presidential election, our people once more trusted Mr. Karzai. It has one reason—they wanted to show their hatred for the warlords. Mr. Karzai hadn't killed anybody." Shahir, the head of the Kilid media group, described the importance of the elections to him: "I see a chance even if I know that most of the game is fake and most people are unaware of their rights. But this is the first step in the process. Our warlords will see how much they are 'cherished' by the people." A woman in Mazar-e Sharif explained, "We want a president whose hands are not wet with the blood of the nation. Someone who will think of the people. It must be someone neutral, who is not a commander."[446]

Some Afghans and members of the international community alike pointed with triumph to unexpected, sky-high turnout, but other measures judge the success of the elections more harshly. Karzai's overwhelming victory says a lot about the will of the electorate. He ran on a platform that included "the strengthening of the security sector and ensuring lasting stability throughout the country . . . the disarmament and demobilization of former combatants . . . [promoting] the rule of law, and the protection of civil liberties and human rights." Hours after

Karzai released this statement, while he was still transitional president, he sacked the warlord Ismail Khan from his post as governor of Herat. People took this as a sign that an elected Karzai would finally eliminate warlords from positions of power in Afghanistan. Malalai Joya told us that "he promised through interviews and in different ways to the people that 'I will never . . . compromise with warlords.'"[447] For example, Karzai told the *New York Times* that "private militias are the country's greatest danger," and that his new struggle with warlords would be "decisive." At the same time, according to the *Times*, "Mr. Karzai spent much of the interview explaining the need for accommodation. He would be tough on the process of disarmament, not on individuals."[448]

J. Alexander Thier, a former legal advisor to Afghanistan's Constitutional and Judicial Reform Commissions, predicted the difficulties of holding free and fair elections in Afghanistan: "Holding elections without the rule of law can undermine democracy by sparking violence, sowing cynicism and allowing undemocratic forces to become entrenched."[449] Almost immediately after the October 9, 2004, elections, the people of Afghanistan experienced the undermining of democracy and the entrenchment of undemocratic forces that Thier foretold. It was not just absence of rule of law that caused this, but the actions of president Karzai himself. In his new cabinet, the elected President Karzai, with support from the United States, strengthened as many warlords as he weakened, dashing the hopes of most voters and ensuring that violence and injustice will remain a part of the institutional structure of Afghanistan, at least for the foreseeable future.

After losing at the polls, several warlords were appointed to government positions. After getting people's hopes up by firing Ismail Khan as governor of Herat, Karzai appointed him minister of energy. To his credit, Karzai sacked the warlords Defense Minister Fahim and Public Works Minister Gul Agha Sherzai, but then appointed Abdul Rashid Dostum, the former defense minister and a presidential candidate, as Afghanistan's army chief of staff. The decision to bring warlords into the central government is referred to as "co-opting," or even "neutralizing" them, with the rationale that joining the government forces warlords to relinquish their past positions and affiliations to political parties. In reality, the government positions serve to legitimize the very men that the Afghan people want tried for war crimes.[450]

The Afghans we spoke to emphasized disarmament of warlords as a way to neutralize their power, rather than appointment to a high office. To this end, the United Nations Assistance Mission in Afghanistan (UNAMA) launched a disarmament program entitled "Disarmament, Demobilization and Reintegration" (DDR) in 2003. DDR was greeted by thousands of women and children who gathered in Kunduz to welcome Karzai with banners that read "DDR will guarantee peace and prosperity for our nation" and "Let's have pens instead of arms."[451] When asked what the most important thing to do to improve security in Afghanistan was, 65 percent of Afghans surveyed said disarmament. This number was much higher, 87 percent, in the province of Mazar-e Sharif, where forces loyal to the two strongest regional commanders, Dostum and Atta Mohammed, often clash.[452] Habiba Sarabi, the first minister of women's affairs and currently governor of Bamiyan Province, predicted, "If the . . . DDR [disarmament] program will not complete, and warlords become again powerful, can you remember the time of 1992? That period will be repeated." Qasimi from Farah Province told us, "I recommend that first of all, the government should collect their [warlords'] weapons and after that, [they must go after] the most criminal people . . . the ones who killed children and women, and those who raped the women. If they have done so, they must go to the judge."[453]

Some, though, remain skeptical of DDR's effectiveness in reducing the prevalence of weapons. Noorani, editor of *Rozgaran*, is one such critic: "Those who have been disarmed, they have just given one Kalashnikov or one of their arms to the DDR process but they have more guns and weapons in their houses and they have [been] paid $200 USD. . . . During the past 20-25 years we have more than 2 million guns and they say that we will disarm 100,000. So where are the rest of the guns?" A female political activist from Kunduz agreed: "the DDR has failed in Afghanistan. Some guns were collected from people but that was symbolic, not real."[454]

It is clear that Afghan democracy cannot truly flourish until the United States no longer finds it in its interest to back armed warlords. Given the current state of affairs, it is hard to fault Noorani for his lack of optimism when, asked if he held out any hope that the warlords will some day lose power, he responded without hesitation, "No, there is no hope." No matter who has official power in Kabul, the U.S. is the real decision maker, something Afghans cannot change by voting.

A PARLIAMENT OF VULTURES

Afghan parliamentary elections were held on September 18, 2005, the first time in thirty years. These elections had the potential to be the most democratic exercises in Afghanistan's history. There was even a slim possibility of the civilian, nonfundamentalist majority in Afghanistan gaining more political power. Human Rights Watch felt that parliamentary and local elections might be "in many ways . . . a better barometer of political progress and women's rights than the presidential election." When pressed, Noorani shared our cautious optimism that the upcoming parliamentary elections could make a difference. According to him, three groups would be represented in the elections: "Firstly, Karzai and his technocrats, [secondly,] another group belonging to Qanooni, Dostum and Mohaqqeq [i.e., warlords], and the third: a group of intellectuals who are unhappy with the failure of Karzai and the warlords." He complained that this third group had little economic power and no support from the world community, and feared that they would not be allowed to run by the warlords.

If the results can be said to be a "barometer of political progress," then political progress in post-Taliban Afghanistan has been uneven. On one hand, 50 of the men elected to the lower house of Parliament (*Wolesi Jirga*, or "House of the People") are considered "independents, or educated professionals."[455] These people with relatively secular and progressive beliefs probably fall into the "technocrat" or "intellectual" categories Noorani mentioned. The parliament also includes sixty-eight women, guaranteeing at least some nonpatriarchal views. It is significant that six were elected in their own right, not via the quota system that guaranteed 25 percent of the 249 seats to women. In particular, Malalai Joya, an outspoken antiwarlord activist (see Chapter 5) got second place in Farah Province, with 7.3 percent of the votes.

On the other hand, about half of the seats in the lower house went to "religious figures or former fighters."[456] Most of the Afghan warlords who were not given a governorship or cabinet post in Hamid Karzai's administration have either been elected to the lower house or appointed by Karzai to the upper house (*Meshrano Jirga*, or "House of Elders"). These men, many of whom still have de facto power in the countryside due to past or present U.S. support, have now been given formal power via the electoral system. They include (in the lower house) Burhanuddin Rabbani, Abdul Rasul Sayyaf, Mohammad Mohaqqeq, Yunus Qanooni, supporters of Abdul Rashid Dostum, four former Taliban commanders, and forty members of Hisb-e-Islami, the party of Gulbuddin Hekmatyar.

Since former Mujahideen are in the majority, it was not surprising that the frontrunners for chair of the lower house were the Northern Alliance leaders Qanooni, Mohaqqeq, Sayyaf, and Rabbani. Amin Tarzi, the Afghanistan analyst for Radio Free Europe/Radio Liberty (RFE/RL), wrote, "The chances of the other contenders, including a third Kabul representative, Shokria Barakzai [the editor of the magazine *Women's Mirror*], do not seem very promising."[457] In the end Qanooni won the post.

In the 102-member upper house, Karzai appointed (among others) Sibghatullah Mojadedi, whose claims on the inferiority of women at the constitutional convention appear earlier in this chapter. Mojadedi, whom Karzai worked for in the anti-Soviet war, is described as a "close ally" of the president and was also picked by Karzai in 2005 to head the Afghan "Commission for Peace." Mojadedi won the chairmanship of the upper house under dubious circumstances. Apparently, he received fifty votes in the initial running, which, since it was not a majority, required a runoff between the two leading candidates. The second-place candidate, Bakhtar Aminzay, a former university chancellor, probably would have won, since the third-place candidate supported him, but Mojadedi threw a tantrum. He "objected strenuously . . . , threatening to walk out, and insisting as the first to declare jihad against the Soviet occupation twenty years ago, he deserved the post." Mojadedi is reported to have told

Aminzay, "If you respected me, you would not have run against me." Aminzay felt pressured to withdraw. "[Mojadedi] was crying and he was unhappy. And the elders advised me to step down."[458]

Karzai also appointed Marshal Mohammed Qasim Fahim to the "House of Elders." One of the most infamous and influential warlords in Afghanistan, Fahim is the former intelligence chief of the Northern Alliance and became military head of the Alliance after the death of Ahmed Shah Massoud. He was chosen as defense minister in Hamid Karzai's transitional administration, but was removed from the post at the end of 2004, supposedly to show that the president was getting tough on warlords. Bringing back to the government a man who still keeps his own private militia shows Karzai's real concern for "the country's greatest danger." One lower-house candidate from Sar-e Pul district complained that, "The commanders have changed their name: they call themselves 'elders' now. But they are still warlords."[459]

It was not surprising that, in a "democratic" contest, so many warlords and other conservative elements made it to the lower house of Parliament. This was because the elections were biased from the start in favor of those with unaccountable power.

First, few warlords were barred from running. According to election rules, individuals commanding private armies were to be disqualified. Throughout 2005, the Electoral Commission received complaints on 500 candidates who had ties to illegal armed groups (out of 5,800 total). By the election date, only thirty-two lower-profile candidates had actually been barred from running. Human Rights Watch reported, "None of the more senior commanders running in the elections, whose records of human rights violations are well-known to Afghans, were disqualified."[460]

In addition to the fact that few commanders were prevented from running, many of their secular and nonviolent opponents were. Many candidates described open threats; others feared retaliation if they ran. Human Rights Watch

> heard consistent reports from around the country of the fear inspired by commanders and their forces, whose past abuses

> remain fresh in the minds of ordinary Afghans. These complaints were heard in almost all regions of the country, and grew stronger as we moved away from urban areas where international security forces were present.[461]

Afghan reporters told HRW about "cases of intimidation involving the Mohaqqeq faction of Hisbi-I-Wahdat." In some cases, "candidates have been threatened anonymously by telephone," which they felt they had no means of addressing via official channels, since "they fear the persons threatening them may in fact be connected to government forces, or have connections with local police or military commanders." One woman candidate in Herat was threatened by a caller, "Don't run in this race. We will hurt you, we will kill you, we may even do something to your family." On another call, she was told "You should stop these things you're doing. . . . There's no need for an introduction, because by the time you know who we are, you won't be alive. Please, do not compete in this election." The candidate complained that, "There are no real mechanisms to protect women's rights, and when women are threatened, they don't have anyone to go to. . . . We can't trust the police."[462]

Even those candidates that were not threatened directly felt intimidated and did not feel free to speak their minds when campaigning, especially when criticizing warlords. A candidate from Takhar told Human Rights Watch, "We *are* afraid. These are powerful people. If I say something criticizing a commander, they can easily send someone to kill me. Who's going to protect me?" A candidate from Ghazni said, "When we give a speech, we don't name these people [local commanders], or criticize them, we just make veiled references to them, and to 'warlordism.'" A candidate in Mazar-e Sharif said similarly, "We refer to past crimes, we talk about the need for expertise instead of guns. That is as much as we can say. To say any more would cause real trouble."[463]

While candidates feared for their lives if they didn't defer to warlords, president Hamid Karzai has shown nothing but full support for the right of warlords to stand for government office. Much of this policy stems from former U.S. ambassador Zalmay Khalilzad, who advised Karzai to "co-opt" the warlords in pursuit of "peace," ignoring justice. Khalilzad endorsed Karzai's decision to appoint Abdul Rashid Dostum as army chief of staff, commenting in March 2005 that the "decision to give a role to . . . regional strongmen is a wise policy." The Independent National Commission for Peace in Afghanistan, a watered-down pro-warlord version of South Africa's Truth and Reconciliation Commission, has furthered this trend. Mojadedi, the commission's chair, has promised former Taliban fighters immunity from prosecution for war crimes. Under this program, initiated with the approval of Khalilzad, even Mullah Omar, the notorious Taliban chief, would be granted immunity if he recants his ways. According to Amin Tarzi of RFE/RL, "Both Mojadedi and Karzai have since backed off of those statements [that Omar could receive amnesty], but distrust has increased and the door of misuse of the reconciliation policy has opened wider."[464] Government acceptance of warlords not only legitimizes them, but forces the choice of disempowering them onto the Afghan people. A candidate from Mazar-e Sharif protested:

> The government says it has to let these men be [parliamentary] candidates because they could make problems. That is not true, but that is what they say. Well if the central government cannot stand up to them, will not stand up to them, how can they expect the people here—who live with these blood-thirsty commanders every day—to vote against them? We should not have to bear the pressure—it is the job of the government.[465]

Many voters themselves were threatened, or had serious reason to fear retaliation if they didn't vote for certain candidates. Human Rights Watch noted that "across the country, [there were] . . . cases in which local commanders or strongmen, or local government officials linked with them, have held meetings in which they have told voters and community leaders for whom to vote. In some cases . . . direct threats have been communicated." Besides these threats from warlord candidates, violence carried out by "remnants" of the Taliban, al-Qa'eda, or other Afghan formations, as well as U.S. soldiers, has created an environment in which it is difficult or dangerous for many Afghans to exercise their democratic rights.

In addition to targeting the U.S. and international troops, antigovernment groups had their sights on moderate Islamic clerics who supported the election process—of whom seven were killed in the run-up to the elections— as well as government officials, foreign aid workers, and people involved with the elections. Citizens were killed for carrying voter registration cards, and electoral workers have been attacked. A total of six candidates were attacked prior to elections, four of whom were killed, and two parliamentarians-elect were killed after the vote.

Even when they were not too afraid to vote against warlords, many voters had difficulty learning the political connections of candidates, because political party affiliations were not allowed on the ballots, due to rules set up by Karzai with the approval of the U.S. In other words, 5,800 candidates were effectively running as independents.

The high warlord participation, intimidation, and difficulty distinguishing commanders and fundamentalists from nonviolent secular candidates led many Afghans to decide not to vote. In all, 6.8 million out of 12.5 million registered voters, or about 54 percent, went to the polls. In Kabul Province, from which hailed Mohaqqeq, Qanooni, and Sayyaf, only 34 percent of the electorate voted. U.S. ambassador Ronald Neumann, who replaced Zalmay Khalilzad in March 2005, said that the low turnout was good, since it meant Afghanistan was as much of a democracy as the United States. "In America, only half of the people vote. If people are getting a little more used to elections, then maybe Afghanistan is turning into a normal country."[466] Hamid Abdullah, who supervised one of Kabul City's polling stations, told the BBC, "I simply did not find a good candidate . . . so I am not voting . . . I personally feel that the turnout is low because people don't like the candidates."[467] A shoe-mender in Kabul told Sam Zarifi of Human Rights Watch,

> I will not vote for any of them. I voted last year for Karzai, and I hoped that things would get better, but now I can barely make enough money for my family. None of the candidates are trustworthy and they do not care about us, just about their own success. . . . Tell the farangis [foreigners] that we need work, not these politicians.[468]

Professor Khalilullah Jamili, who teaches political philosophy and who is also a director of the Cultural Council at Kabul University, told *Asia Times Online*,

> I am facing a hopeless situation. . . . The current parliamentary elections were supposed to bring professionals, intellectuals and real politicians into the parliament so that they could legislate for the good in the country. However, what we perceive is the return of the same people who brought destruction to this country. . . . [M]y political acumen suggests another civil war after six months. Contradictions will emerge and people will point fingers negatively on the people they elected. Guns will remain the last answer for every problem, just like it has in the past.[469]

It appears that Karzai has basically ensured that the Parliament remains little more than a tool for his presidency, as it was designed to be in the constitution. Allowing warlords to run for the lower house and appointing them to the upper house gives them the legitimacy they need, while supposedly giving Karzai bargaining power with them. According to Amin Tarzi, the majority of the delegates now support the president, including most of the warlords.

> Karzai fares well at the outset, but he must navigate very dangerous currents. Some of his allies among the mujahedin may push for reinserting religion—their prerogative—into the politics of the country. [In addition,] Karzai would be placed in a compromising position if, as expected, some members of the Wolesi Jirga who have voiced concern about the crimes committed against the Afghans by some of their colleagues, try to debate past human rights abuses.[470]

Joanna Nathan of the International Crisis Group predicted that the assembly will be a "a weak and fractured, possibly even paralyzed body." Barnett Rubin of New York University said that the elections won't make much of a difference because "until Afghanistan has a functioning, legal economy and basic institutions, there's nothing really for a parliament to do except act as a kind of puppet platform for people's views." This is a best-case scenario, since in all likelihood the large Mujahideen contingent in the Parliament could drive Afghan politics further to the right.[471]

Thus, instead of the nominally more powerful president criticizing or disempowering warlords and other criminals, that task falls to the relatively few brave citizens and parliamentarians who choose to risk their lives.

THE RESULT: A CLIENT "DEMOCRACY"

On Afghanistan's presidential election day, October 9, 2004, President Bush boasted, "A great thing happened in Afghanistan. . . . Freedom is beautiful. Freedom is on the march."[472] In early 2005, Secretary of State Condoleezza Rice met with President Karzai and boasted at a press conference, "there could be no better story . . . than Afghanistan's democratic development."[473] After the Afghan parliament was sworn in, Vice President Dick Cheney asserted that "the victory of freedom in Afghanistan as well as Iraq will be an inspiration to democratic reformers in other lands."[474] But has democracy in Afghanistan really been achieved, and is true democracy even desired by the Bush administration?

There is no doubt that the people of Afghanistan overwhelmingly want democracy and the power to choose their own government. However, the simple act of voting in an election is not sufficient to produce a democracy, no matter how much the population welcomes the opportunity. Deeper examination has revealed that some basic elements of democracy are missing. First, the leaders of the Afghan people were chosen by foreign powers to suit their needs. The presidency has been fraught from the start with deceit and manipulation to keep out the popular former king Zahir Shah and ensure the rise of a U.S. puppet. Even though Karzai was eventually popularly elected, he was chosen as a lesser of two evils—it was either him or one of the warlords. As elected president he has openly broken his promise and, against the wishes of a majority of the people, promoted universally despised warlords into government positions.

Second, the continued prevalence of warlords, used by the U.S. to oust the Taliban, squashes prodemocracy political organizing of women and secular forces, whom they outnumber in the newly-elected Parliament. Warlords continue to rule most of the country outside Kabul, and remain unaccountable to the central government. Ordinary Afghans have little or no protection from persecution by these local and regional commanders.

Third, the constitution proclaims equality for men and women but also upholds the supremacy of Islamic law, which can be interpreted by extremists so as to squash dissent and abuse human rights. Indeed it is already being used to justify repression of women, activists, and journalists by an ultrafundamentalist Taliban-like justice ministry.

Fourth, an outside power—the United States—has leverage over the country's political affairs via Hamid Karzai because the constitution guarantees a strong presidency with power over a potentially more democratic parliament. Furthermore, U.S. troops still have free reign in the Afghan countryside, allying themselves with abusive warlords, committing grave abuses themselves, and weakening the sovereignty of the Afghan people. A 2005 report by the Kabul-based Afghanistan Justice Project pointed out,

> In replicating the same patterns of abuse that have marked the different phases of the conflict in Afghanistan [Soviet occupation, Mujahideen civil war, Taliban era] and allying themselves—for the sake of political expediency—with local commanders who have done the same, U.S. forces have jeopardized prospects for establishing stable and accountable institutions in Afghanistan, have undermined the security of the Afghan people . . . and have reinforced a pattern of impunity that undermines the legitimacy of the political process.[475]

All these factors make conditions extremely difficult for Afghans to decide their own destiny. It remains to be seen if U.S. policy makers will ever allow anything approaching democracy to break out in Afghanistan and interfere with their plans.

PART THREE

RHETORIC VS. REALITY

CHAPTER FIVE

"LIBERATION" RHETORIC AND BURQA OBSESSIONS

OBJECTIFYING AFGHAN WOMEN

> Good morning. I'm Laura Bush, and I'm delivering this week's radio address to kick off a world-wide effort to focus on the brutality against women and children by the al-Qa'eda terrorist network and the regime it supports in Afghanistan, the Taliban. That regime is now in retreat across much of the country, and the people of Afghanistan—especially women—are rejoicing. . . . Because of our recent military gains in much of Afghanistan, women are no longer imprisoned in their homes. They can listen to music and teach their daughters without fear of punishment. Yet the terrorists who helped rule that country now plot and plan in many countries. And they must be stopped. The fight against terrorism is also a fight for the rights and dignity of women.[476]

It was the first time that a first lady had delivered a solo performance during a weekly presidential radio address. Her impassioned speech captured the horror felt by many well-meaning women across the U.S. Mrs. Bush's speech was one of the many instances where a connection was made between the war in Afghanistan and the "liberation" of Afghan women by the Bush administration.

Prior to 9/11 and the ensuing U.S. war in Afghanistan, the oppression of Afghan women was already a hot topic among liberals and feminists, and the subject of numerous petitions floating through the Internet. Documentary films like Saira Shah's *Beneath the Veil* were being aired repeatedly on CNN, exposing shocking scenes of a woman's execution in the Kabul stadium.[477] A 1998 plan by Unocal Corporation to build a pipeline across Afghanistan that would benefit the Taliban was thwarted thanks to the loud protests of mainstream feminist groups like the Feminist Majority and others.[478]

As part of their anti–"Gender Apartheid" campaign, the Feminist Majority also publicized the Taliban's imposition of the burqa (the Afghan veil) to keep women out of sight. While effective at rallying anti-Taliban sentiment, campaigns that focused on the forced wearing of the burqa enabled women's groups to sensationalize the Taliban's abuse by keeping the message simple: Afghan women's oppression was limited to the burqa, and burqa-clad women needed saving by Western governments and their feminist organizations. After the attacks of September 11, 2001, it seemed to some liberals as though Laura Bush had finally caught on by "seizing an issue that had long been of concern to American women at the opposite end of the political spectrum."[479] And better still, her husband, George W. Bush, would now wage a war to "liberate" Afghan women.

The notoriety of the Taliban's abuse of women, together with the U.S. language of "liberation," had convinced many Americans, including well-meaning liberals and feminists, that the 2001 U.S. war on Afghanistan was "the first truly just war since World War II."[480] After all, "liberating" a nation from the grip of a barbaric regime sounded quite noble. Many liberal women's organizations condoned the Bush administration's war as a way for the U.S. to change Afghanistan's regime into one that would benefit women. Eleanor Smeal, the president of the Feminist Majority, accepting Operation Enduring Freedom as a legitimate means of upholding women's rights, announced: "Now, as we seek to remove this terrorist regime that has wreaked havoc, we must return women to their rightful place in society. We must establish a broad-based constitutional democracy that restores women's suffrage and insists that women be leaders and participants in that government."[481] Implying that the Bush administration's war was in response to her group's campaign for Afghan women, Smeal remarked hopefully, "Next time women speak about international issues, they'll [the U.S. government will] listen. . . . Our credibility will have gone up."[482]

By the end of 2001, the reign of the Taliban was over, and with it (we were told), the oppression of Afghan women. In his January 2002 State of the Union Address President Bush declared, "The last time we met in this chamber, the mothers and daughters of Afghanistan were captives in their own homes, forbidden from working or going to school. Today women are free."[483] Two years later, the freedom of Afghan women was still being declared. According to a January 2004 White House press release, "Millions of Afghan women . . . [are] experiencing freedom for the first time."

We showed in Chapter 3 how women were still struggling for their most basic freedoms, demonstrating the mendacity of the Bush administration propaganda. In this chapter we look at the exploitation of Afghan women's predicament by government officials, liberal feminists, and others. Among other things, we explore the historical context of "liberation" rhetoric and the obsession with the burqa as the arbiter of an Afghan woman's freedom.

POLITICS WITHOUT A RISK OR A DOWNSIDE

After 9/11, Karen Hughes, a counselor to President Bush, designed a publicity campaign to capitalize on Afghan women's oppression.[484] This campaign would widely publicize Afghan women's suffering under the Taliban and indirectly justify war. Hughes explained: "I thought focusing on the plight of Afghan women and girls was a way to highlight the cruel nature of the people we were up against."[485] Laura Bush's November 2001 radio debut launched the campaign on the same day that the State Department released a document entitled "The Taliban's War Against Women." This document began with these words: "Prior to the rise of the Taliban, women in Afghanistan were protected under law and increasingly afforded rights in Afghan society." What most Americans did not know was that it was *twenty years* before the Taliban's arrival that women had enjoyed some rights in Afghanistan. No mention was made of the extreme mistreatment of Afghan women by U.S.-

backed Mujahideen in the years right before the Taliban emerged. To bolster the narrow propaganda campaign for war, Mrs. Bush's counterpart in Britain, Cherie Blair, addressed Afghan women's oppression in news conferences, briefings, and media events a week later.[486]

Publicity for the war also involved media training for a handful of Afghan spokeswomen who functioned as token brown female faces that would lend the campaign legitimacy. Two weeks after Laura Bush's radio stint, a group of Afghan women immigrants in the U.S. were thrust into the spotlight by an organization called Vital Voices Global Partnership, a "well connected group that promotes women's leadership around the world."[487] They were hosted by Donna McClarty, the wife of former President Clinton's first chief of staff, and were trained in the art of giving media interviews. High-profile meetings were arranged with Laura Bush, Kofi Annan, and Madeleine Albright as well as a joint hearing with Senator Hillary Clinton. The Afghan immigrant women seemed "stunned and overwhelmed by all the attention."[488]

The campaign was an effective way for the Bush administration to tug at the heartstrings of millions of Americans and portray George W. Bush as the first president bold enough to wage a war to save women. But compared to the extremist Taliban and their attitudes toward women, practically anyone appears progressive, even an ultra-right-wing administration. This could be used to generate political capital. According to the *New York Times* Magazine:

> Promoting the liberation of Afghan women is a political stance without risk and without a downside. It is kind of like walking down the street and seeing a $100 bill lying on the sidewalk. The administration has to pick it up; it would be against human nature not to. It's also the perfect cause for Laura Bush. She can ally herself with women for whom any sort of life other than imprisonment is a liberation but protect herself from feminists and Hillary types like Susan Sontag and Barbara Kingsolver, because her position doesn't require any theory or analysis that might reflect on corporate or multinational goals of G.O.P. sponsors or the failures of American foreign policy over the years.[489]

Speaking out against the oppression of women by the Taliban allowed the Bush administration to score a bipartisan win, attracting both liberals and conservatives to their cause. "I think this is a great chance for them to do a gender gap number without rubbing up against the right wing," said one senator.[490]

A "U.S. COMMITMENT TO AFGHAN WOMEN"

In 2002, with much fanfare, the formation of the U.S.-Afghan Women's Council (UAWC) was announced in post-Taliban Afghanistan. This was to be the culmination of Hughes' publicity campaign of the U.S. "liberation" of Afghan women. According to their Web site, the UAWC was founded "to promote private/public partnerships between U.S. and Afghan institutions and mobilize private resources to ensure Afghan women gain the skills and education deprived them under years of Taliban misrule." Again, only oppression under the Taliban would be addressed, with no mention of women's past and present oppression under U.S.-backed Mujahideen warlords. Headed by Paula Dobriansky, under secretary of state for global affairs, and Habiba Sarabi, the Afghan minister of women's affairs, this council is basically a project of the U.S. State Department, and a perfect showcase for the Bush administration's rhetoric of liberation during the UAWC's yearly visits to Afghanistan. These trips are largely restricted to the capital, Kabul, where the International Security Assistance Force has ensured a relatively secure atmosphere, and spared the American ladies the trauma and violence of the countryside. The UAWC enables high-profile women from the U.S. to highlight their benevolent work on behalf of Afghan women without addressing the reality of Afghan women's lives.

During their first visit in 2003, Karen Hughes was asked about women still wearing the burqa by a reporter, to which she acknowledged that Afghan women were continuing to live in fear. (The burqa is still considered by some U.S. feminists and the mainstream media as the most important measure of Afghan women's freedom, despite strong public critique of this type of cultural-imperialist logic.) Hughes' sympathy knew no bounds and she offered her own presence as an antidote to the fear of women compelled to wear the burqa:

> One of the things that we heard in the meeting is that there is still a substantial amount of fear and so I think one of the whole purposes of a delegation of largely women visiting from the United States of America is to maybe provide some small sense of encouragement to the women of Afghanistan.[491]

One year later, in February 2004, the UAWC delegation was back in Kabul, this time joined by the defense secretary's wife, Joyce Rumsfeld. Their reports of women's freedom were even more optimistic, to help preserve the illusion of "liberation" and progress. Karen Hughes was so impressed by the "different shades of dark hair visible on burqa-free Afghan women" that she remarked, "There's a big change here. . . . There's more shops, there's more energy. There's more women on the streets [*sic*]."[492] A month after the visit, in an online forum, UAWC co-chair Paula Dobriansky repeatedly assured American women of Afghan women's freedom by painting a generalized rosy picture of their situation: "Women have taken on many different professions. Women have gone back to work. There are women journalists. There are women who started up a women's magazine. There are women doctors."[493] Neither Hughes nor Dobriansky mentioned the fact that in the year following the fall of the Taliban, misogynist warlords (e.g. Ismail Khan) were busy reviving Taliban-era repression of women. Nor did they state that Kabul, the site of the UAWC visits, is a relatively safer place for women than the rest of the country.

In March 2005, First Lady Laura Bush made a six-hour visit to Afghanistan in the midst of the UAWC's yearly trip, where she remarked that "the power of freedom is on display across Afghanistan" even though, once again, her only stop was Kabul. While there she informed U.S. soldiers that "thanks to you, millions of little girls are going to school in this country." The State Department has reported this number as about 1 million. Taking with her a highly publicized grant of $21 million for schools, Mrs. Bush's trip was part of the

UAWC's annual public relations exercise to highlight the U.S. "liberation" and to keep the U.S. government's charity to Afghan women in the spotlight.[494]

In 2002–3 the U.S. government funded a film project by Afghan women filmmakers to produce the documentary *Afghanistan Unveiled,* heavily promoted as a sign of women's emancipation. According to the *San Francisco Chronicle,* "People in the West who see "Afghanistan Unveiled" badly want . . . Afghanistan to become a model for how countries can change with outside help."[495] According to the Dobriansky, the film "symbolizes . . . our desire to support the women of Afghanistan."[496] Interestingly, the film is often portrayed as being about "the effects of the repressive Taliban regime and the subsequent U.S. military campaign on the lives of Afghan women and their families." But in fact the film reveals women's struggles continuing beyond Taliban repression: "One woman tells how a local militia commander tried to force her to marry against her will."[497] In their campaign against the Taliban and al-Qa'eda, U.S. forces often work in close collaboration with local militia commanders regardless of their record on human rights and women's rights. The violation of women's rights under U.S.-backed commanders was not mentioned by U.S. government officials as they lauded the film's portrayal of Taliban repression and of women's freedom in post-Taliban Afghanistan. Like the yearly UAWC visits to Kabul, *Afghanistan Unveiled,* as well-intentioned as the filmmakers may have been, was used as yet another public relations tool to promote the U.S.'s "liberation" of Afghan women.

The modestly funded and highly publicized efforts of the UAWC and the State Department are clearly aimed at promoting a perception of U.S. generosity, rather than achieving real progress for Afghan women. At the same time as Mrs. Bush's $21 million "gift" to Afghan women received generous press coverage, another much bigger and less publicized grant of $83 million was made to upgrade the two main U.S. air bases in Afghanistan.[498] Similarly, the State Department's award of $2.5 million for the UAWC to build fourteen provincial Women's Resource Centers is heavily publicized but hardly significant in comparison to what is spent on war fighting and military infrastructure. The UAWC, one of whose goals is to stimulate private-sector economy, actually has no formal budget and instead "relies on its members—White House aides, State Department experts, businesswomen, and educators—to raise money, either U.S. government or private funds."[499] As of this writing, corporate sponsors such as AOL/Time Warner, Daimler-Chrysler-Benz, and other various organizations have provided tens of thousands of dollars each, sometimes through the fundraising efforts of their staffs.[500]

In addition to aiming a spotlight at U.S. "liberation" efforts, the UAWC takes a free-market capitalist approach to assisting Afghan women, in line with Bush's right-wing Republican dominated foreign policy agenda. Within this framework, Afghan women are viewed through the lens of how *they* can fit into a market economy. In an interview with World Vision Radio, State Department spokeswoman Charlotte Ponticelli, who accompanied the UAWC on their annual Kabul delegation in 2005, described the excitement of discovering that Afghan women have marketable skills:

> Connie Duckworth [is] a member of our council. She's a very powerful woman in business—she chairs what's called the Committee of 200—the 200 most powerful women in business group. And she visited Afghanistan with the council about a year ago—her first visit—and she saw what the women were capable of doing. For example weaving rugs—she said: 'You know—there'd be a tremendous market for this in the U.S.'[501]

Ponticelli also described the UAWC's "Women's Resource Centers" throughout Afghanistan. The interviewer, Peggy Wehmeyer, asked: "So if I'm a woman in Afghanistan, I can go into my province and walk into a women's resource center as you call it—and it's kind of like 'One-stop shopping'—I can get most of my needs met there?" Ponticelli agreed: "Absolutely . . . absolutely, that's the goal." Within this framework, if Afghan women can find a way to fit neatly into the U.S.-led global market economy, they may stand a chance at rebuilding their lives.

The UAWC has also partnered with some noncorporate organizations to provide skills and training resources to Afghan women. One partner is the particularly troubling Center for Afghanistan Studies (CAS) at the University of Nebraska. In the 1980s, the Center received funding from the U.S. Agency for International Development (USAID) for a program designed by the CIA to promote anti-Soviet propaganda among Afghan refugees through textbooks that "promoted and strengthened an era of jihad violence" and teacher trainings. The CAS also won a contract with the oil corporation Unocal in the mid-1990s to train hundreds of Afghan men under the Taliban to construct an oil pipeline.[502] Today, the UAWC "has initiated a teacher training exchange that is bringing 30 Afghan women teachers to Nebraska every 6 months for training." Given the history of the CAS to promote U.S. government goals in Afghanistan, it seems a fitting partner for the UAWC.

The UAWC is being touted as the prime example of the U.S. fulfilling its obligations to Afghan women. One State Department press release was entitled "U.S. Commitment to Afghan Women: The U.S.-Afghan Women's Council."[503] With its bare-bones budget, the UAWC makes a negligible difference in the lives of Afghan women. It is not intended to provide direct assistance. Its importance lies in the convenient showcase it provides for U.S. policy, helping the U.S. government to maintain a feminist veneer at the expense of Afghan women's lives, while promoting a free-market capitalist approach to helping women.

During our visit to Afghanistan, we met with Habiba Sarabi, the Afghan chair of the U.S.-Afghan Women's Council, and asked her what she thought of the U.S. media coverage of Afghan women's "liberation" by the U.S.:

> Liberty is something that can't [be brought] from outside. The people themselves should know about their rights. . . . We have a proverb here—Rights is [*sic*] something that we have to take and not to give to someone. So the people of Afghanistan, or Afghan women should have some movement themselves.[504]

Sarabi's comments well represent what most Afghan women told us: that liberation has to come from within the country and cannot be imported into Afghanistan by another nation. She also touched on a widespread concern among Afghan women, which the UAWC never broached:

> Regarding warlordism, we have a lot of difficulties. Until the time the warlords, the people who have power through weapons . . . if the government does not finish their power or the DDR [UN disarmament] program is not completed, or if we can't raise a lot of awareness among women, if we can't promote their education, [then] it's very difficult to give them their liberty. What does liberty mean for Afghan women?[505]

Instead of restricting her concerns for women's freedom to the politically "safe" issues of increasing women's access to education, healthcare, and professions that are marketable to the West, Sarabi additionally focused on the taboo subject of U.S.-backed armed warlords targeting Afghan women, which the U.S. can actually remedy if it chose to. Unfortunately, discussing the U.S. arming of Taliban-like warlords would make the UAWC a less effective public relations tool for the U.S. government's "liberation" of women.

"GENDER APARTHEID" AND THE BLUE BURQA BOOKS

Even before Afghan women's oppression was "discovered" by Karen Hughes and Laura Bush, groups like the Feminist Majority and their spokesperson, Mavis Leno, were calling attention to the Taliban's behavior. The enforcement of the Afghan women's veil or "burqa" was sensationalized and exploited to such an extent that American women would use burqas as props in their demonstrations and publicity campaigns to gain attention among passers-by. Little attempt was made to understand the origins of the garment, its pervasiveness in pre-Taliban Afghanistan, or its context as one of many draconian Taliban edicts. The burqa-clad Afghan woman had become a visual object of horror-filled fascination.

The Feminist Majority Foundation, which launched its "Gender Apartheid" campaign in 1997, constantly used images of mute burqa-clad women on the campaign's Web site and literature. The campaign involved the selling of small pieces of mesh cloth—the eyepieces of the burqa—to raise awareness of Afghan women's oppression. American women were urged to wear a "Symbol of Remembrance for Afghan Women," as though they were paying tribute to the dead. According to the Feminist Majority, "This swatch of mesh represents the obstructed view of the world for an entire nation of women who were once free."[506] To imply that before the Taliban, Afghan women were "free" once more ignores U.S.-backed Mujahideen warlords who launched the most serious attacks on Afghan women's rights from the 1980s through the early '90s. The eyepieces were available for purchase individually or in packets of 10 and 20. Notably, half of the proceeds went towards the huge publicity expenses for the campaign itself (the Feminist Majority has since stopped selling the burqa eyepieces on its Web site).[507]

By perpetuating an oversimplified story of the abuse of women by the Taliban, with the burqa as the main vehicle of that oppression, liberal feminists were setting up Afghan women for only one solution: topple the Taliban and remove the laws on forced veiling, and Afghan women would be free. The brutal war that resulted in thousands of women and children being killed by bombs,[508] indeed led to the defeat of the Taliban regime and the repeal of the mandatory veiling laws. Afghan women are told that they have been liberated, but the overwhelming evidence is that in most parts of the country their oppression continues and, in some cases, is worse.

Furthermore, while many Afghan feminists and secularists may revile the garment, it is a widely accepted part of conservative Afghan tradition. Focusing critique on the burqa as a symbol of oppression reinforces negative Western stereotypes of Muslim culture. According to one critic, "The Western feminist, human rights, and even the Afghan women's groups unwittingly played to Western stereotypic images of Islam and Afghanistan in pressing their cases. Many of those sympathetic to Afghan culture and to Islam worried about the sensationalism surrounding the campaigns. . . . In public forums, Afghanis [*sic*] and other Muslims often raised the issue that the anti–gender apartheid campaign itself was more harmful than beneficial because it was contributing to widespread negative stereotypes."[509]

But the Feminist Majority was not alone in its exploitation. After September 11, 2001, there was a sudden proliferation of what we call the "Blue Burqa Books" (see Figure 5.1). These were a string of newly published books written by mostly Western liberal feminists, capitalizing on the oppression of Afghan women. Typically the book titles involved the words "veil" or "veiled" (like the high-profile U.S.-funded documentary, *Afghanistan Unveiled*) and sported covers of women clad in the standard cornflower blue-burqa. Examples are *Unveiled* by Harriet Logan and *Veiled Threat* by Sally Armstrong. Even books about Afghan women's resistance, like *Veiled Courage* by Cheryl Benard or *Zoya's Story: An Afghan Woman's Struggle for Freedom,* sported the unmistakable blue burqa. Now that the ongoing oppression of Afghan women is no longer fashionable to discuss, as it is perpetrated by U.S. allies and is inconsistent with the supposed "liberation" of Afghan women, there are few if any such books published.[510]

Figure 5.1—The "Blue Burqa Books."

Only a few books were published about Afghan women that defied the "blue burqa" norms. They included Anne Brodsky's book about RAWA, *With All Our Strength* (which has for its cover one of the countless publicly available images of Afghan women marching in RAWA's political demonstrations), Sunita Mehta's *Women for Afghan Women: Shattering Myths and Claiming the Future*, and Melody Ermachild's *Meena: The Martyr Who Founded RAWA*.[511]

Even more fascinating to U.S. audiences than burqa-clad, faceless Afghan women was the famous "unveiled" object of U.S. liberation, Sharbat Gula. The exposed face of Sharbat, photographed as a child in 1984 by photographer Steve McCurry, was considered by *National Geographic* to be "the most recognized photograph" in its history.[512] In 2002 McCurry carried out a highly publicized search for the Afghan girl with the "haunting green eyes."[513] When he found Sharbat, almost two decades after his 1984 piece, she was a married woman who had to ask her husband's permission to allow a second photograph (see Figure 5.2).

National Geographic published a triumphant cover story sporting her troubled face. In the corresponding article, Sharbat's face was coldly dissected: "Time and hardship have erased her youth. Her skin looks like leather. The geometry of her jaw has softened.[514] The eyes still glare; that has not softened." To ensure that she was the "right girl," National Geographic employed biometrics technology, used by the FBI in identifying criminals, to confirm her identity. While her 1984 childhood image was appropriated by the magazine and publicized internationally without her consent, eighteen years later her adult image was bought for the price of financial assistance that the magazine says it is providing to her poverty-stricken family. Interestingly, her

Figure 5.2—*National Geographic*, March 2002: Sharbat Gula made to pose with her 1984 image. © Steve McCurry/Magnum Photo.

words have not been taken as seriously by the American public or *National Geographic* as her image has. Apparently Sharbat Gula does not think much of U.S.-style "liberation" and claims that life was better under the Taliban.[515]

RACIST AND SEXIST LOGIC*

The word "liberation" has obvious implications within today's political context of the U.S. as a superpower waging war on poor, defenseless nations. It conjures up an image of millions of brown faces awaiting the Western savior, as they starve and sustain torture and imprisonment by native tyrants (Mullah Omar, Osama bin Laden, Saddam Hussein) and their cronies (the Taliban, al-Qa'eda, the Baath Party). In Afghanistan, the dark-skinned victims comprised mostly women and children who were supposedly celebrating their impending liberation as bombs began falling on their heads. The idea of a more "advanced" powerful country "liberating" a weaker, "backward" nation and its women, reveals a sense of superiority—it is sexist and racist logic. Going further, Bush and his supporters expected gratitude from these dark-skinned victims of U.S. foreign policy for an act of "liberation" they did not choose, and that could kill them and their families.

U.S. soldiers have been busy "liberating" brown peoples all over the world from the imposition of "communism" and now "terrorism," practiced by their own leaders such as the Taliban and Saddam Hussein. But the rhetoric of "liberation" is not new—it is an age-old trick that disguises and sugarcoats the intentions of the powerful. Older empires claimed to "civilize" their colonies with the same arrogance as today's "liberators," and with the same consequences. For the British imperialists, "possession of an empire . . . encouraged a sense of superiority . . . It also fostered racial arrogance. And yet at the same time, deeply rooted liberal and evangelical ideals produced a powerful sense of imperial duty and mission. The empire existed to civilize and uplift its subjects, or so it champions claimed."[516]

Due to the modern-day rejection of the right of empires to exist,

* Parts of this section originally appeared in Sonali Kolhatkar, "From Afghanistan to Iraq: The Racism of 'Liberation,'" *Znet*, February 10, 2003.

imperialistic behavior is no longer described as such by its practitioners. "Liberation" rhetoric is instead employed to make the imperial project seem benevolent. In other words, the U.S. often engages in what *Atlantic Monthly* correspondent Robert Kaplan calls "Supremacy by Stealth." To Kaplan, the main obstacle to U.S. global hegemony is its own citizenry. "We can dominate the world only quietly: off-camera so to speak." Even though in his view the actions of the American empire are entirely noble ("the preservation—and, wherever prudent, the accretion—of American power" constitutes "the highest morality"), it is difficult to conquer people openly, because "Americans are truly idealistic by nature." Thus, "U.S. foreign policy [must] be robed in idealism, so as to garner public support and ultimately be effective." "Security concerns" necessitate the use of "the idealistic short hand of 'democracy,' 'economic development,' and 'human rights' [to] conceal many harsh and complicated ground-level truths," such as the fact that the U.S. supports misogynistic warlords and a puppet government in Afghanistan.[517]

The most strident criticisms in the major news media of U.S. imperial behavior in Afghanistan are that it is not being done *well* enough. Many liberal commentators, for example, are calling for the U.S. to take its imperial role more seriously. Michael Ignatieff, director of the Harvard Carr Center for Human Rights Policy, uses the derisive term "Nation Building Lite" to describe Bush administration policy towards Afghanistan. He has argued instead "for a committed American imperialism," believing that for the Afghans "their best hope of freedom lies in a temporary experience of imperial rule." This "difficult truth" may not be popular, but "imperialism doesn't stop being necessary just because it becomes politically incorrect." By "committed imperialism," Ignatieff means imperialism that diffuses—not encourages– resistance. He rightly censures the Pentagon for the well-known incident where an Afghan wedding party was bombed, but on grounds that call into question his credentials to teach human rights policy. Ignatieff explains that one of the key ingredients of imperial power is "awe," a fact "the British imperialists understood," and which the U.S. maintains "by the timeliness and destructiveness of American air power." But "awe can be sustained only if the force is just." The bombing of the wedding party was unjust, making it a "major political error" in his opinion (not a war crime or human rights violation). Errors weaken the imperial stranglehold, since "the more errors there are the less awe and the more resistance American power will awaken," making the Afghans less likely to submit to imperial rule, "their best hope of freedom."[518]

AFGHAN WOMEN'S MOVEMENTS: A BRIEF HISTORY

Closer examination reveals that the rhetoric of "liberation" used by the Bush administration, as well as simplistic campaigns by liberal American feminists, ignored the true history of women's rights in Afghanistan, not to mention the existing contemporary women's movements struggling for their rights against fundamentalism and imperialism. Militant and vocal Afghan women who are well organized are not as easy to "liberate" as those who are voiceless and faceless and can be portrayed as dependent on the benevolence of foreigners.

The modern history of social movements in Afghanistan is rarely heard from Bush administration officials, the mainstream media, or liberal feminist groups. In the 1920s, Amanullah, the first Afghan king after independence from Britain, rapidly pushed through Western-style social reforms, particularly in Afghanistan's cities, going as far as to require European-style dress in the capital, Kabul. His reforms eventually sparked a backlash from religious and military leaders, who saw them as weakening their power. It was not until 1959, under the rule of the king's cousin Mohammed Daoud (1953–63), who was serving as regent, that Afghan women were allowed to attend schools and universities, mainly in the cities. The all-encompassing burqa was made an optional garment. The 10-year reign of King Zahir Shah (1963–73), was probably the most democratic in the country's history. Shah established a new constitution in 1964, arguably a step toward "dismantling . . . the monarchy's autocratic powers."[519] By 1965, women were given equal rights and obligations under the law and were allowed to vote in parliamentary elections. This is contrary to the common assumption that Afghanistan never had elections or the women's vote before 2004. By the 1970s, 15 percent of all legislative posts, again mostly in cities, were held by women.

During Shah's reign there were growing student and women's movements, including eight well organized nationwide "parties" (true political parties were outlawed) that the U.S. Embassy considered left-of-center. A May 1973 cable from political officer Albert Fairchild reported on the "Afghan Left," which represented a sort of natural opposition to the fundamentalist mullahs, but were also a feared influence on the king since they were considered potential tools of Soviet policy. According to Fairchild, "Although the Afghan left remains small and fragmented, it has grown considerably over the years following the promulgation of Afghanistan's Constitution in 1964."[520]

Fairchild commented that even though different leftist groups rarely united, the separate groups were well organized and could pose a threat to the current order "in an environment permitting political parties." Since the king was planning on legalizing parties by the end of 1973, this was a distinct possibility. The U.S. political officer dismissed their potency, however, because "the 'democratic experiment' . . . is still an experiment, and the controls over that experiment remain overwhelmingly greater than even the most optimistic spokesmen for the Left would care to admit." The king's son-in-law Sardar Abdul Wali supposedly made the threat: "if the mullahs were unleashed all leftists in the country would be dead within 24 hours," an assertion "most observers accept," according to Fairchild. It is almost as if U.S. strategists in the 1980s took Wali's boast as literal advice on wiping out almost every trace of progressive, or even moderate, forces in Afghanistan, under the pretense that they were all potential Soviet pawns.[521]

The most popular leftist organization, the PDPA, was formed in 1965. By the time of Fairchild's analysis, PDPA had split into two factions, Parcham (Banner) ("the foremost and probably best organized leftist group") and Khalq (the Masses). After Zahir Shah was overthrown, women's rights and other progressive aims were promoted in state propaganda by both the Soviet-influenced governments of Daoud (who was in an uneasy alliance with Parcham) and Taraki (Khalq). But it was difficult to hide the growing internal repression, including politically motivated arrests and killings. Women's rights and other progressive issues were often used cynically as "ideological goals" to advance a political platform. As a Pakistani activist explained, to the official Afghan Left, "women's rights were instrumental, not an aim." To address the lack of a radical women's movement in Afghanistan, Meena, a 20-year-old Kabul University student, founded the RAWA in 1977,[522] making it today "the oldest women's humanitarian and political organization in Afghanistan."[523] According to Amnesty International, RAWA is one of "two Afghan women organizations . . . known to have been formed that are not affiliated to a political party."[524] (The other group is a nonpolitical organization called the Afghan Women's Council).

When Taraki was later overthrown by his deputy, a list was published of 12,000 people who had been killed in Kabul jails after the April 1978 coup, including "professors, teachers, students, civil servants, religious leaders, merchants, and shopkeepers."[525] For example, rather than making it easier to run a feminist organization, the PDPA coup "made security matters worse" for RAWA, requiring changes in "almost everything" about the way the organization operated.[526]

After the Soviet invasion in 1979, the USSR and its puppet government quickly pushed through land reforms, laws giving women more rights, and other moves calculated to placate certain segments of the populace. But many progressive Afghans, like RAWA, "wanted a women's liberation that would arise from the people once they had education and consciousness, not one imposed from above by outside, foreign forces."[527] While leaders expanded rights in the law books, residents of Kabul City who protested "were arrested, interrogated, and tortured in various detention centers." In the countryside, the Soviets commenced an intense aerial bombardment of "suspected resistance hideouts," which included civilian homes.[528] Hundreds of thousands of Afghans fled the country in the first few years of the occupation, most of them becoming refugees in Iran or Pakistan. By the end of the 1980s over 6 million Afghans, more than one-fifth of the population, were refugees.[529]

After the assassination of RAWA's founder, Meena, in 1987, the women's rights organization was driven underground and flourished in the refugee camps of neighboring Pakistan. Keeping alive Meena's legacy, they continued their work, eventually rising to international prominence for speaking out against misogynist fundamentalism, and for their political and humanitarian organizing efforts.

MALALAI JOYA: SPEAKING FOR MILLIONS

Despite the best efforts of the Bush administration to convince Americans and the world that the 2001 U.S. war had "liberated" women and that the U.S. continues to work for the interests of Afghan women, the words of grassroots women activists reveal a very different picture. Their voices are rarely heard in U.S. media lest they expose the lofty claims of freedom and liberation made by Bush administration officials.

Less than two years after the fall of the Taliban, in a large tent in Kabul, a 25-year-old woman made a statement that garnered international headlines:

> My name is Malalai Joya from Farah province. By the permission of the esteemed attendees. . . . I would like to speak for couple of minutes. . . . The chairman of every committee is already selected. Why do you not take all these criminals to one committee so that we see what they want for this nation? These were those who turned our country into the nucleus of national and international wars. They were the most anti-women people in the society who . . . brought our country to this state and they intend to do the same again. I believe that it is a mistake to test those already tested. They should be taken to national and international court. If they are forgiven by our people, the bare-footed Afghan people, our history will never forgive them. They are all recorded in the history of our country.[530]

The event was the 2003 Constitutional *Loya Jirga* in Kabul, convened under the auspices of the U.S. and the UN to ratify a constitution for Malalai Joya's country. The men she spoke of were not the Taliban, but men who were offered as the alternative to the Taliban, elevated to power by the Bush administration: prominent figures in the Northern Alliance, whose past and present record was discussed in Chapters 1 and 3.

A little over a minute after she began speaking, Malalai Joya's microphone was shut off, and some of the men she had targeted rushed toward her threateningly, and shouted slogans of "Death to Communists" and "God is Great," followed by the chairman of the assembly nearly throwing her out saying she had "disturbed this *jirga* and been very rude."[531] Joya's brief outburst has earned her constant death threats and resulted in the loss of her personal security.

Meanwhile, the response she elicited from ordinary Afghans was quite the opposite:

Safia Shahab, a Kabuli in her mid-20s, said Joya is the leader of Afghan women. "Malalai's speech was absolutely correct," she said. "These mujahedin blew Kabul city to pieces in the civil war." Mohammed Nasir, a twenty-five-year-old resident of Khak-i Jabar village near Kabul, is among Joya's big fans after he heard about her speech on the radio. "If I get her picture, I will keep it with me, because she has pulled back the curtain to expose the facts," he said.[532]

In an interview with David Barsamian, Pakistani journalist and author of "Taliban: Islam, Oil and the New Great Game in Central Asia," Ahmed Rashid described what happened:

> I was there and I heard her speak out. And she had enormous support from the floor of the house. It was quite embarrassing even for President Karzai and his supporters, because she was speaking, I think, for millions of ordinary Afghans, who are really fed up with the warlords and the kind of intimidation that they've been carrying out, and also speaking for Afghan women, who in many areas of the country are still facing an enormous intimidation and lack of security. It was a very heartfelt appeal that went to the heart of many Afghans and many of the foreigners who were there.[533]

Malalai Joya, speaking for millions of Afghans, pointed out a reality that defies the U.S.'s rhetoric of "liberation." According to Joya the U.S. had simply returned a different set of misogynists to power. Then–U.S. ambassador to Afghanistan Zalmay Khalilzad described a very optimistic image of the Constitutional *Loya Jirga* of Afghans who "embraced the often difficult and sometimes messy democratic process of debating, listening and compromising. They trusted in the power of their words by openly deliberating the important issues."[534] UAWC cochair Paula Dobriansky concurred, claiming that "women participated actively and were able to question leaders openly and discuss gender related issues." However, when Malalai Joya raised the taboo topic of warlords returning to power, an issue of great importance to the majority of ordinary Afghans, she was silenced. Khalilzad even lauded Joya's actions but portrayed the incident as one where she was ultimately triumphant in her goals: "Malalai Joya refused to be intimidated and went on to play an active role in her working committee."[535] Khalilzad and Dobriansky failed to mention the subsequent threats to her life and the price she has paid for speaking out.

We met Malalai Joya in February 2005, in her office in Farah Province. Armed men stood guard outside. Joya told us what happened after the now-infamous incident at the *Loya Jirga*: "After the *Loya Jirga* my life has completely changed. . . . They [the warlords] called me an infidel, prostitute, communist, and other things. When I came [back] to Farah it was very difficult for me to be safe. They tried a lot to kill me. They even attacked my office." Joya resents having her activities curtailed, being forced to remain indoors. Outdoors, she travels under a burqa with six bodyguards to protect her:[536] "I am very ashamed that now I have special bodyguards. . . . I hate guns because these guns destroyed my country and killed a lot of people but I have no choice." To date, Joya has survived at least four assassination attempts.[537]

She saw the *Loya Jirga* incident very differently from Khalilzad. Her persecution "meant that there was no security, even in the place where the Constitution was being drafted. Even here there was no democracy." She implored us to tell her story in the U.S.:

> You people, you democratic people, should tell the government "why didn't you tell anyone what happened after the *Loya Jirga*? What kind of life she has?" My people who are living in the faraway villages, I know what kind of life they have. I want to tell

> the U.S. government and those people who think that the difficulties of the people of Afghanistan are only the burqa and now they do not have problems. I want *you* people to tell those people "why did they attack this girl in the *Loya Jirga*? Does it mean democracy? Does it mean women's rights?"[538]

Malalai Joya is a passionate young woman whose words seem to flow faster than she can think, despite her broken English. She struggles to accept the faith her people have put in her:

> Even one night after the *Loya Jirga* I understand how much the people of Afghanistan support me. I am honored, I am proud. It isn't me they support—I am [just] a person. It means they support the painful people and suffering women of Afghanistan. They hate the enemies of Afghanistan. They wanted to show their hatred for the enemies of Afghanistan. It was a very hopeful message for me. It gives me a lot of energy. I received a lot . . . of warm messages from the faraway provinces of Afghanistan. I cannot tell you . . . it's difficult for me. Even now as I am talking about the emotions of my people, I cannot control myself [choking back tears]. I said that I am a servant of my people. I am just a person in this country—I am a member of the young generation of this country. Now I accept this risk because of my people. They [warlords] killed a lot of democratic people, a lot of like-minded people. Maybe one day they will kill me. But I will never be afraid.[539, 540]

Two years after her outburst at the *Loya Jirga*, Malalai Joya was elected to Afghanistan's new Parliament at age twenty-seven, winning the second-most votes in her native province of Farah.[541] Becoming a member of Parliament has not silenced her, however. In a news conference at the swearing-in ceremony, she continued her public criticism of the warlords: "I offer my condolences to the people of our country for the presence of warlords, drug lords and criminals [in the Parliament] . . . [The Afghan people recently] escaped the Taliban cage but still they are trapped in the cage of those who are called warlords."[542] Joya was the only MP brave enough to publicly express what most Afghans fear.

THE INCONVENIENCE OF REVOLUTIONARY WOMEN

When Malalai Joya made her 2003 speech at the Constitutional *Loya Jirga* many people assumed that she was a member of the militant underground women's rights organization RAWA. When the abuse of Afghan women was "discovered" by the U.S. public, RAWA gained a brief window of media attention. But the attention was largely focused on their criticism of the Taliban and their documentation of the Taliban's human rights abuses, as this could be harnessed for the cause of war. While Malalai Joya is not a RAWA member and was simply speaking on behalf of Afghan people, her words have a lot in common with the statements of RAWA.

RAWA's strong and consistent critique of both the Taliban and the Northern Alliance was inconvenient from the perspective of the Bush administration, its allies in Afghanistan, and Western women's organizations. To the U.S. government, raising the profile of RAWA's work would also have exposed as hypocritical the empowering of the Northern Alliance as an alternative to the Taliban. Little attention was paid to RAWA's long-term role in Afghan women's resistance from the Soviet occupation through the subsequent Mujahideen rise to power. Admitting that a women's movement for self-determination was alive and active might have lessened the need for a swooping outside military reaction to the Taliban and its misogyny. It may have resulted in financially and morally supporting women's resistance to all oppression, Taliban and otherwise.

In Afghanistan, we found that while RAWA's unwavering stand on women, war, and fundamentalism certainly set it apart as a militant organization, RAWA's basic demands are not uncommon. Its harsh critiques of all fundamentalist armed factions and support for women's rights and democracy were common sentiments in cities and in provinces, even among women and men entirely unaffiliated with it. The Afghanistan Independent Human Rights Commission (AIHRC) concluded in its survey, "A Call for Justice," that a majority of Afghans consider themselves victims of war, whether at the hands of the Mujahideen, the Taliban, and/or the Soviet Union, and want an end to war, and justice for war crimes. The most frequently mentioned human rights desired by respondents included: "ethnic, religious and gender equality; political rights such as the right to participate in free and fair elections; and the right to education." On their Web site, RAWA says it wants a government "based on democratic values and it should [*sic*] ensure freedom of thought, religion and political expression while safeguarding women's rights."[543]

When the concerns of the majority of Afghan people are heard, they are either marginalized or ignored altogether. One unnamed participant in AIHRC's survey complained: "No one has had the courage to take action to bring them [warlords] to justice. No one can defend us against them."[544] "A Call for Justice" was hardly noticed in the U.S.; rarely are the voices of ordinary Afghans heard. In such circumstances, the words of RAWA, Malalai Joya, and others, when heard, are considered out of the ordinary.

Inside Afghanistan, women like Joya and groups like RAWA are obviously problematic to fundamentalist warlords. The price for speaking out is extremely high, as Malalai Joya has discovered. Similarly, RAWA members have for decades traveled undercover, run their projects underground, used pseudonyms, and shunned photographs. RAWA's founder, Meena, paid the ultimate price for her work when she was assassinated in 1987 by men loyal to U.S. beneficiary and notorious warlord Gulbuddin Hekmatyar, collaborating with the KHAD (the Afghan arm of the Soviet KGB).[545]

Even among liberal Americans, outspoken Afghan women are dismissed as being too revolutionary or influenced by Western notions. In an August 2002 article for *The American Prospect*, Noy Thrupkaew wrote a lengthy critique of RAWA, crediting the Feminist Majority and feminist playwright Eve Ensler for RAWA's initial popularity in the United States (the Feminist Majority invited RAWA to a conference in 2000 but has since rarely supported RAWA). Thrupkaew went on to characterize RAWA's viewpoints as more in line with Western feminism than with their own culture:

> With its confrontational, no-holds-barred language and allegiance to a secular society, RAWA reflects much of the Western feminist community's own values—a fact that has earned RAWA strong support in the West but few friends in a strongly Muslim country weary of political battles and bloodshed.[546]

The article quotes several people, most of whom reside in the U.S., accusing RAWA of being too "Western." Sima Wali, who spent twenty-four years outside Afghanistan (until recently), explains: "We are trying to influence the men, many of whom still have Taliban ideology, and they say, 'You are part of these extremists.' It's not time yet. We can't do something extreme and leave Afghan women to deal with it. [RAWA has] a very Westernized radical approach. They are revolutionary."[547] Such critiques do not acknowledge that all RAWA members live in Afghanistan, or Afghan refugee camps, directly under the edicts and abuses of men like those Wali intends to influence. Thrupkaew too fails to note that the greatest difference between RAWA and its critics is that RAWA members choose to struggle within the country, where outspoken protest is the most dangerous. Despite the fact that RAWA gets support not from Western governments or agencies but rather from grassroots supporters internationally,[548] Noy Thrupkaew attributes its popularity to Western groups, and then quotes Western sources who accuse RAWA of being too Western.

One day, after translating the real-life stories of many Afghan women interviewed by her organization, RAWA member Zala commented: "some people say we do too much and are too radical. Listening to all this [stories of Afghan women] it is clear that the words of our critics, especially those who are thousands of miles away, don't matter. . . . They do not understand the reality of life [for Afghans] here."[549]

When the Taliban was in power, Westerners had no problem universalizing the discussion: oppression was a violation of human rights whether in the West or East. Now, for some reason, the discourse on women's rights must be more nuanced and take into account "culture." This is due more to powerful (Western) governments backing the Northern Alliance than to the relativity of values. RAWA's response to

Thrupkaew makes the point that whether it's the Taliban or Northern Alliance, the Soviet Union or the U.S., human rights are universal:

> If democracy and women's freedom is [*sic*] "western values" then why women in the East and especially Islamic countries are not burning forever, in the flames of religion, traditions and culture? . . . [I]n today's "global village" [can] these general and grand humanitarian values such as democracy, secularism and women's freedom be devaluated [*sic*]—according to the fundamentalists—as "western values?" In our view as without air life cannot exists [*sic*], without real democracy and women's freedom, development and progress of a society is not possible.[550]

Another common way of discrediting women like Malalai Joya and the women of RAWA is to accuse them of being "communist" or "Maoist." Among Afghans, who invariably associate communism with the Soviet invasion, these labels are reflexively derogatory. The fundamentalist warlords offended by Malalai Joya's speech denounced her as a communist. RAWA is also sometimes dismissed as a communist or Maoist organization even though most RAWA members are Muslim women and refuse to condemn Islam and religion, as a Maoist organization would (although RAWA condemns religious fundamentalism). Thrupkaew quotes Masuda Sultan, of Women for Afghan Women, a U.S.-based organization: "'most Afghan women don't feel that RAWA represents them,' because of the group's revolutionary rhetoric and alleged ties to Maoism."[551] Yet, when Malalai Joya spoke the same anti-warlord sentiments that RAWA commonly expresses, she received widespread support from Afghans all across the country.

RAWA represents a movement of women in Afghanistan whose analysis is consistent with a secular women's rights–centered ideology that rejects both foreign imperialism and misogynist fundamentalism in all forms. In other words, women's self-determination is part of national self-determination. At the same time, RAWA's basic demands for human rights, women's rights, democracy and an end to fundamentalism are representative of the majority of Afghan people. Few women's organizations in the U.S. that have taken an interest in Afghan women's rights have actually supported the work of any women's movement that openly works for long-term political and social change.* An organized movement of women is too dangerous, too independent of foreign influence to be worthy of serious support by liberal feminist organizations or the U.S. government.

Effort has been more focused on "safe" humanitarian work that can be influenced from outside. For example, the Feminist Majority, in its own words, is working to "Support the Afghan Ministry for Women's Affairs, the Independent Human Rights Commission, and Afghan women–led nongovernmental organizations." These initiatives involve working within governmental structures established by the U.S. and its allies, and with "nonpolitical" humanitarian women's groups who are working within the existing system set up by the U.S. to influence the Karzai government to respect women's rights.

The prevalence of Afghan women's oppression was exploited by the U.S. government to make the case for war. This is not surprising, since the U.S. government is following in the footsteps of previous empires that colonized under the racist pretexts of "civilizing" people. The U.S. is certainly not deviating from its past record in Afghanistan of supporting misogynist thugs under the rhetoric of "freedom." Much effort is expended to continually make the case that U.S. actions have "liberated" Afghan women.

At the same time, many liberal feminists, who could have joined in support of political women's organizations that stand against both the Taliban and the Northern Alliance, and against the U.S.'s war, chose instead to capitalize on Afghan women's oppression through simplistic books and campaigns that used racist and sexist images and words. This is regrettable, given the laudable role played by the Feminist Majority in protesting the Unocal pipeline deal, which would have benefited the Taliban in 1998.

---

* In a June 2006 e-mail conversation with a member of RAWA, we found that aside from our own organization, Afghan Women's Mission, RAWA currently receives modest donations from the following U.S. organizations: Eve Ensler's V-Day, RAWA Supporters, a small Santa Barbara based group, and Compassion Beyond Borders.

What is rarely heard in current feminist discourse hijacked by the U.S. government and uncritically joined by most Western feminist organizations is a more complex analysis of the effects of U.S. policies on women's rights in the first place, as well as Afghan women's own militant resistance to fundamentalism. Alliances with nonpolitical Afghan women's groups enable Western feminists to avoid the questions of long-term movements for self-determination that may defy U.S. policy in the region. Perhaps outspoken women like Malalai Joya or the members of RAWA obviate the need of "liberation" from outside. This in turn could reduce the importance of high-profile anti–"Gender Apartheid" campaigns in favor of women inside Afghanistan who are doing the real work of liberating themselves.

The rhetoric of "liberation" only strengthens the notion that powerful Western nations and their people are superior to the weaker brown nations of the South who need our help in order to survive. Celebrating the resistance of Afghan women, or even admitting that their oppression has not ended, unravels the justification for war and instead rightly places blame on their purported "saviors." Now that U.S. allies are in power, we are told that the country is stabilized and Afghan women are "liberated." No longer does one hear the Bush administration or even just Laura Bush, speaking out about women's rights in Afghanistan. No longer do liberal feminist groups focus all their energies on the "Gender Apartheid" in Afghanistan that still exists. No longer do the mainstream media sport front-page exposès about the mistreatment of Afghan women, despite the fact that the women and men of Afghanistan suffer in silence under new tyrants. Meanwhile, Afghan women continue the hard work of liberating themselves from all forms of fundamentalism and foreign domination.

CHAPTER SIX

THE PROPAGANDA OF SILENCE

THE MASS MEDIA AND GOVERNMENT IMPUNITY

If We see right, We see our Woes
Then what avails it to have Eyes?
From Ignorance our Comfort flows
The only wretched are the Wise
—MATTHEW PRIOR (1664–1721), TO THE HON. CHARLES MONTAGUE

U.S. citizens generally do not know enough about the history of their government's involvement in Afghanistan. They were unaware of the carnage in 1992–96, unable to comprehend the rise of the Taliban during the same period, and unable to understand the causes of the 9/11 attacks in New York and Washington, DC. One reason why we wrote this book is to try to address this ignorance.

A lot of the blame rests with the mainstream corporate news media. For many people the mainstream media is their only window on U.S. government policy, so when news outlets fail to cover Afghanistan, or to cover it sufficiently, the people cannot understand government policies, let alone push to change them.

The media have generally played a powerful role in support of government policy. News coverage of Afghanistan, when it happens at all, is often extremely simplistic, promoting the positive aspects of U.S. policy and ignoring the negative aspects. Sometimes the media ignore events entirely, usually following Washington's lead on whether a story is important or not. Crimes committed by U.S. allies are also not covered sufficiently. Reduction in coverage, what we call the "propaganda of silence," can have as much of a propaganda effect as patriotic platitudes in favor of government actions. The U.S. government has been able to get away with a policy of support for fundamentalists, warlords, misogynists, and drug lords in Afghanistan in part because of the U.S. media's supportive or noncritical role.

In this chapter we review the history of media coverage, mainly looking at the post-Soviet period from 1990 to 1996, when warlords used their U.S.-given weapons and funds to attempt to consolidate their power over Afghanistan; and the post-Taliban period from 2001 to the present, when U.S. troops joined them on the battlefield. We examine the media silence in the years surrounding the 1992–96 war, and the current ignorance of that time period. The U.S. and its Afghan allies were allowed relative impunity after 9/11 because of this "propaganda of silence." We show how media justified the U.S. invasion of Afghanistan by playing on the victimhood of Afghan women and minimizing the criminality of the Northern Alliance. We give examples of the media emphasizing the beneficial aspects of U.S. policies, and covering up, ignoring, or allowing only minute space for evidence of the failure of those policies. Sometimes the government even stifles a media outlet deliberately, as in the *Newsweek* Koran abuse affair in May 2005. Today the media have once again drifted away from Afghanistan, with dramatic consequences for the Afghan people in terms of foreign attention and aid.

THE MEDIA BLACKOUT, 1990–1996

At the beginning of this book we gave the example of a *Free Lance-Star* editorial discussing U.S. post-9/11 actions in Afghanistan that leaves out any context regarding how past U.S. actions have contributed to the present situation. The U.S. was, according to this picture, a newcomer that, with its allies, is now "working to resuscitate the gasping nation." As we have shown, the U.S. government has been far from a newcomer to Afghanistan and has in fact played a leading role in contributing to that nation's problems.[552]

The reason why this picture works, however, is that U.S. citizens are largely ignorant of U.S. actions, particularly the killings and pillage of the years 1990–96 between the end of the Soviet occupation and the Taliban takeover of Kabul. This is because media coverage during this period drastically dropped. A June 2005 report by Human Rights Watch covering the crucial year 1371 (the Afghan calendar equivalent to the period April 1992 to March 1993) notes that "the crimes of this period have not received as much attention as crimes committed during other phases of Afghanistan's wars . . . little information is available today about what happened in Afghanistan during 1371." Either deliberately or unknowingly, the U.S. media silenced the uncomfortable realities of post-Soviet, pre-Taliban Afghanistan, benefiting the U.S. government, which had a hand in causing them.[553]

This claim can be made more precise. Figure 1 shows the history of Afghanistan news coverage from 1975 to 2005, based on a search using the National Newspaper Index (NNI), an online database of five major newspapers (the *Christian Science Monitor*, the *Los Angeles Times*, the *New York Times*, the *Wall Street Journal*, and the *Washington Post*). The height of the graph represents the total number of articles returned by an NNI search under the subject "Afghanistan" for a given month. Key events that caused spikes in news coverage are indicated by the captions near the top of the figure.[554]

The largest surges in news coverage (more than 200 articles in one month) occurred after major changes in superpower involvement: the December 1979 Soviet invasion; the April 1988 Geneva Accords, which precipitated the Soviet withdrawal; and the September 2001 attacks on the U.S. and subsequent American invasion of Afghanistan. Less intense spikes (50–100 articles in one month) are attributable to either turning points in Afghan politics (the fall of Najibullah, the Taliban takeover, the destruction of the Bamiyan Buddha statues) or temporary U.S. involvement (the U.S. Embassy bombings and cruise missile response). But these spikes in mainstream media attention disguise the underlying trend.

The *baseline* article count, the long-term trend underneath the spikes, is a better indication of the ebb and flow of interest in Afghanistan by U.S. decision makers and the media. Prior to 9/11, media focus on Afghanistan had never been great, but the number of articles in the early

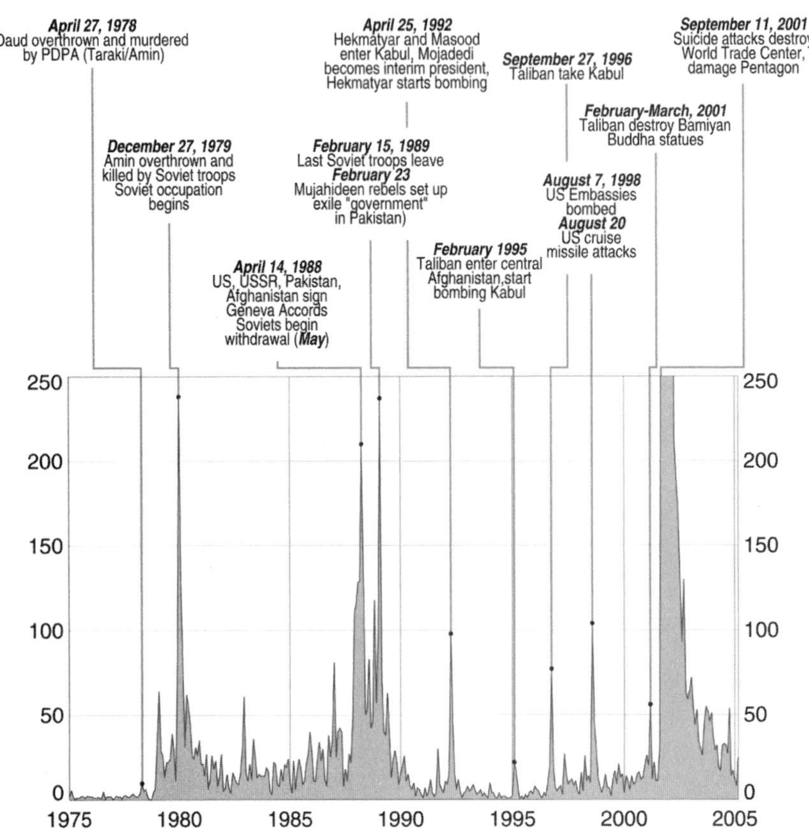

Figure 6.1—Number of articles (monthly totals) with subject "Afghanistan" from a National Newspaper Index search. September 2001 through January 2002 is off the scale of the graph (see Figure 6.3).

1990s was particularly low compared to either the Soviet period (the 1980s) or the Taliban period (late 1990s). One way to measure the long-term trend is to look at the total article count in 5-year intervals (Figure 6.2). The drastic reduction in coverage in the early 1990s is more obvious here than in Figure 6.1. The U.S. media published about 531 articles on Afghanistan in the 1990–94 period of the Mujahideen takeover; about 1/3 as many as during the first half of the Soviet occupation, 1980–84 (1,566 articles); and about 1/5 as many as during the second half of the occupation, 1985–89 (2,805 articles). U.S. newspapers clearly became silent on Afghanistan after the Soviets left. Reporter Ben Macintyre, stationed in Peshawar in 1989, wrote recently, "as Afghanistan fractured into civil war, the country was left to slide into fundamentalism. . . . Long before the rule of the mullahs, the news story had moved on."[555]

According to Human Rights Watch,

> A relatively small number of Afghan and international journalists covered events during this period, and media editors and producers often passed on the stories journalists filed. There were no functioning Afghan news services. No international human rights monitors were deployed in the country at the time, few humanitarian groups were operating, and there was only a modest United Nations presence with no direct mandate to report on the human rights situation.[556]

Human Rights Watch attributes the drop in international attention to the fact that the Afghan wars were "overshadowed by other events,

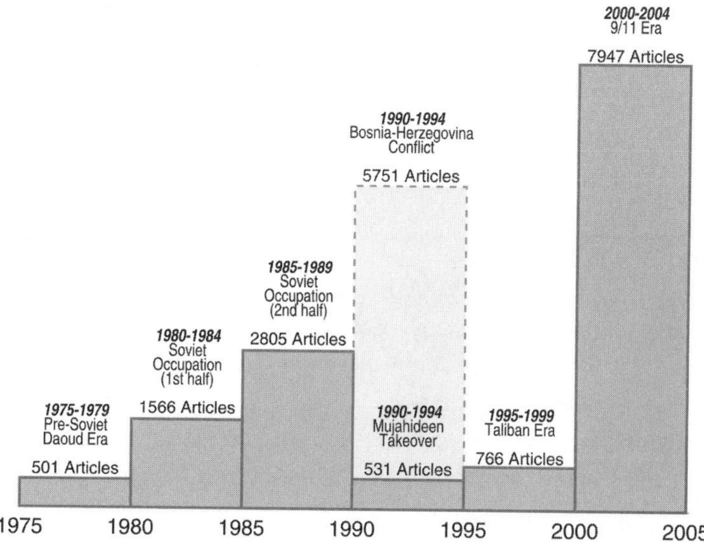

Figure 6.2—National Newspaper Index search results for "Afghanistan," added up over 5-year periods. The results for "Bosnia-Herzegovina Conflict" are also shown for 1990–1994.

including the U.S. presidential campaign between Bill Clinton and George H. W. Bush in 1992, the breakup of the Soviet Union, and war in the former Yugoslavia." It is doubtful that the 1992 U.S. presidential elections could have been responsible for the fivefold reduction in media attention to Afghanistan in 1990–94 as compared with 1985–89, since both periods had presidential elections. We do agree that both the breakup of the Soviet Union and the Yugoslavia war could have redirected the resources of major newspapers away from Afghanistan. For example, Figure 6.2 shows that ten times as many articles were written on the "Bosnia-Herzegovina Conflict" as on Afghanistan during the 1990–94 period, so indeed the breakup of the European nation was considered a more important news story than the destruction of the Central Asian country. Two *New York Times* correspondents (John F. Burns and Elaine Sciolino) who covered Afghanistan in the early 1990s also covered the former Yugoslavia, so for the *Times'* editors the increase in Bosnia coverage meant a conscious decrease in Afghanistan coverage.

Obviously, other stories attracted news agencies away from Afghanistan, but the real question for us is not *what* pulled reporters from Afghanistan, but *why*. Why was the ongoing catastrophe in Afghanistan passed over for other issues? It was surely not that more horrible crimes were being committed elsewhere. For instance, by late 1995, the 40-month Serbian bombardment of Sarajevo had caused between 10,000 and 15,000 civilian deaths. This ugly toll is certainly worthy of international attention. But, during an equivalent period, from 1992 to early 1996, it was estimated that from 25,000 to 45,000 civilians were killed in the Mujahideen and Taliban attacks on Kabul. Even though the Mujahideen had once been championed fervently by the United States government and media, only 10 percent as many stories were published in major U.S. newspapers about their post-Soviet exploits as about the deeds of Serbian commanders.[557]

We think that editors chose to ignore Afghanistan first of all because the country was no longer important to policy makers in Washington. Some newspapers openly agreed with U.S. policy. *The Economist* opined that it made sense to move on:

> All this [the Mujahideen civil war], it may be argued, is sad for the Afghans, but does it matter to the rest of the world? Afghanistan could be deemed to have had its share of attention. For nine years, while the Soviet army was in occupation, it had the status of an international problem. In newspapers and on television David-and-Goliath stories were told of battles between the invaders and the holy warriors known as Mujahideen. The previously obscure towns of Kabul, Herat and Jalalabad fell easily from the lips of instant experts. Then, suddenly, the invaders were gone: driven out by the Mujahideen, some said; or brought home because the Soviet centre was cracking, said the historically minded, just as Rome's legions abandoned the outposts of empire when Rome itself was in trouble. Anyway, problem over.[558]

The media blackout basically mirrored the U.S. government's own waning interest in Afghanistan after the Soviets had left. The drift to other issues like Yugoslavia paralleled Washington's increasing attention to those issues. For example, the U.S. government lent decisive support for a war crimes tribunal for the eastern European country and boosted humanitarian assistance at a time when similar war crimes were being committed with impunity (with U.S.-supplied weapons) in Afghanistan and foreign aid was slowing to a trickle.

Now that Afghanistan no longer "had the status of an international problem," it was not relevant to foreigners, who really only cared about threats to their own interests. Dismissing the Afghan people as unworthy of concern ("All this, it may be argued, is sad for the Afghans, but does it matter to the rest of the world?") betrays the racist component of Western foreign policy and its media, in addition to showing willful ignorance of the Western responsibility for a human rights disaster, still ongoing.

More ominously, we believe that it was convenient for U.S. policy makers that public attention be drawn away from Afghanistan, now that the worst atrocities could no longer be blamed on the USSR, but in part had to be attributed to Washington (the George H. W. Bush administration gave 7,000 tons of captured Iraqi weapons to its Afghan allies as late as mid-1991, while they were laying siege to Kabul). Reporters who attempted to shine a light on U.S. culpability were ridiculed and likely felt pressured into doing selective or uncritical reports. John F. Burns, a *New York Times* reporter who won the Pulitzer prize in 1993 for coverage of Sarajevo, and again in 1997 for his coverage of Afghanistan under the Taliban, wrote in 1990 that it was not easy publishing articles critical of the CIA/ISI protégés. Those who criticized the U.S. Mujahideen allies "became targets" of U.S. officials. Burns wrote a story in the early '90s reporting that Mujahideen rockets were "stirring anti-American sentiment in Kabul," which caused State Department official Howard Schaffer to suggest that Burns had been "duped" by the Najibullah government. Another reporter, James Rupert of the *Washington Post*, described an apparent shift in Afghan public opinion in favor of Najibullah, probably because he wasn't bombing them. Peter Tomsen, Bush's special envoy to the Mujahideen, responded that the report was "unreliable."

This behavior was not confined to officials. Most other reporters refused to probe the character of the U.S.-backed commanders, and even made it difficult for their colleagues to do so. Regarding Gulbuddin Hekmatyar, the prime beneficiary of U.S. funding, most reporters took their lead from U.S. officials:

> [N]ot until his murderous attacks on other rebel groups attracted Washington's condemnation in 1989, did the Peshawar-based reporters—or American diplomats—pay much attention to the sinister nature of Mr. Hekmatyar.

In the American Club for U.S. reporters in Peshawar, Pakistan, according to Burns, "reporters skeptical of an approach that celebrated the rebels' virtues encountered ostracism." Mary Williams Walsh, a reporter for the *Wall Street Journal* who published a piece on "the rebel boosterism she found" among her fellow U.S. reporters had her entry into the club "suspended."[559]

Since most reporters refused to acknowledge the "sinister nature" of U.S.-backed warlords, and then moved on to other stories when the warlords engaged in their worst crimes, the American public had an incomplete picture of the consequences of U.S. actions in Afghanistan. Americans did not understand their government's role in the rise of fundamentalism in the country, which led to the Taliban and paved the way for the 9/11 attacks. And they did not understand why it was wrong for the U.S. to support many of the same criminals to oust the Taliban after 9/11, or promote them to government posts in 2002. Human Rights Watch wrote that "many of the main commanders and political faction leaders implicated in . . . crimes . . . are now officials in the Afghan government." The poor quality of media coverage of the original crimes ensures that the Afghan criminals and the U.S. officials who sponsored them continue to behave with impunity today.[560]

SEPTEMBER 2001: MEDIA RETURN TO AFGHANISTAN TO PROMOTE A U.S. WAR

By late 1994, U.S. media coverage of Afghanistan had dwindled to near zero (Figure 6.1). Then the Taliban arrived, obviously backed by Pakistan, not the U.S. In the mid- to late-1990s, as Afghanistan became less of an embarrassment for U.S. officials, and as Osama bin Laden became more of a concern, the number of press reports slowly rose. After the attacks of September 11, 2001, the number of articles skyrocketed to over 250 in September and around 1,500 in October and November, when the U.S. began its war to take over Afghanistan. It would be charitable to say that the media did not question the Bush administration's motives in the "war on terrorism." In most cases however, they actively promoted U.S. policy.

Exploiting Women's Suffering While Veiling the Causes

In the days after the fall of the Taliban, reporters fell over themselves in a rush to prove that George W. Bush's "liberation" of Afghanistan was a success. Images of women removing their veils were particularly useful (although there were also some images of men cutting off the beards they had been forced to grow by the Taliban). *Business Week*'s cover story on post-Taliban Afghanistan, titled "Liberation," featured the smiling, uncovered face of an Afghan woman. But inside, the magazine's commentary quickly shifted to classic pro-imperialist logic:

> [A]fter a decade in which many of the nation's campuses deprecated the study of Western civilization and embraced multicultural relativism, the liberation of the women and men of Afghanistan makes it clear that there is something very basic and profoundly moving about human freedom. If this is seen by some as American hegemony, so be it . . .[561]

The powerful visual effect of seeing the smiling, uncovered face of an Afghan woman—that the media had only barely finished victimizing after 9/11 (even though the suffering of Afghan women predated that by over a decade)—was presented as a justification for the U.S. war. In Chapter 5 we discussed the Bush administration's rhetoric of "liberation" and how Afghan women were presented as the perfect victims of a brutal regime, on whose behalf the U.S. fought a war of liberation. Bolstering the case for war was the U.S. media, in lockstep with government "liberation" propaganda.

Like the "Blue Burqa Books," newspapers and TV networks bombarded the public with images of blue burqa-clad women, who, once the Taliban fell, were dramatically shown lifting their veils toward freedom. But how real were the scenes of unveiling? *The London Observer* reported the lengths to which reporters would go to capture a scene they were desperate to present:

> Foreign newspaper photographers, under pressure to produce images of the city's rejection of the Taliban, can be seen each day persuading a few women to remove these garments. What the photos do not show is the women putting them back on again moments later.[562]

The unveiling of Afghan women was presented as symbolic of a new era of freedom for all Afghans. An American public ill-informed about Afghanistan's history and culture, and U.S. historical involvement, was perfectly poised to consume the images of women claiming freedom through unveiling. At the very least, it gave a profitable visual portrayal of what a U.S. war had achieved for ordinary Afghans, providing some comfort to those who wanted to be convinced that their tax dollars had funded women's liberation. For others, the unveiling reinforced imperialist and orientalist logic. Again, *Business Week* is an appropriate example:

> The victory over Taliban tyrants is a victory for humanist values. The scenes of joy in the streets of Kabul evoke nothing less than the images of Paris liberated from the Nazis. Women taking to the streets to bask in the Afghan sun, free at last to show their faces. Children gathering to fly kites, a once forbidden pastime. Old people dancing to music, banned for many years. The liberation of Afghanistan from the tyranny of the Taliban is a watershed event that could reverberate for years. The warm embrace by ordinary people of the freedom to do ordinary things is a major victory for Western humanist values.[563]

The media presented a simple picture, easy to swallow: the Taliban forcibly veiled their women, so American forces stormed the country, defeated the Taliban, and unveiled the women. The U.S. media, perhaps unwittingly, presented the baring of women's faces as "a major victory for Western humanist values," reinforcing a sense of cultural superiority and notions of the essential goodness of American foreign policy.

In the long term, this presented a problem, since several years after the fall of the Taliban most Afghan women are still wearing the burqa, particularly in areas outside Kabul, even though the Taliban's laws on forced veiling are technically repealed. Instead of presenting a view of Afghan women that may confuse the U.S. public about Afghan women's freedom (we thought we liberated them!), the media have chosen largely to ignore Afghan women and their continued suffering. This avoids having to confront or revise the exploitative and simplistic portrayals presented in 2001.

Zakia, a young student at Kabul Medical University, told us what she wanted the U.S. media to do:

> My message to the journalists, the cameramen, the photojournalists who come to Afghanistan, is: capture the real story of Afghanistan and tell them to the people of the U.S., [*sic*] not the unimportant things. Those people who say that Afghanistan now has freedom and democracy, and that women have their rights and liberty—they should come and see the situation for themselves.[564]

Part of the problem of course is that Washington's policies have in many ways made things worse for women. When the United States chose to realign itself with the Northern Alliance to eliminate the Taliban government, it was extremely fortunate for U.S. policymakers that the violent campaigns of Alliance members, especially during the early 1990s, were not well known to the U.S. public. Otherwise it would have been much more difficult to sell the Alliance as major players in the next government of Afghanistan.

Ever since the anti-Soviet jihad, the media practically suppressed the intentions of many commanders supported by the U.S. regarding women's rights. Possible warning of what was to come was revealed in an obscure 1988 article in the *New York Times* on page 7 entitled "Afghan Peace Could Herald War of Sexes." It was not an article that would necessarily have caught anyone's eye, given the almost whimsical title, suggesting a confrontation between groups with equal power and status in society. In fact the fears that were expressed in the article by Afghan feminist Masooma Wardak were to come ominously true in a few years under the administration of the Islamic State of Afghanistan under Burhanuddin Rabbani.

> Mrs. Wardak shares a concern felt by women of modern ways among the more than three million Afghan refugees in Pakistan. They fear that fundamentalist mullahs, or religious leaders among the seven parties of the resistance alliance based in Peshawar want to turn back the clock on women's rights when they return to leading positions in this country.[565]

What was entirely left out of the article, which prophesied so well the future of women's rights in Afghanistan, was a deeper probing into the "seven parties of the resistance alliance," not the least of all the fact that the seven Mujahideen groups received open financial and military support from the United States.

After 9/11, the media bolstered the U.S. government's decision to work with the Northern Alliance by highlighting the fact that they were more progressive on women's rights than the Taliban. Twenty-three years after the "war of sexes" article, the *New York Times* published an article in October 2001 entitled "Education Offers Women in Northern Afghanistan a Ray of Hope." The article begins: "Here at least they can ride in the back of trucks if a man deigns to let them. They can shop in the market, although they are allowed to speak to male shopkeepers only if it is absolutely necessary. And they can go to school even if the [range of] professions they can choose from is small—teacher for instance, or midwife." Surely such practices only seem liberal compared to the Taliban. Further reading reveals that "8 young women were allowed to join 300 men studying at the University for the first time, last year" in territory held by the Northern Alliance. Since the NA had been in power in the region for at least six years, the fact that only in 2000 did they allow a handful of women higher education suggests that it was only a token gesture.[566]

The U.S. media put forward a picture of Afghan women's suffering that bolstered the U.S. invasion and passed over the role of the U.S. and its allies the Northern Alliance in causing that suffering. In the eyes of most Americans, the primary cause of the hardships faced by Afghan women was the Taliban.

Demonizing the Taliban

As bad as the Taliban is, the U.S. government went out of its way to make it seem even worse, and the media followed suit. As official enemies of the state, there were few crimes that the Taliban could not be accused of. Under the heading "Psychological War," the *New York Times* published a piece in October 2001, "U.S. Warns Afghans That Taliban

May Poison Relief Food." According to the article, "The Pentagon said today that the Taliban might poison relief food supplies and blame the United States, and warned Afghans not to eat donated food from abroad if it had passed through the hands of the [Taliban]." The Pentagon offered no evidence, but the Times quoted Pentagon spokesperson Rear Admiral John Stufflebeam describing "a pattern of deception by the Taliban, meant to undermine the American air campaign and win international sympathy." In reality the allegations were the *Pentagon's* attempt at deception. A four-sentence blurb the following day, at the bottom of another article (quoting Stufflebeam on the Taliban's ability to cling "doggedly" to power), admitted that the allegations of poisoning food were probably false. "Officials with the World Food Program and United Nations agencies who have delivered aid to Afghanistan for years expressed surprise today at Pentagon allegations that the Taliban might poison relief food supplies." One official from the World Food Program said, "there's not been a single instance that we know of in which the Taliban have tampered with [our deliveries]. Stolen, yes, but not tampered." In the original report, the Pentagon had noted that the warning on Taliban food-poisoning was "a preemptive strike in an intensifying war for public opinion." The lesson here is that in the "war for public opinion" it is not the truth of allegations that matters but the way in which the accusations are presented. The *Times* used large headlines to send a frightening, but false, message, giving the Pentagon a platform in its propaganda war, while conveying the truth the next day in an obscure add-on that would probably be overlooked.[567]

Ironically, the Pentagon itself had considered exactly what it was accusing the Taliban of doing. A September 17, 2001, briefing slide by a special forces general was entitled "Thinking Outside the Box—Poisoning Food Supply," suggesting a potential U.S. tactic in Afghanistan. The slide was supposedly removed by Condoleezza Rice and Donald Rumsfeld before it was shown to President Bush. The *New York Times* never expressed concern that the U.S. considered poisoning Afghan food, but conveyed allegations of the same thing against the Taliban, which were easily proven untrue, thus contributing to the Pentagon's "psychological war."[568]

Another example of the *New York Times* printing false accusations against the Taliban that could have been leveled at the United States concerns children's education. A March 2002 article, "'A' for Afghan, 'S' for Schoolgirl," lauded the generosity of the U.S. government and corporations in donating money to purchase school supplies and textbooks for girls' education in post-Taliban Afghanistan. One passage described a project to edit old textbooks:

> Copies of more than 175 different textbooks for science, math and reading for all levels in both Dari and Pashto were distributed through grants from USAID [U.S. Agency for International Development], Unicef and the University of Nebraska. Nearly five million more are on the way from printing plants in Pakistan. "Our biggest obstacle was editing the material," said Bear McConnell, director of USAID's Central Asia Task Force. The source materials were from Afghan textbooks printed since the 1960's and *altered over the years by different regimes.* Under the Taliban, photographs of people, especially girls, were excised, and *anti-Soviet propaganda was added,* he said [emphasis added].[569]

The passage amounts to a generous rewriting of history in favor of the U.S. government, USAID, and the University of Nebraska. In truth, the anti-Soviet propaganda was in the books from the beginning, when they were originally published from 1984 to 1994 under a $51 million USAID grant to the University of Nebraska's Center for Afghanistan Studies, headed by Thomas Goutierre. The USAID spokesperson quoted in the *New York Times* article must have known about the earlier project, but chose not to mention it. It was not the Taliban, but the U.S. taxpayer that was responsible for unsavory content like the following problem in a fourth-grade mathematics text:

> The speed of a Kalashnikov bullet is 800 meters per second. If a Russian is at a distance of 3,200 meters from a mujahid, and that mujahid aims at the Russian's head, calculate how many seconds it will take for the bullet to strike the Russian in the forehead.[570]

At around the same time as the *New York Times* report, USAID officials told the *Washington Post* that in the U.S.-sponsored books, "Children were taught to count with illustrations showing tanks, missiles and land mines." An aid worker "counted 43 pages containing violent images or passages" in one 100-page book. New versions of the books were printed in the early 1990s, "under increasing pressure from Afghan parents and teachers, and various aid organizations" (Craig Davis), but only the violent images were removed, not the text. Furthermore, older versions of the books remained in circulation, so printing new versions with minor improvements made little difference. During a May 2000 visit to Kabul, Craig Davis found the original books readily available and was able to buy "an entire series of the unrevised textbooks" in a bookshop. The Taliban favored the original versions and kept them in circulation, but "purged human images from the books." This was their only change. Rather than "adding" anti-Soviet propaganda, as purported by the *New York Times*, the Taliban simply left what the U.S.-funded program had already provided.[571]

The original textbook project was defended by the head of the Afghanistan Center at the University of Nebraska, Thomas Goutierre, who told a Canadian Broadcasting Corporation reporter that the books were part of the anti-Soviet war effort.

> We were providing education behind the enemy lines. We were providing military support against the enemy lines. So this was a kind of coordinated effort. . . . [J]ust as important as [the] introduction of stinger missiles was the introduction of the humanitarian assistance [like the textbooks].

Goutierre seems to have few qualms about the effects of U.S. 1980s policy on present-day Afghanistan. "I was interested in being of any type of assistance that I could to help the Afghans get out of their mess and to be frank also anything that would help the United States in order to advance its interests."

An eleven-year-old student in Kabul named Rashid, interviewed for the same CBC program, disagreed. "The Afghan people hate the wars.

This is big mistake to war. [*sic*] This war is not good to small boys and their books." Homa Yousef, an author and history teacher, told the CBC,

> These lessons are like pouring salt in their wounds, referring to guns, tanks and killing. The students themselves say they don't benefit in any way from these lessons, and their level of understanding won't increase by taking these classes. The memories of war will appear again, and most people have lost a father or brother or had their homes looted.[572]

The *New York Times* and other mainstream outlets made it extremely easy for the U.S. government to exaggerate the criminality of its enemies and hide its own participation in the indoctrination of young Afghans into a culture of violence. The *Times* published a story about the 2002 USAID program to scrub the textbooks, and blithely ignored the more important story about the earlier USAID program which created the violent material. In addition, the *Times* relayed faithfully the USAID spokesperson's false claim that the objectionable content was added to the books by the Taliban, sparing the paper's readers the more uncomfortable truth.

Humbling the Media: The Newsweek Affair[573]

The U.S. media generally serve government interests without being told to do so. But, unlike in totalitarian regimes like Nazi Germany or state-socialist dictatorships like Soviet Russia, the United States government does not directly control the mass media, and sometimes media coverage actually exposes government policies and underlying interests. In such cases government officials scold media outlets for "biased" or "irresponsible" journalism, which can lead to media subservience to the power structure. Sometimes media institutions apologize to the government and actually retract their own stories.

A well-known case of media appeasement of a U.S. administration is the *Newsweek* Koran abuse affair. The U.S.-based magazine reported in its May 9, 2005, issue, "sources tell *Newsweek* [that] interrogators [at the U.S. detention center in Guantánamo Bay], in an attempt to rattle suspects, placed Qur'ans on toilets and, in at least one case, flushed a holy book down the toilet." Allegations of Koran abuse were not unheard of. For example, the first British detainee released from Guantanamo told the London *Independent* that "70 percent of the inmates went on a hunger strike after a guard kicked a copy of the Koran." Other examples were reviewed by columnist Molly Ivins, who called the *Newsweek* allegations "old news." This is not to mention the verified accounts of abuse and torture of the prisoners themselves.[574]

But in the current instance, the timing was inconvenient, because a wave of anti-U.S. demonstrations had started spreading across Afghanistan soon after the piece was printed. At times leading to serious violence (at least fifteen people were killed),[575] the protests were planned before the *Newsweek* article, but it is likely that the allegations provided a focus for organizers to rally people around. Perhaps unwittingly at first, most U.S. news media characterized the protests as *caused* by the *Newsweek* piece. The Associated Press said that the article was "the source of anger." Afghan president Hamid Karzai enforced this view, saying that "it is not anti-American sentiment, it is a protest over news of the desecration of the holy Quran."[576]

In reality the protests were caused by long-term anti-U.S. sentiment, as well as frustration with Karzai. Afghan press reports stated that the demonstrations were organized by students and "a large number of educated people participated." Furthermore, "the demonstrations were not spontaneous. They had been well-prepared, and were well organized and well orchestrated."[577] General Richard Myers of the U.S. Joint Chiefs of Staff told reporters, "it's a judgment of our commander in Afghanistan, General Eikenberry, that in fact the violence that we saw in Jalalabad was not necessarily the result of the allegations about disrespect for the Koran . . . but more tied up in the political process and the reconciliation process that President Karzai and his Cabinet is conducting in Afghanistan."[578] RAWA member Selay confirmed to us that the demonstrations went far beyond a simple response to *Newsweek*:

> The recent wave of demonstrations is not something new. Actually in the past one year many Afghan cities witnessed such

> huge demonstrations mainly organized by people who oppose the policies of Mr. Karzai and want to show their opposition to his pro-warlord actions. . . . [T]he desecration of the Koran alone can't move people to protest on such a large scale. Afghans are not more Muslim than the people in other nations that they would risk their lives for it while the Muslims in most other countries did not commit any actions against the *Newsweek* story.[579]

The problem for Washington was that, even though the *Newsweek* piece didn't *cause* the demonstrations, the demonstrations *publicized* stories of U.S. abuse much more than normal, and were damaging U.S. credibility in Afghanistan and the rest of the Islamic world, including Iraq. Secretary of State Condoleezza Rice complained, "It's appalling that this story got out there . . . "[580] According to the *Chicago Tribune*, "the upheaval [due to the protests] kept the Bush administration on the defensive. . . . [T]he violence has disrupted what has been a virtual consensus [in Afghanistan] in support of the U.S. presence." Despite the fact that the protests would have occurred in the absence of the *Newsweek* article, the magazine was made into a scapegoat by the White House and by some of its fellow news media. *Newsweek*, not U.S. policy, was blamed for causing the violence. The conservative group Accuracy in Media said, "blood is on the hands of *Newsweek* magazine." White House spokesperson Scott McClellan said, "[The news item] has caused damage to the image of the United States abroad. . . . [P]eople have lost their lives. It has certainly caused damage to the credibility of the media, as well, and *Newsweek*, itself."[581]

Newsweek defended the publication of the piece, but started to back away from full support for the facts it alleged. In an editorial in the May 23 issue of the magazine, Mark Whitaker wrote that "a top Pentagon spokesman . . . said the Pentagon had investigated other desecration charges by detainees and found them 'not credible.'" *Newsweek* also called into question the original source of the information, saying that he "later said he couldn't be certain about reading of the alleged Qur'an incident in the report we cited, and said it might have been in other investigative documents or drafts." In other words, he saw it somewhere, but not in the cited report. *Newsweek* all but took responsibility for the anti-U.S. sentiment in Afghanistan: "we regret that we got any part of our story wrong, and extend our sympathies to victims of the violence and to the U.S. soldiers caught in its midst."[582]

This wasn't enough for the administration. To fully discredit the protesters and direct attention away from failed U.S. government policies, the article that supposedly "caused" the demonstrations had to be discredited and *Newsweek* humbled. On May 16 at around 11:30 a.m., McClellan called for a full retraction: "I find it puzzling that *Newsweek* now acknowledges that the facts were wrong, and they refuse to offer a retraction. There is a certain journalistic standard that should be met, and in this case it was not met."[583] Condoleezza Rice asserted, "The sad thing was that there was a lot of anger that got stirred by a story that was not very well founded."[584]

That afternoon, *Newsweek* editor Whitaker complied, issuing a statement that read, "Based on what we know now, we are retracting our original story that an internal military investigation had uncovered Qur'an abuse at Guantanamo Bay."[585]

The next day McClellan suggested that *Newsweek* might go even further to atone for its sins by printing pro-U.S. stories and publicizing its "error."

> [W]e would encourage *Newsweek* to do all that they can to help repair the damage that has been done, particularly in the region [around Afghanistan]. And I think *Newsweek* can do that by talking about the way they got this wrong, and pointing out what the policies and practices of the United States military are when it comes to the handling of the Holy Koran.[586]

When asked the following day if he was "trying to dictate to the press," McClellan answered,

> I kind of laugh at it because I don't think that's possible. We have a free media in the United States, and the only point I was

> making yesterday was that . . . I think that there's a responsibility to help repair the damage. And like I said, I've seen *Newsweek* officials out on television shows or appearing on *Nightline*. I mean, I would hope that they would be appearing on Arab networks, as well, and talking to the region about this issue. I think that that would help repair the damage.[587]

According to the U.S. propaganda outlet Voice of America, "The now-discredited *Newsweek* Magazine report about desecration of the Koran by U.S. interrogators at the Guantanamo detention center has sparked much discussion of the credibility of the media and the government's ability to get its side of stories heard." In other words, when media publish unsupportive pieces about U.S. actions, and Afghans refuse to submit to U.S. control of their country, this interferes with "the government's ability to get its side of stories heard," and calls into question "the credibility of the media." The *Whittier Daily News* agreed, editorializing, "[*Newsweek*]'s failure to make appropriate amends right away has placed an enormous burden on the press to re-establish legitimacy." By daring to embarrass the government, *Newsweek* harmed the "legitimacy" of the media. Paul McMasters of the First Amendment Center backed the Bush administration's chastisement of the magazine: "[F]or some government officials regularly stung by negative press, shooting the messengers may not be an option. But making their lives miserable whenever possible is a fairly satisfying second choice."[588]

Adding insult to injury, the Pentagon soon after published a report confirming that "the Koran was stepped on, kicked, soaked with water and accidentally urinated on by guards" at Guantanamo Bay. The "five confirmed cases" of abuse of the Muslim holy book "contradicted earlier claims by the Pentagon that there were no 'credible' allegations of abuse there," according to the *Sunday Times* (London). Since the *Newsweek* article had alleged a specific form of abuse, toilet-flushing (as if that were the only form of abuse they had to answer for), the Bush administration emerged blameless. Jay Hood, the commander of Joint Task Force Guantanamo, stated, "The inquiry found no credible evidence that a member of the Joint Task Force . . . ever flushed a Koran down a toilet. . . . This matter is considered closed." The U.S. media accepted this. *Newsweek* remained chastised, even though the sense of their article, if not the specifics, was vindicated.[589]

DRIFTING AWAY: THE FUTURE OF AFGHANISTAN IN THE U.S. MEDIA

Like in the early 1990s after the Soviet regime was ousted, Afghanistan after the fall of the Taliban was no longer very useful to U.S. policy. The difficulties of "nation building" and the instability caused by the U.S. decision to limit the ISAF and let warlords into the government, as well as the continuing Taliban insurgency and rising popular anti-U.S. sentiment, do not enhance Washington's image as nicely as the retaking of Kabul and the unveiling of Afghan women. Like in the early 1990s, the media have taken the government's lead and "moved on" to other stories and ensured that the U.S. public once again forgets Afghanistan. This is made obvious in Figure 6.3, where the gray shaded graph outlines the monthly number of articles in a National Newspaper Index search on Afghanistan in the post 9/11 era. After an unprecedented high in October 2001, coverage has suffered a continuous drop all the way to the present, with minor spikes due to important events like the March 2002 earthquakes, or the October 2004 Afghan presidential elections. The level of coverage is still somewhat higher than it was in the mid-1990s, but it has returned to what it was in the months prior to 9/11, about 10 to 20 articles per month according to the NNI.

The media exodus has been covered by Lori Robertson, managing editor of the *American Journalism Review*, who noted in June 2003 that

> [Television] coverage has declined since October 2001, when the U.S. launched its war against the Taliban. And the story counts and airtime minutes have continued to plummet. In January 2002, the networks' weekday nightly newscasts aired a total of 106 minutes on Afghanistan, according to Andrew Tyndall, who tracks such numbers for the Tyndall Report. This

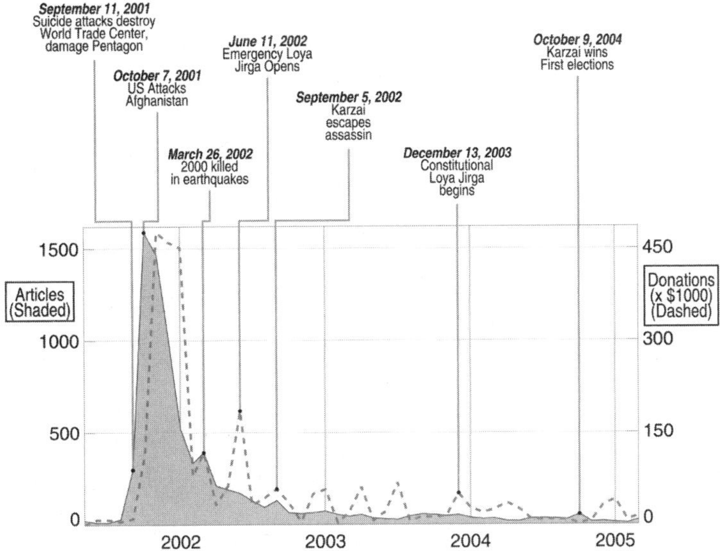

Figure 6.3—National Newspaper Index search results for "Afghanistan" for the period July 2001 to March 2005 (shaded, left scale). Donations for Afghan women's projects through the Afghan Women's Mission for the same period (dashed, right scale). The dates of key events in Afghan politics are indicated.

> January [2003], the count was down to 11 minutes. In March [2003], it was a mere 60 seconds.

By May of 2003, TV networks ABC, CBS, and Fox News, in addition to newspapers *USA Today*, the *Wall Street Journal*, the *Boston Globe*, the *Baltimore Sun*, and the *Washington Times*, had taken their reporters out of Afghanistan. News professionals understand this as toeing Washington's line. Robertson quotes Av Westin, a former ABC News executive: "I think that news judgments at this moment are affected more than ever before by the agenda that comes out of the White House. I don't quite know why." Westin suggested it may be that the media want to appear "patriotic," which in our opinion is a euphemism for "subservient." As we have seen in the early 1990s, the abandonment of Afghanistan by the media when it suited Washington's interests is standard operating procedure. *Washington Post* managing editor Steve Coll, who has covered Afghanistan since the late 1980s, has problems with this kind of journalistic approach. "It may be that the Bush administration has shifted focus. . . . But I don't think we should be in tandem." The *Post* is one of a few newspapers that still keep a reporter in Afghanistan as of this writing.[590]

AJR's Kim Hart did a follow-up piece in its December/January 2005 issue that asserted that since the earlier *AJR* article,

> Afghanistan has become even more of an afterthought. Only two news organizations—*Newsweek* and the *Washington Post*—have full-time reporters in Kabul. . . . Other major newspapers, such as the *Chicago Tribune* and *Los Angeles Times*, rely on stringers in Afghanistan and correspondents based in New Delhi, India, to cover the region, a stark contrast to the hundreds of reporters pouring into Iraq since the war began. The *New York Times* uses a stringer, albeit a full-time one. Television networks have nearly disappeared.

From May 2003 to December 2004, seven news outlets had removed their full-time personnel from Afghanistan. As of this writing, only the *Washington Post*, the *New York Times*, *Newsweek*, and ABC each have one full-time reporter or producer.

As we saw in the early 1990s, the reduction in overall coverage has serious consequences for the Afghan people. First, it is much easier for armed factions (including U.S. forces) to act with impunity if there are no media keeping the spotlight on their actions. Roy Gutman, a correspondent and foreign editor of *Newsday*, commissioned a story to investigate the death of an Afghan soldier in U.S. custody, which was covered by the *Los Angeles Times*, but "was never followed up by other media and quickly forgotten." Gutman complained, "This is something that the news organizations should be all over, but on the whole, nobody's making headlines out of what looks like a systematic pattern of abuse. It seems to me that this is what journalism should be about." Gutman points to the dearth of reporters: "There's a shortage of people there, and once they're there they tend to do the less controversial stories."[591]

Another effect of reduced media coverage and diminished awareness is the reduction in assistance by international donors. In Afghanistan, where the basic needs of the people (food, shelter, health care, and education) depend on international aid, the type of coverage—and even the amount of coverage—can be crucial to the ability of Afghans to survive. Our own experience as codirectors of a U.S.-based nonprofit organization (the Afghan Women's Mission) has been that donations to health, education, and women's empowerment projects have risen and fallen almost in tandem with national news coverage (see Figure 6.3, dashed line). As Dr. P. V. Unnikrishnan opined in the *Financial Times*, "we know from experience in Afghanistan and East Timor that promises [of aid] don't always translate into action. Once the smell and the heat and the blood disappears, and the television cameras move on, the public memory starts to fade. These become unkept promises."[592]

The media cannot be relied on to provide the U.S. public with the information they need in order to understand their government's actions. Both in the early 1990s and in the post-9/11 era the media focus drifted away from Afghanistan at a time when it would be inconvenient to both U.S. administrations for the public's attention to linger there. What media attention is given to Afghanistan is often of a sort that supports Washington policy. Some media outlets that have departed from that standard, *Newsweek* for example, have been disciplined publicly and made an example of. Thus it is little wonder that few Americans have a grasp on the effects of U.S. policy on the Afghan people, and even fewer understand the motives and interests of their government in Afghanistan, the subject of the next chapter.

CHAPTER SEVEN

POWER, PRESTIGE, AND PIPELINES

THE USES OF AFGHANISTAN

Why did the United States invade Afghanistan in 2001, and how does it benefit from remaining there?

Government officials declared publicly their intentions to fight for freedom, democracy, women's rights, and to bring about nation building, and the mainstream media reported it uncritically. The U.S. invasion—less than a month after 9/11—was meant, according to President George W. Bush, as a response to "attacks on our territory, our citizens, and our way of life,"[593] to "punish those who have attacked us," and to "protect our country, protect the good American families."[594] Bush went on to make broader claims, such as: "we wage a war to save civilization, itself,"[595] to "fight against evil,"[596] and to "fight terror." More specifically, Operation Enduring Freedom was intended to "disrupt the use of Afghanistan as a terrorist base of operations,"[597] to "go after Mr. bin Laden,"[598] and to "hunt down the members of the al-Qa'eda organization."[599] Two months later, as the Taliban's defeat appeared imminent, the publicly stated goals became more ambitious. We were told "our military was sent to liberate Afghanistan," and that the "fight against terrorism is also a fight for the rights and dignity of women."[600] In the months that followed the expulsion of the Taliban, the U.S. was "helping to build a free and stable democracy"[601] and we were told that "we will stand with the people of Afghanistan . . . until their hopes of freedom and security are fulfilled."[602]

But these are not the real motives behind U.S. actions. We have already demonstrated that U.S. actions in Afghanistan run counter to the claim of fighting for the "rights and dignity of women" or "building a free and stable democracy." Here we attempt to disentangle why the U.S. initially invaded Afghanistan in 2001, and what its interests are in that country, in the short and long terms. An examination of the true reasons for Washington's presence in Afghanistan, and the benefits it accrues, will allow us to better expose the injustice of U.S. military ventures in general, and to predict the long-term arc of U.S. behavior in the world.

We emphasize that any attempt to discern the "motives" of a government or other complex institution is necessarily speculative and imprecise. For us, the discussion of "motives" really pertains to the intentions of core decision makers in the official halls of power. In our opinion, the "behavior" of the United States and all governments, as well as other institutions that rely on violence (e.g., NATO), is inevitably "motivated" by a desire to consolidate and increase the power of those institutions. This is as true for the invasion of Afghanistan as for any other pivotal act of the U.S. government.

WHY THE U.S. BOMBED AFGHANISTAN: IMMEDIATE OBJECTIVES

We split this chapter into three major sections, dealing with the reasons for going to war, the incidental public relations benefits to the Bush administration of being in Afghanistan, and how the persistence of U.S. troops in Afghanistan bolsters U.S. global standing as a superpower. The division is somewhat arbitrary—obviously, long-term goals influence immediate reactions to events. But, at least in the case of post-9/11 U.S. policy in Afghanistan, we believe that the invasion was brought on directly by the need to respond to the terrorist attacks in Washington and New York, and not by any consideration of incidental benefits to Bush or long-range goals. Former U.S. ambassador Zalmay Khalilzad has said, "[Before 9/11] Afghanistan was marginal to U.S. interests, and then became very central overnight."[603] The evidence seems to agree with this assessment. At first the Bush administration had to switch gears from an Iraq-centered foreign policy, but in time took full advantage of the opportunities that presented themselves in Afghanistan.

All About Oil?

Numerous commentators who are critical of Bush policy have asserted that his oil-hungry administration had an eye toward lucrative oil and gas pipelines through Afghanistan, and 9/11 gave them the perfect excuse to launch a "war for oil." The justification cited for this supposition is the fact that Unocal Corporation was involved with the Taliban in the mid-1990s for the building of an oil and gas pipeline connecting the Caspian Basin to the Indian Ocean. Political cartoonist and writer Ted Rall published an op-ed in the *San Francisco Chronicle* in November 2001 titled "It's About Oil," saying that after 9/11,

> [f]inally the Bushies have the perfect excuse to do what the United States has wanted to do all along—invade and/or install an old-school puppet regime in Kabul . . . this ersatz war by a phony president is solely about getting the Unocal deal done without interference from annoying local middlemen. . . . As Bush would say, 'make no mistake': this is about oil. It's always about oil.[604]

Wayne Madsen, writing for the Centre for Research on Globalization, said, "[T]he War in Afghanistan was primarily about building Unocal's pipeline."[605] While oil and gas pipelines are certainly among U.S. economic concerns in the Central Asian region, there is little evidence to support the claim that oil pipelines were among the major motivations for the October 2001 campaign. It wasn't *all* about oil.

As far as we can tell, the most vocal proponents today of a pipeline through Central Asia are the governments of Afghanistan, Turkmenistan, and Pakistan, and to a lesser extent, India. Turkmen President Saparmurat Niyazov has enthusiastically pushed for a transport system for the 2.83 trillion cubic meters of gas reserves in Turkmenistan's Dauletabad-Donmez field. Pakistani President Pervez Musharraf is eager for his nation's fuel needs to be met more efficiently. And Hamid Karzai is interested in the transit revenues Afghanistan could earn from hosting a pipeline. In May 2002, all three leaders signed a $2 billion deal to construct the pipeline. This deal generated a good deal of speculation among commentators, particularly on the Internet, that it was finally proof of U.S. pipeline motives for invasion.[606] If a gas pipeline through Afghanistan is built, it will be economically beneficial to the Kabul government, and perhaps to the people of Afghanistan. If, however, U.S. firms do not get the contracts to build the pipeline, it is not clear how the Bush administration directly profits from this particular pipeline.

To buttress the theory that the possibility of oil profits drove Bush's invasion of Afghanistan, some have purported Hamid Karzai to be a former adviser to Unocal Corporation. The earliest mention of this can be traced to a December 2001 article in the French magazine *Le Monde*: "[Karzai] acted, for a while, as a consultant for the American oil company Unocal, at the time it was considering building a pipeline in Afghanistan . . ."[607] The *Christian Science Monitor* repeated this claim in 2002: "Cool and worldly, Karzai is a former employee of U.S. oil company Unocal—one of two main oil companies that was bidding for the lucrative contract to build an oil pipeline from Uzbekistan through Afghanistan to seaports in Pakistan."[608] In 2004, writing for *The Nation*, Lutz Kleveman concurred: "Afghan President Hamid Karzai, a former Unocal adviser, signed a treaty with Pakistani leader Pervez Musharraf and the Turkmen dictator Saparmurat Niyazov to authorize construction of a $3.2 billion gas pipeline through the Herat–Kandahar corridor in Afghanistan."[609] In his acclaimed film *Fahrenheit 9/11* Michael Moore repeated the allegation. Karzai's affiliation with Unocal is referenced innumerably on Internet Weblogs and journals.

But Unocal Corporation denies the claim: "Hamid Karzai, the president of Afghanistan, was never a consultant or adviser to Unocal."[610] While Unocal certainly had no qualms about doing business with brutal human rights violators like the Taliban, or the dictatorship in Burma, it is unlikely that they would openly lie about a fact that could be legally challenged. Additionally, Unocal freely admits that U.S. ambassador to Afghanistan Zalmay Khalilzad *was* a consultant for them during the pipeline negotiations.

Despite many hours of research, we did not find any evidence to justify the claims that Karzai had any connection to Unocal. None of the original allegations are referenced. Could it be that *Le Monde* magazine, where the allegation first appeared, accidentally mixed up the past careers of the two main Afghans involved in post 9/11-U.S. policy in their home country, Khalilzad and Karzai? Alternative Radio host David Barsamian asked Pakistani journalist Ahmed Rashid[611] whether there was any substance to the allegations that Karzai was a consultant for Unocal. Rashid, who has written extensively on the Unocal/Taliban deal, set the record straight:

> I've investigated this Unocal allegation very closely, and I don't think Karzai was ever a consultant for them. Unocal, when they were active in Afghanistan in the mid-1990s, met with all sorts of Afghans. And certainly he [Karzai] met with them, along with other Afghans. But he was never on their pay roll. He was not involved with them closely. . . . Unocal had set up a board of advisors around 1994–95 which actually only included Americans. The accusation against Karzai was that he was on this board of advisors. But I know who was on this board of advisors. They were all Americans . . .[612]

A similar line of reasoning suggests that Zalmay Khalilzad, the chief agent of U.S. post-9/11 policy in Afghanistan, had close ties with Unocal, and therefore a pipeline was the ulterior motive for the October 2001 invasion. Khalilzad's connection with Unocal is much easier to substantiate than Karzai's. In fact, he fully admits that he worked on a Unocal-funded project, but disavows any direct contact with the energy giant: "I was asked, not by Unocal but by Cambridge Energy Research Associates . . . if I would do a cost-benefit analysis of building pipelines across Afghanistan. And from then it evolved, but I always went through Cambridge." Certainly, Khalilzad's willingness to sell his skills to a corporation that was working with the Taliban reveals his lack of serious concern for the people of Afghanistan. As *New Yorker* correspondent Jon Lee Anderson wrote, "in many ways, the pipeline project represented the classic Washington revolving door between the corporate world and the foreign-policy establishment." But during his post-9/11 tenure in Afghanistan, there has been no recorded action by Khalilzad that would directly benefit Unocal or any other U.S. energy company. Ultimately, it is difficult to see a causal relationship between Khalilzad's past connection with Unocal and the 2001 decision to bomb Afghanistan.[613]

Although control of energy resources is certainly a long-term goal of U.S. officials and corporations, there is no evidence that Washington entered Afghanistan chiefly to obtain oil and natural gas. The Bush administration has been relatively open about its agenda since taking office. In Afghanistan, it has been transparent about its decision to work with human rights violators like the Northern Alliance, and its willingness to refuse prisoner-of-war status for captured prisoners and disregard for the Geneva Conventions. These and other actions have provoked international criticism. Had oil and gas resources motivated the invasion, U.S. oil and gas companies would likely have immediately and openly sought concessions for the oil and gas pipelines and ensured that resources were under U.S. control so that profits would begin rolling in as soon as possible—as was done in Iraq. After all, no-bid contracts to corporations like Bechtel and Halliburton that have obvious ties to administration officials were openly awarded in Iraq, suggesting that the Bush administration flaunts its greed with relative openness. Conspicuously absent from Afghanistan were Unocal and other U.S. energy corporations. If the war in Afghanistan was really meant to be a "war fought for oil," then why the secrecy—and lack of oil company initiative—compared to Iraq?

That said, even if the U.S. was not motivated initially to invade Afghanistan for oil and gas resources, this does not preclude reaping all possible benefit once the country was under U.S. military control. Now that Afghanistan has entered into a deal with Turkmenistan and Pakistan, having a U.S.-friendly regime in Kabul ensures substantial U.S. political control over the pipeline (even if U.S. corporations don't profit). But we think some U.S. planners take a much broader view of the region. Even more important to the U.S. than the trans-Afghanistan pipeline is a pipeline through Afghanistan's neighbors Azerbaijan and

Georgia to the Black Sea, inaugurated in 2005. As we discuss later, being in Afghanistan provides an excuse to have military bases in the resource-rich Central Asian region. Not only does this enable long-term involvement in profitable projects, it puts U.S. troops in the heart of the traditional geographic dominions of Russia and China.[614]

Furthermore, if Bush really wanted to invade Afghanistan to gain control and/or profits from oil and gas in Central Asia, he would not have required a 9/11. There is nothing to substantiate the allegations that 9/11 provided an "excuse" to invade Afghanistan for any reason. On the contrary, after 9/11, the administration debated invading *Iraq* for four days before realizing that Afghanistan would be a more publicly acceptable target. If Bush were searching for a reason to invade Afghanistan before 9/11, he would not have bothered waiting for the terrorist attacks in New York and Washington (or engineering them, as some have claimed). The actions of bin Laden and al-Qa'eda over the preceding decade provided far more compelling reasons for invading Afghanistan (not that we agree with that course of action) than the elaborately trumped-up "weapons of mass destruction" justification for a war with Iraq.

Imperial Prestige

If oil was not a reason for the post-9/11 bombing campaign, what did the U.S. have to gain from attacking Afghanistan, at least in the short term? An immediate need after 9/11 was to recover imperial prestige swiftly and decisively. In fact, one might say that an attack on Afghanistan was almost *required*. The terrorist attacks demonstrated that the world's most powerful country was vulnerable to a carefully planned assault by a small group of individuals. Without swift punishment, inaction by the U.S. would have damaged its credibility by sending a message that one can get away with attacking it. In an address to the nation on September 20, 2001, Bush was firm, saying, "I will not forget this wound to our country or those who inflicted it. I will not yield; I will not rest."[615] Al-Qa'eda posed a challenge in that it did not really reside in a specific country that the U.S. could easily bomb and destroy. Writing for the conservative *Weekly Standard* soon after 9/11, Charles Krauthammer elucidated: "because it is a sub-state infiltrative entity, the al-Qa'eda network and its related terrorists around the world lack an address. And a fixed address—the locus of any retaliation—is necessary for effective deterrence." But "deterrence," according to Krauthammer, could be easily achieved by launching a war on al-Qa'eda's main host country and its leaders in October 2001:

> If . . . the United States . . . cannot succeed in defeating some cave dwellers in the most backward country on earth, then the entire structure of world stability, which rests ultimately on the pacifying deterrent effect of American power, will be fatally threatened . . . Success therefore requires making an example of the Taliban. Getting Osama is not the immediate goal. Everyone understands that it is hard, even for a superpower, to go on a cave-to-cave manhunt. Toppling regimes is another matter. For the Taliban to hold off the United States is an astounding triumph. Every day that they remain in place is a rebuke to American power.[616]

Less than a month later, Krauthammer's fears were assuaged as the Taliban appeared to be on their way out. Bush triumphantly declared, "Not long ago, al-Qa'eda's leaders dismissed America as a paper tiger. That was before the tiger roared."[617] Within two months the U.S. advertised to the world that anyone considering future attacks would be wise to note the fate of the Taliban and the guests they harbored.

Afghanistan was the perfect nation on which the U.S. could wreak vengeance and rebuild its tarnished reputation. First, assuming that Osama bin Laden was responsible for the 9/11 attacks, a direct link already existed between the Taliban and bin Laden's organization, al-Qa'eda. Second, the Taliban's atrocious human rights record and lack of official recognition as Afghanistan's leaders by most of the world ensured that no one would stand up for the regime if attacked. The only countries in the world that had recognized the Taliban as the legitimate rulers of Afghanistan (Pakistan, Saudi Arabia, and the United Arab Emirates) were staunch U.S. allies who inevitably fell into line as per U.S. wishes. Third, the Taliban's fragile hold on the country and lack of any serious weapons capability made them an easy military target, unable to really fight back. Finally, the U.S. already had armed friends on the ground in the form of the Northern Alliance, to lend Washington an air of legitimacy as it worked with "the Afghans" to take back Afghanistan.

Assured of victory, the U.S. was able to recover its imperial prestige through a quick and decisive military retaliation and assure the world that no one could get away with hurting the most powerful country. Krauthammer succinctly explains: "States line up with more powerful states not out of love but out of fear. And respect."[618] From the bombing campaigns to the treatment of prisoners, the U.S. has acted to maintain "fear and respect" in Afghanistan and Iraq since 9/11.

The Path to Iraq

Insiders revealed that, as the Bush administration scrambled to react to 9/11, there was an attempt to link the terrorist attacks to Iraq. As we explained in Chapter 2, George W. Bush was eager to focus his first term on an Iraqi invasion. But intelligence reports revealed no connection between al-Qa'eda and Iraq. To gratify domestic and international expectations, and to maintain imperial credibility in the face of an outside attack, Afghanistan had to be the first step in what was termed the "Global War on Terrorism," but the tacit assumption was that Iraq would be the second step. As Bush told his Cabinet, "Start with bin Laden, which Americans expect. And if we succeed, we've struck a blow and can move forward" to Iraq.[619]

Less than a year after the 2001 invasion of Afghanistan, the Bush administration began eagerly making the case for the war on Iraq, but this time with the U.S. project in Afghanistan as the template. Speaking to reporters in August 2002, Secretary of Defense Donald Rumsfeld said:

> Wouldn't it be a wonderful thing if Iraq were similar to Afghanistan? . . . If a bad regime was thrown out, people were liberated, food could come in, borders could be opened, repression could stop, prisons could be opened. I mean it would be fabulous.[620]

With most of the evidence for 9/11 pointing directly to al-Qa'eda, invading Iraq in 2001 would have been a public relations disaster for Bush. Time was needed to build a link between 9/11 and Iraq in the minds of the U.S. public. An invasion of Afghanistan provided the necessary ingredients.

Despite the fact that secret administration investigations found "'no compelling case' that Iraq had either planned or perpetrated the attacks" on 9/11, both President Bush and Vice President Cheney have asserted that there was a "collaborative relationship" between Iraq and al-Qa'eda. On November 7, 2002, Bush claimed that Saddam Hussein "is a threat because he's dealing with al-Qa'eda."[621] Apparently the linkage was made often enough in administration statements that the public believed it. In February 2005 a Harris poll found that 64 percent of Americans thought that "Saddam Hussein had strong links with al-Qa'eda," 47 percent believed that "Saddam Hussein helped plan and support the hijackers who attacked the U.S. on September 11, 2001," and 44 percent thought that "several of the hijackers who attacked the U.S. on September 11 were Iraqis." Those numbers have since declined, but the propaganda had already served its purpose, exploiting the 9/11 atrocities to fuel a war against Iraq.[622]

INCIDENTAL BENEFITS: HOW THE BUSH ADMINISTRATION EXPLOITS THE U.S. PRESENCE IN AFGHANISTAN

Prototype for Imperial Democracy

Now that the U.S. has a strong military presence in Afghanistan, the Bush administration can take advantage of the many medium- and long-term benefits.

To help bolster the case for invading Iraq, the administration realized that its actions in Afghanistan represented a useful precedent. To the superficial observer, the U.S. could make the claim that it had successfully implemented "regime change" followed by democratic elections. In Afghanistan, Washington put into practice the same model of imperial domination it would apply later to Iraq (albeit with very different results). This included the many challenges of organizing and implementing voter registration and elections, while carrying out military operations.

In the absence of critical media coverage, Afghanistan served as Bush's foreign policy "success story." The Bush administration was able to demonstrate through its operation in Afghanistan that it can defeat oppressive regimes and enjoy some temporary gratitude from the population. Afghanistan illustrated to potential international critics and the American public that U.S. invasions are carried out with the noblest of goals. Afghanistan's presidential elections were an important showcase for Bush's promise of democracy, even if the end result was a puppet leader and the same criminal warlords.

Often in his speeches, Bush cited Afghanistan and its "success story" immediately before referring to Iraq. Bush told the press:

> [O]ut of, kind of, the desperate straits that the Afghan people found themselves is now a welcoming society beginning to grow. And the same thing is going to happen in Iraq.[623]

During his acceptance speech at the August 2004 Republican National Convention, Bush again made the assertion that the "success" of Afghanistan was what was in store for the people of Iraq:

> Because we acted to defend our country, the murderous regimes of Saddam Hussein and the Taliban are history, more than 50 million people have been liberated, and democracy is coming to the broader Middle East. In Afghanistan, terrorists have done everything they can to intimidate people, yet more than 10 million citizens have registered to vote in the October presidential election, a resounding endorsement for democracy. Despite ongoing acts of violence, Iraq now has a strong prime minister, a national council, and national elections are scheduled for January.[624]

Bush's Reelection Propaganda

Another incidental benefit of having a "successful" U.S.-imposed democracy in Afghanistan was that it could be used in election propaganda to boost public confidence in Bush, perhaps enough to ensure him a second term as U.S. president. Bush averred that the "war on terrorism" was making progress to try to quell public skepticism after billions of dollars were spent on military operations. Even though the U.S.'s use of the rhetoric of "liberation" and "democracy promotion" in Afghanistan and Iraq were quite similar, Iraq didn't turn out to be quite as easy to subjugate as Afghanistan. While the Iraqi population increasingly turned against the U.S. armed presence, war-weary Afghans seemed to tolerate foreign forces in return for relative security. Constant attention to the rising attacks against U.S. soldiers in Iraq forced Bush to direct public focus toward Afghanistan.

Afghanistan's October 2004 presidential election helped deflect attention away from an increasingly chaotic and violent operation in Iraq in the run-up to the November U.S. elections. On October 9, 2004, the day that Afghans went to the polls, Bush remarked at one of his election campaign events:

> The people of that country, who just three years ago were suffering under the brutal regime of the Taliban, went to the polls to vote for their President. . . . It's amazing, isn't it? . . . Our strategy is succeeding. Think about the world the way it was prior to September the 11th. Afghanistan was the home base of al-Qa'eda. . . . Because we led, Afghanistan is an ally in the war on terror and they're having presidential elections today. . . . America has led, many have followed, and the world is safer.[625]

Conservatives like the writers of the *Weekly Standard* did their part right before the U.S. election by lauding the success of Afghanistan's election as a reason to vote for Bush:

> Rather than rending our national fabric with self-reproach, Election Day is a moment to take mature satisfaction in our country's real triumphs. In Afghanistan, four short years ago, murders were plotted for the World Trade Center and the

> Pentagon under the protection of the Afghan government. This year, the plotters and those who protected them have been driven from the country or into remote fastnesses, while vast hordes of Afghans turned out to pay homage to our ideals in a free election. As you part the curtains of your voting booth, remember them.[626]

Voting for Bush was portrayed as tantamount to voting for the continued well-being of the "vast hordes" of Afghan people.

Demonstrating that U.S. Is "Fighting Terrorism"

All U.S. military maneuvers in the twenty-first century have thus far been justified in the name of "fighting terrorism." A U.S. long-term presence in Afghanistan, the former base of al-Qa'eda, ensures that the U.S. public takes this supposed war at least somewhat seriously. Ultimately, *demonstrating* that a war is being waged against "terrorism" is more important than actually waging one.

In reality, to Bush, "fighting terrorism" simply means capturing about thirty individuals. Notwithstanding the difficulty of waging war against an abstract noun, Bush's approach is and has been to "decapitate the beast" by going after "high value targets" or "HVTs," thus ensuring a finite measure of success that can be well publicized each time a single al-Qa'eda leader is caught or killed. According to a *Washington Post* analysis, "Bush conducts the war on terrorism above all as a global hunt for a cast of evil men he knows by name and photograph." Meetings with the president on this strategy were "extremely granular, about individual guys."[627] In May 2005 the "Number 3 man" in al-Qa'eda, Abu Faraj Libbi, was caught. But Libbi was the fourth such "Number 3 man" that intelligence officials named. Each time a suspected al-Qa'eda operative was killed or captured (Mohammed Atef in November 2001, Abu Zubaydah in March 2002, Ramzi Binalshibh in September 2002, Khalid Sheikh Mohammed in March 2003), press reports highlighted it as a specific achievement in the "war on terrorism."[628] And each time the public was assured that the ultimate "decapitation" of Osama bin Laden was close at hand.

Several years after launching the war on Afghanistan, Bush's strategy may not be working too well. The greatest number of "high-value" captures and kills took place in the first year of the war, with fewer such successes in the years since. The *Washington Post* was granted access to classified tallies of the unpublicized "HVT" list, and identified twenty-eight of the approximately thirty names on the list: "Half—14—are known to be dead or in custody. Those at large include three of the five men on the highest echelon: bin Laden, his deputy Ayman Zawahiri and operational planner Saif al-Adel."[629] That means that the "war on terrorism" is ultimately about capturing or killing the fourteen remaining individuals who may or may not be in Afghanistan.

A highly publicized hunt for bin Laden's "Number 2 man," Ayman al-Zawahiri, keeps the "war on terrorism" in the news, with Bush assuring the U.S. public that all is being done to capture bin Laden and other anti-U.S. terrorists. The balance between achieving just enough success, but not too much, is a delicate one. While producing specific results is important to justify U.S. presence in Afghanistan, the longer that bin Laden and his deputy are at large, the longer the continued U.S. military presence (troops or bases) in Afghanistan is required.

The *Washington Post* also suggested that Bush and his vice president Cheney have "inflated the manhunt's success in their reelection bid." In 2003, Director of Central Intelligence George J. Tenet told the U.S. Senate that "more than one third of the top al-Qa'eda leadership identified before the war has been killed or captured."[630] In his January 2004 State of the Union Address, Bush almost doubled this figure: "nearly two-thirds of their [al-Qa'eda's] known leaders have now been captured or killed."[631] During the presidential election campaign later that year, the number was inflated even more, with Bush claiming that "75 percent of known al-Qa'eda leaders have been brought to justice."[632] The 75 percent claim was repeated numerous times in the lead-up to the election, with little scrutiny. One op-ed writer for the *Baltimore Chronicle* noted that "Bush improved his 'terror-fighting' grade from a merely-passing 66 percent to a more respectable 75 percent."[633] Although the number of "High-Value Targets" captured or killed magically increased without corroboration in the press, it is noteworthy that the number of U.S. military and intelligence forces in Afghanistan actually decreased in 2002 and 2003 as the administration prepared to invade Iraq.

As of this writing there are 18,000 U.S. troops "fighting terrorism" in Afghanistan. It is hard to believe that these on-the-ground military operations are aimed at capturing the remaining fourteen "High-Value Targets" on Bush's list. As we described in Chapter 2, U.S. forces work with local and regional commanders to carry out "search and destroy" operations aimed at nebulously defined "suspected terrorists" and to harass, arrest, capture, abuse, and torture local residents based on often inaccurate intelligence. Inside its prisons, U.S. forces carry out inhumane and cruel torture of men who are presumed guilty without any form of court trials. Another ugly consequence of the expanded post-9/11 antiterror policy is that it gives the U.S. government an excuse to ally with extremely repressive regimes that have been battling their own populations under the rubric of "fighting terrorism." Globally the U.S. has extended its "war on terrorism" to countries with terrible human rights records in Africa (Sudan, Ethiopia), Latin America (Colombia), and southeast Asia (Indonesia, the Philippines).

LONG-TERM BENEFITS: EXPANDING U.S. POWER IN CENTRAL ASIA

Shaping NATO into a "Useful Tool of the Americans"

As he was committing the bulk of U.S. forces and resources to the war in Iraq, President Bush turned over increasing authority in Afghanistan to his allies in NATO. An anticipated handover of at least some of the military reins in Afghanistan from the U.S. to NATO forces in 2006 guarantees for the long-term that the country remains under U.S.-friendly control and that NATO has an interest in serving U.S. aims.

The North Atlantic Treaty Organization bound the U.S. with Western European nations since 1953, in response to the growing Soviet-backed communist movement in Eastern Europe. In the years following the fall of the Soviet Union, the usefulness of NATO was called into question. "Warfare by committee, as practiced by NATO, has simply become too cumbersome in an age that requires light and lethal strikes," explained writer Robert D. Kaplan.[634] The events of 9/11 and the U.S. actions that followed provided the perfect opportunity for NATO to reinvent itself and increase its relevance, particularly as a military force at the U.S.'s disposal. NATO and the U.S. are seen to have a common agenda. According to Defense Secretary Rumsfeld, "NATO nations are those—for the most part—those countries on earth that have the same values as we do in North America."[635]

After the 1999 U.S.-led NATO war against the former Yugoslavia, Afghanistan was NATO's first military operation. More significantly, it was the first time NATO involved itself in Asia. Immediately after September 11, 2001, the North Atlantic Council invoked Article V of the North Atlantic Treaty: "an armed attack against one or more [allies] shall be considered an attack against them all." The commitment to assist a NATO ally is not unconditional; rather, each member country will assist the ally under attack with "such action as it deems necessary, including the use of armed force."[636] In October 2001, NATO Secretary General Lord Robertson, in a speech entitled "Is NATO Up to the Challenge?" enthusiastically declared his hope that NATO would be part of whatever response the U.S. decided upon:

> The Article 5 commitment is alive and well; and it applies to U.S. soil just as it applies to Europe. This should leave no room for doubts or second-guessing. We stand together. Europe and North America are one single security space . . . the events of September 11 have not invalidated NATO's pre-September agenda. If anything, they have reinforced the logic of that agenda . . . if the U.S. Congress asks the Europeans "what have you done for me lately?"—we should be ready to give a decent answer.[637]

It should be noted that this statement was made even before the U.S. began bombing Afghanistan and before there was public mention of an invasion of Iraq.

Invoking Article V also appeased Russia, a long-time critic of the clause that rallied together NATO countries against the common menace of the Soviet Union. Now Article V could be applied to another "enemy" common to both NATO countries and Russia. Lord Robertson expressed this openly: [638]

> There is a window of opportunity here that we cannot afford to miss. In Russian eyes, Article 5 has been the quintessential demonstration of NATO's anti-Russian orientation. Now we have invoked Article 5—but in an entirely different context, a context Russia can understand. We must build on this momentum and eradicate the remaining Cold War stereotypes, on both sides.

The common enemy was no longer within Europe, but arose from "unstable failed states and terrorist organizations far from Europe's borders."[639] Defense Secretary Rumsfeld encouragingly stated: "NATO is and will remain the central framework, not only for transatlantic military cooperation, but also for the West's mobilization of its comprehensive collective power to defend its interests."[640]

At a summit in Prague in November 2002, NATO initiated several former Soviet states into the alliance, and launched a radical overhaul of the organization with a focus on finding "a new role for the alliance in a world where the U.S. can—and does—fight wars without it." The overhaul included creating the NATO Response Force, a 20,000-person "strike force" from NATO countries to be used "wherever needed," including outside Europe's borders. One European analyst explained: "the Europeans have to try to turn NATO into a useful tool for the Americans, as a military organization without too many complications that is usable worldwide and is readily deployable."[641]

U.S. Defense Secretary Donald Rumsfeld warned, "If NATO does not have a force that is quick and agile, which can deploy in days or weeks instead of months or years, then it will not have much to offer the world in the 21st century,"[642] by which he meant, "offer the U.S." NATO Secretary General Robertson was ready to deliver, saying, "flexibility and usability are the keynotes"[643] of NATO's overhaul. NATO's ability to provide a "flexible" force for the U.S. is extremely useful in the face of the United Nations' cumbersome machinery of discussion, dialogue, and semi-democratic voting on international military operations. With the NATO Response Force serving as an "indispensable war-fighting instrument"[644] at its disposal, the U.S. can bypass the UN on peace-keeping and other military operations, as well as allow its own forces to focus on the important task of "war fighting."

In Afghanistan, U.S. forces are carrying out their task of hunting Taliban and al-Qa'eda remnants, while the International Security and Assistance Force (ISAF) does the task of peacekeeping and reconstruction. In August 2003, 6,500 NATO troops took over ISAF responsibilities from the United Nations and officially created a role for themselves within a U.S.-led conflict in Asia. In 2004 ISAF forces expanded outside Kabul and formed several "Provincial Reconstruction Teams" in various provinces. The presence of NATO instead of UN forces ensures that the U.S. is surrounded by allies in Afghanistan, with little to no oversight of its brutal operations in the countryside.

The long-term plan is for NATO to take over the bulk of operations in Afghanistan from the U.S. by the end of 2006. According to a Canadian NATO general, "Afghanistan is a 20-year venture." As if to stress that the NATO takeover will be every bit as aggressive as the U.S., the general went on to justify the long-term commitment: "There are things worth fighting for. There are things worth dying for. There are things worth killing for."[645] Since NATO is an alliance of mostly former colonial European powers, it is far less representative of the world's people, than say, the United Nations. By the same token, it is much less accountable to people whose interests do not coincide with those of the new American imperium. As of this writing NATO has already begun discussing options for integrating ISAF and Operation Enduring Freedom under NATO command.[646]

The U.S. attitude toward NATO's post-9/11 military role bolsters the theory that Afghanistan was far less important to the Bush administration than Iraq. Content to let NATO take over Afghanistan (an act that was "less politically charged" than patrolling Iraq),[647] the U.S. relegated NATO's role in Iraq to a minor one: training Iraqi security forces in 2004. This led some to feel that NATO was "underused" or even "sidelined" in Iraq.[648] NATO's training program in Iraq is under the command of a U.S. general, ensuring overall U.S. control of the Iraq operations.[649]

Ultimately, NATO control of Afghanistan serves both U.S. and European interests well. With NATO in charge, the nearly 20,000 U.S. forces in Afghanistan could be freed for subjugating Iraq, where the population is increasingly resistant to U.S. occupation. Meanwhile a "flexible" ally ensures that Afghanistan remains under Western control. The U.S.'s "wars on terrorism" have given the old powers of NATO a new lease on imperial life, and a reason to continue to exist. Both Western communities are once more mobilizing against a new common enemy.

Positioning U.S. Power in the Heart of Asia

The attacks of September 11, 2001, have been cleverly used by the U.S. to position itself militarily and economically into one of the last remaining regions of the world that has eluded its influence. The U.S. established military bases in Central Asia for the first time (Figure 7.1)—geographically closer than ever before to the remaining potential rivals to U.S. power, Russia and China. A permanent U.S. presence in the region could tip the remaining balance of global power in its favor.

In Afghanistan, U.S. air bases in Kandahar, Bagram, and Shindand are already semi-permanent structures—the first two received an $83 million upgrade in 2005.[650] Republican Senator John McCain openly claimed that the U.S. needs permanent military bases in Afghanistan to protect its "vital national security interests" in the region.[651] Justifying the bases to the Afghan public, President Hamid Karzai insisted at a press conference that "the Afghan people want a longer term relationship with the United States." He did not consult with the Afghan people, however, thousands of whom protested in May 2005 against permanent U.S. military bases.[652]

Even as the Taliban regime fell, the U.S. took advantage of Operation Enduring Freedom by establishing several bases in the countries surrounding Afghanistan. In early 2002, then–deputy Secretary of Defense Paul Wolfowitz explained that bases would "send a message to everybody, including important countries like Uzbekistan, that we have a capacity to come back in and will come back in."

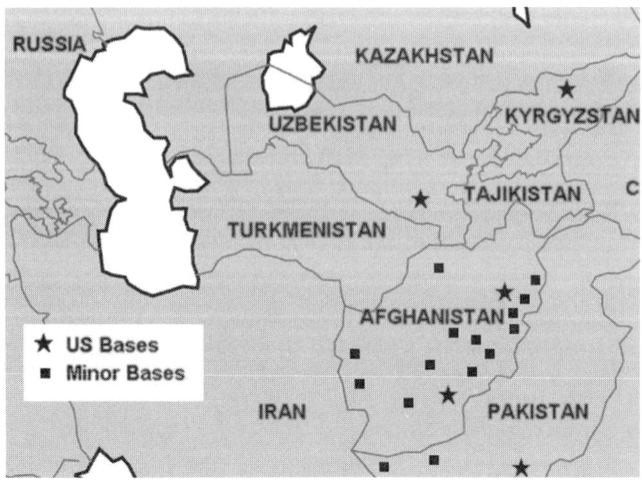

Figure 7.1—January 2005 location of U.S. bases in Central Asia. Based on maps found on the Globalsecurity.org website.

Despite Uzbekistan's horrendous human rights record, the State Department's country profile of Uzbekistan admitted a close alliance with the U.S.:

> Uzbekistan has been a close ally of the United States at the United Nations. Uzbekistan has been a strong partner of the United States on foreign policy and security issues ranging from Iraq to Cuba. . . . Uzbekistan is a strong supporter of U.S. military actions in Afghanistan and Iraq and of the global war against terror. . . . The United States, in turn, values Uzbekistan as a stable, moderate force in a turbulent region.[653]

Using Uzbekistan for military bases has been "undeniably critical" to the U.S., which paid $15 million to Uzbek authorities for use of Karshi-Khanabad airfield since 2001.[654]

Washington's military arrangement with Uzbekistan came at the cost of "protect[ing] Uzbekistan's security," i.e., supporting the violent suppression of Karimov's opposition.[655] In May 2005, government forces killed hundreds of demonstrators in Andijan, Uzbekistan, in what human rights organizations called a "massacre."[656] When the U.S.

government called for an international investigation, in a surprise move, Tashkent responded by evicting the U.S. from one of its most crucial military bases in Central Asia. While Bush *seems* to be putting human rights above its war effort, one senior administration official told the *Washington Post* on condition of anonymity that the intention was to "wait for a cooling-off period."[657]

Tajikistan, which offered the U.S. air-space rights and refueling privileges in 2001, is now being considered as the site for a new U.S. military base.[658, 659] The U.S. also built an air base in Kyrgyzstan, calling it a "transportation hub" for troops and aircraft, initially intended as a temporary base. Although U.S. government officials won't admit it, the Kyrgyz base, like the Afghan bases, is evolving toward permanency.

The U.S. has also engaged with Turkmenistan in its "war on terror." In a 2002 visit to Turkmenistan, U.S. Defense Secretary Rumsfeld remarked, "this country has been cooperative with respect to the global war on terrorism, for which we are grateful and appreciative." Turkmenistan provided land corridors, refueling support, and overflight permissions for U.S. and NATO aircraft. Like Uzbekistan, it has terrible human rights practices. The dictatorial president, Saparmurat Niyazov, who calls himself "Turkmenbashi" (Great Leader of all Turkmen), is described by *Foreign Affairs* as a "totalitarian megalomaniac"[660] whose "domination . . . of all aspects of life in the country and the personality cult he has developed" has resulted in an "appalling" human rights situation.[661] After an attack against Niyazov in 2002, political and civil liberties were severely restricted and there were widespread arbitrary arrests, evictions, detentions, and torture. The government controls all media, and there is no freedom of speech or religion. The rights of women, labor, and non-Turkmens are systematically violated.[662] In 2003, the European Union declared Turkmenistan "one of the worst totalitarian systems in the world."[663]

Broadly speaking, the current U.S. military posture in Central Asia "reflects a major change [after 9/11] in the U.S. vision of who its enemies are and how to confront them." The *Wall Street Journal* described this as "one of the biggest shifts in U.S. military thinking in the past 50 years." In essence, the new strategy entails the placement of U.S. forces "in what Pentagon officials call an 'arc of instability' that runs through the Caribbean Rim, Africa, the Caucasus, Central Asia, the Middle East, South Asia and North Korea." Instead of a single superpower, the new "enemy" apparently resides in countries and regions that are mostly poor and have been "largely cut off from economic globalization. . . . The new strategy assumes that the U.S. is far more likely to send troops into countries that are disconnected from the global economy."[664]

The new Pentagon vision affects the way military bases are conceptualized and troops are deployed. Defense Secretary Rumsfeld remarked that the U.S. was not interested in huge permanent bases, but rather "operating sites" in Asia, which would "not be permanent as a base would be permanent, but would be a place where the United States and coalition countries could periodically and intermittently have access and support."[665] In a speech to the Senate Armed Services Committee, Rumsfeld referred to traditional U.S. military deployment as "static deterrence" against "large armies, navies, and air forces," and went on to describe the new "revolution" in military deployment brought on by the "need to be able to deploy [armed forces] to trouble spots quickly."[666]

Foreign Affairs reported on this new "lily pad" approach, which consists of "small, lightly staffed facilities for use as jumping-off points in a crisis. These 'warm bases,' as they have also been called, would be outfitted with the supplies and equipment to rapidly accommodate far larger forces." The smaller facilities "would be established by negotiating a series of access rights with a wide range of states" and remain connected to larger permanent bases in Germany and Japan.[667] This method gives the U.S. military added flexibility in conflict situations. According to reporter Stephen Blank, "in the event of a crisis, these facilities would expand to accommodate a rapid influx of military personnel and equipment."[668]

In addition, these smaller military facilities are a way for the United States to transition from the use of big bases in Asia, which attract too much attention and often become a point of contention with host countries. *Atlantic Monthly* correspondent Robert Kaplan in his article "How We Would Fight China" comments that big bases are "an intrusive, intimidating symbol of American power, and the only power left to a host-country is to deny us use of such bases." Indeed, the U.S. had no choice but to leave Uzbekistan when told to go in July 2005. Kaplan recommends instead, "unobtrusive bases that benefit the host country much more obviously than they benefit us."[669]

Dotting the Central Asian landscape with military bases sends a clear message to Asian countries that the U.S. is intent on being a force to reckon with in the region. A permanent U.S. presence is a deliberate provocation to not only Central Asian nations, but to the two superpowers in the region—China and Russia—which are also two of the strongest rivals to U.S. hegemony worldwide. The *New York Times* predicted, "too large or too long-term an American military presence [in Central Asia] could alarm Russia and China to the north."[670] In July 2005, the Shanghai Cooperation Organization (SCO) (which includes Kazakhstan, Kyrgyzstan, Tajikistan, Uzbekistan, China, and Russia) asked the U.S. to name a deadline for its use of military bases and airspace in Central Asia.[671] CIA Director George Tenet remarked specifically on Russia's concerns: "Russia remains supportive of U.S. deployments in Central Asia for Afghanistan—but is also wary of the U.S. presence in what Russia considers to be its own backyard."[672] Specifically irking Russia and Iran is the formation of the "Caspian Guard," a collaboration between the U.S., Azerbaijan, and Kazakhstan to ostensibly provide "security" for regional oil resources. According to former chair of the Defense Policy Board Richard Perle, the Guard is designed to "defend the Caspian countries from the threat of Moscow."[673]

What these developments point to is an increased ability for the U.S. to respond rapidly and with overwhelming force to any emerging threat to its interests in Central Asia. Given the importance of Central Asian resources globally, and the roles of Russia and China as powerful international players, the U.S. entry into the game via its "war on terror" in Afghanistan afforded a perfect opportunity for the U.S. to establish itself in the heart of Central Asia.

Pipeline Prospects

> The drive by U.S. companies to exploit these resources already has produced a political realignment of historic dimensions, including an unprecedented American presence in a region that had been under almost continuous Russian control since the mid-19th century.[674]
>
> —WASHINGTON POST

Even before the United States had a military presence in the former Soviet Union, U.S. corporations were doing business there. The chief targets of U.S. investments are the vast oil and gas reserves in the young Central Asian and Caspian states. These untapped resources were described by the U.S. Department of Energy as the "third largest oil and natural gas reserves behind the Middle East and Russia."[675] Despite the fact that controlling the Central Asian reserves was not a major reason for the U.S. invasion of Afghanistan, the expanded American military presence in the recently independent former Soviet states represents a crucial opportunity for the U.S. to assure its dominance and control of energy worldwide.

Current regional players include Russia, Iran, China, and India, all of whom are competing with each other and the U.S. for control of oil and gas. Russia, which already operates its own pipelines in the region, has embarked on an expansion of the Caspian Pipeline Consortium (CPC), which currently operates a pipeline connecting oil fields in western Kazakhstan and Russia with Russia's Black Sea coast. The CPC, led by Russia, includes the governments of Kazakhstan and Oman, as well as Chevron, Shell, Mobil, and other energy companies.[676] For a map of some of the major existing and proposed pipelines, see Figure 7.2.

Iran, the regional power that the U.S. most openly opposes, is also pursuing a pipeline through its territory from the Caspian to its Arabian Sea port. Iran is currently the world's second-largest global supplier of natural gas after Russia. The pipeline would increase this status as well as present an opportunity for neighboring customers Pakistan and India to fuel their growing economies. U.S. anxiety over Iranian regional influence has prompted strong pressure on Pakistan and India to stick to Turkmen gas, via the Turkmenistan–Afghanistan–Pakistan

(TAP) project.[677] Secretary of State Condoleezza Rice remarked at a press conference with the Indian Foreign Minister, Natwar Singh:

> We have made clear our concerns about the Iranian development. We have made clear that at a time when Iran has clearly not yet made a strategic choice to demonstrate to the world that it is prepared to live up to its international obligations, that we would hope that this would be taken into account.[678]

China, with its high-speed economic development, completed a pipeline from Shanghai to the Tarim Basin in August 2004, with plans to link to Kazakhstan, and potentially Turkmenistan and Iran in the near future. China's entry into the oil and gas pipeline game upsets a U.S. desire to extend the Baku–Tblisi–Caspian pipeline to draw on Kazakhstan's oil reserves. The competition could get more heated if India joins China, creating an Asian hub of control over the bulk of Caspian reserves.

Given the longstanding Russian influence on Central Asian and Caspian states, the U.S. and Europe are concerned about "a hypothetical Russian-led alliance of energy exporters, a super-OPEC . . . that would wield extraordinary power over energy markets."[679] To forestall such a development, the U.S. has sponsored a number of pipeline deals to compete with existing Russian projects. Generally, the U.S. and its allies have expended immense political and economic capital to develop pipeline routes that avoid going south through Iran, north through Russia, or east through China, even when such routes would be the most economical. The TAP scheme mentioned earlier is only one of several Western-backed pipelines in the Central Asian and Caspian region. The U.S. and Europe are eager to pipe the energy westward as well, even though it would cost much more than an equivalent Iranian pipeline to the Persian Gulf. After the first TAP pipeline deal collapsed in 1998, the U.S. under Clinton put most of its financial and political weight behind the Baku–Tblisi–Caspian (BTC) pipeline. The $3.6 billion project was built by a consortium of companies led by energy giant BP/Arco

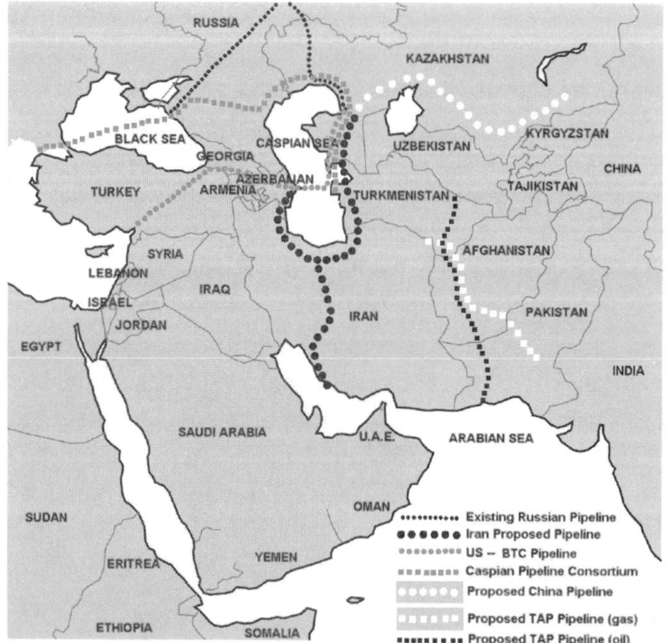

Figure 7.2—Some proposed and existing pipeline routes in Central Asia. Based on maps found at the U.S. Energy Information.

and will bring oil from Azerbaijan via Georgia to Turkey's Mediterranean coast.[680] Inaugurated in 2005, the BTC pipeline is considered the "world's biggest energy scheme."[681]

An op-ed in the *Hindu Newspaper* summarized a scenario in which the U.S. would gain control over the region's oil and gas reserves by:

> (i) replacing Russia's traditional influence over the principal sources of energy in the Caspian region, Kazakhstan, Azerbaijan and Turkmenistan; (ii) establishing political domination of the nearby regions—Georgia, Ukraine, Afghanistan—through which the oil and gas can be taken, bypassing Russia (and Iran), to the international market (principally Western Europe and the U.S.); and (iii) safeguarding the pipelines (by direct military presence, through NATO's eastward expansion, or through

> sponsoring a regional security alliance such as GUUAM (Georgia, Ukraine, Uzbekistan, Azerbaijan, and Moldova), which is led by Ukraine and Georgia at the moment.[682]

Efforts to supplant Russian influence with the principal energy-producing nations have had mixed results. Since Azerbaijan has the largest oil and gas reserves in the former Soviet Union, it figures highly in U.S. calculations. The U.S. has waived economic sanctions in 2002 for Azerbaijan's help in the "war on terror," mostly in the form of airspace flyover rights. According to the State Department, "The United States is committed to aiding Azerbaijan in its transition to democracy and formation of an open market economy."[683] There is more evidence of the second goal being fostered by the U.S. than the first. Azerbaijan has been accorded "Most Favored Nation" trading status. U.S. corporations are involved in three offshore oil projects with the country, including the BTC pipeline, and the U.S. government has sponsored the Caspian Guard to protect their investment. On the democracy side, however, the government of Azerbaijan is notorious for violently suppressing any sort of opposition politics. During the 2005 parliamentary elections there were reports of Azerbaijani police beating up opposition members at rallies. According to Human Rights Watch, "The Azerbaijani authorities are creating an environment of intimidation that flies in the face of the idea of free and fair elections."[684]

Other countries Washington has attempted to draw away from Russia include Turkmenistan, Uzbekistan, and Kazakhstan. The first two have aided and abetted U.S. troop movements in the "war on terror," and Turkmenistan is of course involved with the TAP pipeline. Uzbekistan has since rejected the U.S. presence. Kazakhstan, on the other hand, seems to be rising in U.S. favor. The country's oil and gas reserves are second only to those in Azerbaijan (out of the former Soviet states). Kazakhstan has been singled out by the Bush administration as having the potential "to lead Central Asia toward a future of democracy."[685] President Nursultan Nazarbayev has responded by becoming an ardent promoter of U.S. foreign policy. Kazakhstan is the only Central Asian country that sent troops to Iraq in support of the U.S. occupation.

Kazakh Foreign Affairs Minister Kassymzhomart Tokayev told the Heritage Foundation,

> [W]e stand ready to legally and politically protect interests of the United States in Kazakhstan and the entire region. . . . So far as the United States presence in Central Asia is concerned, we view it as one of the important factors of regional stability, strengthening the independence and sovereignty of Kazakhstan as well as that of other countries in the region.[686]

It remains to be seen how exclusive the Kazakh-U.S. relationship is, given the continuing close ties between Kazakhstan and Russia.

As time passes and media attention wanes from Afghanistan, we anticipate that the rhetorical reasons that led the U.S. to enter Afghanistan (imperial prestige, stepping-stone to Iraq, demonstrating imperial democracy, election propaganda, war on terror demonstration) will give way to more material interests (enhancing U.S. power, keeping NATO serving U.S. interests, dominating energy reserves). The latter set of interests primarily benefits U.S. military and corporate elites. The likely consequences for ordinary U.S. citizens are not so pleasant, however. As the U.S. military reduces its troop contingent in Afghanistan in 2006, it is possible that it might attempt to enhance its presence in the countries to the north, possibly to guard new pipeline routes. This may spark a new era of Cold War–style tensions with China and Russia, including the renewed threat of nuclear war. In addition, the U.S. occupations of Iraq and Afghanistan, and military cooperation with Azerbaijan and Pakistan represent an obvious threat to a defiant Iran, whose own embryonic nuclear program could in the future be the stated cause of a U.S. invasion. A continued unaccountable Western military presence in Afghanistan and surrounding countries is sure to create new cadres of anti-Western terrorists. It is entirely probable that these policies will result in the tragedy of September 11, 2001, repeating itself.

EPILOGUE

FROM THE BELLY OF THE BEAST

ACTIVISM AND SOLIDARITY

We hope this book has convinced you that the U.S. government has always acted in its own self-interest in Afghanistan. Through its military policies the U.S. has harmed Afghans directly by bombs, imprisonment, and torture, and indirectly by arming misogynist and fundamentalist warlords. The U.S. has interfered in the politics of Afghanistan, overseeing the installation of a puppet president and a government heavily saturated with criminal warlords, and this has had a deep impact on the democratic development of the country. Afghan women, whose horrific oppression garnered international outrage, were used by the Bush administration to sell a war to the U.S. public and then discarded when no longer convenient. The people of Afghanistan are far from liberated, yet the American public remains ignorant of their continued suffering, or of the culpability of the U.S., thanks to the pliability of the American media.

As a result Afghanistan is still a very dangerous place for the ordinary people who live there. The Taliban and al-Qa'eda forces have steadily intensified their attacks since 2002. In fact, 2005 has been the most violent year since the U.S. began its operations, with 91 U.S. troops and 1600 Afghans killed.[687] In late 2005/early 2006, dozens of people were killed in suicide bomb attacks, an unheard-of phenomenon in Afghanistan. The heavy-handed tactics of the U.S. military have helped to recruit foot soldiers for Taliban, al-Qa'eda, and other reactionary forces who are among the most visible and powerful opponents of U.S. imperialism.

As always, the Afghan people pay the price for decisions made by the U.S. and are now caught between the agendas of Islamic fundamentalism (warlords, Taliban, al-Qa'eda) and Western imperialism (U.S., NATO). While our suffering as a nation does not compare to the twenty-five years of Afghan suffering, we are caught in the friction between these same two forces. Americans learned on 9/11 that eventually we too pay the price for our government's policies. Democratic action in both nations can be the only long-term antidote to both Islamic fundamentalism and U.S. imperialism.

Given how our government has played the most consistently destructive role of any foreign power in Afghanistan, Americans who are already active in opposing the U.S. war in Iraq and elsewhere must not forget Afghanistan in their activism and political expression. It is imperative that we confront U.S. policies in Afghanistan and the surrounding region. Living in the "belly of the beast," as it were, it is up to us as Americans to change our government's policies. We certainly have far more power to do so than the Afghan people. Since this book is written by Americans, and is addressed primarily to Americans, the question arises: what should Americans demand of their government regarding its policies toward Afghanistan? Should Americans call for an immediate withdrawal of U.S. troops (as has been called for in Iraq)? Is it that simple? We don't think so, at least not yet. If the U.S. withdraws immediately, the warlords and the still-active Taliban movement will most certainly devour the country. But if the U.S. stays, the Afghan people will continue to suffer a violation of their rights and sovereignty at the hands of American soldiers. Furthermore, the continued presence of U.S. troops and their violent actions only inspire more violence on the part of the Taliban and al-Qa'eda. There is no easy path to recovery from the decades of war, foreign interference, and the accompanying chaos, but we can and must begin by discerning what Afghans themselves want.

THE U.S. PRESENCE: FEARED BUT NEEDED TEMPORARILY

There is little media analysis of how ordinary Afghans really feel about the actions of the U.S. military in their country. Afghans have historically defied any attempt at foreign subjugation. But they seem to have accepted a foreign troop presence in the face of so many decades of war.

In December 2005, an ABC News survey revealed that 65 percent of Afghans want the U.S. to leave their country, but "only after security is restored."[688] The uncomfortable reality is that, as long as disarmament of warlord factions is incomplete, the presence of foreign troops is believed by Afghans to provide some measure of security against warlords and their private armies.

Zakia, a student activist at Kabul University, echoed a common sentiment: "if American troops will be here, we will be safe." But she had no illusions about the U.S. historic and current record in Afghanistan. She recognized the irony that U.S. policies have led to so much war in her country that most Afghans will accept any alternative to chaotic warlord violence, including the presence of foreign troops:

> America knew that Afghan people are very powerful and very brave. So they even destroyed the bravery of Afghan people. They had such bad policies in Afghanistan, such bad things happened in Afghanistan, that all people are now not brave, they are just beggars. . . . [T]hat's why they need American troops.[689]

Friba of RAWA had this to say about the need for foreign troops:

> We, and the majority of Afghans, are still of the opinion that, even though the U.S. government is in Afghanistan for its own interests, even though the U.S. relies on the most dirty elements and parties in Afghanistan, even though the U.S. wants to install its puppet regime and puppet parliament in Afghanistan, still for the time being it is in the benefit of Afghanistan that the U.S. stay here for a limited time. Because the day the U.S. forces leave Afghanistan, the bloody years of 1992–96 will be repeated, as the warlords have weapons and money today [which they didn't have as much of under the Taliban].[690]

Poll numbers indicate that most Afghans favor a continued U.S. presence because they fear the warlords and Taliban/al-Qa'eda even more than the U.S. occupation. The ABC News poll seems to confirm this assessment: 91 percent of respondents considered the Taliban (41 percent), drug traffickers (28 percent), or warlords (22 percent) to be the greatest danger to Afghanistan, compared with 4 percent who felt that way about the U.S. This does not mean, however, that the U.S. government is warmly accepted. The same poll revealed that 30 percent of Afghans feel that attacks against the U.S. forces are justified.[691]

In fact, the violent actions of U.S. soldiers have galvanized a growing anti-U.S. sentiment. Indefinite imprisonment, torture, and murder of prisoners have resulted in surges of anger and outrage throughout the country. While we rarely hear of sustained widespread opposition to U.S. and NATO forces, there have been many large demonstrations against U.S. policies and Hamid Karzai's government across Afghanistan.

In May 2005, these large demonstrations were finally noticed and widely reported, but they were blamed on *Newsweek* reports of Koran desecration by U.S. soldiers, as we have discussed. Thousands of students and others took to the streets and dozens were killed by Afghan and U.S. forces. Reports indicate that the demonstrators were unarmed and shouted anti-U.S. and anti-Karzai slogans and burned U.S. and Pakistani flags and effigies. While they were not organized by the Taliban or warlords, the protests were joined belatedly by fundamentalists, who were also unhappy with a foreign troop presence that undermines their monopoly on power.[692]

RECOMMENDATIONS

In our opinion, the following things need to happen for the Afghan people to have a chance at a stable existence with real sovereignty.

Disarm the Warlords and Help Bring Them to Justice

During our trip to Afghanistan, we found widespread support for disarmament among people of diverse backgrounds.

In 2004 the Afghanistan-based Human Rights Research and Advocacy Consortium published a study called *Take the Guns Away*, which showed that 88 percent of Afghans wanted the government to do more to reduce the powers of commanders, with 65 percent saying that disarmament was the most important step toward improved security in Afghanistan.[693] Mariam, a middle-aged woman living in the remote western Farah Province told us what she thought of the U.S. policies of bombing Afghanistan from the air and supporting warlords on the ground: "My message to your government is only this—we never said that you should kill these fundamentalists and Taliban—we only said that you should not send rifles—you should disarm them. . . . This is my message."[694]

Wasay Engineer of the Solidarity Party of Afghanistan told us that many of Afghanistan's problems could be solved if private militias were completely disarmed:

> The disarming process is the best thing to bring peace in Afghanistan. . . . If disarming takes place there will be justice in Afghanistan, there will be a good constitution and law in Afghanistan, then after that we can do lots of economic projects for Afghanistan. It is important to disarm first to enable justice—that will then improve the economic and financial part of the country and the society will progress day by day.[695]

Currently the United Nations is carrying out a project of "Disarmament, Demobilization, and Reintegration" (DDR), which aims to "honorably decommission the Afghan Military Forces."[696] The DDR program has the potential for comprehensive disarmament if generously funded. The American public should demand that the U.S. government refocus its military expenditures into the DDR program in order to disarm its allies—the same men it armed in the '80s and again after 9/11.

The U.S. could also support future efforts led by the Afghan government to bring the armed warlords to trial for past crimes against humanity. In 2005 the Afghanistan Independent Human Rights Commission (AIHRC), a government funded agency, conducted a survey, *A Call for Justice*,[697] which concluded that a majority of Afghans consider themselves victims of human rights violations, and a significant portion desire some form of administration of justice such as a war crimes tribunal. Forty-four percent of Afghans surveyed said they would like the international community to be involved in such trials. Nader Nadery, the spokesman for AIHRC told us:

> The first thing that we want is to get rid of these people [warlords]. But if you reappoint them at the same position, people will slowly, after a year or so, realize that nothing has changed and the ministers can do nothing sitting at the top of a system which is corrupt. . . . If we don't remove the bad guys and reform the system we will not be able to achieve a democratic Afghanistan in the future. . . . The Afghans expect the U.S. to help them bring these perpetrators to justice and remove them from office rather than provide political support for these people to be in power.[698]

End the U.S. Occupation

> [M]any in Afghanistan are of the opinion that even the U.S.'s very trumpeted "war against drugs and terrorism" and campaign to "promote democracy" are bogus because the U.S. has forged a unity with the most infamous, anti-democratic, religious, terrorists and drug mafia forces in the history of Afghanistan.[699]
>
> —MALALAI JOYA, WOMEN'S RIGHTS ACTIVIST AND MEMBER OF THE AFGHAN WOLESI JIRGA (LOWER HOUSE OF PARLIAMENT).

If the U.S. continues on its current path, it is likely that it will overstay its welcome very soon. The rising movement against U.S. troops indicates that increasingly Afghans see the U.S. as more of a problem than a solution, and the pragmatic acceptance of American troops is being reconsidered. After the May 2005 countrywide demonstrations, over 1000 people demonstrated in July outside the main U.S. base at Bagram calling for an end to arbitrary house break-ins and arrests and for treating Afghans with more dignity. There is no reason to expect such actions to end, given that U.S. policy will probably not change any time soon. When we were in Afghanistan, we were told that the U.S. is considered like a "bitter medicine" by Afghans: despite all the horrible side effects, the overall result will be better than if the medicine is not taken. But there is only so much people can take. As Friba told us, "when you drink a bitter medicine but it still does not eliminate or even reduce your illness, you may come to the point to reject taking those medicines. And the Afghan people will soon come to this conclusion."[700]

The occupation of all foreign troops should end, *but only after disarmament is complete and Afghans feel safe in their own country*. We recommend that the United States end its futile "war on terror," stop backing any and all warlords, armed militias, and those with violent backgrounds in Afghanistan, and instead focus on taking back the weapons provided over decades. If there was indeed nationwide disarmament of private militias, there would be little reason for the U.S. to offer protection against armed forces, and consequently to stay in Afghanistan. The end of U.S. occupation should include the permanent closure of all U.S. bases in the country, whose purpose has more to do with the desire to challenge Russia and China than to help the Afghan people. Such a course of action is very unlikely unless it is demanded by the American public.

Expand International Security Forces and Strengthen the Afghan National Army

Withdrawing U.S. forces may reduce new recruits to resurgent Taliban/al-Qa'eda forces, but it will not entirely diminish them. Nor will it be able to forestall a resurgence in warlord militia strength. In the absence of international attention, the Taliban easily took over Afghanistan in the mid-'90s, and could do so again. Immediately after the Taliban's fall in 2001, the U.S. and international community had an opportunity to fill the military vacuum in the country with peacekeeping forces to help civil society recover from decades of war. However, this window of opportunity was lost as the U.S. prevented an expansion of the United Nations–led ISAF (International Security Assistance Force) outside Kabul and instead focused tens of thousands of troops to hunt and kill Taliban/al-Qa'eda remnants. This tactic has clearly failed to bring about security in Afghanistan. Today, the safest city in the country is Kabul, the city most heavily patrolled by foreign peacekeepers and Afghan National Army troops.

The American public ought to demand that the U.S. government, together with NATO and the United Nations, expand peacekeeping forces throughout the country. To avoid the appearance of Western imperial occupation, the UN, a far more representative body than NATO, should resume a central role. Ideally, such forces should comprise troops from countries that have not sponsored violence in Afghanistan.[701] These troops would be the only foreign presence in the country and their mandate would be strictly limited to preventing attacks on civilians by all armed groups. Their presence would have to be temporary, contingent upon the gradual strengthening of the Afghan National Army, which would eventually take over nationwide security.

Many progressive activists in the U.S. will balk at our suggestion for an international military occupation of Afghanistan, even a temporary one. Evidence of misconduct by peacekeeping forces in other countries is certainly a warning against even this kind of force. However, we see no other solution to Afghanistan's desperate need for security throughout the country.

Support Secular, Democratic Afghan Groups

While Washington continues its destructive policies, our officials and media make it seem as if the only groups in Afghanistan critical of the U.S. are religious fundamentalists. But these groups do not enjoy popular support[702] and are co-opting social justice movements to their own ends. Regarding the May 2005 protests, Selay of RAWA told us,

> [O]f course the fundamentalists, especially the party of Gulbuddin and al-Qa'eda, try to make use of these protests and guide it according to their own wishes. . . . If the situation continues like this, we will see larger and more violent protests by people. Of course the Taliban and al-Qa'eda will try to make use of this situation more then others. Unfortunately democratic-minded forces of Afghanistan are very weak and are not being supported by the international community, so are not in the position to lead these protests in the best possible way.[703]

The prodemocracy movements in Afghanistan need support from the international community and in particular from Americans. People of conscience in the United States can counterbalance our government's violent policies in Afghanistan by backing nonviolent, democratic, human rights–based indigenous Afghan groups. There are various worthy organizations in Afghanistan doing the hard work of providing education, health care, and skills training, as well as expanding human rights and women's rights, and even politically agitating against warlordism and fundamentalism. We list some at the end of this chapter.

Pay Reparations

In addition to supporting the political infrastructure of a new democratic culture in Afghanistan, the people of the United States owe it to the Afghan people to pay for the full reconstruction of the physical infrastructure of the country, destroyed as a direct result of intense, ongoing conflict supported and fueled by U.S. policies from the 1980s to the present. Afghans have received only a small fraction of international aid per capita compared with people in other conflict situations such as Bosnia, Kosovo, and East Timor.[704] A trust fund should be set up for the reconstruction of Afghanistan, with contributions from the countries that fueled the past quarter century of war: the U.S. and its allies (Great Britain, France, Egypt, Saudi Arabia, Pakistan, UAE, China), Russia, Iran, and India. The Afghan government's reconstruction requests should be fully funded.[705]

Increase and Improve Media Coverage

Many Afghans we met expressed the fear that the U.S. public was forgetting about them once more, just like after the Soviet withdrawal in the early 1990s. Sadly, it seems as though this apprehension is justified. Indeed, a Harris poll conducted in July 2005 revealed that fewer Americans pay attention to Afghanistan (62 percent) than Iraq (85 percent).[706] Part of the blame lies with the poor media coverage of Afghanistan. As we showed in Chapter 6, the U.S. mainstream media has drastically dropped its coverage of Afghanistan, and whatever coverage exists is usually patently uncritical of U.S. policy and actions.

We urge Americans to seek out information on Afghanistan, and to pressure their local and national media institutions to pay greater attention to Afghanistan. For example, groups that regularly release detailed and well-researched reports include the Afghanistan Justice Project, the Afghanistan Research and Evaluation Unit, the Afghanistan Independent Human Rights Commission, Human Rights Watch, Amnesty International, and the International Crisis Group. Independent community media organizations that often provide alternatives to mainstream coverage should be encouraged to do the same.

We think the American public will take seriously a media discourse critical of U.S. policy in Afghanistan. The July 2005 Harris poll showed that only one-third of respondents agreed that "things in Afghanistan are moving in the right direction," whereas 68 percent said that either "things are moving in the wrong direction" (27 percent) or were not sure (41 percent). When respondents were asked if they were "confident . . . that U.S. policies in Afghanistan will be successful," a plurality (45 percent) said they were "not confident," and only 25 percent were "confident." The remaining 30 percent were "not sure." A majority of respondents (67 percent) said "the situation for U.S. troops in Afghanistan" was either "getting worse" (30 percent) or that there was "no real change" (37 percent).

Remember Afghanistan

Unlike the occupation and military maneuvers in Afghanistan, the U.S. war on Iraq has sparked a serious antiwar movement. U.S.-sponsored injustices in Afghanistan are comparable to those in Iraq, Haiti, Colombia, Palestine, or East Timor, and thus should be addressed alongside the many other worthy causes that U.S. progressives have taken up. We urge all antiwar activists reading this book to remember Afghanistan in their activism. U.S. organizers should mention Afghanistan in their posters, flyers, announcements, newsletters, and other widely distributed materials. Too often U.S.-based activists leave out any mention of Afghanistan in their indictments of U.S. foreign policy. If Afghanistan is ignored, it is certain that U.S. government impunity will continue.

However, it is crucial that in our desire to highlight Afghanistan, we not fall into the same traps of exploitation and sensationalism that the mainstream media and conservative and liberal groups are guilty of. Objectifying Afghan women by their clothing is not appropriate. Wearing a burqa at an antiwar rally does not make sense as a gesture of solidarity, nor is it appropriate for non-Afghans to do so. It deprives Afghan women of their agency in the same way as the Bush administration did to help justify its war in 2001. Thousands of Afghan women have bravely marched with bare faces and fists in the air in their political demonstrations, demanding their rights. Such an image that defies stereotyping and exploitation is what we recommend.

During our time in Afghanistan, we met many brave and resilient people. The thought of them drives our activism and our desire for justice for the Afghans. They defied our expectations, moved us to tears with the stories of their losses, and earned our deep respect for their determination to nurture democracy and human rights in such a desperate situation. Mariam, who lost her husband as a result of cruel U.S. policies in the 1980s, challenged us:

> We are also human beings. We are women. We want our rights, we want education. We also want all these things that your people want. I also want to be free like you people, to go freely to America, and to Japan and to other countries to visit and see other people, to see how they live. For how long should we be living in these rooms with no freedom and such cruelty?

We hope the American people will look at themselves and their government and think about the answer to Mariam's question. More than that, we need to fight for a world in which Mariam no longer needs to ask this of us.

ANTIFUNDAMENTALIST, PRO–HUMAN RIGHTS HUMANITARIAN ORGANIZATIONS IN AFGHANISTAN RUN BY WOMEN

Revolutionary Association of the Women of Afghanistan (www.RAWA.org) is a women-led group that has been organizing poor women, refugees, students, and others to struggle for their rights in a nonviolent manner since 1977. They run scores of social and political projects throughout Afghanistan and in Pakistan's refugee camps, organize annual political demonstrations and publish a quarterly political magazine. The authors have been raising funds for RAWA's projects since 2000 and highly recommend RAWA as being on the forefront of political and social struggle in Afghanistan.

Humanitarian Assistance for the Women and Children of Afghanistan (www.HAWCA.org) was established in 1999 as a "nonpolitical" organization providing support to Afghan women and children. HAWCA's vice president, Habiba Sarabi, went on to be appointed the first female governor in Afghanistan in 2005. HAWCA runs a number of health, educational, and micro-finance projects in Afghanistan and Pakistan.

Organization for Promoting Afghan Women's Capabilities (www.geocities.com/OPAWC), is run by Malalai Joya, a young and spirited social worker and elected member of Parliament, who gained international attention when she denounced warlords in Afghanistan's 2003 Constitutional *Loya Jirga* (Chapter 5). OPAWC funds medical teams in fourteen Afghan provinces and runs a number of schools and literacy projects.

NOTES

1. Editorial, "Afghan Spring," *Free Lance-Star*, May 23, 2004, http://www.freelancestar.com/News/FLS/2004/052004/05232004/1371798.
2. Ibid.
3. Rachel Stohl and Michael Stohl, "Fatally Flawed? U.S. Policy Toward Failed States," *Defense Monitor*, October 2001; Press Conference: Prime Minister Tony Blair and President George Bush, April 6, 2002, http://www.number-10.gov.uk/ output/Page1711.asp.
4. "'War lite' is all very well. Empire lite is a mistake," *Economist* (London), August 14, 2003; The White House, "The National Security Strategy of the United States of America," September 2002.
5. Sebastian Mallaby, "The Reluctant Imperialist: Terrorism, Failed States, and the Case for American Empire," *Foreign Affairs*, March/April 2002; Martin Wolf, "We cannot ignore failing states," *Financial Times* (London), June 8, 2004.
6. James Dobbins et al., *America's Role in Nation-Building: From Germany to Iraq* (Santa Monica: RAND, 2003), 129.
7. Mariam, in conversation with the authors, Farah, Afghanistan, February 22, 2005.
8. Amnesty International, *Human Rights Defenders in Afghanistan: Civil Society Destroyed*, ASA 11/012/1999, 1 November 1999, http://web.amnesty.org/library/Index/ENGASA110121999?open&of=ENG-PAK; Afghanistan Justice Project, *Casting Shadows: War Crimes and Crimes Against Humanity: 1978–2001*, (Kabul: The Afghanistan Justice Project, 2005), 62.
9. Anne E. Brodsky, *With All Our Strength: The Revolutionary Association of the Women of Afghanistan* (New York: Routledge, 2003), 90–92.
10. Qasimi, in conversation with the authors, Farah, Afghanistan, February 23, 2005.
11. Tim Golden, "In U.S. Report, Brutal Details of 2 Afghan Inmates' Deaths," *New York Times*, May 20, 2005.
12. *A Call for Justice: a National Consultation on past Human Rights Abuse* (Kabul: Afghanistan Independent Human Rights Commission, January 29, 2005), http://www.aihrc.org.af/Rep_29_Eng/rep29_1_05call4justice.pdf.
13. Alex Whiting, "Afghanistan still the 'sick man' of Asia," *Reuters Alertnet*, June 20, 2005.
14. *Afghanistan: National Human Development Report 2004* (United Nations Development Programme, 2005), http://undp.org.af.
15. "U.S. Adults Paying Less Attention to the Events in Afghanistan than Those in Iraq," *Harris Poll*, July 26, 2005, http://harrisinteractive.com/harris_poll/index.asp?PID=587.
16. Craig Baxter, in *Afghanistan: A Country Study*, http://countrystudies.us/afghanistan/27.htm; U.S. Embassy (Kabul), "The Afghan Left," Airgram (Confidential), May 22, 1973, in National Security Archive Electronic Briefing Book No. 59, ed. William Burr, October 26, 2001, http://www.gwu.edu/~nsarchiv/NSAEBB/NSAEBB59.
17. Harold H. Saunders and Henry A. Applebaum (National Security Council Staff), "Coup in Afghanistan," Memorandum (Secret), July 17, 1973, in National Security Archive Elec-

tronic Briefing Book No. 59, ed. William Burr, October 26, 2001, http://www.gwu.edu/~nsarchiv/NSAEBB/NSAEBB59.

18. Steve Galster, "Afghanistan: The Making of U.S. Policy, 1973–1990," October 9, 2001, in The September 11th Sourcebooks, Vol. II: *Afghanistan: Lessons from the Last War*, National Security Archive, http://www.gwu.edu/~nsarchiv/NSAEBB/NSAEBB57/essay.html#8.
19. Ibid.
20. Ibid.
21. *Le Nouvel Observateur* (French version), January 15–21, 1998, 76, trans. William Blum, http://www.counterpunch.org/brzezinski.html.
22. Galster, "The Making of U.S. Policy."
23. Anthony Austin, "Soviet, Recounting Afghan Events, No Longer Ties Ex-Leader to CIA," *New York Times*, January 15, 1980; cited in William Blum, *Killing Hope* (Monroe, ME: Common Courage, 1995), 343.
24. Blum, *Killing Hope*, 342.
25. Toufiq, in conversation with the authors, Farah, Afghanistan, February 23, 2005.
26. Jimmy Carter, *State of the Union Address 1980*, January 23, 1980; http://www.jimmycarterlibrary.org/documents/speeches/su80jec.phtml.
27. Barnett Rubin, *The Fragmentation of Afghanistan: State Formation and Collapse in the International System*, 2nd Ed. (New Haven: Yale, 2002), x.
28. *Policy, Responsibility, and Platforms of the Revolutionary Association of the Women of Afghanistan*, Tabistan 1359 (RAWA: Summer 1980), cited in Hafizullah Emadi, *Repression, Resistance, and Women in Afghanistan* (Westport: Praeger, 2002), 109; Barnett R. Rubin, "Afghanistan: The Forgotten Crisis," *Writenet* (UK), February 1996, http://www.fuhem.es/portal/areas/paz/observatorio/informes/afganistan1.htm.
29. Tim Weiner, *Blank Check: The Pentagon's Black Budget* (New York: Warner, 1990), 149; Barnett Rubin, *The Search for Peace in Afghanistan: From Buffer State to Failed State* (New Haven: Yale, 1995) 113–14; House Committee on Foreign Affairs, *United States Policy Toward Afghanistan*, 101st Cong., 2nd sess., 1990, 157–158; Brodsky, *With All Our Strength*, 90–92.
30. Robert D. McFadden, "Bin Laden's Journey from Rich, Pious Boy to the Mask of Evil," *New York Times*, September 30, 2001.
31. Paul Berman, *Terror and Liberalism* (New York: W.W. Norton & Company, 2004), 16–17; for more details on how U.S. policy led to the terror networks of the 1990s, see John K. Cooley, *Unholy Wars: Afghanistan, America, and International Terrorism* (3rd Ed.) (London: Pluto, 2002); Mahmood Mamdani, *Good Muslim, Bad Muslim* (New York: Pantheon, 2004), 119–177; and William Blum, *Rogue State: A Guide to the World's Only Superpower* (Monroe: Common Courage, 2000), 33–37.
32. Barnett Rubin, *Search for Peace*, 113–114; United States Department of State, *Afghanistan and Pakistan*, March 1980, Cited in Galster, *The Making of U.S. Policy*; Rubin, *Search for Peace*, 34–5.
33. Milton Bearden, "Afghanistan, Graveyard of Empires," *Foreign Affairs*, November/December 2001.
34. George Gallup Jr., *The Gallup Poll: Public Opinion 1980* (Wilmington: Scholarly Resources, 1981), 17–18; Orrin Hatch, "Don't Forget the Afghans," *New York Times*, November 22, 1985; Bill Bradley, "Captive Afghanistan, 6 Years Later: Fighters Need U.S. Aid," *New York Times*, December 27, 1985.
35. James Nathan, "Don't Arm the Afghans," *New York Times*, September 6, 1980.
36. Barnett Rubin, *Fragmentation*, ix.

37. Eduard Shevardnadze, Speech to the Plenary Session of the Supreme Soviet, October 23, 1989, http://history.hanover.edu/courses/excerpts/111shev.html; House Committee on Foreign Affairs, *Policy Toward Afghanistan*, 25.
38. John Kifner, "Afghans in Exile Losing Influence to Rebels in Field," *New York Times*, June 12, 1988; Richard S. Erlich, "Mujahideen Vow to Execute Afghan Communists," *Washington Times*, January 21, 1988.
39. Rubin, *Fragmentation*, x; Kifner, "Afghans in Exile"; Clifford Krauss, "U.S. Renews Hope for Afghan Peace," *New York Times*, October 16, 1990; Rubin, *Search for Peace*, 113–14.
40. House Committee on Foreign Affairs, *Policy Toward Afghanistan*, 116.
41. John F. Burns, "Now They Blame America," *New York Times Magazine*, February 4, 1990, 24.
42. Associated Press, "Rocket Hits Bus Station in Kabul; 23 Reported Killed," *Los Angeles Times*, October 11, 1989.
43. House Committee on Foreign Affairs, *Policy Toward Afghanistan*, 42–3.
44. House Committee on Foreign Affairs, *Recent Developments in U.S. Policy Toward Afghanistan*, 102nd Cong., 1st sess., 1991, 27; Rubin, *Search for Peace*, 113–14.
45. Thomas Friedman, "U.S. Urges Afghan Factions to Avoid Violent Anarchy," *New York Times*, April 17, 1992; "Then There Were Three," *Economist*, May 30, 1992, 39.
46. Radek Sikorsky, "Afghanistan Revisited," *National Review*, August 23, 1993, 40; Editorial, *Los Angeles Times*, September 20, 1991.
47. Edward A. Gargan, "Rival Rebels Fight in Afghan Capital Day After its Fall," *New York Times*, April 27, 1992; Edward A. Gargan, "Rebels' Leader Arrives in Kabul and Forms an Islamic Republic," *New York Times*, April 29, 1992; Associated Press, "U.S. Officials Discuss New Link With Kabul," *New York Times*, June 15, 1992.
48. "The New Style," *Economist*, May 9, 1992, 35; Ahmed Rashid, "Behind the Veil, Again," *Far Eastern Economic Review*, June 4, 1992, 29; Fitwai-e-Sharia-e-Satr wa Hijab," Kabul, August 27, 1993. Cited in Emadi, *Repression*, 124.
49. "No Peace in Kabul," *Time*, August 24, 1992, 13; Associated Press, "Those Still in Kabul Cope With a Broken City," *New York Times*, September 6, 1992.
50. U.S. Department of State Dispatch, "Department Statements," October 5, 1992, 760.
51. Michael Griffin, *Reaping the Whirlwind: The Taliban Movement in Afghanistan* (Sterling: Pluto, 2001), 30.
52. "Afghanistan: Foreign-Sponsored Human Rights Disaster Ignored by the World," *Amnesty International*, November 29, 1995, ASA 11/016/1995.
53. John F. Burns, "With Kabul Largely in Ruins, Afghans Get a Respite from War," *New York Times*, February 20, 1995; "Afghanistan: International Responsibility for Human Rights Disaster," *Amnesty International*, November 1995, ASA 11/09/1995.
54. Griffin, *Whirlwind*, 26.
55. Paul Lewis, "UN Sets Up War-Crimes Panel for Charges of Balkan Atrocities," *New York Times*, October 7, 1992.
56. Editorial, "In Dubious Battle in Afghanistan," *New York Times*, February 4, 1990.
57. General Accounting Office, "Peace Operations: U.S. Costs in Support of Haiti, Former Yugoslavia, Somalia, and Rwanda" (Washington: GAO), NSIAD-96-38, March 6, 1996.
58. Kenneth Katzman, *Afghanistan: Current Issues and U.S. Policy*, Congressional Research Service Order Code RL30588 (Washington: Library of Congress, updated August 27, 2003), 35.
59. John F. Burns, "Outside Hands Still Stir the Afghan Pot," *New York Times*, February 26, 1995.
60. Burns, "Afghans Get Respite."

61. "When Hekmatyar failed to deliver for Pakistan, the administration began to support a new movement of religious students known as the Taliban." The September 11th Sourcebooks, Volume VII: *The Taliban File*, ed. Sajit Gandhi, National Security Archive Electronic Briefing Book No. 97, September 11, 2003, http://www.gwu.edu/~nsarchiv/NSAEBB/NSAEBB97/index.htm; A thorough history of the Taliban movement is given in Ahmed Rashid, *Taliban: Militant Islam, Oil, and Fundamentalism in Central Asia* (New Haven: Yale, 2000).
62. U.S. Embassy (Islamabad), Cable (Secret), "The Taliban: What We've Heard," January 26, 1995, Freedom of Information Act Release to the National Security Archive; U.S. Embassy (Islamabad), Cable (Confidential), "Meeting with the Taliban in Kandahar: More Questions than Answers," February 15, 1995, Freedom of Information Act Release to the National Security Archive. See http://www2.gwu.edu/~nsarchiv/NSAEBB/ NSAEBB97/index.htm; Michael Dobbs, "Analysts Feel Militia Could End Anarchy," *Washington Post*, September 28, 1996.
63. U.S. Department of State, Cable (Confidential), "Dealing with the Taliban in Kabul," September 28, 1996, Freedom of Information Act Release to the National Security Archive; see http://www2.gwu.edu/~nsarchiv/NSAEBB/NSAEBB97/index.htm.
64. Dobbs, "Anarchy"; Editorial, *Los Angeles Times*, September 30, 1996.
65. Kathy Gannon, Associated Press, "Taliban Rebels Take Hold as Streets of Kabul Revive," *Washington Post*, September 28, 1996; U.S. Department of State, *Daily Press Briefing #156*, September 27, l996 (Briefer: Glyn Davies).
66. Rashid, *Taliban*, 166; U.S. Embassy (Moscow), Cable (Confidential), "A/S Raphel Consultations with Deputy FM Chernyshev," May 13, 1996, Freedom of Information Act Release to the National Security Archive; Elaine Sciolino, "State Dept. Becomes Cooler to the New Rulers of Kabul," *New York Times*, October 23, 1996; U.S. Department of State, *Daily Press Briefing #156*.
67. Katzman, *Afghanistan: Current Issues*, 38.
68. Sciolino, "State Dept. Becomes Cooler"; House Committee on International Relations, Subcommittee on Asia and the Pacific, *U.S. Interests in the Central Asian Republics*, 105th Cong., 2nd sess., 1998, 39.
69. Lisa Girion, "Unocal to Settle Rights Claims," *Los Angeles Times*, December 14, 2004.
70. House Committee on International Relations, *U.S. Interests in the Central Asian Republics*, 41.
71. Sciolino, "State Dept. Becomes Cooler"; Susan Page, "Clinton camp mobilizing to keep women's vote," *USA Today*, October 15, 1996; Dan Morgan and David B. Ottaway, "Women's Fury Toward Taliban Stalls Pipeline," *Washington Post*, January 11, 1998.
72. Morgan and Ottaway, "Women's Fury"; Thomas W. Lippman, "UN Ambassador Will Deliver Message to Afghan Faction," *Washington Post*, April 9, 1998; Kenneth J. Cooper, "U.S. Wins Promise of Peace Talks in Afghanistan," *Washington Post*, April 18, 1998.
73. Zalmay Khalilzad and Daniel Byman, "Afghanistan: The Consolidation of a Rogue Regime," *Washington Quarterly* 23:1, 65–78, Winter 2000.
74. James Risen and David Johnston, "Experts Find No Arms Chemicals at Bombed Sudan Plant," *New York Times*, February 9, 1999; Michael Barletta, "Chemical Weapons in the Sudan: Allegations and Evidence," *Nonproliferation Review*, Fall 1998; Vernon Loeb, "Because of a Cupful of Soil, the U.S. Flattened this Sudanese Factory," *Washington Post*, July 25, 1999.
75. *The 9/11 Commission Report*, Authorized Edition (New York: W. W. Norton & Company, 2004), 116.

76. Craig Turner, "Self-defense Claim Should Hold Up, Experts Say," *Los Angeles Times*, August 21, 1998; Paul Richter, "U.S. Says Raids a Success, Warns of More Strikes," *Los Angeles Times*, August 22, 1998.
77. Paul Richter, "Raids a Success"; *The 9/11 Commission Report*, 116; Editorial, "U.S. Air Raids Necessary," *Los Angeles Times*, August 21, 1998.
78. Office of the UN Coordinator for Afghanistan, "Vulnerability and Humanitarian Implications of UN Security Council Sanctions in Afghanistan," December 2000.
79. UK Ministry of Defense, "Pictures of ISAF: The Indira Gandhi Hospital," March 2002, http://www.operations.mod.uk/fingal/photo_gallery_indira_gandhi_hospital.htm.
80. Ambassador Nancy Soderberg, "Statement in the Security Council on Adoption of Further Sanctions Against the Taliban in Afghanistan," U.S. Mission to the UN, December 20, 2000, http://www.un.int/usa/00_206.htm.
81. *The 9/11 Commission Report*, 126; Human Rights Watch, "Afghanistan: Ban Weapons To All Warring Factions," December 15, 2000, http://hrw.org/english/docs/2000/12/15/afghan623.htm.
82. United Nations General Assembly/Security Council, *The situation in Afghanistan and its implications for international peace and security*, Report of the Secretary-General, A/55/633-S/2000/1106, November 20, 2000.
83. "The Taliban Dilemma: More Sanctions Against the Taliban?" *Economist*, December 16, 2000.
84. "The Taliban Dilemma," *Economist*.
85. Revolutionary Association of the Women of Afghanistan, "UN Sanctions Amplifies the Agony of Our Misery-Stricken People," January 21, 2001, http://pz.rawa.org/rawa/unsanc.htm.
86. "Aid Workers Question Afghan Sanctions,"Associated Press, March 24, 2001.
87. Charles Recknagel, "Pakistan Fails to Observe UN Sanctions on Taliban," Radio Free Europe/Radio Liberty, April 2001; Barbara Crossette, "Russia Seeks Sanctions Against Pakistan for Aid to Taliban," *New York Times*, April 9, 2001; Farhan Bokhari, "U.S. Officials to Visit Afghanistan," *Financial Times*, April 20, 2001.
88. Agence France-Presse, "U.S. Officials Make Quiet Trip to Afghanistan, First Since 1998," April 18, 2001; BBC News, "U.S. Officials on Afghanistan Visit," April 18, 2001.
89. Talat Aslam, "Shift in U.S. Policy as Envoys Visit Afghanistan," *Dawn* (Pakistan), April 18, 2001.
90. Syed Talat Hussain, "U.S. Official Praises Taliban's Measures: Poppy Eradication," *Dawn* (Pakistan), May 5, 2001.
91. It is interesting that the 9/11 Commission also believed that Bush would have been quite capable of manufacturing a pretext to invade Afghanistan: "If a president wanted to rally the American people to a warlike effort, he would need to publicize an assessment of the growing al-Qa'eda danger. Our government could spark a full public discussion of who Usama Bin Laden was. . . . Recent examples of such debates include calls to arms against such threats as Serbian ethnic cleansing . . . [and] Iraqi weapons of mass destruction . . . We believe American and international public opinion might have been different . . . had they been informed of these details."

    See *The 9/11 Commission Report*, Authorized Edition (New York: W. W. Norton & Company, 2004), 341.
92. James Risen, "To Bomb Sudan Plant, or Not: A Year Later, Debates Rankle," *New York Times*, October 27, 1999.
93. *The 9/11 Commission Report*, 120; National Security Archive, "Bush Administration's First Memo on al-Qa'eda Declassified," National Security Archive Electronic Briefing

Book No. 147, ed. Barbara Elias, February 10, 2005, http://www.gwu.edu/~nsarchiv/NSAEBB/ NSAEBB147/index.htm.

94. *The 9/11 Commission Report*, 126–133; James Risen, "U.S. Pursued Secret Efforts to Catch or Kill bin Laden," *New York Times*, September 29, 2001; Michael Elliott, "They Had a Plan: Long Before 9/11, the White House Debated Taking the Fight to al-Qa'eda," *Time*, v160, i7, p28, August 12, 2002.
95. Richard Sale, "Pakistan Restricts Transit of Terrorists in Wake of Cole Attack," United Press International, November 20, 2000; Ahmed Rashid, "The Hard Road to Revenge," *Far Eastern Economic Review*, December 7, 2000; Elliott, "They Had a Plan."
96. U.S. National Security Council Counterterrorism Security Group (Classified), "A Strategy for Eliminating the Threat from the Jihadist Networks of Al Qida; Status and Prospects," December 2000, see National Security Archive, "First Memo on al-Qa'eda Declassified," http://www.gwu.edu/~nsarchiv/NSAEBB/NSAEBB147/index.htm; Elliott, "They Had a Plan"; *9/11 Commission Report*, 206.
97. *9/11 Commission Report*, 204–5.
98. *9/11 Commission Report*, 207–8; George Arney, "U.S. 'Planned Attack on Taleban'," *BBC Online*, September 18, 2001, http://news.bbc.co.uk/1/hi/world/south_asia/1550366.stm; Jonathan Steele et al., "Threat of U.S. Strikes Passed to Taliban Weeks Before NY Attack," *The Guardian* (London), September 22, 2001, http://www.guardian.co.uk/Archive/Article/ 0,4273,4262511,00.html.
99. Richard Clarke, interviewed by Leslie Stahl, "Did Bush Press For Iraq-9/11 Link?" CBS News, March 20, 2004, http://news4colorado.com/topstories/topstories_story_080210238.html.
100. *9/11 Commission Report*, 335; Bob Woodward, *Bush at War* (New York: Simon & Schuster, 2002), 43.
101. Department of Defense, [Title Excised], Cable (Confidential), October 4, 2001, in Sajit Gandhi, ed., The September 11th Sourcebooks, Volume VII: *The Taliban File*, National Security Archive Electronic Briefing Book No. 97, September 11, 2003, http://www.gwu.edu/~nsarchiv/NSAEBB/NSAEBB97/index.htm.
102. Woodward, *Bush at War*, 98.
103. George W. Bush, "Address to a Joint Session of Congress on Terrorist Attacks," September 20, 2001; George W. Bush, "Address to the Nation Announcing Strikes Against Al Qaida Training Camps and Taliban Military Installations in Afghanistan," October 7, 2001; George W. Bush, "Remarks Following a Meeting With the Homeland Security Council and an Exchange With Reporters," October 29, 2001; George W. Bush, "Remarks Following Discussions With Prime Minister Tony Blair of the United Kingdom and an Exchange With Reporters," November 7, 2001; All Bush speeches and remarks can be found in the *Weekly Compilation of Presidential Documents*, http://www.gpoaccess.gov/wcomp/index.html.
104. Elisabeth Bumiller, "President Rejects Offer by Taliban for Negotiations," *New York Times*, October 15, 2001; George W. Bush, "Exchange With Reporters on Returning From Camp David, Maryland," October 14, 2001.
105. John F. Burns, "Taliban Envoy Talks of a Deal Over bin Laden," *New York Times*, October 16, 2001.
106. Woodward, *Bush at War*, 103, 98, 63; Michael R. Gordon, "Allies Preparing for a Long Fight as Taliban Dig In," *New York Times*, October 28, 2001.
107. Marc Herold, *A Dossier on Civilian Victims of United States' Aerial Bombing of Afghanistan: A Comprehensive Accounting* (rev. ed.), Cursor.org, March, 2002, http://www.cursor.org/stories/civilian_deaths.htm.

108. Herold, *Dossier on Civilian Victims*; "Afghanistan: U.S. Bombs Kill Twenty-three Civilians," Human Rights Watch, Press Release, October 26, 2001; "Afghanistan: New Civilian Deaths Due to U.S. Bombing," Human Rights Watch, Press Release, October 30, 2001; Murray Campbell, "Bombing of Farming Village Undermines U.S. Credibility," *Toronto Globe and Mail*, November 3, 2001.
109. Richard Lloyd Parry, "A Village is Destroyed. And America Says Nothing Happened," *The Independent* (London), December 4, 2001.
110. David Zucchino, "The Americans . . . They Just Drop Their Bombs and Leave," *Los Angeles Times*, June 2, 2002.
111. Scott Baldauf, "Afghans Flee Kandahar Bombing," *Christian Science Monitor*, December 6, 2001.
112. David Zucchino, "The Americans . . ."; Doug Struck, "Casualties of U.S. Miscalculations," *Washington Post*, February 11, 2002; Susanne M. Schafer, "Raid May Have Involved Mistaken Deaths, Beatings of Innocents," Associated Press, February 11, 2002.
113. "Cluster Bombs in Afghanistan," Human Rights Watch Backgrounder, HRW.org, October 2001; Andrew Buncombe, "Don't confuse food parcels with cluster bombs, warns U.S.," *The Independent* (UK), October 31, 2001; "UN Slams Use of Cluster Bombs as 8 Die," *The News International* (Pakistan), October 26, 2001.
114. "Cluster Bombs in Afghanistan," Human Rights Watch Backgrounder, HRW.org, October 2001.
115. Suzanne Goldenberg, "Long After the Air Raids, Bomblets Bring More Death," *The Guardian* (London), January 28, 2002.
116. "Afghanistan: UN to clear coalition cluster bombs," UN Office for the Coordination of Humanitarian Affairs, IRINnews.org, January 2, 2002, http://www.irinnews.org/report.asp?ReportID=18295&SelectRegion=Central_Asia; "Fatally Flawed: Cluster Bombs and Their Use by the United States in Afghanistan," Human Rights Watch Report Vol. 14, No. 7 (G), HRW.org, December 2002, http://hrw.org/reports/2002/us-afghanistan/.
117. Jonathan Steele, "Forgotten Victims," *The Guardian* (London), May 20, 2002.
118. "Afghanistan: Air-dropping food rations is not enough," *Solidarités* (Paris), October 8, 2001; Agence France-Presse, "UN's Robinson Calls for Suspension of Air Strikes," October 12, 2001; Laura Flanders, "Killer Food Drops," WorkingforChange.com, October 8, 2001; Matt Peacock, "Tony Blair Departs for Middle East Again," ABC Radio (Australia), October 10, 2001, http://www.abc.net.au/am/stories/s387218.htm; "After the start of the bombing of Afghanistan: a Christian Aid perspective," ChristianAid.org.uk, October 10, 2001, http://www.christianaid.org.uk/afghanistan/0110food.htm; "MSF Rejects Link of Humanitarian and Military Actions," Médecins Sans Frontières, Press Release, October 8, 2001, http://www.msf.org/countries/page.cfm?articleid=70FD6D4D-3B90-407D-81F5119552D7CD9E.
119. Andrew Buncombe, "Don't confuse food parcels."
120. Cynthia McKinney, Statement on Afghanistan, House International Relations Subcommittee on International Operations and Human Rights, October 31, 2001, http://www.house.gov/international_relations/107/75925.pdf.
121. Chris Tomlinson, "U.S. Bombs Wipe Out Farming Village," Associated Press, December 3, 2001.
122. Christopher Hitchens, "The End of War," *The Nation*, November 29, 2004.
123. David Zucchino, "The Americans . . ."
124. Nicholas Kristof, "A Merciful War," *New York Times*, February 1, 2002.
125. Stephen Thorne, "New Foreign Policy Adopts 3-D Approach," *Canadian Press*, December 31, 2004.

126. Afghanistan Facilities, GlobalSecurity.org, http://www.globalsecurity.org/military/facility/afghanistan.htm (accessed March 12, 2006).
127. Amin Tarzi, "Establishing Security in Afghanistan: The Role of Provincial Reconstruction Teams," Radio Free Europe/Radio Liberty, January 30, 2003.
128. Afghanistan Facilities, GlobalSecurity.org.
129. Stephen Thorne, "New Foreign Policy."
130. Larry Thompson and Michelle Brown, "Security on the cheap: PRTs in Afghanistan," RefugeesInternational.org, July 7, 2003, http://www.refugeesinternational.org/content/article/detail/887/.
131. Afghanistan Facilities, GlobalSecurity.org.
132. Donna Miles, "Commander Reports Steady Progress in Eastern Afghanistan," American Forces Press Service, January 3, 2005.
133. Terry Boyd, "PRTs: The Public Face of Special Ops," *Stars and Stripes* (European Edition), February 12, 2004.
134. "Provincial Reconstruction Teams in Afghanistan," Position Paper Adopted by Interaction's Afghanistan Reconstruction Working Group, Interaction.org, April 23, 2003, http://www.interaction.org/files.cgi/1541_FINAL_PRT_POSITION_PAPER.pdf.
135. Carlotta Gall, "In Afghanistan, Violence Stalls Renewal Effort," *New York Times*, April 26, 2003.
136. Jim Teeple, "U.S. Military Efforts Focus on Security, Rebuilding in Afghanistan," Voice of America, May 5, 2003, http://www.voanews.com/english/archive/2003-05/a-2003-05-05-29-U.S.cfm.
137. Edward Girardet, "Security for Aid Workers—A Missing Link," *Christian Science Monitor*, December 20, 2004.
138. Ewen MacAskill, "Pentagon forced to withdraw leaflet linking aid to information on Taliban," *The Guardian* (London), May 6, 2004.
139. David Rohde, "G.I.s in Afghanistan on Hunt, but Now for Hearts and Minds," *New York Times*, March 30, 2004.
140. James Dunnigan, "Getting Afghans to Talk Without Torture," StrategyWorld.com, April 16, 2005.
141. Pamela Constable, "Army Veterinarians Make a Field Call: Whirlwind Treatment of Afghan Herds Aims to Win Hearts of Rural People," *Washington Post Foreign Service*, March 7, 2004.
142. Carsten Stormer, "Winning hearts, minds and firefights in Uruzgan," *Asia Times* (Hong Kong), August 6, 2004.
143. David Rohde, "G.I.s in Afghanistan."
144. Kathleen T. Rhem, "Civil Affairs: Winning Hearts and Minds in Afghanistan," *American Forces Press Service*, October 17, 2002.
145. Kenny Gluck, "Coalition forces endanger humanitarian action in Afghanistan," MSF.org, May 6, 2004, http://www.msf.org/countries/page.cfm?articleid=409F102D-A77A-4C94-89E0A47D7213B4D5.
146. Stephen Graham, "Aid Workers Killed in Afghanistan," Associated Press, August 4, 2004.
147. Diderik van Halsema, "Six days surrounding MSF's decision to withdraw from Afghanistan," MSF.org, August 1, 2004, http://www.msf.org/countries/page.cfm?articleid=AA5AE5CF-05EA-4D43-8DB12C6450CBEA7C.
148. Pamela Constable, "With Strong Tribal Structure and Foreign Aid, Paktia Province Is Seen as Model for Others," *Washington Post*, October 1, 2003.
149. Carmela Baranowska, *Taliban Country* (video) 2004, see www.talibancountry.com.
150. Baranowska, *Taliban Country*.

151. John Sifton, "Enduring Freedom: Abuses by U.S. Forces in Afghanistan," Human Rights Watch, HRW.org, March 2004, http://www.hrw.org/reports/2004/afghanistan0304/.
152. Sifton, "Abuses by U.S. Forces."
153. R. Jeffrey Smith, "Army Files Cite Abuse of Afghans: Special Forces Unit Prompted Senior Officers' Complaints," *Washington Post*, February 18, 2005.
154. Daniel Cooney, "GIs Who Burned Fighters' Bodies to Be Disciplined," Associated Press, November 27, 2005.
155. Eric Schmitt, "Army Examining an Account of Abuse of 2 Dead Taliban," *New York Times*, October 20, 2005.
156. George Negus, "Stephen Dupont Interview," *Dateline* (Australia), October 19, 2005, transcript at http://news.sbs.com.au/dateline/index.php?page=transcript&dte=2005-10-19&headlineid=1037.
157. Syed Saleem Shahzad, "Osama Adds Weight to Afghan Resistance," *Asia Times*, September 11, 2004; Syed Saleem Shahzad, "Revival of the Taliban," *Asia Times*, April 9, 2005.
158. Negus, "Stephen Dupont Interview."
159. USA Special Operations Command (web site), "Psychological Operations," Fact Sheet, viewed March 11, 2006, http://www.soc.mil/usacapoc/psyopfs.shtml.
160. Andrew North and Bilal Sarwary, "The 'Enemy Central' Province in Afghanistan," BBC News (Online), December 8, 2005, http://news.bbc.co.uk/go/pr/fr//2/hi/south_asia/4508052.stm.
161. ABC News Poll, "Life in Afghanistan," December 7, 2005.
162. Sgt. Robert M. Storm, "Marines conduct spoiling attack in advance of upcoming elections," *Marine Corps News*, August 21, 2005, http://www.marines.mil/marinelink/mcn2000.nsf/0/18322DACC7E6A0378525706C003A1CA9?opendocument.
163. Kent Harris, "Vicenza-Based Troops in Afghanistan Aggressively Taking Fight to the Enemy," *Stars & Stripes* (Mideast Edition), June 28, 2005.
164. Dana Priest, "CIA Holds Terror Suspects in Secret Prisons," *Washington Post*, November 2, 2005.
165. Jane Mayer, "Outsourcing Torture: The secret history of America's "extraordinary rendition" program," *The New Yorker*, February 14, 2005, http://www.newyorker.com/fact/content/?050214fa_fact6.
166. "His Year in Hell," CBS News, January 21, 2004, http://www.cbsnews.com/stories/2004/01/21/60II/main594974.shtml.
167. Kari Lydersen, "Torture Survivor Fights U.S., Canada for Railroading to Jordan, Syria," *The New Standard*, February 15, 2005.
168. Priest, "CIA Holds Terror Suspects."
169. U.S. Department of State Bureau of Democracy, Human Rights, and Labor, *Uzbekistan: Country Reports on Human Rights Practices* (report for the year 2000), February 23, 2001, http://www.state.gov/g/drl/rls/hrrpt/2000/eur/858.htm.
170. U.S. Department of State Bureau of Democracy, Human Rights, and Labor, *Uzbekistan: Country Reports on Human Rights Practices* (reports for the years 2000–2004), http://www.state.gov/g/drl/rls/hrrpt/.
171. Nick Paton Walsh, "U.S. looks away as new ally tortures Islamists," *The Guardian* (London), May 26, 2003.
172. Jacquelyn K. Davis and Michael J. Sweeney, "Central Asia in U.S. Strategy and Operational Planning: Where Do We Go from Here?" Institute for Foreign Policy Analysis, February 2004.
173. Don Van Natta Jr., "U.S. Recruits a Rough Ally to Be a Jailer," *New York Times*, May 1, 2005.
174. Ibid.

175. Reed Brody, "The Road to Abu Ghraib," Human Rights Watch, HRW.org, June 2004, http://www.hrw.org/reports/2004/usa0604/usa0604.pdf.
176. Gordon Corera, "Guantánamo Bay's unhappy anniversary," BBC News, January 11, 2006, http://news.bbc.co.uk/2/hi/americas/4603346.stm.
177. Christopher Bollyn, "Red Cross Hit Hard by Suicide Bombers," *American Free Press*, April 12, 2004.
178. "Harsh detention for Afghan prisoners," BBC News online, January 16, 2002, http://news.bbc.co.uk/1/hi/world/south_asia/1752863.stm.
179. "U.S.: Geneva Conventions Apply to Guantánamo Detainees," Human Rights Watch Press Release, HRW.org, January 11, 2002, http://hrw.org/press/2002/01/us011102.htm.
180. "Harsh detention for Afghan prisoners," BBC News online, January 16, 2002, http://news.bbc.co.uk/1/hi/world/south_asia/1752863.stm.
181. "U.S.: Geneva Conventions Apply," Human Rights Watch.
182. "U.S.: Geneva Conventions Apply," Human Rights Watch.
183. "Secretary Rumsfeld Media Stakeout at NBC," News Transcript, Department of Defense, Defense.gov, January 20, 2002, http://www.defense.gov/transcripts/2002/t01222002_t0120so.html.
184. George W. Bush and Tony Blair, "President Bush, Prime Minister Blair Discuss War on Terrorism," Press Conference Transcript, July 17, 2003, http://www.whitehouse.gov/news/releases/2003/07/20030717-9.html.
185. Ron Fournier, "Going Backwards: Bush Orders Terrorist Trials by Military Tribunal," Associated Press, November 13, 2001.
186. Peter Slevin and George Lardner Jr., "Bush Plan for Terrorism Trials Defended," *Washington Post*, November 15, 2001.
187. U.S. Attorney General John Ashcroft, Department of Justice Press Conference, November 15, 2001.
188. Martha Baskin, "Guantanamo Prisoner First to Challenge Military Tribunals," *The New Standard*, June 27, 2004.
189. "81 Afghan prisoners released," Associated Press, January 17, 2005.
190. Miranda Leitsinger, "Guantánamo prison passes fourth anniversary with construction of prison," Associated Press, January 15, 2006.
191. "U.S. frees some 85 suspected Afghan militants," Reuters, May 1, 2005.
192. "18 Guantánamo detainees sent home to Afghanistan," Associated Press, April 19, 2005.
193. Neil A. Lewis and Eric Schmitt, "Inquiry Finds Abuses at Guantánamo Bay," *New York Times*, May 1, 2005.
194. "Red Cross Blasts Guantánamo," BBC News online, October 10, 2003, http://news.bbc.co.uk/2/hi/americas/3179858.stm.
195. Neil A. Lewis, "Red Cross Criticizes Indefinite Detention in Guantánamo Bay," *New York Times*, October 10, 2003.
196. "Red Cross Blasts Guantanamo," BBC News online.
197. Moazzam Begg, "A letter from Guantanamo: In full," BBC News online, January 11, 2005.
198. "Guantánamo torture scandal deepens," AlJazeera.net, December 22, 2004.
199. Neil A. Lewis and Eric Schmitt, "Inquiry Finds Abuses at Guantánamo Bay," *New York Times*, May 1, 2005.
200. David Stout, "Bush Picks Alberto Gonzales to Replace Ashcroft at Justice Dept," *New York Times*, November 10, 2005.
201. James Yee, *For God and Country: Faith and Patriotism Under Fire* (New York: Perseus Books Group, 2005), 113.

202. Yee, *For God and Country*, 70–72.
203. Ibid., *For God and Country*, 101–2.
204. Tim Golden, "In U.S. Report, Brutal Details of 2 Afghan Inmates' Deaths," *New York Times*, May 20, 2005.
205. R. Jeffrey Smith, "Army Files Cite Abuse of Afghans: Special Forces Unit Prompted Senior Officers' Complaints," *Washington Post*, February 18, 2005.
206. Golden, "Afghan Inmates' Deaths."
207. Ibid.
208. Ibid.
209. Ibid.
210. John J. Lumpkin, "U.S. Investigates 8 Afghan Prison Deaths," Associated Press, December 13, 2004.
211. Douglas Jehl, "Army Details Scale of Abuse of Prisoners in an Afghan Jail," *New York Times*, March 12, 2005.
212. Associated Press, "Report: 108 Died In U.S. Custody," March 16, 2005.
213. M. Cherif Bassiouni, "Report of the Independent Expert on the Situation of Human Rights in Afghanistan," Economic and Social Council, United Nations, March 11, 2005, 16.
214. M. Cherif Bassiouni, 17.
215. Kevin Clarke, "Rights mandate for Afghanistan to end," *National Catholic Reporter*, May 13, 2005.
216. Deborah Horan, "Ex-UN envoy: U.S. feared discovery of prison abuse," *Chicago Tribune*, April 29, 2005.
217. Tim Golden, "Afghan Inmates' Deaths."
218. Douglas Jehl and Andrea Elliot, "Cuba Base Sent Its Interrogators to Iraqi Prison," *New York Times*, May 29, 2004.
219. Over 90 percent of Afghans chose either the Taliban, drug traffickers, or warlords as the "Greatest Danger to Afghanistan." ABC News poll, "Life in Afghanistan," ABC News, December 7, 2005.
220. Lt. Gen. David Barno, Briefing on Provincial Reconstruction Teams, USAID Headquarters, Washington, DC, December 15, 2005, http://www.usaid.gov/press/speeches/2005/sp051215.html.
221. Afghanistan Justice Project, *Casting Shadows: War Crimes and Crimes Against Humanity: 1978-2001*, (Kabul: The Afghanistan Justice Project, 2005), 157.
222. Qasimi, private speech recorded by the authors, Farah, Afghanistan, February 23, 2005.
223. Bob Woodward, *Bush at War* (New York: Simon & Schuster, 2002), 317.
224. Michael Gordon, "Alliance of Convenience: Rebels Useful to the U.S.," *New York Times*, October 23, 2001.
225. Woodward, *Bush at War*, 267; Barry Bearak, "Who Betrayed Haq? Candidates are Many," *New York Times*, October 28, 2001.
226. Woodward, *Bush at War*, 248; Norimitsu Onishi, "G.I.'s had Crucial Role in Battle for Kandahar," *New York Times*, December 14, 2001; Jane Perlez and Steven Lee Myers, "U.S. Plucks Rebel Figure from Afghan Redoubt for 'Consultations,' then Returns Him," *New York Times*, November 6, 2001.
227. Barry Bearak, "Leaders of the Old Afghanistan Prepare for the New," *New York Times*, October 25, 2001; "Peshawar Assemblage," *Dawn* (Karachi), October 27, 2001; John F. Burns, "Afghan Gathering in Pakistan Backs Future Role for King," *New York Times*, October 26, 2001.
228. House Committee on International Relations, *U.S. Diplomatic Efforts in the War Against Terrorism*, 107th Cong., 1st sess., October 24, 2001, 39–40.

229. Ibid.
230. George W. Bush, "Remarks Following Discussions with President Pervez Musharraf of Pakistan and an Exchange With Reporters in New York City," November 10, 2001, *Weekly Compilation of Presidential Documents* 37, no. 46: 1644.
231. John F. Burns, "Afghan Region's Politics Snarl U.S. War Plan," *New York Times*, October 12, 2001; Michael Gordon, "Alliance of Convenience."
232. Charles M. Sennott and Ellen Barry, "The Fast Fall of the Taliban," *Boston Sunday Globe*, November 18, 2001; Woodward, *Bush at War*, 313–315.
233. Rupert Cornwell, "West Tries to Put Brave Face on Kabul's Capture," *The Independent* (London), November 14, 2001; Andrew Grice, "Blair Embarrassed by the Quick Surrender of Capital," *The Independent* (London), November 14, 2001.
234. Woodward, *Bush at War*, 310; George W. Bush, "The President's News Conference With President Vladimir Putin of Russia," November 13, 2001, *Weekly Compilation of Presidential Documents* 37, no. 46: 1655.
235. David E. Sanger with James Dao, "U.S. to Press Afghan Rebels Not to Form Government," *New York Times*, November 18, 2001.
236. Dan Chapman, "Many Afghans Haunted by Northern Alliance's Past," *Atlanta Journal-Constitution*, November 12, 2001.
237. Dexter Filkins with Barry Bearak, "A Tribe Is Prey to Vengeance After Taliban's Fall in North," *New York Times*, March 7, 2002; Agence France-Presse, "We Felt Safer Under the Taliban, say Kabul Residents," January 25, 2002; Rory McCarthy and Nicholas Watt, "Alliance Accused of Brutality in Capture of Kunduz," *The Guardian* (UK), November 27, 2001.
238. Michael Ware, "Meet the New Boss, Same as the Old Boss," *Time*, January 14, 2002.
239. RAWA Statement, "The People of Afghanistan do not Accept domination of the Northern Alliance! RAWA's Appeal to the UN and World Community", RAWA.org, November 13, 2001, http://www.rawa.org/na-appeal.htm.
240. *A Call for Justice: a National Consultation on past Human Rights Abuse* (Kabul: Afghanistan Independent Human Rights Commission, January 29, 2005), http://www.aihrc.org.af/Rep_29_Eng/rep29_1_05call4justice.pdf.
241. Andrew Maykruth, "Northern Alliance's Entrance in Kabul, Afghanistan, Produces Mixed Emotions," *Knight Ridder/Tribune Business News*, November 15, 2001; BBC News Interview with Dick Cheney, November 15, 2001, http://www.whitehouse.gov/vicepresident/news-speeches/speeches/ vp20011115.html.
242. PBS, "Filling the Vacuum: The Bonn Conference," *Frontline*, PBS, December, 2001, http://www.pbs.org/wgbh/pages/frontline/shows/campaign/withus/cbonn.html.
243. "RAF flies Northern Alliance representatives to Bonn," UK Ministry of Defense, November 26, 2001, http://www.operations.mod.uk/veritas/bonn_flight.htm.
244. "Key Afghan warlords reject Bonn deal," BBC News online, December 6, 2001.
245. Sarah Chayes, "Afghanistan's Future, Lost in the Shuffle," *New York Times*, July 1, 2003.
246. Norimitsu Onishi, "Afghan Warlords and Bandits are Back in Business," *New York Times*, December 28, 2001.
247. Diego A. Ruiz Palmer, "The Road to Kabul," *NATO Review*, Summer 2003, http://www.nato.int/docu/review/2003/issue2/english/art3.html.
248. Steven Erlanger, "Afghans Plunge into Talks, Differing on Peacekeepers," *New York Times*, November 29, 2001.
249. Michael R. Gordon, "Less Ambitious Security Force Is Favored by Afghan Leaders," *New York Times*, December 5, 2001.
250. C. J. Chivers with Michael R. Gordon, "In Lawless Land, Narrow Role for Security Force," *New York Times*, December 23, 2001.

251. William J. Durch, "Peace and Stability Operations in Afghanistan: Requirements and Force Options," The Henry L. Stimson Center, June 28, 2003.
252. William J. Durch, "Peace and Stability Operations"; John F. Burns, "UN Aide Asks More Security Troops for Afghanistan," *New York Times*, January 25, 2002.
253. U.S. Department of Defense, Special Briefing on the Unified Command Plan (transcript), Defense.gov, April 17, 2002, http://www.defense.gov/transcripts/2002/t04172002_ t0417sd.html.
254. Agence France-Presse, "British Troops Shot at in Afghanistan, U.S. Against ISAF Expansion," February 21, 2002.
255. Ari Fleischer, White House Press Briefing, January 28, 2002.
256. Richard Tomkins, "Anxiety over Afghan Security," United Press International, June 3, 2002; Fahmi Howeidi, *Al Ahram Weekly*, October 23, 2002.
257. Agence France-Presse, "U.S. Against ISAF Expansion"; Woodward, *Bush at War*, 321.
258. Secretary Rumsfeld and Gen. Franks, News Briefing (transcript), Defense.gov, August 15, 2002, http://www.defense.gov/transcripts/2002/t08152002_t0815sd.html; *Human Rights and Reconstruction in Afghanistan* (Brooklyn: Center for Economic and Social Rights, May 2002), http://cesr.org/node/view/499; "Majority of Afghans Say Country Heading in Right Direction, Despite Security, Economic Concerns," AsiaFoundation.org, July 13, 2004, http://www.asiafoundation.org/ Locations/afghanistan_survey.html; Noorani (editor of *Rozgaran*), in conversation with authors, Kabul, Afghanistan, February 16, 2005.
259. Reuters, "First Anti-American Protest Held in Afghan Capital," May 6, 2003.
260. U.S. Department of State, Office for Afghanistan Reconstruction, "Progress in Afghanistan," March 24, 2003, http://www.state.gov/p/sa/rls/fs/18939.htm; United States Department of State, Bureau of Consular Affairs, "Travel warning: Afghanistan," January 9, 2006, http://travel.state.gov/travel/cis_pa_tw/tw/tw_2121.html.
261. *World Report 2003: Afghanistan*, Human Rights Watch, HRW.org, http://www.hrw.org/wr2k3/asia1.html.
262. *Newsweek*, "The Death Convoy of Afghanistan," August 26, 2002.
263. House Subcommittee on Europe and the Middle East and Asian and Pacific Affairs, Hearing, March 7, 1990, Appendix 2, responses submitted by Barnett R. Rubin to questions submitted by the subcommittee, 141.
264. Human Rights Watch, "Afghanistan: The Massacre at Mazar-i Sharif."
265. Press Release, "Physicians for Human Rights Reveals Appalling Conditions at Shebarghan Prison in Afghanistan," Physicians for Human Rights, January 28, 2002, http://www.phrusa.org/research/afghanistan/report_release.html.
266. *Newsweek*, "Death Convoy."
267. Ibid.
268. *Democracy Now!*, "Premiere of *Afghan Massacre: Convoy of Death*," Democracynow.org, May 23, 2003, http://www.democracynow.org/afghanfilm.shtml.
269. Andrew North, "Karzai warning to Herat governor," BBC News online, May 11, 2004, http://news.bbc.co.uk/2/hi/south_asia/3700257.stm; Ahmed Zia Siamak, "Khan Stifles Local Press," Institute for War and Peace Reporting, Afghan Recovery Report No. 20, July 25, 2002.
270. Ian MacWilliam, "New Afghan governor takes up post," BBC News online, August 16, 2003, http://news.bbc.co.uk/1/hi/world/south_asia/3157393.stm.
271. "All Our Hopes are Crushed: Violence and Repression in Western Afghanistan," *Human Rights Watch* 14, no. 7 (C), November 2002.
272. "Afghanistan: Torture and Political Repression in Herat: U.S. and U.N. Warlord Strategy Fails the Afghan People," *Human Rights Watch*, November 5, 2002.

273. "All Our Hopes are Crushed."
274. "'Killing You is a Very Easy Thing For Us': Human Rights Abuses in Southeast Afghanistan," *Human Rights Watch Report* 15, no. 05 (July 2003): 10.
275. "'Killing You is a Very Easy Thing,'" 10–11.
276. "Warlords Clash in North Afghanistan," BBC News online, May 1, 2002, http://news.bbc.co.uk/1/hi/world/south_asia/1962372.stm.
277. Madeleine Coorey, "Up to 100 Die in Violence as Afghan Aviation Minister Assassinated," *Agence France-Presse*. March 21, 2004.
278. "Afghan Warlord Calls for Sackings," *The Guardian* (London), April 10, 2004.
279. Stephen Graham, "Afghan Warlord's Troops Overrun City," Associated Press, April 9, 2004.
280. Donald Rumsfeld, "Department of Defense News Briefing," (transcript), May 8, 2002, http://www.defenselink.mil/transcripts/2002/t05082002_t0508sd.html.
281. Associated Press, "Fighting in Eastern Afghanistan Kills 40," April 28, 2002.
282. Pamela Constable, "Land Grab in Kabul Embarrasses Government," *Washington Post*, September 16, 2003.
283. Lawrence Smallman, "UN Rep Wants Afghan Ministers Out," Aljazeera,net, September 11, 2003, http://english.aljazeera.net/NR/exeres/B78FED6B-8A36-47BE-8D75-B40B1A32F7F2.htm.
284. Carlotta Gall, "Housing Plan for Top Aides in Afghanistan Draws Rebuke," *New York Times*, September 21, 2003.
285. Afghan Independent Human Rights Commission, "Your House Is Not Yours, Don't Insist Otherwise You Will be Jailed and Tortured," AIHRC.org.af, September 2003, http://www.hewad.com/news1.htm.
286. "UN U-turn on Afghan land grab", BBC News online, September 14, 2003, http://news.bbc.co.uk/2/hi/south_asia/3108324.stm.
287. Chris Kraul, "U.S. Military May Intervene If Afghan Violence Continues," *Los Angeles Times*, May 13, 2003.
288. Norimitsu Onishi, "Afghan Warlords and Bandits Back in Business," *New York Times*, December 28, 2001.
289. Ahmed Rashid, "Peace Proves Elusive Outside Kabul as Calls Surface to Curb Warlords," *Wall Street Journal*, February 15, 2002.
290. Carol Off, "In the Company of Warlords," CBC.ca, March 2, 2002, http://www.cbc.ca/national/news/afghanwarlords/index.html.
291. Associated Press, "Bush: War On Drugs Aids War On Terror," December 14, 2001.
292. Colin Brown and Andrew Clennell, "Opium Trade Booms in 'Basket-case' Afghanistan," *The Independent* (UK), July 28, 2004.
293. Agence France-Presse, "Northern Alliance Main Opium Producer: UN," October 16, 2001.
294. Paul Harris, "Victorious Warlords Set to Open the Opium Floodgates," *Observer International* (UK), November 25, 2001.
295. Alfred W. McCoy, *The Politics of Heroin: CIA Complicity in the Global Drug Trade* (Chicago: Lawrence Hill Books, 2003), 479.
296. John Cooley, *Unholy Wars* (London: Pluto Press, 1999), 5, 129.
297. Alfred W. McCoy, *Opium History Up To 1858 A.D.*, 1994, http://www.opioids.com/opium/history/.
298. Agence France-Presse, "Afghanistan is Again the World's Largest Opium Producer, UN," October 25, 2002.

299. United Nations Office on Drugs and Crime, and Government of Afghanistan Counter Narcotics Directorate, *Afghanistan Opium Survey 2004* (Vienna: UNODC, 2004), http://www.unodc.org/pdf/afg/afghanistan_opium_survey_2004.pdf.
300. Christopher Adams, "UK 'risks losing war on Afghan drugs'," *Financial Times* (UK), July 30, 2004.
301. United Nations Office on Drugs and Crime, *Afghanistan Farmer's Intentions Survey 2003/2004*, (Vienna: UNODC, February 2004), 33, http://www.unodc.org/pdf/afg/afg_fis_report_2003-2004.pdf.
302. The "Gross Income from Opium per hectare" was $4,600, compared with the "Gross Income from Wheat per hectare" of $390. See *Afghanistan Opium Survey 2004*.
303. M. Cherif Bassiouni, *Report of the Independent Expert on the Situation of Human Rights in Afghanistan* (New York: United Nations Economic and Social Council, March 11, 2005).
304. Ibid.
305. David Rodhe, "Education Offers Women in Northern Afghanistan a Ray of Hope," *New York Times*, October 3, 2001.
306. Richard Lacayo, "About Face for Afghan Women," *Time.com* Web Exclusive, November 25, 2001, http://www.time.com/time/world/article/0,8599,185651,00.html.
307. Ian MacWilliam, "Women Protest Over Afghan Security," BBC News online, August 9, 2003, http://news.bbc.co.uk/2/hi/south_asia/3138263.stm.
308. Anna Badkhen, "Reports of Rape, Looting by Afghan Militiamen: Warlord's Followers Terrorize the Helpless," *San Francisco Chronicle*, February 15, 2002.
309. Chris Stephen, "The First Rush of Freedom," *Guardian Unlimited*, November 13, 2001.
310. James Astill, "Death by burning: the only escape for desperate Afghan women," *The Guardian* (London), April 24, 2004.
311. Kimberley Sevcik, "Why Did This Woman Set Herself on Fire?" *Marie Claire*, February 2004.
312. Nasreen, in conversation with the authors, Herat, Afghanistan, February 22, 2005.
313. Golnaz Esfandiari, "Self-Immolation of Women on the Rise in Western Provinces," Radio Free Europe/Radio Liberty, March 1, 2004.
314. "Afghanistan, 'We Want to Live as Humans': Repression of Women and Girls in Western Afghanistan," *Human Rights Watch* 14, no. 11 (C) (December 2002).
315. Evelyn Leopold, "Post-Taliban Warlords Oppress Afghan Women," Reuters, December 17, 2002.
316. "'We Want to Live as Humans,'" Human Rights Watch.
317. Ibid.
318. "Afghanistan, 'No One Listens to Us and No One Treats Us as Human Beings': Justice Denied to Women," Amnesty International, AI INDEX: ASA 11/023/2003, October 6, 2003.
319. Ibid.
320. Thomas Holdich, *The Indian Borderland* (London: Methuen, 1901), 366. In John Griffiths, *Afghanistan: Key to a Continent* (Boulder: Westview Press, 1981), 36.
321. Percy Sykes, *A History of Afghanistan*, vol. 2 (1940; New Delhi: Munshiram Manoharlal, 2002), 177.
322. C. W. Wade, letter to John Colvin, Private Secretary to Lord Auckland, 1837. In Percy Sykes, *A History of Afghanistan*, vol. 1 (1940; New Delhi: Munshiram Manoharlal, 2002), 405.
323. Sir Hamilton Grant, Letter to Afghan Government, 1919. In Sykes, *A History of Afghanistan*, vol. 2, 359.
324. W. H. Macnaughten, "The Simla Manifesto," in Sykes, *A History of Afghanistan*, vol. 2, 339.

325. Sykes, *A History of Afghanistan*, vol. 2, 3.
326. Craig Baxter, *The Reign of King Amanaullah, 1919–29*, in Peter R. Blood, ed., *Afghanistan: A Country Study*, Revision of 5th Edition (only published online) (Washington: Federal Research Division, Library of Congress, 1997), http://countrystudies.us/afghanistan/18.htm.
327. Craig Baxter, *Tajik Rule, January—October 1929*, in Blood, *Afghanistan: A Country Study*, http://countrystudies.us/afghanistan/20.htm.
328. Jawaharlal Nehru, *Glimpses of World History*, orig. published 1934–5 (New Delhi: Oxford University Press, 14th Impression, 1999), 782–3.
329. Nick Cullather, "Damming Afghanistan: Modernization in a Buffer State," *Journal of American History* 512 (September 2002); Arthur M. Schlesinger, *The Vital Center: The Politics of Freedom* (London: Deutsch, 1970), 233, cited in Cullather.
330. Nick Cullather, "Damming Afghanistan."
331. Cullather, "Damming Afghanistan"; Hafizullah Emadi, *State, Revolution, and Superpowers in Afghanistan* (New York: Praeger, 1990), 41, cited in Cullather.
332. Jane Perlez and Steven Lee Myers, "U.S. Plucks Rebel Figure from Afghan Redoubt for 'Consultations,' Then Returns Him," *New York Times*, November 6, 2001.
333. InfoTrac Web, *National Newspaper Index*, http://www.gale.com/tlist/sb5089.html (available in the U.S. through public libraries). The first article with Karzai's name is John Kifner, "For Afghans, a Major Goal is Credibility," *New York Times*, April 27, 1989. The second article is John Daniszewski and Richard Boudreaux, "Afghans Explore Idea of Post-Taliban Council," *Los Angeles Times*, October 12, 2001.
334. Douglas Frantz, "In Quiet Corners, the Roots of Afghan Rebellion," *New York Times*, October 18, 2001.
335. Mark Landler, "Hailed Abroad, Karzai Is Ignored at Home," *New York Times*, February 2, 2002.
336. Meena Siddiqui (human rights attorney), in conversation with the authors, Kabul, Afghanistan, February 17, 2005.
337. Landler, "Hailed Abroad."
338. Norimitsu Onishi, "G.I.'s Had Crucial Role in Battle for Kandahar," *New York Times*, December 15, 2001.
339. Norimitsu Onishi, "For Afghan Clan, a Full Circle Back to Power," *New York Times*, December 9, 2001.
340. Norimitsu Onishi, "G.I.'s Had Crucial Role."
341. Zakia, Medical Student at Kabul University, in conversation with the authors, Kabul, Afghanistan, February 19, 2005.
342. PBS, "Filling the Vacuum."
343. Rory McCarthy and Ewen MacAskill, "King's Aide Is Favourite to be Next Leader," *The Guardian* (London), December 3, 2001.
344. Samia Nkrumah, "An Opportunity to Seize," *Al-Ahram* (Cairo), December 20-26, 2001.
345. Norimitsu Onishi, "G.I.'s Had Crucial Role."
346. Steven Erlanger, "After Arm-Twisting, Afghan Factions Pick Interim Government and Leader," *New York Times*, December 6, 2001.
347. Abdul Sattar Sirat, The Long Way for Peace in Afghanistan, The Afghan Observer (online), January 13, 2004, http://afghanobserver.com/Articles/Sirat_WorldCouncil.htm.
348. Khalilzad and Byman, "Consolidation of a Rogue State."
349. U.S. Embassy in Kabul, "Dr. Zalmay Khalilzad: U.S. Ambassador to Afghanistan," Press Release, November 24, 2003, http://usembassy.state.gov/afghanistan/wwwhbiozal.html.

350. Sahar Saba (Foreign Affairs Committee Member, RAWA), in conversation with the authors, Pasadena, CA, March 2004; Rachel Morarjee, "'Viceroy' Khalilzad Leaves Controversial Legacy in Afghanistan," *Agence France-Presse*, April 6, 2005; Andrew North, "Zalmay Khalilzad: Afghan 'Viceroy'," BBC News, April 6, 2005, http://news.bbc.co.uk/2/hi/south_asia/4416245.stm; Habiba Sarabi, Afghan Minister of Women's Affairs, in conversation with the authors, Kabul, Afghanistan, February 19, 2005.
351. Joe Stephens and David B. Ottaway, "Afghan Roots Keep Adviser Firmly in the Inner Circle," *Washington Post*, November 23, 2001.
352. Department of State, "Biography of Zalmay Khalilzad," State.gov, http://iraq.usembassy.gov/iraq/ambassador.html (accessed March 14, 2006).
353. Project for a New American Century, Statement of Principles, http://www.newamericancentury.org/statementofprinciples.htm (Khalilzad is one of the statement's signatories).
354. Patrick E. Tyler, "U.S. Strategy Plan Calls for Insuring No Rivals Develop in a One-Superpower World," *New York Times*, March 7, 1992; Jon Lee Anderson, "American Viceroy: Zalmay Khalilzad's Mission," *The New Yorker*, December 19, 2005.
355. Robert Fisk, "This Looming War Isn't About Chemical Warheads or Human Rights: It's About Oil," *The Independent* (UK), January 18, 2003.
356. Stephens and Ottaway, "Afghan Roots Keep."
357. Amy Waldman, "In Afghanistan, U.S. Envoy Sits in Seat of Power," *New York Times*, April 17, 2004.
358. North, "Zalmay Khalilzad: Afghan Viceroy"; Amin Tarzi, "Chief Justice Asks U.S. President to Keep Afghan Envoy, Sparking Controversy and No Result," *RFE/RL Afghanistan Report*, April 11, 2005, http://www.rferl.org/reports/afghan-report/2005/04/12-110405.asp.
359. Anderson, "American Viceroy."
360. *A Call for Justice: a National Consultation on past Human Rights Abuse* (Kabul: Afghanistan Independent Human Rights Commission, January 29, 2005), http://www.aihrc.org.af/Rep_29_Eng/rep29_1_05call4justice.pdf.
361. Anderson, "American Viceroy"; Scott Johnson, "Our Mr. Fix-It in Iraq," *Newsweek*, August 29, 2005.
362. Khalilzad and Byman, "Consolidation of a Rogue State."
363. Omar Zakhilwal and Adeena Niazi, "The Warlords Win in Kabul," *New York Times*, June 21, 2002.
364. Zakhilwal and Niazi, "The Warlords Win."
365. Reuters, "U.S. State Department Releases Afghan Poll," June 16, 2001; Sahar Saba (Foreign Affairs Committee Member, RAWA), in conversation with the authors, Pasadena, CA, March 2004.
366. Pamela Hess, "Afghan Council Postponed, King Steps Aside, *United Press International*, June 10, 2002.
367. U.S. Department of State, "Khalilzad Says Loya Jirga was Delayed Due to Confusion," June 12, 2002 (transcript of June 10 press conference), http://usinfo.state.gov/regional/nea/sasia/afghan/text/0612envoy.htm.
368. Carlotta Gall, "Former King Rules Out All But a Symbolic Role," *New York Times*, June 10, 2002.
369. U.S. Department of State, "Khalilzad Says Loya Jirga."
370. BBC News, Interview with Zahir Shah, June 9, 2002.
371. Agence France-Presse, "Ex-King of Afghanistan Agreeable to an Assembly Nomination," May 28, 2002.
372. Zalmay Khalilzad, "Afghanistan: Time to Reengage," *Washington Post*, October 7, 1996.
373. Hess, "Afghan Council Postponed."

374. Omar Zakhilwal, "Stifled in the Loya Jirga," *Washington Post*, June 16, 2002.
375. Hess, "Afghan Council Postponed."
376. Gall, "Former Afghan King."
377. David Rohde, "Afghan Leader Expected to Get Extended Term, *New York Times*, May 26, 2002.
378. BBC News (online), "Tempers Flare at Loya Jirga," June 12, 2002, http://news.bbc.co.uk/1/hi/world/south_asia/2039665.stm.
379. Scott Baldauf, "Afghanistan's troubled start to democracy: Vote rigging has some Pashtun leaders calling for a boycott of the June 10 Loya Jirga," *Christian Science Monitor*, May 28, 2002.
380. Susan B. Glasser and Peter Baker, "Surge of Violence Threatens Plans for Afghanistan," *Washington Post*, April 12, 2002.
381. Human Rights Watch, "Afghanistan: Return of the Warlords," *Human Rights Watch Briefing Paper*, June 2002, http://hrw.org/backgrounder/asia/afghanistan/warlords.pdf.
382. J. Alexander Thier, "The Politics of Peace Building," in *Nation Building Unravelled? Aid, Peace and Justice in Afghanistan*, Antonio Donini, Norah Niland, and Karin Wermester, eds. (Bloomfield, CT: Kumarian Press, 2004) 39–60.
383. Human Rights Watch, "Loya Jirga off to Shaky Start," June 13, 2002.
384. Human Rights Watch, "Afghanistan: Return of the Warlords," June 6, 2002.
385. Michael Gordon, "CIA Sees Threat Afghan Factions May Bring Chaos," *New York Times*, February 21, 2002.
386. Phillip Smucker, "New Afghan Leader Faces a Rogues Gallery Government," *Christian Science Monitor*, June 21, 2002.
387. Zakhilwal and Niazi, "The Warlords Win."
388. Carlotta Gall, "Karzai, Seeking Ethnic Balance, Names Minister to Lead Police," *New York Times*, June 23, 2002.
389. Smucker, "Rogues Gallery Government."
390. Human Rights Watch, "Afghanistan: Analysis of New Cabinet," June 20, 2002.
391. Jonathan Steele, "The West Is Walking Away from Afghanistan—Again," *The Guardian* (London), June 24, 2002.
392. Zakhilwal and Niazi, "The Warlords Win."
393. U.S. Department of State, "Khalilzad Says Loya Jirga."
394. Hamid Karzai, Interview with BBC, approx. June 14, 2002.
395. U.S. Embassy (Kabul), "King Zahir's Experiment: Some End-of-Tour Observations," Airgram (Confidential), August 1, 1970. In William Burr ed. National Security Archive Electronic Briefing Book No. 59, October 26, 2001, http://www.gwu.edu/~nsarchiv/NSAEBB/NSAEBB59/.
396. U.S. Embassy (Kabul), "Afghanistan's Clerical Unrest; A Tentative Assessment," Airgram (confidential), June 24, 1970. In William Burr, ed., National Security Archive Electronic Briefing Book no. 59, October 26, 2001, http://www.gwu.edu/~nsarchiv/NSAEBB/NSAEBB59/.
397. Scott Baldauf, "Guerrilla Chiefs to Undercut Karzai," *Christian Science Monitor*, December 12, 2003.
398. John Sifton, "Flawed Charter for a Land Ruled by Fear," *International Herald Tribune*, January 7, 2004.
399. Sifton, "Flawed Charter."
400. In January 2004 the aid organization CARE cited "more attacks on civilians in the past three months than in the 20 months following the Taliban's fall." CARE, Press Release, January 15, 2004.

401. Pamela Constable, "Attacks, U.S. Airstrikes Cast a Pall over Progress Toward Constitutional Assembly," *Washington Post*, December 8, 2003; P. Haven, "U.S.: Taliban Would Attack Afghan Council," Associated Press, December 9, 2003; C. Gall, "U.S. Acknowledges Killing 6 More Afghan Children," *New York Times*, December 11, 2003.
402. Zalmay Khalilzad, "Afghanistan's Milestone," *Washington Post*, January 6, 2004.
403. Farhan Bokhari, "Centralised presidency in Afghanistan suits U.S. best," *Gulf News*, December 25, 2003.
404. International Crisis Group, "Afghanistan: The Constitutional Loya Jirga" (Kabul/Brussels: ICG), December 12, 2003, http://www.crisisweb.org/home/getfile.cfm?id=1050.
405. Waheedullah Massoud, "Karzai Refuses to Compromise as Afghan Assembly Threatened by Boycott", *Agence France-Presse*, December 31, 2003.
406. Associated Press, "Last-Ditch Effort Secures Afghan Charter," January 4, 2004.
407. Ibid.
408. Carlotta Gall, "Afghanistan's Constitution Council Adjourns in Disarray," *New York Times*, January 1, 2004.
409. George W. Bush, "Efforts To Globally Promote Women's Human Rights," State.gov, March 12, 2004, http://www.state.gov/p/nea/rls/rm/30393.htm.
410. Wasay Engineer, representative of Solidarity Party of Afghanistan, in conversation with the authors, Kabul, Afghanistan, February 17, 2005.
411. Masuda Sultan, "Afghan Constitution a Partial Victory for Women," WomensENews.org, January 14, 2004.
412. Hafizullah Gardish, "Chief Justice Under Scrutiny," Institute for War and Peace Reporting, ARR no. 54, March 28, 2003.
413. Nina Shea, "Sharia in Kabul? A theological iron curtain is descending across Afghanistan," Center for Religious Freedom, October 28, 2002.
414. Agence France-Presse, "Islam 'only source' of law in Afghanistan," May 4, 2003.
415. Agence France-Presse, "Western-style rule 'unacceptable,'" June 10, 2002.
416. Malalai Joya, elected representative of Farah Province to constitutional *Loya Jirga*, in conversation with the authors, Farah City, Afghanistan, February 23, 2005.
417. Meena Siddiqui, in conversation with the authors, Kabul, Afghanistan, February 17, 2005.
418. Agence France-Presse, "Islam 'only source.'"
419. Human Rights Watch, "Killing You is a Very Easy Thing for Us: Human Rights Abuses in Southeast Afghanistan," *Human Rights Watch* 15, no. 5, July 2003.
420. Hamid Karzai, Press Conference (translated), Radio Afghanistan, June 25, 2003.
421. Noorani (editor of *Rozgaran*), in conversation with the authors, Kabul, Afghanistan, February 16, 2005.
422. Gulalai Habibi, editor of *Shafaq*, in conversation with the authors, Kabul, Afghanistan, February 20, 2005.
423. George W. Bush, Remarks at the 2004 Republican National Convention, WhiteHouse.gov, September 2, 2004, http://www.whitehouse.gov/news/releases/2004/09/20040902-2.html.
424. Paul Krugman, "America's Lost Respect," *New York Times*, October 1, 2004.
425. Carol Harrington and Jared Ferrie, "Afghan Vote Threatens Bush's Credibility," *Toronto Star*, August 13, 2004.
426. Associated Press, "Rumsfeld Hails Free Afghan Elections," August 12, 2004.
427. Christina Bennet, Shawn Wakefield, and Andrew Wilder, "Afghan Elections: The Great Gamble," Afghanistan Research and Evaluation Unit, November 2003.
428. Human Rights Watch, "The Rule of the Gun: Human Rights Abuses and Political Repression in the Run-up to Afghanistan's Presidential Election," Human Rights Watch

Briefing Paper, HRW.org, September 2004, http://www.hrw.org/backgrounder/asia/afghanistan0904/index.htm.

429. Human Rights Watch, "The Rule of the Gun."
430. The Human Rights Research and Advocacy Consortium, *Take the Guns Away: Afghan Voices on Security and Elections* (Kabul: HRRAC, September 2004), 9.
431. David Zucchino, "U.S. general lauds security success but remains wary," *Los Angeles Times*, October 10, 2004.
432. Agence France-Presse, "Kabul to get $1.2bn under Bush plan," September 8, 2003.
433. Pamela Constable, "Envoy to Afghanistan is a Force of Nurture," *Washington Post*, October 11, 2003.
434. RAWA, "Let Us Struggle Against War and Fundamentalism and for Peace and Democracy!" Statement on International Women's Day, RAWA.org, March 8, 2002, http://www.rawa.org/mar8-02en.htm; *A Call for Justice*, 78.
435. Ron Synovitz, "Afghanistan: Analysts Say Enforcement of Law on Political Parties Will Test Karzai," Radio Free Europe/Radio Liberty, October 15, 2003.
436. Pamela Constable, "Karzai Faces Revolt In Fragile Coalition," *Washington Post*, October 11, 2003.
437. Paul Watson, "U.S. Hand Seen in Afghan Election," *Los Angeles Times*, September 23, 2004.
438. Editorial, "Don't Let Violence Halt Balloting in Iraq and Afghanistan," *Newsday*, September 28, 2004; Reynolds, "Test for Afghan Democracy."
439. Christina Bennet, Shawn Wakefield, and Andrew Wilder, "Afghan Elections: The Great Gamble," Afghanistan Research and Evaluation Unit, November 2003.
440. CBC News Online, "Afghanistan's presidential election," October 12, 2004, http://www.cbc.ca/news/background/afghanistan/afghanelection.html.
441. Noorani (editor of *Rozgaran*), in conversation with the authors, Kabul, Afghanistan, February 16, 2005.
442. Qasimi (elected delegate to *Loya Jirga*), in conversation with the authors, Farah Province, Afghanistan, February 23, 2005.
443. Zakia (student activist at Kabul University), in conversation with the authors, Kabul, Afghanistan, February 19, 2005.
444. Human Rights Research and Advocacy Consortium, "Take the Guns Away."
445. James Ingalls and Sonali Kolhatkar, "Elections in Afghanistan," *Z Magazine*, November 2004.
446. Wasay Engineer (Solidarity Party spokesperson), in conversation with the authors; Malalai Joya, in conversation with the authors; Nir Rosen, "Afghanistan: Ballots and Bullets, Part 4," *Asia Times* (Hong Kong), October 9, 2004; Human Rights Research and Advocacy Consortium, "Take the Guns Away," 12.
447. Malalai Joya (elected representative of Farah Province to constitutional *Loya Jirga*), in conversation with the authors, Farah City, Afghanistan, February 23, 2005.
448. Carlotta Gall and David Rohde, "Afghan President Describes Militias as the Top Threat," *New York Times*, July 12, 2004.
449. J. Alexander Thier, "What Elections Mean for Afghanistan," Hoover Institution, September 29, 2004, http://www.oover.stanford.edu/pubaffairs/we/2004/thier09.html.
450. *A Call for Justice: a National Consultation on past Human Rights Abuse* (Kabul: Afghanistan Independent Human Rights Commission, January 29, 2005), http://www.aihrc.org.af/Rep_29_Eng/rep29_1_05call4justice.pdf.
451. United Nations Assistance Mission in Afghanistan, *Official Launch Ceremony of Disarmament, Demobilization and Reintegration (DDR) Programme Kunduz*, Photo Gallery, October 24, 2003, http://www.unama-afg.org/news/_photos/DDR/_imgpages/Image1.htm (accessed March 14, 2006).

452. Human Rights Research and Advocacy Consortium, "Take the Guns Away," 5.
453. Habiba Sarabi (former Minister of Women's Affairs), in conversation with the authors; Qasimi, in conversation with the authors, February 23, 2005.
454. Noorani, in conversation with the authors, February 17, 2005; "The Rule of the Gun: Human Rights Abuses and Political Repression in the Run-up to Afghanistan's Presidential Election," Human Rights Watch Briefing Paper, HRW.org, September 2004, http://www.hrw.org/backgrounder/asia/afghanistan0904/index.htm.
455. Carlotta Gall, "Islamists and Mujahedeen Secure Victory in Afghan Vote," *New York Times*, October 23, 2005.
456. Ibid.
457. Amin Tarzi, "Rivals Compete for Parliament Speaker Post," RFE/RL, November 18, 2005
458. Carlotta Gall, "Afghans Demonstrate Two Different Styles of Democracy," *New York Times*, December 20, 2005.
459. Human Rights Watch, *Afghanistan on the Eve of Parliamentary Elections*, September 2005, 15.
460. Ibid., 3.
461. Ibid., 9.
462. Ibid., 11–12.
463. Ibid., 13.
464. Amin Tarzi, "Is Reconciliation With The Neo-Taliban Working?" RFE/RL, June 2, 2005.
465. Human Rights Watch, *Afghanistan on the Eve*, 17.
466. Daniel Cooney, "Millions Go to Polls to Vote in Afghanistan," Associated Press, September 19, 2005.
467. Soutik Biswas, "Puzzle of the Stay-Away Voters," BBC News (online), September 19, 2005, http://news.bbc.co.uk/go/pr/fr/-/1/hi/world/south_asia/4258514.stm.
468. Sam Zarifi, "Afghan Election Diary," Human Rights Watch, September 16, 2005, http://www.hrw.org/campaigns/afghanistan/blog.htm#blog16.
469. Syed Saleem Shahzad, "Afghanistan Sees New Elections, Old Faces," *Asia Times Online*, September 17, 2005, http://www.atimes.com/atimes/Central_Asia/GI17Ag02.html.
470. Amin Tarzi, "New Parliament Must Cope with Deep Divisions," RFE/RL, December 20, 2005.
471. ADN Kronos International, "Elections Will Create Weak and Divided Parliament, Says Expert," September 7, 2005; David Brunnstrom, "Afghan Vote a Milestone but Democracy Fragile," Reuters, September 12, 2005.
472. George W. Bush, Remarks at Victory 2004 Rally in Chanhassen, Minnesota, Center City Park, WhiteHouse.gov, October 9, 2004, http://www.whitehouse.gov/news/releases/2004/10/20041009-8.html.
473. Joel Brinkley and Carlotta Gall, "Rice Calls Afghans Inspiring, but Election Is Delayed Again," *New York Times*, March 18, 2005.
474. Associated Press, "Cheney Attends Afghanistan Parliament Ceremony," December 19, 2005.
475. The Afghanistan Justice Project, *Casting Shadows*, 158.
476. Laura Bush, Radio Address, November 17, 2001.
477. Raymond Whitaker, "The Women's War," *The Independent* (UK), October 4, 2001. Note: The execution of Zarmeena was first captured on film by a member of RAWA. See RAWA, "Public Execution of an Afghan Woman (Zarmeena) by Taliban," November 16, 1999, http://www.rawa.org/zarmeena.htm.
478. Deborah Prussel, "Feminists take on UNOCAL—opposition to company's plan to build pipeline in Afghanistan where Taliban denies rights to women," *The Progressive*, October 1998.

479. Vanessa Gezari, "U.S. women's panel takes aid to Afghans," *Chicago Tribune*, January 9, 2003.
480. Richard Falk, "Defining a Just War," *The Nation*, October 11, 2001.
481. "Hill Activity Increases on Behalf of Afghan Women," *Ms. Magazine Online*, November 7, 2001, http://www.msmagazine.com/news/uswirestory.asp?id=5925.
482. Sharon Lerner, "What Women Want: Feminists Agonize Over War in Afghanistan," *Village Voice* (New York), October 31–November 6, 2001, http://www.villagevoice.com/news/0144,lerner,29544,1.html.
483. George W. Bush, State of the Union Address, January 29, 2002, http://www.whitehouse.gov/news/releases/2002/01/20020129/11.html.
484. "[Karen Hughes] found a role for herself in convincing Bush to demonstrate his compassionate side by highlighting the plight of Afghani [*sic*] women under the Taliban. To this day, Bush spends a few minutes in every speech talking about how U.S. forces "liberated" the women of Afghanistan from the tyranny of Taliban rule." James Carney, "Karen Hughes: Exit the High Prophet," *Time.com*, April 24, 2002, http://www.time.com/time/columnist/carney/article/0,9565,233342,00.html. See also Elizabeth Bumiller, "An Influential Bush Advisor, Karen Hughes, Will Resign," *New York Times*, April 24, 2002.
485. Ellen Goodman, "Demonizing the women's march," *Boston Globe*, May 2, 2004.
486. Elizabeth Bumiller, "First Lady to Speak about Afghan Women," *New York Times*, November 16, 2001.
487. Elizabeth Bumiller, "Afghan Women Trade Shadows for Washington's Limelight," *New York Times*, November 30, 2001.
488. Bumiller, "Afghan Women Trade."
489. Jane Smiley, "Women's Crusade," *New York Times* Magazine, December 2, 2001.
490. Elizabeth Bumiller, "The Politics of Plight and the Gender Gap," *New York Times*, November 19, 2001.
491. U.S. Department of State, "U.S.-Afghan Women's Council holds first meeting in Kabul," press conference, January 8, 2003, http://usinfo.state.gov/sa/Archive/2004/Jan/29-250159.html.
492. Margaret Coker, "Bush Adviser Spearheads Aid Effort for Afghan Women," *Palm Beach Post-Cox News Service*, February 29, 2004.
493. Paula Dobriansky, "Ask the White House" online interactive forum, March 10, 2005, http://www.whitehouse.gov/ask/20040310.html.
494. Deb Reichmann, "First Lady Drops In On Afghanistan," Associated Press, March 30, 2005.
495. Jonathan Curiel, "Afghanistan, Through Eyes of Young Women," *San Francisco Chronicle*, December 3, 2003.
496. Paula Dobriansky, Remarks at a PBS Reception and Screening of *Afghanistan Unveiled*, National Press Club Ballroom, Washington, DC, December 1, 2004, http://www.state.gov/g/rls/rm/2004/39476.htm.
497. Independent Television Service, "Independent Lens' 'Afghanistan Unveiled' Chronicles Life of Women During Taliban Era," press release, September 1, 2004.
498. Associated Press, "U.S. bases in Afghanistan get $83 million upgrade," March 28, 2005.
499. Coker, "Bush Adviser Spearheads."
500. U.S. Department of State, "U.S. Implements More Than 175 Programs on Behalf of Afghan Women," press release of the January 8, 2004.
501. Charlotte Ponticelli, Interview with Peggy Wehmeyer, World Vision Radio, May 30, 2004.
502. Brooke Williams, "Windfalls of War: University of Nebraska at Omaha," The Center for Public Integrity, October 30, 2003.

503. U.S. Department of State Office of the Senior Coordinator for International Women's Issues, "U.S. Commitment to Afghan Women: The U.S.-Afghan Women's Council," press conference, January 2004, http://www.state.gov/g/wi/28108.htm.
504. Habiba Sarabi, in conversation with the authors (corrected for grammar), Kabul, Afghanistan, February 19, 2005.
505. Ibid.
506. Feminist Majority Foundation, "Mavis Leno to Chair Feminist Majority Foundation's Campaign to Stop Gender Apartheid," Feminist Daily News Wire, October 21, 1998,
507. Ibid.
508. Marc Herold, *A Dossier on Civilian Victims of United States' Aerial Bombing of Afghanistan: A Comprehensive Accounting* (rev. ed.), Cursor.org, March 2002, http://www.cursor.org/stories/civilian_deaths.htm.
509. Nancy Gallagher, "The International Campaign Against Gender Apartheid in Afghanistan," *UCLA Journal of International Law and Foreign Affairs* (2000–2001), 5, 367.
510. Harriet Logan, *Unveiled* (New York: Regan Books, 2002); Sally Armstrong, *Veiled Threat* (New York: Four Walls Eight Windows, 2002); Cheryl Benard, *Veiled Courage* (New York: Broadway Books, 2002); John Follain and Rita Cristofari, *Zoya's Story: An Afghan Woman's Struggle for Freedom* (New York: William Morrow, 2002).
511. Anne E. Brodsky, *With All Our Strength: The Revolutionary Association of the Women of Afghanistan* (New York: Routledge, 2003); Sunita Mehta, ed., *Women for Afghan Women: Shattering Myths and Claiming the Future* (New York: Palgrave MacMillan, 2002); Melody Ermachild Chavis, *Meena, Heroine of Afghanistan* (New York: St. Martin's Press, 2003).
512. "Magazine rediscovers Afghan girl," *Chicago Tribune*, March 17, 2002.
513. Gregg Zoroya, "'National Geographic' tracks down Afghan girl," *USA Today*, March 13, 2002.
514. Cathy Newman, "A Life Revealed," *National Geographic*, March 2002.
515. David Braun, "How They Found National Geographic's "Afghan Girl," *National Geographic News*, March 7, 2003.
516. Lawrence James, *The Rise and the Fall of the British Empire* (New York: St. Martin's Press, 1994), xiv.
517. Robert Kaplan, "Supremacy by Stealth," *Atlantic Monthly*, July/August, 2003.
518. Michael Ignatieff, "Nation Building Lite," *New York Times* Magazine, July 28, 2002.
519. Michael Griffin, *Reaping the Whirlwind: The Taliban Movement in Afghanistan* (Sterling: Pluto, 2001), 88.
520. U.S. Embassy (Kabul), "The Afghan Left," Airgram (confidential), May 22, 1973. In William Burr ed., *National Security Archive Electronic Briefing Book* no. 59, October 26, 2001, http://www.gwu.edu/~nsarchiv/NSAEBB/NSAEBB59.
521. U.S. Embassy (Kabul), "The Afghan Left."
522. For the story of Meena's life, we recommend Chavis, *Meena*.
523. "Sahar Saba: Women's rights in post-Taliban Afghanistan," CNN.com, November 19, 2001, http://archives.cnn.com/2001/COMMUNITY/11/19/saba.cnna/.
524. Amnesty International, "Women in Afghanistan: A Human Rights Catastrophe," London, 1995. AI Index: ASA, November 3, 1995, http://www.amnesty.org/ailib/intcam/afgan/afgtoc.htm.
525. Amnesty International, *Amnesty International Reports* (London: AI, 1980), 177. In Hafizullah Emadi, *Repression, Resistance, and Women in Afghanistan* (Westport: Praeger, 2002), 104.
526. Brodsky, *With All Our Strength*, 49–57.
527. Ibid. 54.

528. Emadi, *Repression*, 112.
529. Amnesty International, *Protect Afghan Civilians and Refugees*, ASA 11/012/2001, October 9, 2001.
530. MalalaiJoya.com, *Text of Malalai Joya's Historical Speech in the Loya Jirga*, December 17, 2003. See http://www.malalaijoya.com/.
531. Paul Haven, "Afghan constitutional council embroiled in controversy, marred by angry sparring," Associated Press, December 17, 2003.
532. Bashir Gawkh and Danish Karokhel, "Joya Speech Breaks Wall of Silence," Institute for War and Peace Reporting, *Afghan Recovery Report* no. 90, December 22, 2003.
533. Ahmed Rashid interview by David Barsamian, "Afghanistan and Pakistan: Countries in Crisis," February 16, 2004, transcript, Alternative Radio.
534. Zalmay Khalilzad, "Afghanistan's Milestone," *Washington Post*, January 6, 2004.
535. Ibid.
536. Hamida Ghafour, "One Woman's Words Defy Might of Afghan Warlords," *Daily Telegraph* (UK), July 14, 2004.
537. BBC Online, "Profile: Malalai Joya," November 12, 2005, http://news.bbc.co.uk/2/hi/south_asia/4420832.stm.
538. Malalai Joya, in conversation with the authors (corrected for grammar), Farah City, Farah province, Afghanistan, February 23, 2005.
539. Ibid.
540. Gawkh and Karokhel, "Joya Speech Breaks Wall of Silence."
541. Sayed Salahuddin, "Female foe of warlords faces them in Afghan assembly," *Reuters*, October 6, 2005.
542. Carlotta Gall, "Newly Elected Parliament Convenes in Afghanistan," *New York Times*, December 19, 2005.
543. RAWA, "RAWA's Standpoints," 1997–2006, http://www.rawa.org/points.html.
544. *A Call for Justice: a National Consultation on past Human Rights Abuse* (Kabul: Afghanistan Independent Human Rights Commission, January 29, 2005), http://www.aihrc.org.af/Rep_29_Eng/rep29_1_05call4justice.pdf.
545. See Chavis, *Meena*.
546. Noy Thrupkaew, "What Do Afghan Women Want?" *The American Prospect*, vol. 13, issue 15, August 26, 2002.
547. Ibid.
548. The authors of this book are directors of the Afghan Women's Mission, which collects funds for RAWA's projects.
549. Anne E. Brodsky, *With All Our Strength: The Revolutionary Association of the Women of Afghanistan*, (New York: Routledge, 2003), 276.
550. RAWA, "RAWA's Answer to Noy Thrupkaew," EquityFeminism.com, October 18, 2002, http://rawa.fancymarketing.net/prospect.htm.
551. Thrupkaew, "What Do Afghan Women Want?"
552. Editorial, "Afghan Spring," *The Free Lance-Star*, May 23, 2004, http://www.freelancestar.com/News/FLS/2004/052004/05232004/1371798.
553. Human Rights Watch, *Blood-Stained Hands: Past Atrocities in Kabul and Afghanistan's Legacy of Impunity* (New York, 2005), 2, http://hrw.org/reports/2005/afghanistan0605/.
554. InfoTrac Web, National Newspaper Index, http://www.gale.com/tlist/sb5089.html (available in the U.S. through public libraries). The NNI begins in 1980 (except *for Los Angeles Times*). We estimated the 1975–79 monthly coverage for the five newspapers using the *New York Times* archive (http://pqasb.pqarchiver.com/nytimes/advancedsearch.html?) and scaling the *NYT* results for that period by the ratio between NNI and *NYT* in 1980, the first year both archives had in common.

555. Ben Macintyre, *The Man Who Would Be King: The First American in Afghanistan*, (New York: Farrar, Straus and Giroux, 2004), 5.
556. Human Rights Watch, *Blood-Stained Hands: Past Atrocities in Kabul and Afghanistan's Legacy of Impunity* (New York, 2005), 2, http://hrw.org/reports/2005/afghanistan0605/.
557. John F. Burns, "Afghan Capital Grim as War Follows War," *New York Times*, February 5, 1996.
558. "A Tank, a Tank, My Kingdom for a Tank (Afghanistan civil war)," *The Economist* (London), February 26, 1994.
559. Robin Wright and John M. Broder, "U.S. Will Send Iraqi Arms to Afghan Rebels," *Los Angeles Times*, May 19, 1991; John F. Burns, "Afghanistan: Now They Blame America," *New York Times* Magazine, February 4, 1990.
560. Human Rights Watch, *Blood-Stained Hands*, 3.
561. Bruce Nussbaum, "Liberation; The victory over Taliban tyrants is a victory for humanist values," *Business Week*, December 3, 2001.
562. Chris Stephen, "The First Rush of Freedom," *The Observer* (London), November 18, 2001.
563. Bruce Nussbaum, "Liberation."
564. Zakia, in conversation with the authors, Kabul, Afghanistan, February 19, 2005.
565. Henry Kamm, "Afghan Peace Could Herald War of Sexes," *New York Times*, December 12, 1988.
566. David Rohde, "Education Offers Women in Northern Afghanistan a Ray of Hope," *New York Times*, October 3, 2001.
567. Thom Shanker and Eric Schmitt, "U.S. Warns Afghans that Taliban May Poison Relief Food," *New York Times*, October 25, 2001; New York Times, "Workers Report No Food Tampering." See Jane Perlez, "Tenacious Taliban Cling to Power With Tactics, Cunning, and Help from Old Friends," *New York Times*, October 26, 2001.
568. Bob Woodward, *Bush at War* (New York: Simon & Schuster, 2002), 100.
569. Kari Haskell, " 'A' for Afghan, 'S' for Schoolgirl," *New York Times*, March 31, 2002.
570. Cited in Craig Davis, " 'A' is for Allah, 'J' is for Jihad," *World Policy Journal*, Spring 2002, http://www.worldpolicy.org/journal/articles/wpj02-1/Davis.pdf. For a detailed review of the University of Nebraska textbook project, see Mark Vasina and Tajuddin Tajj Millatmal, "An Overview of the UNO Afghan Center's Actions in Afghanistan," *Nebraska Report* (Nebraskans for Peace Newsletter), March 2005, http://www.nebraskansforpeace.org/Documents/2005/2005marchreport.pdf.
571. Joe Stephens and David B. Ottaway, "From U.S., the ABC's of Jihad," *Washington Post*, March 23, 2002, http://www.washingtonpost.com/ac2/wp-dyn/A5339-2002Mar22; Davis, "'A' is for Allah."
572. CBC News Online (Carol Off, Reporter), "Back to School in Afghanistan," May 6, 2002, http://www.cbc.ca/news/background/afghanistan/schools.html.
573. The idea that scapegoating *Newsweek* allowed the U.S. government to avoid taking responsibility for its actions was originally stated in Robert Jensen and Pat Youngblood, "Scapegoating Newsweek," AlterNet, May 17, 2005, http://www.alternet.org/mediaculture/22022/.
574. Molly Ivins, "Desecration of Koran Old News," *Courier Post*, May 19, 2005, http://www.courierpostonline.com/columnists/cxiv051905a.htm.
575. BBC Online, "*Newsweek* withdraws Koran report," http://news.bbc.co.uk, May 17, 2005.
576. Musadeq Sadeq, "Anti-U.S. Riot Turns Deadly in Afghanistan," Associated Press, May 11, 2005.
577. B. Raman, "Afghan Violence Linked to Hizbut Tehrir," *Asia Times*, May 14, 2005, http://www.atimes.com/atimes/Central_Asia/GE14Ag01.html.

578. U.S. Department of Defense, News Transcript, "Secretary of Defense Donald H. Rumsfeld and Air Force General Richard Myers, Chairman, Joint Chiefs of Staff," May 12, 2005.
579. Selay (member of RAWA), e-mail to authors, May 21, 2005, http://www.politicalconscience.net/wordpress/?p=12.
580. Associated Press,"Newsweek Urged To Repair Damage," CBS News, May 17, 2005.
581. James Rupert, "Anti-U.S. Protests Spread in Islamic World," *Chicago Tribune*, May 14, 2005; Steve Holland, "White House Says *Newsweek* Report Damaged U.S. Image," Reuters, May 16, 2005; The White House, "Press Gaggle by Scott McClellan," May 16, 2005.
582. Mark Whitaker, The Editor's Desk, *Newsweek*, May 23, 2005, http://msnbc.msn.com/id/7857154/site/*Newsweek*/.
583. The White House, "Press Gaggle by Scott McClellan," May 16, 2005.
584. Associated Press,"Newsweek Urged To Repair."
585. Whitaker, The Editor's Desk, *Newsweek*, May 23, 2005.
586. The White House, "Press Briefing by Scott McClellan," May 17, 2005.
587. The White House, "Press Briefing by Scott McClellan," May 18, 2005.
588. Paul K. McMasters, "Press Pays a Price for Anonymous Sources," American Press Institute, May 19, 2005, http://www.americanpressinstitute.org/content/6580.cfm; Editorial, "Freedom of the Press Confers Responsibility," *Whittier Daily News*, May 17, 2005.
589. Sarah Baxter, "Pentagon Admits Prison Guards Abused Koran," *The Sunday Times* (London), June 5, 2005; http://www.timesonline.co.uk/article/0,,2089-1641253,00.html; Richard A. Serrano, "Pentagon: Koran Defiled," *Los Angeles Times*, June 4, 2005; for the results of the official investigation into Koran abuse, see United States Southern Command, News Release, *Koran Inquiry: Description of Incidents*, June 3, 2005, http://www.southcom.mil/pa/Media/Releases/PR050603a.pdf.
590. Lori Robertson, "Whatever Happened to Afghanistan?" *American Journalism Review*, June 2003, http://www.ajr.org/Article.asp?id=3041.
591. Kim Hart, "Quitting Kabul," *American Journalism Review*, December/January 2005.
592. P. V. Unnikrishnan and Ray Marcelo, "Stop All the Clocks," *Financial Times* (London), January 28, 2005.
593. George W. Bush, Letter to Congress on American Response to Terrorism, Office of the Press Secretary, WhiteHouse.gov, October 9, 2001, http://www.whitehouse.gov/news/releases/2001/10/20011009-6.html.
594. George W. Bush, Remarks at the California Business Association Breakfast, October 17, 2001, http://www.whitehouse.gov/news/releases/2001/10/20011017-15.html.
595. White House Office of the Press Secretary, "President Discusses War on Terror in Address to the Nation," World Congress Center, Atlanta, Georgia, WhiteHouse.gov, November 8, 2001, http://www.whitehouse.gov/news/releases/2001/11/20011108-13.html.
596. White House Office of the Press Secretary, "Remarks by the President To the Warsaw Conference on Combatting Terrorism," WhiteHouse.gov, November 6, 2001.
597. George W. Bush, Letter to Congress, October 9, 2001.
598. Dick Cheney, Interview by Tim Russert, Camp David, Maryland, *Meet the Press*, MSNBC, WhiteHouse.gov, September 16, 2001, http://www.whitehouse.gov/vicepresident/news-speeches/speeches/vp20010916.html.
599. White House Office of the Press Secretary, "President Discusses War on Terror," November 8, 2001.
600. Laura Bush, Radio Address, Crawford, Texas, WhiteHouse.gov, November 17, 2001, http://www.whitehouse.gov/news/releases/2001/11/20011117.html.

601. George W. Bush, "Turning Back the Terrorist Threat: America's Unbreakable Commitment," Heritage Lecture #809, The Heritage Foundation, November 19, 2003.
602. George W. Bush, Address to the United Nations General Assembly, United Nations Headquarters, New York, New York, WhiteHouse.gov, September 21, 2004, http://www.whitehouse.gov/news/releases/2004/09/20040921-3.html.
603. Jon Lee Anderson, "American Viceroy," *The New Yorker*, December 19, 2005.
604. Ted Rall, "It's About Oil," *San Francisco Chronicle*, November 2, 2001.
605. Wayne Madsen, "Afghanistan, the Taliban and the Bush Oil Team," Centre for Research on Globalisation (CRG), GlobalResearch.ca, January 23, 2002, http://globalresearch.ca/articles/MAD201A.html.
606. BBC Online, "Afghanistan: the pipeline war?" BBC.co.uk, October 29, 2001, http://news.bbc.co.uk/1/hi/world/south_asia/1626889.stm.
607. Chipaux Francoise, "Hamid Karzaï, Une Large Connaissance Du Monde Occidental," *Le Monde* (France), December 6, 2001.
608. Ilene R. Prusher, Scott Baldauf, and Edward Girardet, "Afghan power brokers," *Christian Science Monitor*, June 10, 2002, http://www.csmonitor.com/2002/0610/p01s03e-wosc.html.
609. Lutz Kleveman, "Oil and the New 'Great Game,'" *The Nation*, February 16, 2004.
610. Unocal, "Controversial new movie repeats old and false allegations about Unocal," Unocal.com, June 30, 2004, http://www.Unocal.com/uclnews/2004news/063004.htm.
611. See Ahmed Rashid, *Taliban: Militant Islam, Oil, and Fundamentalism in Central Asia* (New Haven: Yale, 2000). This bestselling book was considered required reading after 9/11 for anyone interested in learning about Afghanistan.
612. Ahmed Rashid interview by David Barsamian, "Afghanistan and Pakistan: Countries in Crisis," February 16, 2004, transcript, Alternative Radio.
613. Anderson, "American Viceroy."
614. "Russian-American Rivalry Head to Caspian," Russian News and Information Agency Novosti, April 15, 2005.
615. George W. Bush, Address to a Joint Session of Congress and the American People, United States Capital, Washington, DC, WhiteHouse.gov, September 20, 2001, http://www.whitehouse.gov/news/releases/2001/09/20010920-8.html.
616. Charles Krauthammer, "The Real New World Order: The American and the Islamic challenge," *Weekly Standard*, vol. 7, no. 9, November 12, 2001.
617. George W. Bush, "We're Fighting to Win—And Win We Will," Remarks on the USS *Enterprise* on Pearl Harbor Day, WhiteHouse.gov, December 7, 2001, http://www.whitehouse.gov/news/releases/2001/12/20011207.html.
618. Krauthammer, "The Real New World Order."
619. Bob Woodward, *Bush at War* (New York: Simon & Schuster, 2002), 43.
620. Michael Gordon, "Iraqi Opposition Gets U.S. Pledge to Oust Hussein for a Democracy", *The New York Times*, August 11, 2002.
621. *The 9/11 Commission Report*, 334; Fairness and Accuracy in Reporting, "Fox News Spins 9/11 Commission Report," June 22, 2004, http://www.fair.org/activism/fox-commission.html.
622. Harris Poll, "Sizeable Minorities Still Believe Saddam Hussein had Strong Links to al-Qa'eda, Helped Plan 9/11, and had Weapons of Mass Destruction," Harris Poll #95, December 29, 2005.
623. George W. Bush and Hamid Karzai, Press Availability, The Rose Garden, Washington DC, June 15, 2004, http://www.whitehouse.gov/news/releases/2004/06/20040615-4.html.

624. George W. Bush, Remarks at the 2004 Republican National Convention, Madison Square Garden, New York, NY, September 2, 2004, http://www.whitehouse.gov/news/releases/2004/09/20040902-2.html.
625. George W. Bush, Remarks at Victory 2004 Rally in Chanhassen, Minnesota, Center City Park, WhiteHouse.gov, October 9, 2004, http://www.whitehouse.gov/news/releases/2004/10/20041009-8.html.
626. Charles H. Fairbanks Jr., "Afghanistan Reborn," *Weekly Standard*, vol. 10, issue 8, November 1, 2004.
627. Barton Gellman and Dafna Linzer, "Afghanistan, Iraq: Two Wars Collide," *Washington Post*, October 22, 2004.
628. Paul Haven, "Libyan is 4th Al-Qa'eda No. 3 captured so far," Associated Press, May 8, 2005.
629. Gellman and Linzer, "Two Wars Collide."
630. George J. Tenet, "The Worldwide Threat in 2003: Evolving Dangers in a Complex World," Testimony before Senate Select Committee on Intelligence, February 12, 2003.
631. George W. Bush, State of the Union Address, January 20, 2004, Office of the Press Secretary, Washington, DC.
632. Presidential Candidates' Debate, Sponsored by the Miccosukee Tribe of Indians of Florida, University of Miami, Coral Gables, Florida, September 30, 2004. Transcript available at http://www.debates.org/pages/trans2004a.html.
633. Alice Cherbonnier, "The 75% Solution," *Baltimore Chronicle*, October 26, 2004.
634. Robert D. Kaplan, "How We Would Fight China," *Atlantic Monthly*, June 2005.
635. Donald H. Rumsfeld, press conference, NATO Air Base, Geilenkirchen, Germany, DefenseLink.mil, June 7, 2002, http://www.defenselink.mil/speeches/2002/s20020607-secdef.html.
636. Article V of the North Atlantic Treaty states, in full: "The Parties agree that an armed attack against one or more of them in Europe or North America shall be considered an attack against them all and consequently they agree that, if such an armed attack occurs, each of them, in exercise of the right of individual or collective self-defense recognized by Article 51 of the Charter of the United Nations, will assist the Party or Parties so attacked by taking forthwith, individually and in concert with the other Parties, such action as it deems necessary, including the use of armed force, to restore and maintain the security of the North Atlantic area. Any such armed attack and all measures taken as a result thereof shall immediately be reported to the (U.N.) Security Council. Such measures shall be terminated when the Security Council has taken the measures necessary to restore and maintain international peace and security." North Atlantic Treaty Organization, "North Atlantic Treaty," Washington, DC., April 4, 1949, http://www.nato.int/docu/basictxt/treaty.htm.
637. Lord Robertson (NATO Secretary General), "Is NATO up to the Challenge?" NATO.int, October 1, 2001, http://www.nato.int/docu/speech/2001/s011001a.htm.
638. Ibid.
639. R. Nicholas Burns (U.S. ambassador to NATO), "Launching NATO's Transformation at Prague," speech (transcript), Berlin, Germany, State.gov, October 30, 2002, http://www.state.gov/p/eur/rls/rm/2002/14907.htm.
640. Donald H. Rumsfeld, "The Future of NATO and Iraq," Prepared Statement for the Senate Armed Services Committee, Washington, DC, DefenseLink.mil, April 10, 2003, http://www.defenselink.mil/speeches/2003/sp20030410-depsecdef0142.html.
641. Peter Ford, "Expanded NATO Looks for New Role," *Christian Science Monitor*, November 22, 2002.
642. George Cahlink, "Shaking Up the Alliance," Airforce Magazine Online, vol. 87, no. 10, October 2004.

643. Lord Robertson (NATO Secretary General), "Media Statement at the Meeting of the North Atlantic Council," Warsaw, Poland, NATO.int, September 24, 2002, http://www.nato.int/docu/speech/2002/s020924b.htm.
644. Kaplan, "How We Would Fight China."
645. CBC News, "General warns of 20-year mission in Afghanistan," August 8, 2005.
646. Agence France-Presse, "U.S. presses NATO to prepare takeover of Afghanistan military operations," October 13, 2004.
647. BBC Online, "NATO expands Afghanistan mission," BBC.co.uk, February 10, 2005, http://news.bbc.co.uk/1/hi/world/south_asia/4254391.stm.
648. Kathleen Knox, "NATO: Prague Conference Convenes To Discuss Potential Alliance Role In Greater Mideast," Radio Free Europe/Radio Liberty, October 20, 2003.
649. Adam Ereli (deputy spokesman), "NATO Iraq Training Role," U.S. Department of State, State.gov, September 22, 2004, http://www.state.gov/r/pa/prs/ps/2004/36397.htm.
650. Stephen Graham, "U.S. Bases in Afghanistan Get $83M Upgrade," *The Guardian* (London), March 28, 2005.
651. Stephen Graham, "McCain Calls for Permanent Afghan Bases," Associated Press, February 22, 2005.
652. Daan van der Schriek, "Afghan riots bode ill for U.S. long-term plans," International Relations and Security Network, May 13, 2005.
653. U.S. Department of State, Background Note: Uzbekistan, February 2005. Wording changed in July 2005, http://www.state.gov/r/pa/ei/bgn/2924.htm. See Sergei Blagov, "An iron fist, without the glove," *Asia Times*, May 17, 2005, http://www.atimes.com/atimes/Central_Asia/GE17Ag02.html.
654. Robin Wright and Ann Scott Tyson, "U.S. Evicted From Air Base In Uzbekistan," *Washington Post*, July 30, 2005.
655. Eric Schmitt and James Dao, "U.S. Is Building up its Military Bases in Afghan Region," *New York Times*, January 9, 2005.
656. Human Rights Watch, "Bullets Were 'Falling Like Rain': The Andijan Massacre, May 13, 2005" Human Rights Watch, June 7, 2005.
657. Wright and Tyson, "U.S. Evicted."
658. Lionel Beehner, "ASIA: U.S. Military Bases in Central Asia," Council on Foreign Relations background Q & A, July 26, 2005, http://www.cfr.org/publication/8440/asia.html#3.
659. "Tajikistan Says Can Host U.S. Military after Closure of Base in Uzbekistan," *Moscow News*, September 16, 2005, http://www.mosnews.com/news/2005/09/16/tajikus.shtml.
660. Thomas Carothers, "Promoting Democracy and Fighting Terror," *Foreign Affairs*, January/February 2003.
661. Amnesty International, "Turkmenistan." In Amnesty International Report 2004, http://web.amnesty.org/report2004/tkm-summary-eng.
662. U.S. Department of State, "Turkmenistan: Country Reports on Human Rights Practices," State.gov, February 25, 2004, http://www.state.gov/g/drl/rls/hrrpt/2003/27870.htm.
663. European Parliament, *Resolution on Turkmenistan, including Central Asia*, Strasbourg, October 23, 2003.
664. Greg Jaffe, "Pentagon Prepares to Scatter Soldiers in Remote Corners," *Wall Street Journal*, May 27, 2003.
665. Stephen Blank, "U.S. Strategic Priorities Shifting in Central Asia," EurasiaNet, March 25, 2004.
666. Donald H. Rumsfeld, Testimony to the Senate Armed Service Committee, Washington, DC, Thursday, September 23, 2004.

667. Kurt M. Campbell & Celeste Johnson Ward, "New Battle Stations?" *Foreign Affairs*, September/October 2003.
668. Blank, "U.S. Strategic Priorities."
669. Kaplan, "How We Would Fight China."
670. Schmitt and Dao, "U.S. Is Building."
671. Matthew Clark, "Will U.S. be asked to leave key military bases?" Christian Science Monitor, July 5, 2005.
672. Douglas Jehl, "C.I.A. Says Russia Could Try to Reassert Itself After a Putin Victory," New York Times, March 14, 2004.
673. Andrea R. Mihailescu, "UPI Energy Watch," United Press International, May 11, 2005.
674. Dan Morgan and David B. Ottaway, "Azerbaijan's Riches Alter the Chessboard," Washington Post, October 4, 1998.
675. Michael Cohen, "Country Analysis Briefs: Caspian Sea Region," Energy Information Agency, U.S. Department of Energy, May 24, 2005, http://www.eia.doe.gov/cabs/caspian.html.
676. Caspian Pipeline Consortium, "CPC Shareholders Progress Toward Pipeline Expansion Plan Approval," press release, May 20, 2005. Pipeline route maps are based on U.S. Energy Information Agency, "Country Analysis Briefs: Caspian Sea Region," U.S. Department of Energy, July 2002, http://www.eia.doe.gov/emeu/cabs/caspgrph.html (obsolete). See also

    Norman D. Livergood, "The New U.S.-British Oil Imperialism," December 18, 2005, http://www.hermes-press.com/impintro1.htm (accessed March 14, 2006).
677. Sunit Arora, "If not Iran, maybe Turkmen gas: Aiyar gets Pak invite," Indian Express, June 6, 2005.
678. Condoleezza Rice, "Remarks With Indian Minister of External Affairs Natwar Singh Following Meeting," State.gov, April 14, 2005, http://www.state.gov/secretary/rm/2005/44662.htm.
679. Robert V. Barylsky, "Russia, the West, and the Caspian Energy Hub," Middle East Journal, Spring 1995.
680. Kieran Cooke, "Caspian oil set for fast flow to the West," BBC.co.uk, May 5, 2005.
681. Ibid.
682. M. K. Bhadrakumar, "The Great Game for Caspian Oil," The Hindu (India), April 20, 2005.
683. U.S. Department of State, Bureau of European and Eurasian Affairs, "Azerbaijan Background Notes," December 2005, http://www.state.gov/r/pa/ei/bgn/2909.htm.
684. Human Rights Watch, "Azerbaijan: Police Violence Mars Election Campaign," October 4, 2005.
685. U.S. Department of State, "Rice Urges Kazakhstan to Lead Central Asia on Democratization," October 13, 2005, http://usinfo.state.gov/eur/Archive/2005/Oct/13214264.html.
686. Kassymzhomart Tokaev, "Kazakhstan: The Democratic Path for Peace and Prosperity," speech to Heritage Foundation, August 23, 2005, http://www.heritage.org/Research/RussiaandEurasia/wm877.cfm.
687. UN Office for the Coordination of Humanitarian Affairs, "Afghanistan: Year in Review 2005—Fragile progress, insecurity remains," January 11, 2006.
688. ABC News Poll, "Life in Afghanistan," ABC News, December 7, 2005.
689. Zakia (student at Kabul University), in conversation with the authors, Kabul, Afghanistan, February 19, 2005.
690. Friba (member of RAWA), e-mail to authors, May 25, 2005; James Ingalls, "Protests Were Grassroots, But Afghans Still Want Troops . . . For Now," political conScience (Web log), May 26, 2005, http://www.politicalconscience.net/wordpress/?p=14.

691. ABC News Poll, "Life in Afghanistan."
692. B. Raman, "Afghan violence linked to Hizbut Tehrir," Asia Times, May 14, 2005.
693. The Human Rights Research and Advocacy Consortium, Take the Guns Away: Afghan Voices on Security and Elections (Kabul: HRRAC, September 2004).
694. Mariam, in conversation with the authors, Farah, Afghanistan, February 22, 2005.
695. Wasay Engineer (Solidarity Party spokesperson), in conversation with the authors, Kabul, Afghanistan, February 17, 2005.
696. United Nations Development Programme, "Afghanistan's New Beginnings Programme," www.undpanbp.org.
697. A Call for Justice: a National Consultation on past Human Rights Abuse (Kabul: Afghanistan Independent Human Rights Commission), January 29, 2005, http://www.aihrc.org.af/Rep_29_Eng/rep29_1_05call4justice.pdf.
698. Nader Nadery (spokesman for the Afghanistan Independent Human Rights Commission), in conversation with the authors in Kabul, Afghanistan (edited for grammar), February 19, 2005.
699. Malalai Joya, e-mail to authors, February 11, 2006.
700. Reuters, "Afghans Protest Outside U.S. Base Over Arrests," July 26, 2005; Friba (member of RAWA), e-mail to authors.
701. The list of countries that should not be part of the peacekeeping force would include the United States, Israel, the United Kingdom, France, Egypt, Saudi Arabia, The United Arab Emirates, Pakistan, Russia, India, China, and Iran.
702. ABC News Poll, "Life in Afghanistan."
703. Selay (member of RAWA), e-mail to authors, May 21, 2005; RAWA, "RAWA's View of Afghanistan Protests," Znet, May 28, 2005, http://www.zmag.org/content/showarticle.cfm?SectionID=40&ItemID=7958.
704. James Dobbins et al., "The UN's Role in Nation-Building: From the Congo to Iraq," Rand Corporation, 2005, http://www.rand.org/pubs/monographs/2005/RAND_MG304.sum.pdf.
705. Documents describing the Afghan government's reconstruction plan and budget are located on the Web site at http://www.af.
706. Harris Poll, "U.S. Adults Paying Less Attention to the Events in Afghanistan than Those in Iraq," The Harris Poll #57, July 26, 2005, http://harrisinteractive.com/harris_poll/index.asp?PID=587.

ACKNOWLEDGMENTS

This book is dedicated to the people of Afghanistan.

We would like to thank Rahul Mahajan, David Barsamian, and Robert Jensen for faithfully supporting us and encouraging us to write this book. Even when we were beginning to doubt our abilities, their confidence and advocacy kept us on track. We would especially like to thank Rahul for commenting on a draft of the manuscript, and David for gracing these pages with a foreword.

We are indebted to our dear sisters in RAWA for teaching us so much about the realities in Afghanistan. Without them, we would not have even thought of this project. Their heroic struggle is a tremendous source of inspiration.

We would also like to acknowledge the unbelievably brave Malalai Joya. Meeting her was one of the high points of our lives.

We thank Gayatri Patnaik and Jill Petty for believing in this book.

We thank our parents for always encouraging us to think critically about the world and to follow our dreams.

The authors finally thank their loving spouses for tolerating them during the writing of this book.

INDEX

ABC. *See* American Broadcasting Company
abduction, of women, 112–16
Abdullah, Abdullah, 91, 125, 136
Abdullah, Hamid, 163
Abdullah, Syad, 31
Abu Ghraib, xviii, 78, 80
Accountability Department, Afghan Government, 145
Accuracy in Media, 215
acid, throwing of, xv, 9
ACLU. *See* American Civil Liberties Union
Action Against Famine, 36
Adams, Brad, 150
"Afghan Elections: The Great Gamble" (AREU), 149
Afghan Information Center, 13
Afghanistan
  1970s, 3–7
  1980s, 7–12
  1990-1996, 12–22
  1992-1996, xv, 21, 29, 95, 197
  1996-1998, 22–29
  1998-2001, 29–38
  2001, winter in, 54
  air strikes against, 47, 141, 183, 231
  bombing of, 41, 49–57
  as buffer state, 4, 117–20
  as client democracy, 165–66
  as constitutional monarchy, xiv
  constitution of, 126, 130, 138–43, 143, 145, 146, 147, 164, 166, 184–85
  countryside of, 62–69
  decision to attack, 47
  as destroyed state, 38
  as failed state, xii–xiv, 21, 37
  functionality of, 230
  independence of, 118–19
  interest in, 49, 199–200, 203
  as international problem, 203
  Iraq v., 42, 47, 83
  as Islamic Republic, 144
  modern boundaries of, 117–18
  national army of, 100, 103, 105, 116, 257–58
  police force of, 100, 102
  quality of life in, ix
  reconstruction of, 259
  remembering, 260–61
  as rogue state, 29–38, 37, 41
  sovereignty of, xiv, 254
  as Soviet client democratic republic, xiv
  strategic importance of, 25
  as success story, 233
  U.S. targeting of, 41–49
  Yugoslavia v., 21–22
Afghanistan Independent Human Rights Commission (AIHRC), 96, 109, 115, 191, 195, 255–56, 260
Afghanistan Justice Project, 83, 166, 260
Afghanistan Research and Evaluation Unit (AREU), 149, 153, 160
Afghanistan Unveiled, 175
Afghan Left, 185–86
Afghan Massacre: Convoy of Death, 104–5
Afghan resistance, 122
  Mujahideen v., 13, 15
Afghans
  educated, xiv
  feminist, xviii
  progressive, 185–86
  public opinion of, 13, 68, 101, 204
  safety of, 98
  war weariness of, 83, 86
Afghan, Sediq, 101

Afghan Transitional Authority, 98, 133
Afghan Women's Council, 186
Afghan Women's Mission, 221
Aftab, 147
Ahmad, Eqbal, vii
Ahmad, Faiz, 9
Ahmad, Mir, 53
AIHRC. *See* Afghanistan Independent Human Rights Commission
air strikes, 47, 141, 183, 231
AJR. See American Journalism Review
al-Adel, Saif, 236
Al Ahram Weekly, 100
Albright, Madeleine, 172
Amanullah, 119–20, 184
American Broadcasting Company (ABC), 219–20, 253–54
American Civil Liberties Union (ACLU), 76
American Club, of Peshawar, 204
American Journalism Review (AJR), 218, 220
The American Prospect, 192
Americans. *See also* United States (U.S.)
 ignorance of, xii, 197–98, 203, 221, 251
 interests of, xix–xx
 as warlords, 82–84
America's Role in Nation Building (RAND), xiii
Amin, Hafizullah, 6
Aminzay, Bakhtar, 159
Amnesty International, 20–21, 49, 115, 260
Anderson, John Lee, 130, 227
Annan, Kofi, 34–35, 172
antigovernment groups, 162
antiwar movement, U.S., 260
Arar, Maher, 69–70
arc of instability, 244
AREU. *See* Afghanistan Research and Evaluation Unit
Ariana airline, 32–33
Armstrong, Sally, 180
Ashcroft, John, 74
Asia Foundation, 101
Asia Times, 67, 163
Asia, U.S. power in, 241–45, 250
Atlantic Monthly, 183, 244
Attaullah, Haji, 126
awe, 183–84
Azerbaijan, 228, 245, 248–50
Baath Party, 182
Bacha-i-Saqqao, 120
Bagram Air Base, 74, 78, 80, 82
Baku-Tblisi-Caspian pipeline (BTC), 247, 249
Baltimore Chronicle, 236
Baltimore Sun, 219
Bamiyan Buddha statues, 199
Barakzai, Shokria, 159
Baranowska, Carmela, 62–63
Barker, Paul, 59
Barno, David, 82
Barsamian, David, 188, 227
Bassiouni, M. Cherif, 80–82, 112
Baxter, Craig, 4
Bearden, Milton, 11
Bechtel, 228
Begg, Moazzam, 76–77
Benard, Cheryl, 180
Beneath the Veil (Shah, Saira), 169
Berger, Sandy, 30
Berman, Paul, 10
Black, Cofer, 51
Black Sea, 229
Blair, Cherie, 172
Blair, Tony, xii, 93, 110
Blank, Stephen, 244
blasphemy, 144, 147
blue burqa books, 180–81, 206
bodies, burning of, 66
bombing
 1993 World Trade Center, 29
 2001 World Trade Center, xi–xiv, xvi, xix, 3–38, 29, 41, 49–51, 57, 87–88, 197–98, 205, 224–25, 229, 232, 250
 of Afghanistan, 41, 49–57
 of Khobar Towers, 29
 suicide, 251
 U.S. goals for, 49–50, 51
 of USS *Cole*, 29, 33, 44
 of wedding party, 183
Bonn Conference, 97–98, 103, 124–27, 131, 148
Bonn Process, 126, 138–39, 151
Bosnia, 99, 259
Boston Globe, 219
Boucher, Richard, 20
Boyce, Michael, 51
BP/Arco, 247
Bradley, Bill, 12

Brahimi, Lakhdar, 99, 126, 141
Brand, Willie, 79–80
bribery, 60, 84, 153
British empire, 117–20, 182
Brodsky, Anne, 181
Brzezinsky, Zbigniew, 6–7
BTC. *See* Baku-Tblisi-Caspian pipeline
buffer state, 4, 117–20
Burns, John F., 15, 21, 90, 202, 204
burqa, xvii, 114, 170–71, 173–74, 179, 184, 190, 261
Bush at War (Woodward), 46
Bush, George H.W., 202
Bush, George W., 50–51, 92–94, 143, 165, 170–72, 178. *See also* United States
  Administration of, xiii, xvii, 16–17, 22, 37, 41–42, 72–73, 82, 87, 91, 101, 127, 148–49, 165, 187, 196, 215
  democracy and, 165
  drug trade and, 110
  exploitation of Afghan women by, xvii–xviii
  gratitude, expectation of, 182, 233
  Iraq and, 231–32
  public relations campaign of, 171–78, 224, 231–35
  RAWA and, 191
  reelection campaign of, 151, 233–35
  war, justification for, 223
  wars of, ix
  women's rights and, 171–73
Bush, Laura, 169–72, 196
Business Week, 148–49, 205, 207
Byman, Daniel, 127

A Call for Justice (AIHRC), 192, 255
Cambridge Energy Research Associates (CERA), 129, 227
Camp Delta, 71, 78. *See also* Guantanamo Bay
Camp X-ray, 71. *See also* Guantanamo Bay
Canadian Broadcasting Corporation (CBC), 212–13
candidates, 152–53, 163
CARE. *See* Cooperative for Assistance and Relief Everywhere
Carter, Jimmy, 6–7
CAS. *See* Center for Afghanistan Studies
Caspian Guard, 245, 249
Caspian Pipeline Consortium (CPC), 246
Catholic Agency for Overseas Development, 55
CBC. *See* Canadian Broadcasting Corporation
CBS. *See* Columbia Broadcasting System
Center for Afghanistan Studies (CAS), 177, 211–12
Center for Economic and Social Rights (CESR), 101
Center for Research on Globalization, 225
Central Intelligence Agency (CIA), 6, 9, 14, 19–20, 29, 69–70, 87–89, 177, 204
CERA. *See* Cambridge Energy Research Associates
CESR. *See* Center for Economic and Social Rights
chadori, 114
Champion, James, 69
chastity checks, 114
Chayes, Sarah, 97
checkpoints, 109
Cheeks, Gary, 59
Cheney, Dick, 47, 74, 96, 128, 165, 232, 236
Chernyshev, Albert, 26
Chevron, 246
Chicago Tribune, 215, 220
children's education, 211–13
China, 229, 245–47, 250, 257
Chowkar-Karez, Afghanistan, 51–52, 56–57
Christian Science Monitor, 123, 136, 199, 226
CIA. *See* Central Intelligence Agency
Civil Affairs Units. *See* Provincial Reconstruction Teams
civilians
  attacks on, 280n400
  casualties, vii, 14–15, 20, 51–55, 140–41, 202
  targeting of, 56–57, 67
civilization, saving of, 223
civil society, xvii, 136
Clarke, Richard A., 42–47, 87
client democracy, 165–66
Clinton, Hillary, 172
Clinton, William J., 26, 28, 44
  Administration of, 24, 30–31, 41–44, 87, 127
  campaign of, 202
cluster bombs, xvi, 53–54, 56. *See also* land mines

Cohen, William, 30
Cold War, 3, 121–22, 239, 250
collateral damage. *See* civilians, casualties
Coll, Steve, 219
Colombia, 237
Columbia Broadcasting System (CBS), 219
Combined Task Force Thunder, 58
Commission for Peace, 159
communism, 182, 194
conservatives, 234
constitution, 126, 130, 138–43, 164
  1964, 184–85
  amendments to, 146
  article 22 of, 143
  article 34 of, 147
  article 35 of, 145
  article 54 of, 145
  equality in, 166
  women and, 143
constitutional monarchy, xiv
Cooperative for Assistance and Relief Everywhere (CARE), 59, 280n400
co-option
  of social justice, 258
  of warlords, 156, 161
corporations, absence of, 228
Counterterrorism Center, of CIA, 51
countryside, 62–69, 117
CPC. *See* Caspian Pipeline Consortium
crimes
  civil, 108–12
  against humanity, 255
  war, 103–8, 152, 156, 192
  against women, 112–16
Cullather, Nick, 121
cultural ignorance, 66
Cypress Group, 97. *See also* Northern Alliance

dam projects, 121–22
Daoud Khan, Mohammed, 4–5, 120–22, 184–85
Daud, Mohammed, 105
Dauletabad-Donmez field, 225
Davies, Glyn, 25–26
Davis, Craig, 212
DDR. *See* Disarmament, Demobilization and Reintegration
Dean, John, 74
decentralized government, 142
Delenda, 43, 45
democracy, 117, 141, 148–50, 208, 223–24, 249
  Bush Administration and, 165
  client, 165–66
  elements of, 165
  idealism and, 183
  imperialism as, 49, 232–33
  promotion of, 234
  undermining of, 156
Democracy Now!, 105
demonstrations
  anti-U.S., 101, 214–15, 254, 256
  against Karzai, H., 101, 254
  by religious leaders, 139
  by women, 113, 261
destroyed state, 38
development. *See* economic development
Dilawar, 78–80
disarmament, 156–57, 254–57
Disarmament, Demobilization and Reintegration (DDR), 157, 255
Dobbins, James F., 126
Dobbs, Michael, 25
Dobriansky, Paula, 173–75, 189
Doctors Without Borders, 55, 59–60. *See also* Medecins Sans Frontieres
Doran, Jamie, 104–5
Dostum, Abdul Rashid, vii, 17–10, 23, 27, 43, 87, 104–5, 107, 134, 150, 156–57, 159, 161
drug trade, 108–12
  Bush, G.W., 110
  eradication of, ix
  sanctions and, 110
Duckworth, Connie, 176
Dunbar, Charles F., 138
Dupont, Stephen, 66–67
Durand, Henry, 119
Durand line, 120, 122
Durand, Mortimer, 118
Durch, William J., 99

East Timor, 259
economic development, 121, 183
Economist, xiii, 17–18, 35–36, 202–3
education, 145, 192
  children's, 211–13
  women's, 209

elders, 160. *See also* warlords
elections
aftermath of, 153–58
observer of, 135
parliamentary, 126, 158–65
presidential, 126, 148–53, 165
security during, 151, 156
timing of, 149, 151
violence preceding, 162
women and, 153–54
embassies, 1998 attacks on, xvi, 29–30, 41–42
"Enduring Freedom: Abuses by U.S Forces in Afghanistan" (HRW), 65
enemy combatants, 69–73
Engineer, Wasay, 144, 155, 255
Ensler, Eve, 192, 195
equality, women's and men's, 166, 184, 192
Ermachild, Melody, 181
Etemadi, Mustafa, 143
Ethiopia, 237
ethnicities, 24, 87, 118
exploitation, 261
extraordinary rendition, 69–73
extremists, as tool, 10
eyepieces, burqa, 179

factional fighting, 103–8
Fahim, Mohammed, 88, 107, 123, 136, 147, 156, 159–60
Fahim, Qasim, 108
Fahrenheit 9/11, 226
failed state, xii–xiv, 21, 37
Fairchild, Albert, 4
Far Eastern Economic Review, 44
Fellner, Jamie, 72
Feminist Majority, 28, 99, 170, 178–80, 192, 195
feminists
Afghan, xviii, 96, 191–96, 259
Western, xvii, 28, 169–71, 178–82, 184, 191–93, 195–96
Filochowski, Julian, 55
Financial Times, 221
First Amendment Center, 217
Fisk, Robert, 128
Fleischer, Ari, 100
flyover rights, 249
food aid, 55
poisoning of, 210
Food and Agriculture Organization, 35
food drops, 55–56
Foreign Affairs, 243–44
For God and Country: Faith and Patriotism Under Fire (Yee), 77
Fox News, 219
Franks, Tommy, 98
freedom. *See also* democracy; liberation
of expression, 147
imperialism as, 184
of press, 147–48, 216
Free Lance-Star, xi–xii
free market capitalism, 176–77
Friba, 253
Friedman, Thomas, 17
Friends of Afghanistan, 128
fundamentalists. *See* Mujahideen; Northern Alliance

Gailani, Syed Ahmad, 8, 90, 97
gender apartheid campaign, xvii, 170, 178–82, 196. *See also* feminists, Western
Geneva Accords, 199
Geneva conventions, 68, 72–73, 82, 104, 228. *See also* international law
Georgia, 229, 248
Georgia, Ukraine, Uzbekistan, Azerbaijan, and Moldova alliance (GUUAM), 249
globalization, economic, 244
Gonzalez, Alberto, 77
Gorbachev, Mikhail, 13
Gordon, Michael, 88
Goutierre, Thomas, 211–12
Griffin, Michael, 20–21
ground war, xvi
Guantanamo Bay, 69, 71–73, 75–79, 213–14, 216–17
Guardian, 46, 55, 125, 137
Gula, Sharbat, 181–82
Gulf News, 141
Gulf War, 15–16, 47
Gutman, Roy, 220
GUUAM. *See* Georgia, Ukraine, Uzbekistan, Azerbaijan, and Moldova alliance

Habibi, Gulalai, 148
Habibullah, 78–80

Halliburton, 228
van Halsema, Diderik, 61
Hamdan, Salim Ahmed, 74
Hamilton, Lee, 15
Haq, Abdul, 88–91
Haq, Ehsanul, 125
Hart, Kim, 220
Harvard Carr Center for Human Rights Policy, 183
Hatch, Orrin, 12
HAVA. *See* Helmand and Arghandab Valley Authority
HAWCA. *See* Humanitarian Assistance for the Women and Children of Afghanistan
Hazaras, 87, 122, 131, 143
Hekmatyar, Gulbuddin, xiv–xv, 9, 14, 16–20, 22–23, 88, 91, 104, 159, 192, 204
Helmand and Arghandab Valley Authority (HAVA), 121
Herat, Afghanistan, 114
Heritage Foundation, 250
heroin. *See* drug trade
Herold, Marc, 51
high value targets (HVTs), 235–37
Hilferty, Bryan, 140–41
Hindu Newspaper, 248
Hisb-e-Islami, 88, 104, 159
Hisbi-i Wahdat, 20, 161
Hitchens, Christopher, 56
Holdich, Thomas, 117
Hood, Jay, 217
Hoon, Geoff, 53
House of Elders, 159–60. *See also* parliament
House of Representatives International Relations Committee, 91
House of Representatives International Relations Subcommittee on International Operations and Human Rights, 56
House of the People, 158. *See also* parliament
Howeidi, Fahmi, 100
HRW. *See* Human Rights Watch
Hughes, Karen, 171, 173–74, 178, 283n484
human development index, xix
humanitarian aid, ix, xix, 55
  bribery with, 60
  donors, reduction in, 221
  militarization of, 57–62
  per capita, 259
  safe, 195
  theft of, 108
  workers, targeting of, 61
Humanitarian Assistance for the Women and Children of Afghanistan (HAWCA), 262
humanitarian organizations, 262
human rights, 80–81, 143, 164, 175, 183, 230, 237, 255, 259
  abusers, 152
  Mujahideen and, viii, 87
  Northern Alliance and, 94, 103–8
  reporting on, 201
  Taliban and, 27, 230
  Turkmenistan and, 243
  UN investigator of, 80–81
  universality of, 193–94
  U.S. and, 24, 25, 38, 71
  Uzbekistan and, 70–71, 242–43
Human Rights Research and Advocacy Consortium, 150, 154, 254
Human Rights Watch (HRW), viii, 34, 51–52, 65, 68, 70, 72, 106, 114, 135–37, 137, 139, 147, 150, 158, 160–63, 199, 201, 205, 249, 260
  World Report, 102
humiliation, of detainees, 64, 69, 76
hunger strikes, 75
Hussein, Saddam, 16, 182, 232, 233
HVTs. *See* high value targets

ICRC. *See* International Committee of the Red Cross
idealism, of democracy, 183
IDPs. *See* internally displaced people
Ignatieff, Michael, 183
ignorance, xii, 66, 197–98, 203, 221, 251
imperialism
  appearance of, 258
  British, 117–20, 182
  as democracy, 49, 232–33
  freedom as, 184
  fundamentalism v., 251–52
  in media, 206–7
  prestige of, 229–31
  resistance to, 183–84, 194
  U.S., 182–84, 229, 251–52
  women's liberation and, viii

IMU. *See* Islamic Movement of Uzbekistan
indefinite detention, 69–73
independence, of Afghanistan, 118–19
Independent, 52, 113, 128, 214
Independent National Commission for Peace in Afghanistan, 161
Inderfurth, Karl F., 28
India, 120, 225, 246
Indira Gandhi Pediatric Hospital, 32–33
Indonesia, 237
inflation, 36
Initial Response Force (IRF), 77–78
insecurity, enforcement of, 97–103
instability, arc of, 244
Institute for Foreign Policy Analysis, 71
intellectuals, 158
  persecution of, 9
intelligence errors, 52–53
Inter-Action, 59
internally displaced people (IDPs), 112. *See also* refugees
international bodies, 100. *See also* United Nations
International Committee of the Red Cross (ICRC), 75–76
International Crisis Group, 135, 137, 141–42, 145, 164, 260
international humanitarian organizations, 36, 59–60
international law, 31, 72–73. *See also* Geneva conventions
International Medical Aid, 36
International Security Assistance Force (ISAF), 58, 98–101, 105, 173, 218, 240, 257–58
Inter-Services Intelligence Directorate (ISI), 8–9, 14, 19, 22, 29, 48, 89, 125, 204
Iran, 5, 102, 125, 246, 250
  revolution in, 7
Iraq, 42, 47, 83, 129–30, 224, 228–29, 234, 237, 238, 240–41, 249, 250, 252, 260
  Bush, G.W. and, 231–32
  path to, 231–32
IRFing. *See* Initial Response Force
ISAF. *See* International Security Assistance Force
Islamic Law, xvii, 23–24, 126, 130, 143–48, 166
  media and, 147
  public opinion on, 146
  women and, 144–46
Islamic Movement of Uzbekistan (IMU), 70
Islamic Teaching. *See* Vice and Virtue Squad
Ivins, Molly, 214

Jamiat-i Islami, 13
Jamili, Khalilullah, 163–64
Janan, 62–63
jang saalaraan. *See* warlords
jihadi. *See* Mujahideen
Joint Election Management Body, 153
Joint Task Force Guantanamo, 217
Jospin, Lionel, 36
Joya, Malalai, viii, 140, 146, 155–56, 158, 187–92, 194, 196, 262
justice, 73–75
  peace v., 138, 161
  for warlords, xix, 143, 152, 192, 254–56

Kabul, Afghanistan
  attack on, 23, 202
  destruction of, 21
  luxury in, ix
  Northern Alliance, occupation by, 92–97
  peacekeepers, restriction to, 98
  Sarajevo v., 21
  security in, 173
  siege of, 15, 19–21
Kabul University, 253
Kabul Weekly, 123
Kama Ado, Afghanistan, 52, 57
Kandahar, Afghanistan, 23–24, 52, 93
Kaplan, Robert, 183, 238, 244–45
Karimov, Islam, 242
Karmal, Babrak, 4, 6
Karzai, Hamid, vii, 9, 95
  appointments of, 105
  bodyguards of, viii
  at Bonn Conference, 125
  on democracy, 149
  demonstrations against, 101, 254
  election of, 117
  emergence of, 123
  foreign control of, 119

ISAF recommendations of, 99
Khalilzad, Z. and, 129
Koran abuse and, 214–15
legitimization of, 133–34
at *Loya Jirga*, 132–34, 137, 141–42
Mujahideen and, 124
operating budget of, 109
opponents of, 152–53
platform of, 155
political parties enactment by, 152
popular support for, 123, 151
press, freedom of, 147
as puppet, 123–24
Unocal and, 226–28
U.S. and, xvii, 89, 101–2, 124, 153, 166, 241
victory of, 153–55
warlords, support of, 164
warlords v., 154–55
Kazakhstan, 245–49
Keegan, John, 95
Keith, Kenton, 56
Kelly, John, 13–16
Keshwar Kamal, Meena, 9, 186, 192. *See also* Revolutionary Association of the Women of Afghanistan
KHAD, 192
al Khadimat, Makhtab, 10, 29
Khalili, Karim, 87, 136, 147
Khalilzad, Zalmay, xvii, 105, 131, 133, 141, 151, 188–89, 224
bribery by, 153
Karzai, H. and, 129
Unocal and, 226–28
as U.S. viceroy, 127–30
warlords and, 161–62
Khalis, Yunus, 88
Khalq, 4–6, 185. *See also* Progressive Democratic Party of Afghanistan
Khan, Abdur Rahman, 118
Khan, Ahmed, 65
Khan, Alif, 71–72
Khan, Ismail, 87, 97, 105–7, 114, 137, 150, 155–56, 174
Khan, Nadir. *See* Nadir Shah
Khan, Naimatullah, 127
Khan, Padsha, 107–8
Khobar Towers, bombing of, 29
Kilid media group, 155
"Killing You is a Very Easy Thing for Us" (HRW), 106, 147
Kleveman, Lutz, 226
Koran
abuse of, xviii, 213–18, 254
handling of, 77
Korengal valley, 68
Kosovo, 259
Kothari, Miloon, 108–9
Krauthammer, Charles, 229–31
Kristof, Nicholas, 57
Krugman, Paul, 149
Kunduz, Afghanistan, 103–4
Kyrgystan, 243

bin Laden, Osama, 9–10, 29–32, 37, 41–44, 57, 87, 182, 205, 223, 229, 235–36
disrespect by, 51
September 11, 2001 and, 51
surrender of, 50
land appropriation, 108–12
land-mines, xvi, 54. *See also* cluster bombs
land reforms, 186
Lavrov, Sergei, 35
laws of war, 68, 72–73
Leno, Mavis, 178
Lesser, Ian, 31
Libbi, Abu Farraj, 235
liberation, 223, 233–34, 251
civilization v., 182, 195
free market capitalist approach to, 176–77
of women, viii, xviii, 113, 169–84, 187–88, 195–96, 205–8
lily pad approach, 244
Logan, Harriet, 180
London Observer, 206
Los Angeles Times, 18, 25, 31–32, 52, 123, 153, 199, 220
Loya Jirga, 85, 91, 154
1949, 120
boycott at, 142–43
constitutional, 18, 126, 138–43, 187–89, 191
emergency, 105, 126, 131–37
Karzai, H., 132–34, 137, 141–42
Malalai Joya at, 140, 155, 187-191
manipulation of, 131–34
outcome of, 136–37
representatives, selection of, 139–40
security at, 189
violence preceding, 134–38

Macintyre, Ben, 201
Maclean's, 91
Madsen, Wayne, 225
Mahdawi, Mir Hussein, 147
Majrooh, Sayed Bahauddin, 13–14
Manawi, Ahmed Fazel, 147
Maresca, John, 27–28
Martinkus, John, 66
mass murder, 103–8
Massoud, Ahmed Shah, 17–18, 20, 23, 27, 43–44, 87–88, 160
Mayer, Jane, 69
McCain, John, 241
McClarty, Donna, 172
McClellan, Scott, 215–16
McCoy, Alfred, 111
McCurry, Steve, 181
McKinney, Cynthia, 56
McMasters, Paul, 217
Medecins du Monde, 36
Medecins Sans Frontieres (MSF), 61. *See also* Doctors Without Borders
media
  1990-1996 blackout of, 198–205
  1992-1996, coverage during, xv
  credibility of, 217
  criticality of, 233, 259
  criticisms of, 183
  future coverage by, 218–21, 250
  government policy and, 197–98, 199, 202–3, 213, 219, 221
  historical statistics of, 199–201, 218
  humbling of, 213–18
  imperialism in, 206–7
  increase in coverage by, 259–60
  independent, 260
  Islamic Law and, 147
  pliability of, 251
  post-9/11, xvi, 205–18
  promotion of U.S. war by, 205–18
  propaganda of silence in, 197–98, 201
  public awareness and, 221
  RAWA and, 191
  reduction in coverage by, 220–21, 259
  reporters, removal of, 219–20
medicines, 33
Meena. *See* Keshwar Kamal, Meena
Meena: The Martyr Who Founded RAWA (Ermachild), 181
Mehmooda, 155
Mehta, Sunita, 181
Meshrano Jirga. See House of Elders
military responses
  injustice of, 224
  justification of, 57
military, U.S.
  abuse by, 64–65, 252
  accountability of, 100
  bases, 69, 78, 229, 241–45, 257
  in countryside, 99–103, 166
  manipulation of, 63, 65
  persistence in Afghanistan, 224, 236, 252–54
  provocation by, 66–69
  PRTs, 57–61, 102
  Psychological Operations, 66–68
  public opinion of, 241, 252–54
  tribunals, 73–74
militia, 175, 257. *See also* private armies
Miller, Marty, 27
Ministry for the Promotion of Virtue and Prevention of Vice, xv, 18, 144. *See also* Vice and Virtue Squad
Ministry of Women's Affairs, 127, 134, 137, 195
mission cilivilitrice, viii
Mobil, 246
Mohammad, Atta, 107, 150, 157
Mohammed, Jaan, 62–63
Mohammed Lala, Noor, 64
Mohammed, Niaz, 65
Mohammed, Wali, 63–64
Mohaqqeq, Mohammad, 150, 159, 163
Mojadedi, Sibghatullah, 18, 144, 159, 162
Le Monde, 226–27
Moore, Michael, 226
MSF. *See* Medecins Sans Frontieres; Doctors Without Borders
Mudoh, Afghanistan, 52, 57
Mujahideen. *See also* Northern Alliance; warlords
  Afghan resistance v., 13, 15
  criticism of, 204
  in government, 159
  human rights abuses of, viii
  human rights and, 87
  Karzai, H., 124
  Saudi backing of, 8, 16–17
  Taliban and, vii

Taliban v., 23
U.S. backing of, xiv–xvi, 3, 6, 8–16, 202–3, 209
victims of, 96, 192
women and, xv, 3, 172, 179, 209
de Mul, Erick, 36
Mullah Omar, 125, 162, 182
Musharraf, Pervez, 48, 92, 94, 225–26
Muslim culture, stereotypes of, 179–80
al-Mutairi, Nasser Nijer Naser, 75
Myers, Richard, 53, 71, 214

Nadery, Nader, 256
Nadir Shah, 120
Naik, Niaz, 46
Najibullah, Mohammed, xv, 13, 15–17, 25, 32, 43, 87, 120, 123, 125, 199, 204
Nasir, Mohammed, 188
Nathan, James, 12
Nathan, Joanna, 164
national army, Afghan, 100, 103, 105, 116, 257–58
National Geographic, 181–82
National Islamic Front of Afghanistan, 8
National Newspaper Index, 123, 199–200, 218–19
National Organization for Women, 28
nation building, xiv, 95, 218, 223
lite, 49, 183
The Nation, 56, 226
natural gas, 25, 42, 129, 228, 246. *See also* oil
Nazarbayev, Nursultan, 249
negative symmetry, 16
neoconservative, 128
Neumann, Ronald, 163
news. *See also* media
judgments, 219
opinion v., 137
Newsday, 150, 220
Newsweek, xviii, 105, 130, 198, 220, 221
Koran abuse story by, 213–18, 254
scapegoating of, 287n573
The New Yorker, 69, 130, 227
New York Times, xviii, 10, 12–15, 17–18, 22, 57, 76, 78–80, 82, 88–90, 95, 98, 112, 123, 125, 129, 134, 137, 149, 156, 172, 199, 202, 204, 208–13, 220, 245
Niazi, Adeena, 131, 136–37
Nightline, 217
9/11 Commission, 30, 46, 267n91
Report, 31, 34
Niyazov, Saparmurat A., 26, 225–26, 243
nomads, 122
"No One Listens To Us and No One Treats Us as Human Beings: Justice Denied to Women" (Amnesty International), 115
Noorani, 101, 147–48, 154, 157–58
North Atlantic Treaty Organization (NATO), 258
Article V of, 238–39, 290n636
expansion of, 248
Response Force, 239–40
U.S., tool for, 237–41
Northern Alliance. *See also* Mujahideen; warlords
ascendance of, xvi–xvii
Bonn Conference delegates of, 97
CIA and, 87–88
election interference by, 135
empowerment of, 187
formation of, 87
in government, 124, 130, 138, 142–43
human rights and, 94, 103–8
Kabul, occupation of, 92–97
legitimization of, 130
sanctions and, 34
U.S. and, 43–44, 47, 90, 92–95, 97, 103, 193, 228, 231
war crimes of, 103–8
women and, 112–16, 208–9
nuclear war, 250

Observer, 110
oil, 25–26, 42, 129, 177, 225–29, 246–50. *See also* pipeline project
Olympic games 1980, 12
Oman, 246
OPAWC. *See* Organization for Promoting Afghan Women's Capabilities
operating sites, 244
Operation Avalanche, 140–41
Operation Enduring Freedom, xvi, xviii, 49, 51, 53, 117, 170, 241
opinion, news v., 137
opium. *See* drug trade

Organization for Promoting Afghan Women's Capabilities (OPAWC), 262
Oxfam, 36, 59

Pahlawan, Abdul Malik, 104
Pakistan, 6, 8, 16, 37, 90, 92, 102, 125, 205, 225–26, 228, 250
  formation of, 120
  ISI of, 8–9, 14, 19, 22, 29, 48, 89, 104, 125
  Northwest Frontier Province of, 122
  Taliban, backing of, 22, 47–48
Parcham, 4, 6, 185. *See also* Progressive Democratic Party of Afghanistan
parliament, 141
  elections of, 126, 158–65
  human rights debates in, 164
  lower house of, 158
  representation within, 158
  strength of, 143, 164
  upper house of, 159–60
  warlords in, viii
Parry, Richard Lloyd, 52
Pashtunistan, 9, 48, 120, 122
Pashtuns, 9, 87–91, 95, 118, 120, 131
Pashtun, Yusuf, 105
patriotism, 219
PDPA. *See* Progressive Democratic Party of Afghanistan
peace, justice v., 138, 161
peacekeepers, 98–101, 240, 257–58, 293n701
Pentagon, 52–53, 56–57, 67, 72, 183, 210, 217, 235, 244
  Defense Planning Guidance, 128
Peshawar Assembly, 89–90
Peshawar Group, 97. *See also* Northern Alliance
Peshawar, Pakistan, 204
Philippines, 237
PHR. *See* Physicians for Human Rights
physical infrastructure, reconstruction of, 259
Physicians for Human Rights (PHR), 54, 104
pipeline project, xvi, 26–27, 42, 129, 170, 177, 195, 225–29. *See also* oil
  BTC, 247, 249
  prospects of, 246–50
  TAP, 246–47, 249
poisoning, of food aid, 210
police force, Afghan, 100, 102
political parties, 145, 163, 185
political parties law, 152
The Politics of Heroin (McCoy), 111
Ponticelli, Charlotte, 176
poppy growing. *See* drug trade
Powell, Colin, 47, 90–91
powerful states, weak states v., xii, 231
POWs. *See* prisoners of war
president. *See also* Karzai, Hamid
  candidates for, 152–53
  election of, 126, 148–53, 165
  strength of, 141–42, 166
press, freedom of, 147–48, 216
prisoners
  hunger strikes by, 75
  release of, 74–75
  treatment of, 231, 237
prisoners of war (POWs), 72, 228
private armies, 160, 257. *See also* militia
Progressive Democratic Party of Afghanistan (PDPA), 4–5, 83, 185–86
progressives, 160, 258
Project for a New American Century, 128
Project on the Future of Peace Operations, 99
propaganda, vii, 210, 217, 232, 233–35
  of silence, 197–98, 201
Provincial Reconstruction Teams (PRTs), 57–61, 102, 240
PRTs. *See* Provincial Reconstruction Teams
Psychological Operations, 66–68
public awareness, 234, 259–60
  media, reliance on, 221
  U.S., 197, 206, 208, 221
"Public Execution of an Afghan Woman (Zarmeena) by Taliban," 283n477
public opinion
  Afghan, 13, 68, 101, 204
  American, 11–12
  on disarmament, 254–55
  on human rights abusers, 152
  Islamic Law and, 146
  Karzai, H. in, 123, 151
  on military bases, 241
  on security situation, 101
  U.S. military, actions of, 252–54
  war for, 210

Qadir, Haji Abdul, 136
Qadiri Sufi order, 8
al-Qa'eda, 29, 41, 87–88, 182, 223, 229–30, 235
 9/11 and, 232
 1998 embassy attacks by, xvi
 recruits for, 257
 strategy against, 44–45
 surrender of, 50
Qanooni, Yunus, 98, 108, 125, 153, 159, 163
Qasimi, 157
Qazi, 147
Quasimi, 85–86
Quraishi, Najibullah, 104–5
Qu'ran. *See* Koran

Rabbani, Burnhanuddin, 13, 18–20, 23–25, 27–28, 87, 91, 125, 144, 159, 208
racism, 66, 76, 79, 82, 182–84, 203
Radio Free Europe, 37, 159
Rahman, Abdul, 75
rape, xiv, xv–xvi, 103, 112–16
Raphel, Robin, 26
Rashid, Ahmed, 109, 227
RAWA. *See* Revolutionary Association of the Women of Afghanistan
Reagan, Ronald, 13, 127–28
Reaping the Whirlwind (Griffin), 21
recommendations, of authors, 254–61
Reconciliation Commission, 18
refugees, 36, 186. *See also* internally displaced people
Refugees International, 58
regime change, vii, 41, 232
religious conservatives, 139. *See also* Mujahideen; Northern Alliance
relocation projects, 122
reparations, 259
reporters, removal of, 219–20
representative government, 94. *See also* democracy; elections
Republican National Convention, 233
revenge attacks, 95–96
Revolutionary Association of the Women of Afghanistan (RAWA), viii, 8–9, 36, 96, 127, 130, 132, 155, 181, 214, 253, 258, 262, 283n477
 considered as communists, 194
 critiques of, 192–93
 founding of, 186
 fundamentalism and, 194–95
 inconvenience of, 191–96
Reynolds, Andrew, 148, 151, 153
Reza, Ali, 147
Rice, Condoleezza, 45–46, 95, 165, 210, 215–16, 247
Richardson, Bill, 28, 31
risk, politics without, 171–73
Robertson, George, 238–39
Robertson, Lori, 218–19
Robillard, Rafael, 59
Robinson, Mary, 55
rogue state, 29–38, 37, 41
Rohrabacher, Dana, 27–28
Rome Group, 97, 125. *See also* Northern Alliance
royal family, 4. *See also* Zahir Shah, Mohammed
Roy, Arundhati, viii
Rozgaran, 101, 147–48, 154, 157
Rubenstein, Leonard S., 54
Rubin, Barnett, 8–9, 11, 14, 16, 103, 164
Rumsfeld, Donald, 45–47, 52, 73, 89, 99–101, 107–8, 128, 210, 231, 238–39, 239, 243–44
Rumsfeld, Joyce, 174
Rupert, James, 204
Russia, 32, 125, 229, 239, 245–47, 249–50, 257. *See also* Union of Soviet Socialist Republics
 Treaty of Friendship with, 119

Saba, Sahar, 127, 132
salt pit, 70
Samar, Sima, 134, 137, 144
sanctions, 32–37
 drug trade and, 110
 smart, 33
San Francisco Chronicle, 175
Sarabi, Habiba, 127, 137, 157, 173, 177–78, 262
Sarajevo, 21, 202, 204
Sattar, Abdul, 46
Sattar Sirat, Abdul, 93, 125
Saudi Arabia, Mujahideen, backing of, 8, 16–17
Sayyaf, Abdul Rasul, vii, xiv, 16, 20, 23, 159, 163

Schaffer, Howard, 204
Schlesinger, Arthur, 121
SCO. *See* Shanghai Cooperation Organization
search and destroy operations, 237
secular government, desire for, 146
secular organizations, 8, 165, 258–59
security, ix, 151
  disarmament and, 157
  during elections, 151, 156
  in Kabul, 173
  lack of, 97–103
  Loya Jirga and, 189
  from U.S. military, 253
Selay, 214
self-immolation, xvii, 112–16
Sellers, Terry, 60
sensationalism, 261
September 11, 2001, xi–xiv, xvi, xix, 41, 49, 87–88, 198
  before, 3–38
  casualties of, 51, 57
  causes of, 197, 205
  as excuse, 225, 229
  exploitation of, 232
  bin Laden and, 50
  al-Qa'eda and, 232
  repetition of, 250
  response, need for, 224
sexism, 182–84
Shafaq, 148
Shahab, Safia, 188
Shah, Saira, 169
Shah Shuja, 118–19, 123, 125
Shaker Qala, Afghanistan, 53–54
Shanghai Cooperation Organization (SCO), 245
Sharia Law. *See* Islamic Law
Sheberghan prison camp, 104
Shell, 246
Sherzai, Gul Agha, 97, 105, 107, 156
Shevardnadze, Eduard, 12–13
Shifa pharmaceutical plant, 30–31, 43
Shinwari, Fazl Hadi, 75, 97, 130, 144–47
Siddiqui, Meena, 123, 146
Sifton, John, 139
Sikorsky, Radek, 18
silence, propaganda of, vii
Simla Manifesto, 118–19
Singh, Natwar, 247
Smeal, Eleanor, 170
social justice, co-option of, 258
social reforms, 184
Soderberg, Nancy, 33–34
soldiers, attacks on, 234, 254. *See also* military, U.S.
Solidarity Party of Afghanistan, 144–45, 155, 255
southern strategy, 88
Soviet Union. *See* Union of Soviet Socialist Republics
spokeswomen, for publicity campaign, 172
Steele, Jonathan, 55
Stohl, Michael, xii
Stohl, Rachel, xii
The Strategy for Eliminating the Threat from the Jihadist Networks of al Qida, 44
Stufflebeem, John, 53, 210
Sudan, 237
suicide bombings, 251
Sultan, Masuda, 194
Sunday Times, 217
Supreme Council for the National Unity of Afghanistan, 91
Supreme Court, 144–45
Sykes, Percival, 118

Taggart, Chris, 26
Tajikistan, 243
Tajiks, 24, 87, 118, 122, 131
Take the Guns Away, 254
Taliban, 182, 205, 233, 251, 257
  amnesty for, 130
  demonizing of, 42, 209–13
  destruction of, 45, 49–50
  fall of, 230
  human rights and, 27, 230
  Mujahideen and, vii
  Mujahideen v., 23
  opposition to, 88–90
  Pakistan, backing by, 22, 47–48
  as preferable alternative, 22–29
  rise of, vii, 205
  sanctions and, 34, 37
  stability from, 82
  take-over by, xvi, 199
  U.S. and, 23–25, 37, 42, 45
  U.S., comparison to, 82–84
  victims of, 96, 192

women and, xv–xvi, 22–23, 25, 28–29, 170–71, 173
"Taliban: Islam, Oil and the New Great Game in Central Asia" (Rashid), 188
"The Taliban's War Against Women," 171
TAP. *See* Turkmenistan-Afghanistan-Pakistan pipeline
Taraki, Noor Mohammed, 4–6, 185–86
Tarzi, Amin, 159, 162, 164
tax appropriation, 108–12
technocrats, 158
television, 144, 206, 219
Tenet, George J., 236, 245
Terror and Liberalism (Berman), 10
terrorism, 182
fighting, 235–37
war on, xvi, xviii, 77, 95, 153, 205, 231, 234, 235–36, 237, 241, 243, 249, 257
terrorists, xii, 30, 38, 73–74, 82, 223, 233, 250
capture of, 235–37
textbooks, 211–13
Thier, J. Alexander, 137, 156
Thomas, Donald, 60
Thrupkaew, Noy, 192–94
Time, 19, 45, 96
Tokayev, Kassymzhomart, 250
Tomsen, Peter, 204
Toronto Star, 149
torture, 69, 237
normalization of, 75–82
travel warning, 102
Treaty of Friendship, with Russia, 119
tribal assets. *See* Central Intelligence Agency; Mujahideen; Northern Alliance; warlords
Turkey, 248
Turkmenistan, 225, 228, 243, 246, 248, 249
Turkmenistan-Afghanistan-Pakistan pipeline (TAP), 246–47, 249
Tutwiler, Margaret D., 17–18
Tyndall, Andrew, 218

UAVs. *See* unmanned aerial vehicles
UAWC. *See* U.S.-Afghan Women's Council
Ukraine, 248
UN. *See* United Nations
UNAMA. *See* UN Assistance Mission in Afghanistan
UN Assistance Mission in Afghanistan (UNAMA), 157
UN Children's Fund (UNICEF), 35
UN Development Program (UNDP), xix
UNDP. *See* UN Development Program
unexploded ordinance, 54. *See also* landmines; cluster bombs
UNICEF. *See* UN Children's Fund
Union of Soviet Socialist Republics (USSR), 120. *See also* Russia
blaming of, 203
bleeding of, 10
breakup of, 202
influence of, 3–4, 120
invasion by, xi, xiii, 3, 6–8, 12–13, 122, 186, 194, 199
trapping of, vii
U.S., negative symmetry with, 16
withdrawal of, xv, 16–17, 203
United Front. *See* Northern Alliance
United Nations (UN), 239–40, 255, 258
human rights investigator, 80–81
United States (U.S.). *See also* Bush, George W.
Afghan women, commitment to, 173–78
Asia, position in, 241–45, 250
bombing, goals of, 49–50, 51
CIA of, 6, 9, 14, 19–20, 29, 69–70, 87–89, 177, 204
citizens, consequences for, 250, 252
credibility of, 5, 7, 215, 229
demonstrations against, 101, 214–15, 254, 256
Department of Energy, 246
Department of State, 4–5, 11, 17, 19–20, 22, 24–25, 70, 101, 138, 171, 174–75, 177, 204, 249
energy resources, importance of, 228
extremists, use of, 10
fighting terrorism, demonstration of, 235–37
foreign policy objectives of, 49, 183, 203
hegemony of, 245
human rights and, 24, 25, 38, 71
idealism and, 183
image of, 218
immediate objectives of, 224–32
imperialism of, 182–84, 251–52
incidental benefits to, 232–37

initial involvement of, xi
international body v., 100
invasion by, 199, 223, 229
justice of, 73–75
justification by, 223
Karzai, H. and, xvii, 89, 101–2, 124, 153, 166, 241
long-term benefit to, 237–50
Middle East, control of, 7, 30
military, abuse by, 64–65
military, accountability of, 100
military, countryside operations of, 99–103, 166
military, manipulation of, 63, 65
military, provocation by, 66–69
most favored nation of, 249
motives of, 223–24
Mujahideen, backing of, xiv–xvi, 3, 6, 8–16, 202–3, 209
National Security Strategy of, xiii
NATO, as useful tool, 237–41
Northern Alliance and, 43–44, 47, 90, 92–95, 97, 103, 193, 228, 231
policy repercussions of, vii
power, promotion of, 130, 224
pre-9/11 policy of, 3–38
public awareness in, 197, 206, 208, 221, 234, 259–60
public opinion in, 11–12
responsibility of, xiii–xiv, xvi, xviii–xix, 10, 21–22, 38, 102, 198, 204, 205, 251, 253
rhetorical v. material interests, 250
self-interest of, 251
Special Forces, 65, 105
stability from, 82
Taliban and, 23–25, 37, 42, 45
Taliban, comparison to, 82–84
troops, abuse by, xviii
USSR, negative symmetry with, 16
warlords, backing of, 100, 178
withdrawal of, 252, 256–57
women's rights and, 38, 195–96
universality, of human rights, 193–94
University of Nebraska, 211–12
unmanned aerial vehicles (UAVs), 44
UN Mine Action Programme, 54
Unnikrishnan, P.V., 221
Unocal Corporation, xvi, 26–27, 42, 128–29, 170, 177, 195, 225–28
UN Office for the Coordination of Humanitarian Affairs, 32
UN Security Council (UNSC), 32, 34–35
resolution 1267, 32
resolution 1333, 33
Unveiled (Logan), 180
unveiling, of Afghan women, 205–7
UN World Food Program, 55, 109
Uruzgan, Afghanistan, 62
U.S.. *See* United States
U.S.-Afghan Women's Council (UAWC), 173–78, 189
budget of, 177
corporate sponsors of, 176
free market capitalism and, 176–77
U.S. Agency for International Development (USAID), 177, 211–13
USAID. *See* U.S. Agency for International Development
USA Today, 219
USS *Cole*, bombing of, 29, 33, 44
USSR. *See* Union of Soviet Socialist Republics
Uzbekistan, 47, 70–71, 226, 241–43, 249
Uzbeks, 24, 87, 118, 131, 143

values
humanist, 207
relativity of, 193
Vance, Cyrus, 5
Van Patot, Karen Tissot, 61
Veiled Courage (Benard), 180
Veiled Threat (Armstrong), 180
Vendrell, Francesc, 35, 99
Vice and Virtue Squad, 115. *See also* Ministry for the Promotion of Virtue and Prevention of Vice
violence, culture of, 213
Vital Voices Global Partnership, 172
Voice of America, 217
voters
intimidation of, 150, 154, 162–63
registration of, 149, 233
turnout of, 153–55, 163
"Vulnerability and Humanitarian Implications of UN Security Council Sanctions in Afghanistan," 32

Wade, C.W., 118
Wali, Sardar Abdul, 185
Wali, Sima, 193
Wall Street Journal, 123, 199, 204, 219, 243
Walsh, Mary Williams, 204
war
  on abstract noun, 235
  by committee, 237
  crimes, 103–8, 152, 156, 192
  laws of, 68, 72–73
  nuclear, 250
  for oil, 225
  prisoners of, 72, 228
  psychological, 209–10
  for public opinion, 210
  on terror, xvi, xviii, 77, 95, 153, 205, 231, 234, 235–36, 237, 241, 243, 249, 257
  victims of, 192
  weariness, 83, 86, 154, 192, 234
  women as justification for, xvii–xviii, 171–72, 195, 198, 223, 251, 261
war crimes tribunal, 203, 255–56
Wardak, Masooma, 208
Wardak, Taj Mohammad, 107–8
warlords, 86–87. *See also* Mujahideen; Northern Alliance
  as allies, 87–88
  Americans as, 82–84
  as candidates, 150
  co-opting of, 156, 161
  criticism of, 161
  disarmament of, 156–57, 254–57
  as elders, 160
  empowerment of, xviii, 138, 142–43, 159
  in government, viii, 152, 154–59, 161–62, 165, 190, 218, 251
  justice for, xix, 143, 152, 192, 254–56
  Karzai, H., support for, 164
  Karzai, H. v., 154–55
  Khalilzad, Z. and, 161–62
  neutralizing of, 156–57
  pre-*Loya Jirga* violence of, 134–38
  sinister nature of, 204
  U.S. backing of, 100, 178
  U.S. military, manipulation of, 63, 65
  women's rights and, 148, 178
Washington Post, 24–25, 53, 123, 128, 133, 137, 141, 148, 151–52, 199, 204, 212, 219–20, 235–36, 243
Washington Quarterly, 127
Washington Times, 219
weak states, powerful states v., xii, 231
weapons, xv
  of mass destruction, 229
wedding party, bombing of, 183
Wedgewood, Ruth, 31
Weekly Standard, 229
Wehmeyer, Peggy, 176
Westin, Av, 219
Whitaker, Mark, 215–16
white man's burden, viii
Whittier Daily News, 217
With All Our Strength (Brodsky), 181
Wolesi Jirga. See House of the People
Wolfowitz, Paul, 47, 128, 241
women, 165–66
  abduction of, 112–16
  acid, throwing on, xv, 9
  agency of, 261
  American, 169, 179
  Bush, G.W., use by, 171–73
  capitalization on oppression, 180
  constitution and, 143
  crimes against, 112–16
  demonstrations by, 113, 261
  dress code for, 114–15
  education of, 209
  grassroots activists, 187
  imprisonment of, xvii, 146
  Islamic Law and, 144–46
  as justification for war, xvii–xviii, 171–72, 195, 198, 223, 251, 261
  liberation of, viii, xviii, 113, 169–84, 187–88, 195–96, 205–8
  movements, history of, 184–87
  Mujahideen and, xv, 3, 172, 179, 209
  Northern Alliance and, 112–16, 208–9
  objectification of, ix, 261
  in parliament, 158, 184
  political instrumentality of, 185–86
  Rabbani government and, 18–19
  revolutionary, 191–96
  rights of, xv, 3, 8, 28, 38, 131, 137, 143, 148, 158, 171–73, 175, 185–86, 223, 259
  self-immolation by, xvii, 112–16
  suffering, causes of, 205–9
  suffering, exploitation of, 205–9
  Taliban and, xv–xvi, 22–23, 25, 28–29, 170–71, 173

unveiling of, 205–7, 218
U.S. commitment to, 173–78
U.S. concern with, 38
victimization of, 206
as voters, 153–54
warlords and, 48, 178
Zahir Shah and, 184
Women for Afghan Women, 194
Women for Afghan Women: Shattering Myths and Claiming the Future (Mehta), 181
Women's Mirror, 159
Women's Park, 113
Women's Resource Centers, 175–76
Woodward, Bob, 46–47, 88
World Bank, 42
World Food Program, 210
World Trade Center
1993 bombing of, 29
2001 bombing of, xi–xiv, xvi, xix, 3–38, 29, 41, 49–51, 57, 87–88, 197–98, 205, 224–25, 229, 232, 250

Yee, James, 77–78
Yousef, Homa, 213
Yugoslavia, 21–22, 202–3, 238

Zadran, Amanullah, 134
Zahir Shah, Mohammed, xvii, 4, 11, 13–14, 27, 90–91, 93, 120, 122, 131–35, 137–38, 165, 184–85
Zakhilwal, Omar, 131, 136–37
Zakia, 253
Zawahiri, Ayman, 236
Zia ul Haq, 9
Zia-Zarifi, Salman, 68, 136–37, 163
Zoya's Story: An Afghan Woman's Struggle for Freedom, 180

ABOUT THE AUTHORS

SONALI KOLHATKAR and JAMES INGALLS are the codirectors of the Afghan Women's Mission, a U.S.-based non-profit organization that raises funds for and awareness of the projects of the Revolutionary Association of the Women of Afghanistan (RAWA). Their writings have appeared in *Z Magazine* and *Foreign Policy in Focus,* and on Alternet and Common Dreams. In February 2005, Kolhatkar and Ingalls traveled to Afghanistan to witness firsthand the results of U.S. policy, and to understand how ordinary Afghans felt about the war. Sonali Kolhatkar is the host and producer of *Uprising*, a daily drive-time program on KPFK Pacifica Radio in Los Angeles. James Ingalls is a Staff Scientist at the Spitzer Science Center at the California Institute of Technology.

DAVID BARSAMIAN is the founder and director of Alternative Radio, www.alternativeradio.org.